# HTML5

*Your visual blueprint™ for designing rich web pages and applications*

## Adam McDaniel

WILEY

John Wiley & Sons, Inc

...Visual blueprint™ for designing rich web
...applications

...ned by

John Wiley & Sons, Inc.
111 River Street
Hoboken, NJ 07030-5774

www.wiley.com

Published simultaneously in Canada

Copyright © 2012 by John Wiley & Sons, Inc., Indianapolis, Indiana

Wiley publishes in a variety of print and electronic formats and by print-on-demand. Some material included with the standard print versions of this book may not be included in e-books or in print-on-demand. If this book refers to media such as a CD or DVD that is not included in the version you purchased, you may download this material at http://booksupport.wiley.com. For more information about Wiley products, visit www.wiley.com.

Library of Congress Control Number: 2011939648

ISBN: 978-0-470-95222-1

Manufactured in the United States of America

10 9 8 7 6 5 4 3 2 1

## Trademark Acknowledgments

Wiley, the Wiley logo, Visual, the Visual logo, Visual Blueprint, Read Less - Learn More and related trade dress are trademarks or registered trademarks of John Wiley & Sons, Inc. and/or its affiliates. All other trademarks are the property of their respective owners. John Wiley & Sons, Inc. is not associated with any product or vendor mentioned in this book.

## Contact Us

For general information on our other products and services please contact our Customer Care Department within the U.S. at 877-762-2974, outside the U.S. at 317-572-3993 or fax 317-572-4002.

For technical support, please visit www.wiley.com/techsupport.

WILEY   Sales | Contact Wiley at (877) 762-2974 or fax (317) 572-4002.

**Arc de Triomphe**

Commissioned by the Emperor Napoleon in 1806 to commemorate his imperial armies, this familiar landmark is the world's largest triumphal arch. It dominates the famed Champs-Elysées and bears the names of hundreds of Napoleon's generals along with four spectacular relief sculptures. From its summit, tourists view a breathtaking panorama of Paris.

Discover more about the city and its monuments in *Frommer's Paris 2011* (ISBN 978-0-470-61441-9), available wherever books are sold or at www.Frommers.com.

# Credits

**Acquisitions Editor**
Aaron Black

**Senior Acquisitions Editor**
Stephanie McComb

**Project Editor**
Dana Rhodes Lesh

**Technical Editor**
Paul Geyer

**Copy Editor**
Dana Rhodes Lesh

**Editorial Director**
Robyn Siesky

**Business Manager**
Amy Knies

**Senior Marketing Manager**
Sandy Smith

**Vice President and Executive Group Publisher**
Richard Swadley

**Vice President and Executive Publisher**
Barry Pruett

**Project Coordinator**
Kristie Rees

**Graphics and Production Specialists**
Carrie A. Cesavice
Joyce Haughey
Andrea Hornberger
Jennifer Mayberry

**Quality Control Technicians**
Lindsay Amones
Melanie Hoffman
Lauren Mandelbaum
Rob Springer

**Proofreading**
Melissa D. Buddendeck

**Indexing**
Potomac Indexing, LLC

**Screen Artist**
Jill A. Proll

**Cover Art Illustrator**
David Gregory

# e Author

⁣⁣⁣⁣⁣⁣⁣⁣⁣⁣⁣⁣⁣⁣⁣⁣⁣⁣⁣⁣ has been designing, developing, modifying, and maintaining computer programs of one ⁣⁣⁣⁣⁣⁣⁣⁣ another since 1993, and he has been an active proponent of HTML since being introduced to the ⁣⁣⁣⁣⁣⁣ in 1994.

⁣⁣⁣⁣⁣ that time, Adam has led a team of developers implementing an eCommerce fulfillment engine for a virtual ⁣⁣⁣⁣⁣ ping mall, designed hundreds of corporate websites, and developed front-end HTML and back-end CGI ⁣⁣⁣⁣⁣ infrastructure for CADVision, at the time one of the largest ISPs in Western Canada. In 2001, Adam moved into the software security sector, working for Hitachi ID Systems for over eight years, designing and implementing software security recommendations for various Fortune 500 companies across the United States and Europe. Soon afterwards, based on his past CGI experience, Adam wrote his first book, *Perl and Apache: Your visual blueprint to developing dynamic Web content*. Most recently, Adam rejoined the HTML world as the lead OS architect for Jolicloud, a Paris-based company, contributing to its HTML5 Linux operating system.

As Adam is always interested in new technologies and architectures, his other development credits include an open-source offline HTML reader for the Palm OS platform, contributions to the Linux Kernel, and other utility and specialty programs. In 2006, Adam produced the Array.org Netbook Kernel software download and website, allowing users to download an optimized build of the Linux kernel, specific for the Ubuntu Linux distribution.

# Author's Acknowledgments

This book is the product of many significant people, without all of whom, this project would never have been possible.

My expert Wiley editors were instrumental in shepherding this book into what you see today. Aaron Black, my acquisitions editor, kept this project on schedule, and I am grateful to him for introducing me to the publishing industry. Dana Lesh, my project editor, gracefully offered feedback and direction and prevented this book from degrading into a garbled mess of inconsistent ideas and broken sentences. Also, thank you Neil Salkind and Andrew Kim of StudioB; this is the first project we have worked on together, and I look forward to many more.

I would also like to thank the Jolicloud HTML5 team: Tariq Krim, Brenda O'Connell, Romain Huet, Jeremy Selier, and Cedric Duclos. The desktop revolution offered by HTML5 and cloud computing is something few people could have foreseen, it was great being on the ground floor with you all. In addition, thank you Adam Buckeridge for your help with the book's example site design and Derek Brans for your HTML5 and jQuery expertise.

To the HTML5 architects, designers, and developers from Mozilla, Opera, Google, and Apple who took the lead in identifying the future of the Internet, shaping the HTML5 standard, and promoting it, thank you. The web certainly would not be as awesome without your resources and innovation.

Finally, to my beautiful wife Shauna, without your many years of love, support, and encouragement, and even your devil's advocate ("I don't think this you've thought this through") feedback, I would be lost, overwhelmed, and probably homeless. As this project was in the homestretch, your patience and understanding is what allowed it to succeed. You always keep me grounded and focused, and I cherish the life and family we have built together.

This book is dedicated to my firstborn — my daughter, Brielle. Although today you are very young, one day you may choose a career that has not even been invented yet. By then, I hope that I have inspired you to explore new technologies, ask questions, investigate problems, and find innovative solutions in whatever path you take.

# How to Use This Visual Blueprint Book

## Whom This Book Is For

This book is for advanced computer users who want to take their knowledge of HTML to the next level.

## The Conventions in This Book

### ① Steps

This book uses a step-by-step format to guide you easily through each task. Numbered steps are actions you must do; bulleted steps clarify a point, step, or optional feature; and indented steps give you the result.

### ② Notes

Notes give additional information — special conditions that may occur during an operation, a situation that you want to avoid, or a cross-reference to a related area of the book.

### ③ Icons and Buttons

Icons and buttons show you exactly what you need to click to perform a step.

### ④ Extra or Apply It

An Extra section provides additional information about the preceding task — insider information and tips for ease and efficiency. An Apply It section takes the code from the preceding task one step further and allows you to take full advantage of it.

### ⑤ Bold

**Bold** type shows text or numbers that you must type.

### ⑥ Italics

*Italic* type introduces and defines a new term.

### ⑦ Courier Font

`Courier font` indicates the use of scripting language code such as statements, operators, or functions, and code such as objects, methods, or properties.

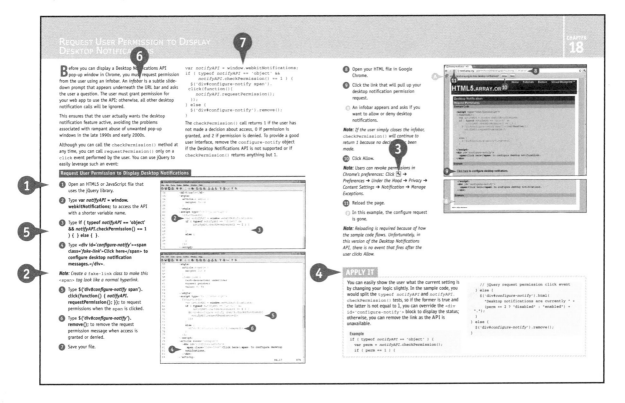

# TABLE OF CONTENTS

# TABLE OF CONTENTS

## Chapter 8   Using jQuery with HTML5

# TABLE OF CONTENTS

# TABLE OF CONTENTS

## Chapter 18  Displaying Desktop Notifications

## Appendix A  HTML5 Reference

H TML, or Hypertext Markup Language, is a programming language designed, documented, and maintained by the World Wide Web Consortium (W3C). A *markup language* is a programming language that uses special tags to embed words and commands in and around regular text.

HTML5 is the latest version of HTML available today for the World Wide Web. It is a new specification that builds on the previous HTML 4.01 and XHTML 1.1 specifications, providing you with the tools that you need to produce the next generation of websites.

As a whole, HTML5 also relies on other technologies, such as Cascading Style Sheets version 3 (CSS3) and JavaScript as the magic to make websites really pop and move. So much do these three disciplines complement each other that they all fall under the "HTML5" banner.

## HTML: The Living Standard

The W3C was in charge of HTML since its inception in 1994, but by 2004, the W3C had become complacent in developing the next generation of the language. In response, a new organization called the Web Hypertext Application Technology Working Group (WHATWG) was founded by industry affiliates to direct the future of HTML.

By April 2007, WHATWG published a working draft of HTML5 to the W3C and began promoting it to web browser vendors. Today, that working draft has been renamed to "HTML: The Living Standard" and the term *HTML5* refers to a snapshot of that standard. Because WHATWG is a community-driven body, the process is completely open to define the future of the HTML living standard.

HTML5 in the media has actually grown to include features that are not directly controlled by the W3C HTML5 or WHATWG HTML specifications but by web browser vendors. As such, one HTML5 browser may add a new HTML5-like feature or API, thus appearing to enhance the specification to the public. Google's Notification API is an example of this.

Until these rogue features are merged with WHATWG's standards, they tend not to be implemented on competing HTML5 web browsers, and support remains limited.

## Audience

This book is written for web developers who already have experience with HTML 4.01 or earlier, JavaScript, and CSS. If you are a developer who has previously created websites with images, hyperlinks, and tables and want to move on to the next level, this book is for you.

There has been a lot of talk about HTML5 in the technology press: New web browsers, web applications, and mobile devices have already started producing new and creative sites, applications, animations, videos, and interfaces with HTML5. Now it is your turn.

## New Features of HTML5

The actual list of features currently defined in the HTML5 scope is always changing. This is because HTML5 is still technically an "experimental technology," and even in mid-2011, it is reported that its standard will not be finalized until 2014. This book covers the most stable and anticipated features of HTML5, but by the time you read this, there may be even more to discover online.

### The Semantic Layout

A new group of HTML tags enables you to build your web page using a *semantic* layout. This means that logically grouped sections of your page can have equally logical HTML tags. For example, web page headers and footers can be wrapped in `<header>` and `<footer>` tags; navigational toolbars can use `<nav>` tags; large sections are enclosed in `<section>`; and actual content is written within `<article>` tags.

Producing a web page in this way will make understanding the source code easier for you and easier for automated programs to parse.

The semantic layout is described in Chapter 2, "Getting Started with HTML5 Page Layout."

**New Features of HTML5** (continued)

## New User Interface Tags

HTML5 introduces a few new user interface (UI) tags that you can use to make browsing your website a richer experience. New features include <mark> for highlighting, <figure> and <figcaption> for providing new details to images, and <meter> and <progress> to display a static and moving progress bar.

WHATWG has also used this opportunity to deprecate older HTML tags that have become obsolete or are simply better implemented in CSS. Tags such as <center>, <font>, <frame>, <strike>, <tt>, and <u> are now ignored.

All new and removed tags are summarized later in this chapter. You can learn how to use the new tags in Chapter 3, "Using New HTML5 User Interface Tags and Attributes."

## New CSS3 Visual Enhancements

CSS enables you to customize any HTML element's dimension, color, font, text, image, alignment, and layout. For CSS3, there are easier ways to locate and isolate individual tags to apply these custom styles in your website. You can even create interesting 2D and 3D transformations, transitions, and animations.

The new CSS3 visual enhancements are showcased in Chapters 4, "Styling with CSS3," and 5, "Enhancing Your Web Page Visually with CSS3."

## Flexible Box Model and Multi-Column Layout

There are two new ways to create tablelike layouts in CSS3 and HTML5. The Flexible Box Model allows you to organize web page data into multiple rows or columns within a new display: box object. The multi-column layout allows you to structure data into multiple columns of variable height and width.

These new methods are demonstrated in Chapter 6, "Creating Boxes and Columns with CSS3."

## Intelligent Form Inputs

Form input fields enable your users to submit data back to your website. Because some fields must accept only specific formats — such as numbers and dashes for telephone numbers — in HTML 4.01 and earlier, you had to sanitize data inputs in JavaScript or with web server code. In HTML5, you can now instruct the web browser to restrict input fields to specific formats.

For example, you can enforce numbers only, number ranges, dates, email addresses, and URLs. You can even specify custom pattern-matching rules for obscure format restrictions.

The intelligent form inputs are explained in Chapter 7, "Creating HTML5 Form Inputs."

## jQuery, Browser Events, and Custom Data Attributes

JavaScript is the scripting language that can be leveraged on any modern web browser. In HTML5, you can alter web browser events, use custom data attributes, and dynamically hide and display entire sections of HTML code, all to produce a dynamic user experience.

jQuery is particularly well suited for simplifying the flow of HTML5 events and custom data attributes within JavaScript, as JavaScript code can be fickle depending on the web browser.

The jQuery library, new events, and custom data attributes are itemized in Chapter 8, "Using jQuery with HTML5."

## The Chrome Inspector

The Chrome Inspector is a debugger built right into the Google Chrome web browser. It enables you to examine and manipulate HTML, CSS, and JavaScript code in real time, and you can even audit your website for network and resource activity. This is an incredibly useful tool for anyone who wants to master HTML5.

The Chrome Inspector is delineated in Chapter 9, "Inspecting and Debugging Your Website."

## Canvas Graphics

The Canvas API gives you complete control over every pixel, color, animation, and user interaction with the web browser; it is literally a blank canvas to create anything. Effectively, the Canvas API was designed to compete directly against Adobe Flash, providing all logic within the trusted and open confines of JavaScript. Several mobile platform companies have publicly embraced HTML5 and its Canvas API as a 100% replacement of Flash.

Although the Canvas API is restricted to 2D graphics and plotting, HTML5 does have an experimental specification called *WebGL* that can generate enhanced 3D graphics within your web browser.

The Canvas API is illustrated in Chapter 10, "Drawing with the HTML5 Canvas."

continued

### Built-in Audio/Video Support

Whereas the Canvas API replaces Flash drawing and animations, the new audio and video support built into HTML5 replaces Flash movies and multimedia.

Although different HTML5 web browsers support different file encoding formats — or *codecs* — you can easily produce content and convert it into the necessary formats to reach the widest-possible HTML5 audience.

The built-in audio and video tags are presented in Chapter 11, "Adding HTML5 Multimedia."

### Drag-and-Drop Events

Using a combination of HTML5 events, JavaScript, and CSS, you can interact with the user in ways only experienced directly on the desktop. With a drag-and-drop interface, you can allow your users to use their mouse or touchscreen to visually interact with your website in creative new ways.

Ultimately, by combining drag-and-drop events, audio, video, and the Canvas API, you have everything you need to create HTML5 web applications and games!

A drag-and-drop example is outlined in Chapter 12, "Using Drag and Drop in HTML5."

### Storage Databases

For years, *cookies* have been used as a medium to store information on the user's web browser. Because a cookie consists of only simple key/value data chunks, web developers have had to utilize clever techniques so that they could handle more complex data structures. Although HTML5 reimplements cookies as the Web Storage API, it goes the next step by introducing the Web SQL and IndexedDB APIs as relational databases.

The various storage databases are explored in Chapter 13, "Storing Data Using a Client-Side Database."

### Offline Detection and Synchronization

No longer do you *need* to actually be connected online in order to use a website. HTML5 now provides you with the ability to produce a web application that can detect whether it is connected online and, if not, instruct the web browser to retrieve your website from its internal *application cache*.

When the user comes back online, all data that is new on the cache can be automatically uploaded and resynchronized with your web server software. This effectively produces the illusion that your web application is always available, regardless of whether the Internet itself is or not.

Offline detection and synchronization is covered in Chapter 14, "Providing Offline Access to Web Applications."

### Geolocation

Because so many smartphones have HTML5 mobile web browsers built in, you can leverage the Geolocation API and provide information and guidance based on the user's physical location.

This information can easily be tied to other third-party services, such as Google Maps, to provide an instant overhead map of the surrounding streets and buildings.

Coverage of the Geolocation API is located in Chapter 15, "Using Geolocation."

### Web Workers

JavaScript by its nature is a synchronous, single-threaded environment. This means only one script can run at a time on your website. Web Workers are a new way to create multiple threads of the JavaScript runtime environment, all running as separate scripts, asynchronously in your website. Each thread has the capability to send messages to the others within the JavaScript stack, enabling you to offload a CPU-intensive process in the background but leave the UI free and responsive.

JavaScript Web Workers are discussed in Chapter 16, "Running Secondary JavaScript Threads Using Web Workers."

### WebSockets

WebSockets are designed to be low-level, persistent communication channels between a web browser and web server. Whereas Ajax is a technology that hacks together an asynchronous XML request to the web server over the HTTP protocol, WebSockets are designed to be more efficient, using their own dedicated channel and protocol.

The WebSockets API is explained in Chapter 17, "Communicating with WebSockets."

## New Features of HTML5 (continued)

### Notifications

The Notifications API enables you to pop up subtle display notification messages outside of the web browser itself. This API was developed by Google for the purpose of displaying new email notifications from its Gmail service. As such, this API is available only in WebKit-based browsers, such as Chrome and Chromium.

Although this may sound ripe for abuse, notifications cannot appear from a website or web application without the user first agreeing to receive them. Unlike pop-up windows, which have plagued the Internet since the 1990s, this feature is off by default and can be enabled only when requested on a per-domain basis.

The Notifications API is revealed in Chapter 18, "Displaying Desktop Notifications."

## Fallbacks and Drawbacks

Just because you have new access to a rich set of tools and features in HTML5, it does not mean that you need to use everything everywhere. Furthermore, not every HTML5 web browser supports every HTML5 specification. Unless you specifically mandate that your website is HTML5 only, you should think about users who have not yet upgraded their web browsers. Will implementing a new HTML5 feature ensure accessibility to your website for all web browsers? Can you use a combination of HTML, CSS, and JavaScript to emulate the feature? If the answer is "no" to either question, you need to ask yourself if such a feature is appropriate.

### Static HTML5 on Older Browsers

Fortunately, earlier HTML standards have instructed web browsers to ignore HTML tags that they do not understand but display the text contained within the unknown tag anyway. This means that content described within `<header>`...`</header>` and `<mark>`...`</mark>` tags will still appear to the end user, but it may appear unformatted and not in context.

For most new HTML5 features described in this book, a fallback method is available to at least *partially* display a usable web page to older web browsers. Assuming your site is uncomplicated, you can produce a 100%-compliant HTML5 web page that renders basically the same on non-HTML5 web browsers.

### Enhanced HTML5 on Older Browsers

A drawback of HTML5's enhanced content is that there is no easy fallback for non-HTML5 web browsers. In fact, even most browsers that are partially HTML5 compliant cannot display all of the same enhanced HTML5 tags exactly as specified by WHATWG. The end result may be a bit of a mess: Your site may work with one browser, partially work with another, and completely fail with a third.

You will need to decide if a new, enhanced HTML5 feature, such as 3D transition effects, the Canvas API, or HTML5 videos, is actually worth it. If a user's browser fails to render an HTML5 video tag, what exactly is lost? What if it is an advertisement or featured content?

Ideally, all enhanced features of HTML5 will *complement* your website but not make the site dependent on them.

## The Future of HTML5

Until HTML5 has reached official status, as a standard it is constantly evolving. Even today, there are several new features that have been specified by WHATWG that have not been implemented by any of the HTML5 web browsers. Later in this chapter, you will learn how to compare web browsers for overall HTML5 levels of support; even today's best HTML5 web browser, Chrome, scores only 288 out of 400 points for overall HTML5 compliance!

New features will be added, just as features on the current HTML5 docket will be removed. In addition, web browser developers will continue to provide complementary APIs and specifications of their own, outside of the W3C, that will be touted as a new "HTML5" feature.

There are several blogs and tutorial websites that demonstrate the latest and greatest HTML5 features. You can use this book as an introduction to the technology, plus the current incarnation of its supporting specifications, but the following resources are great for keeping tabs on the latest information: http://html5.org, www.whatwg.org/html, www.html5rocks.com, www.html5tutorial.net, www.w3schools.com/html5, and www.w3.org/html/planet.

**B** y mid-2008, the first web browsers built on the new WHATWG HTML5 specification were being released for end users. The first such web browser was Firefox 3 from the Mozilla Foundation. Actual support was far from the complete HTML5 specs, but it could handle the new Canvas API, some semantic markup tags, and new mouse interaction events. Google Chrome soon followed in April 2009, and today there are about a half dozen HTML5 web browsers, with Chrome leading the pack in terms of overall HTML5 compliance.

All HTML5-aware web browsers are fully compatible with earlier HTML specifications. This backward-compatibility helped to encourage user adoption rates and provided a means for the standard to be tested and grow into the next generation of HTML.

## Desktop Web Browsers

Traditional PC desktop and laptop computers typically employ highly powered CPU chips, a large monitor display, a full-sized keyboard, and multibutton mouse. This is the environment in which the desktop web browser was born and where HTML5 flourishes today.

### Mozilla Firefox

Firefox emerged from the ashes of the now-defunct Netscape and Mozilla web browsers in November 2004, providing a viable, open-source alternative to the then-dominant Internet Explorer market. After a number of successful releases, Firefox enjoys a stable 30% market share, second overall of all Internet users. Firefox uses the Gecko layout engine.

The Mozilla Foundation, the organization behind Firefox, is a founding member of WHATWG. Firefox is available on the widest range of operating system platforms, including Windows 2000 and later, Mac OS X 10.4 and later, and Linux.

Firefox 3 was the first browser to embrace HTML5 and has always been a strong supporter. Even today's latest release, Firefox 4, includes the platform's best contribution to the HTML5 bandwagon. It features major Gecko enhancements, such as a faster JavaScript engine, WebGL 3D support, and GPU-based hardware acceleration.

### Google Chrome

The web browser produced by Google, called *Chrome,* always has featured HTML5 support. First released in April 2009, it has come a long way in a very short period of time. As of June 2011, Chrome is estimated to own 15 to 20% of the browser market share, and this is still growing. Google Chrome is available for Windows (XP, Vista, and 7), Mac OS X, and Linux operating systems, and it features the WebKit layout engine.

A very close relative to Google Chrome is a web browser called Chromium because both use the same code base and WebKit engine. Because Chrome is an open-sourced browser, anyone is free to build and release it. *Chromium* is the name assigned to third-party builds of the browser source, whereas the name *Chrome* can be applied only to official Google builds. Effectively, Chrome and Chromium are the same base code, the only difference being that Chromium can be customized and released by individuals — outside of Google's quality control — to apply features for specific operating systems or environments.

### Opera

Originally conceived in 1994 as a research project in Norway, Opera was soon spawned into its current namesake company, Opera Software ASA. A founding member of WHATWG, Opera released its first HTML5-aware web browser, Opera 10, in June 2009.

The Opera 11 layout engine, Presto, features a mixed level of better-yet-worse HTML5 support, at least when compared to other HTML5 web browsers. It handles the new intelligent form inputs much better than any other browser but is still lacking when it comes to semantic tags and drag-and-drop support.

## Desktop Web Browsers (continued)

### Apple Safari

Apple, the third and final founding member of WHATWG, is a staunch proponent of HTML5. Part of this stems from the longstanding dispute with Adobe over Flash support, but part is from the rich UI capabilities that Apple software is known for.

Apple has invested the most resources into its WebKit layout engine, first announcing it in 2003 as an open-sourced web page renderer forked from KHTML, the KDE layout engine. Today, Apple still oversees its development, but there are many high-profile contributors, including Google and Nokia.

Safari is the web browser Apple ships on its Mac OS X desktop and iOS mobile operating systems, and it is also available for Windows XP, Vista, and 7. The first version of Safari to support HTML5 was released as Safari 4. The most recent version, Safari 5, provides improved support for many HTML5 features.

### Microsoft Internet Explorer

Internet Explorer, once the top web browser in terms of innovation and market penetration, has fallen steadily since its peak of a 90% market share in early 2006. Internet Explorer 6, 7, and 8 are still used today by many legacy Internet users, but the level of HTML5 support is poor at best. Overall market share in mid-2011 hovers around 38%, its earlier share first eaten away by Firefox and then by Chrome.

To counter this trend, Microsoft released its first web browser to tout HTML5 compatibility, Internet Explorer 9, in March 2011. It uses an enhanced Trident layout engine to provide Microsoft's first foray into HTML5. Early results are impressive, with integrated CPU and GPU support and other significant speed improvements; Microsoft is clearly attempting to assert Internet Explorer 9 as the top HTML5 web-browsing experience.

Internet Explorer 9 is available only for the Windows Vista, Windows 7, and Windows Server 2008 platforms. It is not available for Windows users who are still running older operating systems, such as XP and Server 2003.

## Mobile Web Browsers

Mobile computers — available as smartphones, netbooks, tablets, and other ultracompact PCs — have experienced significant growth over the past few years. These are devices with lower-powered CPUs, smaller displays, a thumb-sized keyboard (or none at all), a touchscreen or trackpad, and cellular connectivity. These devices have special web browsers designed for these limitations, yet many offer some of the best level of HTML5 support available.

Many desktop web browser vendors have produced mobile versions of their platforms, featuring the same HTML5 layout engine. WebKit powers Google Android and Apple Safari (for the iPhone, iPad, and iPod touch) browsers, Presto for Opera Mobile, Nintendo Wii, and Nintendo DSi, and Gecko for Firefox Mobile.

Of note is Trident for Windows Phone 7. This layout engine is not the same version featured in Internet Explorer 9 but rather an earlier version closely based on Internet Explorer 6. As such, Windows Phone 7 offers one of the poorest mobile HTML5 browsing experiences among smartphones.

Finally, there are also vendors that compete only in the mobile browser market. This includes the RIM BlackBerry devices, whose recent versions feature the BOLT web browser, and the HP WebOS browser. Both of these companies use the WebKit layout engine on their smartphones and tablets.

## The Best Overall Support?

If you are noticing a trend here with WebKit, you are not alone. WebKit overall today provides the best level of HTML5 support and is the most widely adopted layout engine, thanks to its open-source license. Ultimately, all WebKit-based browsers can be treated roughly as equal in terms of HTML5 support;

however, WebKit itself is under constant, independent development. Newer versions of WebKit browsers will feature a more recent version of the engine, and each WebKit release brings us one step closer to HTML5 nirvana.

It is important to note that HTML5 implies a transitional period between HTML 4.01 and the new standard. Furthermore, even HTML5-aware web browsers do not support the HTML5 specification perfectly. This means that you need to provide some sort of backward compatibility with all HTML5 features you use, providing that you do not want to alienate your users based on their choice of web browser.

This book stresses backward compatibility wherever possible. However, you should discourage your users from using outdated web browsers so that you can avoid these types of compatibility issues. You will learn how to best use an HTML5 tag and how to safely implement its HTML 4 fallback.

## Mixing HTML Standards and Web Browsers

A single web page can follow only a single HTML standard. In other words, mixing standards on a single page is not possible; you must decide if a page is HTML 4, HTML5, or based on some other markup language. This instructs the web browser on which etymology to use and how to interpret your web page.

### HTML 4 on HTML5 Web Browsers

It is safe to assume that all HTML5 web browsers will honor HTML 4 websites, but only if the appropriate HTML 4 document type declaration is found. This maintains backward compatibility with the vast majority of websites on the Internet.

The HTML 4 declaration instructs the web browser to run in HTML 4 standards mode, thus rendering the older standard correctly. An example of an HTML 4 document type declaration is

```
<!doctype html public "-//W3C//DTD HTML 4.01//EN"
  "http://www.w3.org/TR/html4/strict.dtd">
```

### HTML5 on HTML5 Web Browsers

When an HTML5 web browser encounters the HTML5 document type declaration, new features and APIs are automatically activated in the browser and made available for that website. However, because not all browsers are created equal, a subset of HTML5 tags may not be implemented in certain browsers. Effectively, the browser needs to fall back to HTML 4 compatibility when it encounters an HTML5 feature that it does not understand.

An example of an HTML5 document type declaration is simply

```
<!doctype html>
```

Following is a list of the latest HTML5 web browsers, as of mid-2011, and their current state of HTML5 support. Note that there are some HTML5 specifications that are not supported by any of these browsers, specifically video subtitle support, and the Microdata, FileWriter, and Device APIs.

### Google Chrome

Google Chrome, as of milestone version 14, provides one of the best levels of HTML5 support available. For multimedia support, it does understand Ogg Theora and WebM encoded videos; however, MPEG-4 and H.264 are to be removed due to patent restrictions.

It does not yet understand some new tags such as `<ruby>`, `<time>`, and `<command>`, all of which it silently ignores.

In forms, Chrome is behind in adopting some intelligent form inputs, such as the `color`, `date`, `datetime`, `datetime-local`, `month`, `week`, and `time` input types; for these, it falls back to the generic `<input type=text>` behavior. It silently ignores the `<fieldset>`, `<datalist>`, and `<keygen>` form elements.

Chrome cannot yet handle the new seamless `<iframe>` attribute, instead falling back to the HTML 4.01 specification for `<iframe>`.

## Mixing HTML Standards and Web Browsers (continued)

### Mozilla Firefox

Mozilla Firefox has better HTML5 support as of its 5.0 release than the previous 3.6 or 4.0 builds but still places second overall in terms of support. For multimedia, it cannot decode MPEG-4 or H.284 formats, but it can handle Ogg Theora and WebM videos. It also lacks AAC and MP3 audio decoding support, but it does handle PCM and Ogg Vorbis correctly.

Furthermore, Firefox does not yet understand some new tags such as `<ruby>`, `<time>`, `<details>`, and `<command>`, all of which it ignores.

In forms, Firefox 5 does not yet handle new inputs, such as the `color`, `date`, `datetime`, `datetime-local`, `month`, `week`, `time`, `number`, and `range` input types; for these, it falls back to the generic `<input type=text>` behavior. It also ignores the `<keygen>`, `<progress>`, and `<meter>` form elements.

It cannot yet handle the new seamless or sandboxed `<iframe>` attributes, instead falling back to the HTML 4.01 specification. Finally, there is no support for the WebGL API.

### Apple Safari

Apple Safari, as of version 5.1, offers overall very good HTML5 support, but it too is not perfect. There is great support for QuickTime multimedia video and audio, which supports H.264, MP3, and AAC, with Ogg Vorbis and Theora plus WebM supported with a QuickTime plug-in.

It also does not yet understand some new tags such as `<time>`, `<details>`, and `<command>`, all of which it ignores.

There is good support for the new intelligent input types. However, the color, date, and time-based types are not yet fully supported. Most of these attributes do work, but there is still incomplete support for the `<fieldset>`, `<progress>`, and `<meter>` form tags.

Safari cannot handle the new seamless `<iframe>` attribute. Also, there is no support for the WebGL 3D, FileReader, or IndexedDB APIs.

### Opera

Opera, as of version 11.5, offers fairly good HTML5 support. For multimedia, it does not support decoding MPEG-4 or H.284 formats, but it can decode Ogg Theora and WebM videos. It also

lacks AAC and MP3 audio decoding support, but it does handle PCM and Ogg Vorbis correctly.

It has a good understanding of the semantic layout; however, it does not yet understand some new tags such as `<ruby>`, `<details>`, and `<command>`, all of which it ignores.

In forms, Opera has the best-available support for the new input types. Nearly every type specified by the HTML5 specification is supported.

There is no support for the new `<iframe>` attributes. Finally, there is no support in JavaScript for the drag-and-drop, session history, WebGL, FileReader, IndexDB, or WebSocket APIs.

### Microsoft Internet Explorer

Microsoft Internet Explorer, as of version 9, is the company's first foray into HTML5. Its level of support is not great, but it is about halfway there. For multimedia, Internet Explorer cannot understand the Ogg Theora and WebM formats, but it can decode MPEG-4 with H.264 video. It also lacks Ogg Vorbis audio decoding support, but it does handle MP3 correctly. Ogg Vorbis, Theora, and WebM can be added with the help of a DirectShow filter.

In forms, Internet Explorer cannot handle any of the new intelligent form input types; everything falls back to the generic `<input type=text>`. It also ignores the new `required` attribute, along with all new form elements.

There is no support for the new `<iframe>` attributes. Finally, there is no support for the drag-and-drop, session history, Web Applications, WebGL, FileReader, IndexedDB, WebSQL, or Web Workers APIs.

### HTML5 on non-HTML5 Web Browsers

When a non-HTML5 web browser opens your HTML5 web page, one of three things may happen, depending on the HTML5 tag used. First, content will appear, but it may be displayed in the wrong order or in the wrong place. Second, JavaScript-enhanced features may not work entirely or may produce an error message. Third, content or features may be missing entirely.

Your job as a web developer is to minimize these potential risks by coding your HTML5 website with appropriate fallbacks for non-HTML5 web browsers whenever possible.

As mentioned earlier, the World Wide Web Consortium is the standards body charged with maintaining and developing markup languages, prior to HTML5, on the Internet.

## SGML

The Standard Generalized Markup Language (SGML) is a document structure language that dates back to the mid-1980s. Its syntax is remarkably flexible, yet its implementation is very program specific. Every SGML file must begin with formal declarations — this defines all *elements* and *attributes* that can be used within — followed by the document itself. The elements and attributes, when found, dictate how the document text can be *marked up* to define formatting, layout, structure, and purpose.

Syntax is controlled by a structure of *standalone tags* — with element names and a forward slash, all within angle brackets — and *container tags* — which have a starting and ending element tag, with the forward slash in the latter. Marked-up text can then be defined within the container tags, as follows:

```
<element/>
<element>text</element>
```

One or more optional attributes can then be added to further extend an element's definition. The value itself must use single or double quotes:

```
<element key="value"/>
<element key="value">text</element>
```

Tags can be nested within each other, producing an SGML document. This format was standardized by the ISO (International Organization for Standardization) as ISO 8879 in 1986.

## HTML

HTML is the most commonly used dialect among web browsers and web servers on the Internet. Effectively, HTML is a derivative of SGML but with predefined tag names, structure, and display standards.

### HTML Tags

In 1991, Tim Berners-Lee, an engineer at CERN, published an internal document called "HTML Tags" that used SGML as its basis point. He took the complicated declaration syntax from SGML out and predefined a series of element names.

HTML further simplified beyond SGML by removing the forward slash from standalone tags and relaxed the requirement of nesting tags properly. Even the quotes for attribute values were no longer required:

```
<element>
<element name=value>
<element name=value>text</element>
```

It was using the tags from the "HTML Tags" document that the first web browser, NCSA Mosaic, was implemented. Some tags from this era still exist today, such as <title>, <h1> to <h6>, <p>, <ul>, <li>, and <a>; however, the actual structure of HTML documents was still very loose and not clearly defined.

### HTML 2.0

In November 1995, HTML 2.0 became the first official specification of HTML published. This standard provided the modern structure of <html>, <head>, and <body> tags, plus new text-formatting tags such as <pre>, <blockquote>, <b>, <i>, <tt>, <br>, and <hr>. HTML now supported embedding image files with <img> and submitting data with <form>. After this release, additional features such as tables, image maps, and internationalization were added.

### HTML 3.0

Never officially adopted, the draft HTML 3.0 specification was deemed too large and daunting for the two major web browser vendors of its time, Netscape and Microsoft, to fully implement. This included many new display features, including tables, figures, and mathematical formulas.

However, both companies decided to implement their own proprietary features into their HTML 3.0-compatible web browsers, such as stylized fonts, colors, backgrounds, and even an early version of JavaScript. This led to a major disconnect between the HTML 3.0 draft authors, web browsers, websites, and users in terms of who produced the best online experience.

## HTML 3.2

Published in January 1997, HTML 3.2 dropped some complexity from HTML 3.0 and reconciled many proprietary features onto common ground. This officially added new stylized attributes such as `bgcolor`, `text`, `link`, and `background` for `<body>`, plus new text-formatting tags such as `<center>`, `<div>`, and `<font>`. Java applet support was added, but JavaScript was still not yet sanctioned.

## HTML 4.0 and 4.01

Published in December 1997, HTML 4.0 was the first standard that offered variations: *strict*, in which tags that were deprecated from HTML 3.2 and earlier were not allowed; *transitional*, in which deprecated tags were allowed; and *frameset*, which was like transitional except that the new `<frameset>` tag replaced `<body>`. The frameset allowed for the web browser's display area to be subdivided into independently controlled views, each with their own URL.

Although the overall HTML 4.0 standard was solid, the new framing features were treated by web developers as an overcomplicated solution to a nonexistent problem and were often abused and shunned from use.

HTML 4.01 was released in December 1999 as a minor clarification update that addressed questions and problems implementers had about the specification.

### ISO HTML

The ISO officially adopted HTML 4.01 (strict) as ISO 15445 in 2000. The standards published by the ISO span hundreds of industries and jurisdictions, so acceptance meant that HTML 4.01 was solidified as the *de facto* standard for all participants on the World Wide Web.

Very shortly after HTML 4.01 was published, development of HTML was forked. The Extensible Markup Language (XML) produced XHTML 1.0. XML, by definition, used the same structure of markup tags as HTML, except that the element names were completely open and free and available ad hoc to custom platform definitions. Effectively, XML documents were like simplified SGML documents.

First published in January 2000, XHTML moved HTML closer to its SGML roots but required web developers to use stricter rules to define their websites.

For example, all element names had to be represented in lowercase; attribute values had to be properly quoted; standalone tags had to end in a forward slash (`<element/>`); and nested container tags had to be opened and closed in the correct order. For existing web developers, it was difficult to give up the freedoms HTML offered, just for the badge of "XHTML compliance."

XHTML suffered in its adoption due to incomplete and buggy implementations of programs attempting to follow its stricter standard.

As the W3C was promoting "proper XHTML use," a group of web browser vendors became concerned that the W3C was not preparing for the next generation of websites and web applications. In 2004, these vendors formed WHATWG, an organization to spearhead the development of HTML5, as mentioned earlier in the chapter.

HTML5 is actually a collection of new technologies that build upon HTML 4.01. Some extend the elements available to add in new features; others extend the Document Object Module (DOM) by adding new JavaScript APIs.

In April 2007, WHATWG presented to the W3C its first HTML5 draft, which the W3C adopted.

Officially, in early 2011, WHATWG decided that the term *HTML5* will be the last HTML-based standard to actually have a number attached. Instead, simply put, *HTML* should be used to refer to all standards, including whatever comes afterward. HTML5 is now, according to both the W3C and WHATWG, simply a snapshot of "HTML: The Living Standard."

# Introducing the New and Changed HTML5 Tags and Attributes

HTML5 has introduced several new tags and attributes from the previous HTML 4.01 standard. This was done by WHATWG to prepare the Internet for the future paradigm of web applications. The new standard includes better page structure definitions through semantic markup tags, new features such as the Canvas API, multimedia APIs, and new UI objects, and better text input through customizable text input types.

Some tags and attributes were even changed slightly from HTML 4.01. This was done to better define how they are to be used in the real world and to make them easier to use.

Note the following tables describe only the changes from HTML 4.01 to HTML5. A more-complete list of HTML5-supported tags and attributes can be found in Appendix A, "HTML5 Reference."

| New Tag(s) | Description |
|---|---|
| `<article>`, `<aside>`, `<header>`, `<footer>`, `<nav>`, `<section>` | New semantic markup tags to define the flow and structure of a web page. |
| `<audio>`, `<video>` | New multimedia tags to embed audio and video resources. |
| `<bdi>` | Applied to text that should change bidirectionally, right to left. |
| `<canvas>` | An object to render dynamic graphics in JavaScript. |
| `<command>` | Represents a command the user can activate. |
| `<details>` | Represents additional information that builds on `<summary>`. |
| `<datalist>` | Applies to the new `list` attribute, used in `<input>`, to create pull-down combo boxes. |
| `<embed>` | Defines a plug-in object. |
| `<figure>`, `<figcaption>` | Create a single `figure` block to complement a main document. |
| `<hgroup>` | Groups multiple `<h1>`..`<h6>` headers together. |
| `<keygen>` | Defines control for public and private key pair generation. |
| `<mark>` | Highlights text with a yellow background and is customizable in CSS. |
| `<meter>` | A static progress bar that shows an absolute measurement. |
| `<output>` | A placeholder for dynamic script output. |
| `<progress>` | A progress bar that can demonstrate activity via JavaScript. |
| `<ruby>`, `<rt>`, `<rp>` | Applied around ruby annotations. |
| `<time>` | Represents a date and/or timestamp. |
| `<wbr>` | Represents a line-break opportunity within single words. |

| Existing Tag(s) | New Attribute(s) | Description |
|---|---|---|
| `<a>`, `<area>` | `media` | Define what type of CSS media a link applies to. |
| `<area>` | `hreflang, rel` | Defines the language an image map refers to. |
| `<base>` | `target` | Represents a new browsing context name for relative hyperlinks. |
| `<input>`, `<select>`, `<textarea>`, `<button>` | `autofocus` | Automatically focus an input object after the page is loaded. |
| `<input>`, `<textarea>` | `placeholder` | A short hint or keyword that applies to an text input element. |
| `<html>` | `manifest` | Gives the address of the web page's application cache manifest. |
| `<input>`, `<output>`, `<select>`, `<textarea>`, `<button>`, `<fieldset>` | `form` | Link a data-entry element to a specific form externally from its `<form>` tag. |
| `<input>` | `required` | Specifies that an input element is required when the form is submitted. |
| `<fieldset>` | `disabled` | Allows you to recursively disable a `<fieldset>` element group. |
| `<iframe>` | `sandbox` | Applies additional security restrictions to content imported in an `iframe`. |
| `<iframe>` | `sameless` | Renders the `iframe` element seamlessly in the parent document. |
| `<iframe>` | `srcdoc` | Defines the literal source content document text. |
| `<input>` | `autocomplete` | Allows the web browser to save the form values when submitted, autopopulating them if the user returns to the same form. |
| `<input>` | `list` | Applies the new `<datalist>` element values into an text input element. |
| `<input>` | `min, max` | Indicates a numeric range of allowed values. |
| `<input>` | `multiple` | Allows the user to enter multiple values for a single text-input field. |
| `<input>` | `pattern` | Defines a regular expression pattern required by allowed values. |
| `<input>` | `step` | Indicates a numeric step factor for allowed values. |
| `<link>` | `sizes` | Specifies the number of icon link type attributes. |
| `<menu>` | `label` | Applies a text label identifier to a menu element group. |
| `<menu>` | `type` | Defines a menu type as a toolbar, context menu, or list. |
| `<meta>` | `charset` | Specifies the character encoding used. |
| `<ol>` | `reversed` | Boolean to create a descending ordered list. |
| `<style>` | `scoped` | Allows you to limit the depth of CSS definitions. |
| `<script>` | `async` | Executes a JavaScript script asynchronously. |

continued

| New Input Type Attribute Value | Description |
|---|---|
| email | Restricts text input to a valid email address. |
| color | Displays a color input box. |
| search | Defines a search field. |
| tel | Restricts text input to a telephone number. |
| url | Restricts text input to a valid URL. |
| date | Restricts text input to a valid date by year, month, and day. |
| month | Restricts text input to a valid month by year and month. |
| week | Restricts text input to a valid week number. |
| time | Restricts text input to a valid time by hour, minute, seconds, and milliseconds. |
| datetime | Restricts text input to a valid date and time. |
| datetime-local | Restricts text input to a valid date and time without a time zone. |
| number | Restricts text input to a number. |
| range | Restricts text input to a valid numeric range. |

| New Global Attribute | Description |
|---|---|
| contenteditable | Indicates that an element is editable by the user. |
| contextmenu | Applies a specific context menu to an individual element. |
| data-* | Allows you to embed custom data values as attributes that will be accessible in JavaScript. |
| draggable | Defines an element that can be selected in a drag-and-drop operation. |
| hidden | Defines an element as being hidden from the user's display. |
| spellcheck | Allows the web browser to check spelling and grammar of editable text. |

| Changed Tag(s) | Description |
|---|---|
| `<a>` | Without an `href` attribute, represents a placeholder for a link. |
| `<address>` | Scoped only by the `<section>` tag. |
| `<b>`, `<strong>` | Represent text that should be stylistically offset from normal text. The traditional bold effect is applied via CSS. |
| `<cite>` | Represents a title of work being referenced. |
| `<head>` | No longer allows the `<object>` element to be found within. |
| `<hr>` | Represents a paragraph-level break and no longer a literal line. |
| `<i>` | Represents text that should be typographically different from normal text. The traditional italic effect is applied via CSS. |
| `<menu>` | Represents toolbars and context menus only. |
| `<s>` | Represents content that is no longer accurate or relevant. |
| `<small>` | Represents small print. |

| Tag | Changed Attribute | Description |
|---|---|---|
| `<img>` | `border` | Must be 0 if used; otherwise, use CSS `border-width: size` declaration. |
| `<script>` | `language` | Omit and use `type` attribute instead. |

According to WHATWG, HTML5 must redefine how some legacy HTML tags are being used — especially the tags that apply cosmetic alterations and are better suited as CSS definitions. However, rather than deprecate these HTML tags, WHATWG and W3C have decided instead to flag them as obsolete.

The difference between these two is that obsolete tags are still required by web browsers to be supported, but web developers — people like you — are now required not to use them! In other words, if you use any of these obsolete tags in your HTML5 website, HTML5 Validator tools will mildly complain, but HTML5 web browsers will happily comply.

| Obsolete Tag(s) | Replacement |
|---|---|
| `<acronym>` | Use the `<abbr>` tag. |
| `<applet>` | Use the `<object>` tag. |
| `<basefont>` | Use CSS `body { font-family: font }` rule. |
| `<basefont>, <font>` | Use CSS `font-family: font` declaration. |
| `<big>` | Use CSS `font-size: 1.3em` declaration. |
| `<center>` | Use CSS `text-align: center` declaration. |
| `<dir>` | Use the `<ul>` tag. |
| `<frame>, <frameset>, <noframes>` | Use the `<iframes>` tag and CSS `position: fixed` declaration. |
| `<isindex>` | Use the `<input>` tag. |
| `<strike>` | Use CSS `text-decoration: line-through` declaration. |
| `<tt>` | Use CSS `font-family: monospace` declaration. |
| `<u>` | Use CSS `text-decoration: underline` declaration. |

| Tag(s) | Obsolete Attribute(s) | Replacement |
|---|---|---|
| `<a>, <embed>, <img>, <option>` | name | Use the `id` attribute instead. |
| `<a>, <link>` | charset | Use a proper content-type header on the linked resource. |
| `<a>` | shape, cords | Use `<area>` for image maps. |
| `<area>` | nohref | Simply omit the `href` attribute. Do not specify `nohref`. |
| `<body>` | alink, link, vlink | Use CSS `a:active, a:link, a:visited` selectors with the `color` property. |
| `<body>` | text | Use CSS `body { color: color }` rule. |
| `<body>` | background | Use CSS `body { background-color: color }` rule. |
| `<body>` | marginheight, marginwidth | Use CSS `body { margin: height width }` rule. |
| `<br>` | clear | Use CSS `clear: direction` declaration. |

| Tag(s) | Obsolete Attribute(s) | Replacement |
|---|---|---|
| `<col>`, `<colgroup>`, `<tbody>`, `<td>`, `<tfoot>`, `<th>`, `<thead>`, `<tr>` | char, charoff | No available replacement. |
| `<col>`, `<colgroup>`, `<tbody>`, `<td>`, `<tfoot>`, `<th>`, `<thead>`, `<tr>` | valign | Use CSS `vertical-align:` *type* declaration. |
| `<dl>`, `<menu>`, `<ol>`, `<ul>` | compact | Use CSS `font-size: 0.7em` declaration. |
| `<link>` | target | No longer necessary. |
| `<head>` | profile | No longer necessary. |
| `<hr>` | noshade | Use CSS `hr { border-style: none; background-color: gray }` rule. |
| `<hr>` | size | Use CSS `hr { height:` *size* `}` rule. |
| `<hr>` | width | Use CSS `hr { width:` *percent* `}` rule. |
| `<html>` | version | No longer used. |
| `<iframe>` | frameborder | Use CSS `iframe { border-width:` *size* `}` rule. |
| `<iframe>` | marginheight, marginwidth | Use CSS `iframe { margin:` *marginheight marginwidth* `}` rule. |
| `<iframe>` | scrolling | Use `<iframe seamless>`. |
| `<img>`, `<iframe>` | longdesc | Use an `<a href=`*longdesc*`>` tag. |
| `<img>`, `<object>` | hspace, vspace | Use CSS `margin:` *hspace vspace* declaration. |
| `<li>`, `<ol>`, `<ul>` | type | Use CSS `list-stype-type:` *type* declaration. |
| `<meta>` | scheme | No available replacement. |
| `<object>` | archive, classid, codebase, codetype, declare, standby | No longer used. |
| `<param>` | valuetype, type | No replacement; just use `name` and `value` attributes. |
| `<table>` | cellpadding | Use CSS `table { padding:` *size* `}` rule. If zero, add `border-collapse: collapse` declaration. |
| `<table>` | cellspacing | Use CSS `td, th { padding:` *size* `}` rule. |
| `<table>` | frame | Use CSS `table { border-side:` *size* `solid }` rule. |
| `<table>` | rules | Use CSS `td, th { border-side:` *size* `solid }` rule. |
| `<table>`, `<object>` | border | Use CSS `table, object { border-width:` *size* `}` rule. |
| `<table>`, `<td>`, `<th>`, `<col>`, `<colgroup>`, `<pre>` | width | Use CSS `width:` *size* declaration. |
| `<table>`, `<tr>`, `<td>`, `<th>`, `<body>` | bgcolor | Use CSS `background-color:` *color* declaration. |
| `<td>` | axis, scope | Use the `scope` attribute on `<th>` instead. |
| `<td>`, `<th>` | abbr | No available replacement; use more concise text in the `<th>` column header. |
| `<td>`, `<th>` | height | Use CSS `td, th { height:` *size* `}` rule. |
| `<td>`, `<th>` | nowrap | Use CSS `td, th { white-space: nowrap }` rule. |
| `*` | align | Use CSS `text-align:` *direction* declaration. |

**Y**ou can use an HTML5 Validator tool to verify how well a website supports HTML5. There are many validation tools available online, but they should all conform to the most recent HTML5 specifications. One such tool produced by the W3C is called *the W3C Markup Validation Service,* at http://validator.w3.org.

The W3C Markup Validation Service is fairly thorough. It enables you to verify a website against non-English character-encoding types and older markup languages, such as HTML versions 4.01, 3.2, and 2.0, various XHTML standards, MathML, Scalable Vector Graphics (SVG), and Synchronized Multimedia Integration Language (SMIL).

When you connect, you must submit the URL of the site that you want to validate. The tool will download the HTML source code for the site, autodetect the encoding and document type, and analyze it for compliance. It rates any infractions by severity, groups together like errors and warnings, and provides you with an explanation on how to resolve the problem.

The preceding section, "Understanding Obsolete HTML Tags and Attributes," states that the HTML5 specification dictates a series of obsolete tags and attributes and yet allows web browsers to maintain compatibility. Although this is a convenience for the end user as the browser is more forgiving, the W3C Markup Validation Service will not be. As such, even if an HTML5 website you produce looks perfect in an HTML5 web browser, expect to find warnings and errors here.

How do you decide which warnings and errors are safe to ignore? The simple answer is to test your HTML5 pages yourself, in as many web browsers as possible. If it looks correct, leave it. HTML is designed to be forgiving of errors; however, XHTML is not. This tool follows the XHMTL mantra in that everything must be to-the-letter correct.

## Validate a Website for HTML5 Compliance

**1** In a web browser, type **http://validator.w3.org** and press Enter.

The W3C Markup Validation Service website loads.

**2** Enter the URL of the site that you want validate and press Enter.

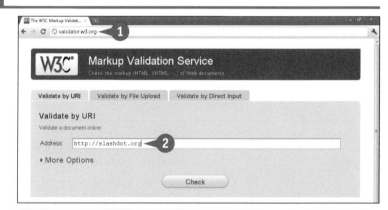

**A** A summary of the validation appears.

**3** Scroll down to see the specifics.

**B** Here is an example of an error message.

**C** Here is a warning message.

**④** Click a link for more specific documentation, such as this element.

*Note: Depending on the failure, not all warnings or errors will have a link to documentation.*

*Note: You can use Ctrl+click to open a link in a new tab.*

The documentation for the HTML5 feature appears.

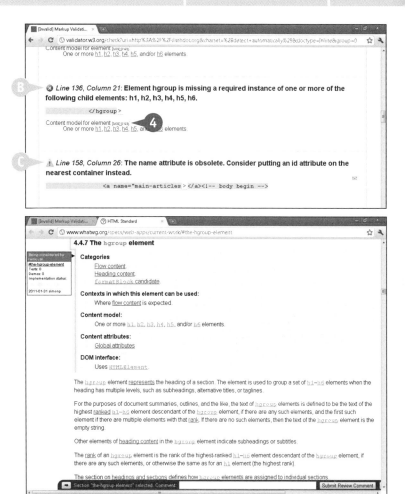

As pointed out earlier, even if an HTML5 web page fails validation, it may still render correctly in your browser. This is because the HTML5 specifications state that deprecated tags must be avoided by the web developer but may be honored by web browsers. This is a critical requirement of maintaining backward compatibility with earlier HTML versions. Ideally, this tool should be used not to report errors, but for you to judge if a warning or error is appropriate given your target audience.

Other tools the W3C has created include the Semantic Data Extractor, at www.w3.org/2003/12/semantic-extractor.html, and the CSS Validation Service, at http://jigsaw.w3.org/css-validator/. The Extractor enables you to view the outline of an HTML5 website's semantic layout tags, such as <header>, <footer>, <section>, <article>, and <aside>, and displays the simplified outline and summary. The semantic layout method is described further in Chapter 2.

The CSS Validation Service compares multiple versions of CSS, including HTML5's counterpart, CSS3, and rates your website for CSS compliance. CSS is introduced in Chapter 4.

The complete list of W3C tools can be found at the W3C Quality Assurance page, www.w3.org/QA/Tools/.

The HTML5 Test, at www.html5test.com, is a website that enables you to validate how well today's web browsers support the *most current* HTML5 specification. As mentioned, HTML5 is the "living standard," so the official specifications of today may differ tomorrow. Because WHATWG wants HTML5 to evolve over time, you can count on the HTML5 Test to verify sites using the latest specifications available.

The HTML5 Test is not designed to be an all-inclusive verifier of every HTML5 feature. It quantifies HTML5 support at a high level and provides you with the ability to compare different web browsers side by side. It works by identifying when a tested feature is supported by your browser, but it does not validate that your web browser actually *interprets* a feature correctly. Therefore, there is a chance the HTML5 Test site will say that your browser supports a feature, but that feature may not conform perfectly to the WHATWG specifications.

The HTML5 Test assigns a score out of 400 points to your browser. Bonus points are earned based on above-and-beyond levels of support. Your web browser's score is calculated using hundreds of tests from various test classes, including new parsing rules; canvas support; audio/video capabilities; new HTML5 elements; new HTML5 form features; enhanced user interaction support, such as drag-and-drop; microdata support, such as native binary execution; web application capabilities; and new security features.

The HTML5 Test site also verifies specifications related to — but not defined within — the official HTML5 specs. These include geolocation support, WebGL for 3D drawing, interserver communications, local files, browser storage, JavaScript Web Workers, local devices, miscellaneous text, and scrolling enhancements.

For each test, the HTML5 Test site offers a link to the official W3C HTML5 specification page. This describes the technical details of each feature tested.

## Validate a Web Browser for HTML5 Support

**1** In the first web browser that you want to validate, type **www.html5test.com** and press Enter.

The HTML5 Test website loads.

**A** The web browser's score appears here.

**Note:** *The score in this example shows that the web browser is HTML5 compatible.*

**2** Scroll down to the individual test results.

**B** This shows the score of specific test groups.

**3** Click here to expand a test.

**C** This is a successful test for an individual HTML5 feature.

**D** This is a failed test for an individual HTML5 feature.

**Note:** *You can click the test's name to open the official W3C specification for that specific HTML5 feature.*

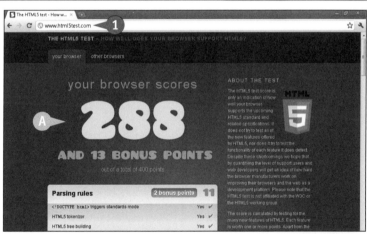

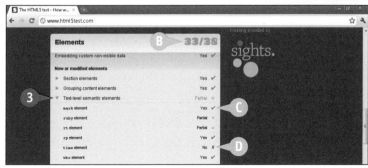

**4** In the second browser that you want to validate, type **www.html5test.com** and press Enter.

The HTML5 Test website loads.

**E** The web browser's score appears here.

*Note: This score shows that this web browser is not HTML5 compatible.*

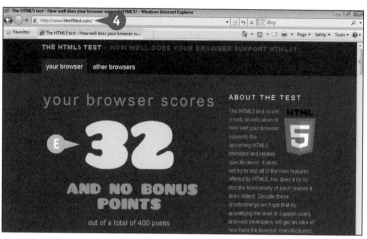

**5** Scroll down to browse the individual test results.

**F** Here are some test classes that failed HTML5 support.

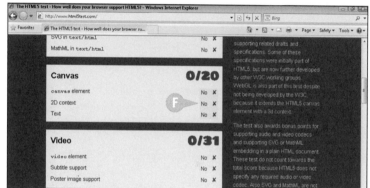

## EXTRA

The HTML5 Test scores bonus points to your browser based on features it supports but are not a part of the official HTML5 specification. Most bonus points are awarded when the browser supports additional multimedia codecs.

Here is a summary of HTML5 Test results using various web browser applications and versions:

| Web Browser | HTML5 Test Score | Web Browser | HTML5 Test Score |
|---|---|---|---|
| Android 2.2 | 156 | Internet Explorer 8* | 32 |
| Android 2.3 | 182 (+1 bonus point) | Internet Explorer 9 | 130 (+5 bonus points) |
| Android 3.1 | 222 (+3 bonus point) | iOS Safari 4.0.2 | 195 (+7 bonus points) |
| Chrome 10 | 273 (+13 bonus points) | iOS Safari 4.3 | 206 (+7 bonus points) |
| Chrome 14 | 326 (+13 bonus points) | OS X Safari 5.0.4 | 228 (+7 bonus points) |
| Firefox 3.0* | 57 | OS X Safari 5.1 | 293 (+7 bonus points) |
| Firefox 3.6* | 155 (+4 bonus points) | Opera 11.50 | 296 (+7 bonus points) |
| Firefox 4 | 240 (+9 bonus points) | Windows Phone 7* | 17 |
| Firefox 5 | 286 (+9 bonus points) | WebOS 1.4.5 | 140 (+5 bonus points) |
| Internet Explorer 6* | 17 | | |

*Does not officially support HTML5.

21

**I**f you need to use Internet Explorer — even an old, outdated version such as Internet Explorer 6 — you can install the Google Chrome Frame (GCF) plug-in. This will enable you to experience all the features of Google Chrome, such as enhanced HTML5 support.

Some computer experts actually recommend using this plug-in as standard practice because Internet Explorer's security and JavaScript features are rather outdated, compared to most modern web browsers.

The GCF plug-in will work only on Internet Explorer 6, 7, and 8, using Windows XP SP2 or greater, Windows Vista, and Windows 7. Once installed, the plug-in can be activated to render web pages in multiple ways.

Without any special configuration, the GCF will activate only on websites that have a specific `meta` tag identifier, stating HTML5+GCF compatibility:

```
<meta http-equiv="X-UA-Compatible"
  content="chrome=1">
```

For websites that lack this `meta` tag, you can activate GCF on the workstation for any website you want using the Registry. The `AllowUnsafeURLs` value enables you to initiate GCF on all URLs that literally begin with "gcf:."

```
[HKEY_CURRENT_USER\Software\Google\
  ChromeFrame]
"AllowUnsafeURLs"=dword:00000001
```

Using this, when you type in a GCF-prefixed URL, such as gcf:http://*www.mydomain.com*, the GCF plug-in will activate and render the web page with Chrome and HTML5.

## Support HTML5 in Internet Explorer with a Plug-in

**1** Open Internet Explorer 6, 7, or 8.

**2** Type **www.google.com/chromeframe** and press Enter.

**3** Click Get Google Chrome Frame.

**4** Agree to the Terms of Service and click Run if prompted.

**Ⓐ** The Google Chrome Frame Installer launches.

**5** Click Finish when the installation is complete.

**6** Restart Internet Explorer.

**7** Type **gcf:about:version** and press Enter.

**Ⓑ** The Google Chrome "About" page appears within Internet Explorer.

**Note:** *Internet Explorer is now HTML5 compatible but only on sites with the special* `X-UA-Compatible` `meta` *tag.*

**8** Press ⊞+R.

The Run dialog appears.

**9** Type **regedit.exe** and press Enter.

The Registry Editor opens.

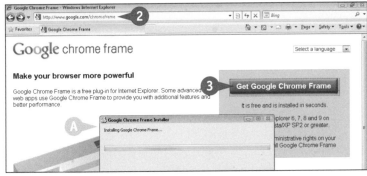

⑩ Click HKEY_CURRENT_USER →
Software → Google →
ChromeFrame to expand the
Registry tree.

*Note:* *You may need to create the*
*ChromeFrame key by right-clicking*
*and clicking New → Key.*

⑪ Right-click and click New →
DWORD.

⑫ Type **AllowUnsafeURLs** and
press Enter.

⑬ Double-click AllowUnsafeURLs.

The Edit DWORD Value dialog
box appears.

⑭ Type **1**.

⑮ Click OK.

⑯ Back in Internet Explorer, type
**gcf:** before an HTML5 website
URL and press Enter.

The HTML5 Web page is
rendered by Google Chrome
Frame.

*Note:* *Internet Explorer is now HTML5*
*compatible for all sites with "gcf:" in*
*the URL.*

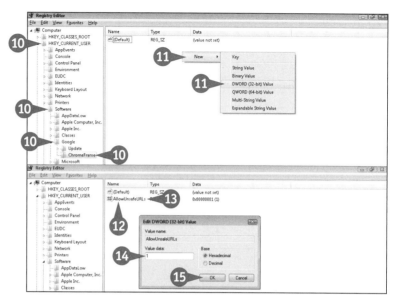

The Google Chrome Frame is available in stable, beta, and experimental builds. The procedure in this section
describes how to install the latest stable release.

If your website is already verifying whether the user is running Internet Explorer, you can promote the Google
Chrome Frame as a way to view HTML5 websites within Internet Explorer.

You can also enable GCF as the default renderer for Internet Explorer on all sites, regardless of the `meta` tag or
the "gcf:" URL prefix. You can do so by setting the `IsDefaultRenderer` value in the Registry as follows:

```
[HKEY_CURRENT_USER\Software\Google\ChromeFrame]
"IsDefaultRenderer"=dword:00000001
```

Internet Explorer will need to be restarted after applying this all-encompassing setting. After that, all websites you
visit will use GCF, and as such, the HTML Test, www.html5test.com, will report the best-possible score, showing
that GCF is active.

# CREATE AN HTML5 WEB PAGE

A web page identified as an *HTML5 web page* means different things to different web browsers, depending on whether the browser itself supports HTML5, along with which specific features. Chapter 1, "Introducing HTML5," discusses how to identify which features an HTML5 browser supports; you can use this information later in building your web page, but first, you must identify that your page is designed for HTML5.

Every HTML5 web page requires a special `doctype` element as the first element on the page. The whole line becomes a `doctype` *declaration*, or DTD. If you are familiar with HTML 4.01, the DTD was a long, cumbersome string that described which version of HTML or XHTML the page supported. For example, the following describes a web page designed for the HTML 4.01 Transitional standard:

```
<!doctype html public "-//W3C//DTD HTML 4.01
   Transitional//EN" "http://www.w3.org/TR/
   html4/loose.dtd">
```

In HTML5, the DTD tag has been simplified immensely:

```
<!doctype html>
```

The `doctype` element is required for legacy reasons. It ensures that the browser runs in *standards mode*, which basically ensures that it follows the latest HTML specification that it is coded for, as closely as possible.

So, when an HTML5 browser sees this, it knows that the page supports the new HTML5 standard, which is the latest version that it understands. When an HTML 4.01 browser sees this, it knows to follow HTML 4.01 Transitional standard, as this is what it falls back to when the `doctype` *legacy string,* the latter part of the DTD plus the URL, is missing.

Following the DTD, other HTML container tags that you are already familiar with from HTML 4.01 and earlier, such as `<html>`, `<head>`, `<title>`, and `<body>`, are still valid and required.

## Create an HTML5 Web Page

① Open a text editor.

② Type **<!doctype html>**.

③ Type **<html>**.

④ Type **</html>**.

**Note:** The `html` element must be begin on the second line and end on the last line of your web page.

⑤ Type **<head>**.

⑥ Type **</head>**.

⑦ Type **<body>**.

⑧ Type **</body>**.

**Note:** The `head` and `body` tag groups must follow one another. All unique page content appears within one or the other.

⑨ Type **<title>***Page Title***</title>** within the head tag group.

⑩ Insert some content within the body tag group.

⑪ Save the HTML5 web page as *pagename*.html.

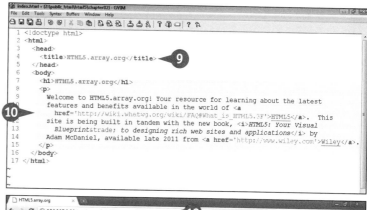

⑫ Open the *pagename*.html file in an HTML5 web browser.

Ⓐ The title appears.

Ⓑ The body content appears.

**Note:** *Because this HTML5 example follows HTML 4.01 standard, this particular page will render correctly in a pre-HTML5 browser as well.*

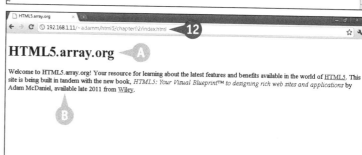

---

## APPLY IT

Note that in HTML5 and HTML 4.01, the doctype element and attributes are not case sensitive. So you can use <!DOCTYPE HTML>, and it will still be considered valid.

The doctype element is also used by third-party validator services to check for compliance against the various HTML standards, as described in Chapter 1. There is one caveat, though: An HTML 4.01 browser will not understand HTML5 tags, but your doctype element will say that it supports the latest HTML specification, according to this older browser. So how do you test an HTML5 web page for compliance against earlier standards, such as HTML 4.01 Transitional?

### TRY THIS

Go to the W3C Markup Validation Service, at http://validator.w3.org, type in an HTML5 website URL, and click More Options.

Select a non-HTML5 Document Type option, such as HTML 4.01 Transitional, and run the test.

### RESULT

The number of errors and warnings will increase, compared to the same test run with an HTML5 Document Type option. This indicates the HTML5-specific code that is not perfectly HTML 4.01 compliant.

As you start to implement the HTML5 features described in this book, this test can produce more and more supposed failures. Fortunately, fallback procedures inherent with HTML5 tag structure will prevail, allowing the page to render correctly, and these errors become benign.

# Understanding the Semantic Layout in HTML5

**T**he new *semantic layout* in HTML5 refers to a new class of elements that is purely designed to help you understand where and how text is defined in your web page and its context. All semantic tags must appear within the `<body>`...`</body>` container tag group.

Each semantic element has no specific output, color, or design; they are purely here to help you, the web developer, understand the context in which HTML code and text belong on your page. Each element can be stylized with CSS, however, which is described later in the section "Assign CSS Styles to Layout Elements." Until then, each element will be invisible, and its text will appear drab and monotone when viewed in an HTML5 web browser.

It is important to note that the new semantic layout elements are all optional and are only provided for your benefit as a web developer. They are designed to help you visualize and understand where appropriate content goes and how it is to be stylized with CSS.

## <header>...</header>, <footer>...</footer>

The `<header>` and `<footer>` tag groups are most commonly found immediately after `<body>` begins and before `<body>` ends, respectively. They indicate content that appears at the top and the bottom of your web page:

Most websites' headers typically contain a site logo image, introductory text, navigation, and possibly a search form. Footers, by contrast, may contain additional secondary navigation, legal or copyright notices, and any final closing images or text.

```
<body>
  <header>[Page header]</header>
  [Page content]
  <footer>[Page footer]</footer>
</body>
```

## <section>...</section>

The `<section>` tag group describes the different sections of content on your web page. You can use as many section groups as you need. All sections must be found directly within the `<body>` tag group, preceded and succeeded by a single `<header>` and `<footer>` tag group, if used:

How do you decide what makes a unique section? Different major, unrelated components of your website should each make up a single section. For example, you may create a navigational section, an article content section, a search section, and so on.

```
<body>
  <header>[Page header]</header>
  <section>[First Section]</section>
  <section>[Second Section]</section>
  <section>[Third Section]</section>
  ...
  <footer>[Page footer]</footer>
</body>
```

## <nav>...</nav>

The <nav> tag group describes the navigational links users can use to traverse your website. The nav tag is most commonly found within <section>, creating a navigational section, but may also be used within the <article>, <header>, and <footer> tag groups:

```
<section>
  <header>[Navigational section header]</header>
  <nav>[Navigational links...]</nav>
  <footer>[Navigational section footer]</footer>
</section>
```

It is most common for a <nav> tag group to contain only an unordered list of <a href="url">...</a> links, specially stylized by CSS, as described later in this chapter in the section "Declare a Navigation Layout Element."

## <article>...</article>

The <article> tag group houses actual content, with different groups indicating standalone articles of content, all stored within a single section designed to hold all articles:

```
<section>
  <header>[Article section header]</header>
  <article>[First article...]</article>
  <article>[Second article...]</article>
  <article>[Third article...]</article>
  ...
  <footer>[Article section footer]</footer>
</section>
```

This might seem unusual at first, but imagine a typical newspaper as an analogy. A newspaper has multiple sections, such as World News, Local News, Sports, and Classifieds, with each containing several unique articles related to the section.

For your website, if you only have one logical article within a single section, you could bypass the <article> tag and define the content directly within the <section> group, but this goes against the spirit of the semantic layout in HTML5.

continued ➤

## `<hgroup>...</hgroup>`

The optional `<hgroup>` tag is designed to appear within the `<article>` container, when the container contains more than one heading tag — `<h1>`, `<h2>`, and up to `<h6>` — in a row. A good example of this is an article title, followed by a subtitle, and the article author:

If your article has only one heading element, you can ignore the `<hgroup>` tag group and place it directly within the `<article>` group.

```
<article>
  <hgroup>
    <h1>[Article title]</h1>
    <h2>[Article subtitle]</h2>
    <h3>[Article author]</h3>
  </hgroup>
  [Article content...]
</article>
```

## `<p>...</p>`

The paragraph tag you should already be familiar with. It can appear anywhere within any of the earlier tags, except `<hgroup>`, and describes an individual paragraph composing the article's content. You can use as many paragraph tag groups as there are paragraphs of text:

Prior to HTML5, poorly written HTML pages used a standalone `<p>` tag indicating a paragraph break. I myself was often guilty of this infraction. Never do this in HTML5. A `<p>` tag must always indicate the start of the paragraph, and `</p>` indicates the end.

```
<article>
  <hgroup>[Article headers]</hgroup>
  <p>[First paragraph text]</p>
  <p>[Second paragraph text]</p>
  ...
</article>
```

## `<figure>...<figcaption>...</figcaption></figure>`

The optional `<figure>` tag is designed to appear only within the `<article>` container, straddled by paragraphs:

```
<article>
  <hgroup>[Article headers]</hgroup>
  <figure>
    [Image related to the article]
    <figcaption>[Figure image description]</
figcaption>
  </figure>
  <p>[Paragraph text]</p>
  ...
</article>
```

For a `<figure>` to "stand out," CSS would need to be applied. This example is described later in this chapter in the section "Declare Figure and Aside Layout Elements."

## `<aside>...</aside>`

The optional `<aside>` tag is designed to appear only within the `<article>` container, straddled by paragraphs. It represents content that is related to the article but not a part of the article's reading text order. For example, in a news-related website, an `<aside>` tag could hold an interesting image, quote, or poignant text — basically something that summarizes the article yet stands out from the article's main text. This is designed to catch the reader's eye, enticing him or her to read the article itself:

```
<article>
  <hgroup>[Article headings]</hgroup>
  <figure>[Figure image]</figure>
  <p>[Paragraph text]</p>
  <aside>[Supporting article text or quote]</aside>
  <p>[Paragraph text]</p>
  ...
</article>
```

Naturally, for an `<aside>` to stand out, CSS would need to be applied to make its font larger than the regular article, limited to a specific width, and boxed in with a subtle black border. This example is described later in this chapter in the section "Declare Figure and Aside Layout Elements."

The `header` and `footer` elements are new in the HTML5 semantic layout design, although their idea has been around for quite some time. Previously, a simple `<div>` tag, or even a table, would create headers and footers. These elements are purely optional, but they help you understand your page layout at a glance:

```
<body>
   <header>
      Body header content
   </header>
   Main body content
   <footer>
      Body footer content
   </footer>
</body>
```

Use `<header>` and `<footer>` within any semantic layout element. For example, you could use the `<section>` tag, described later in this chapter in "Declare Section and Article Layout Elements," and assign the section a header or footer, if you so choose.

The `header` and `footer` elements will not receive any special treatment from the web browser, just like `<div>...</div>` tags. The real benefit to semantic elements lies in the ability to understand the purpose of the code within and to easily assign CSS styles.

When first establishing a header or footer, or any semantic layout element, assign it a temporary CSS border. This will help give you an idea about the boundaries of the header and footer when rendered by the web browser. Later, after you are happy with the complete layout of the web page, you can remove the temporary CSS and apply a proper design layout.

## Declare Header and Footer Layout Elements

**1** Scroll to one line after the `<body>` tag.

**2** Type **<header>**.

**3** Insert HTML content for the top of the page.

**4** Type **</header>**.

**5** Scroll to one line above the `</body>` tag.

**6** Type **<footer>**.

**7** Insert HTML content for the bottom of the page.

**8** Type **</footer>**.

**9** Scroll to the `<head>` tag group.

**10** Type **<style type='text/css'>**.

**11** Type **header, footer { border: 1px solid gray; }** to create a temporary border.

**Note:** *A border around any tag helps you to visualize its boundaries in a web browser.*

**12** Type **</style>**.

**13** Save the HTML file.

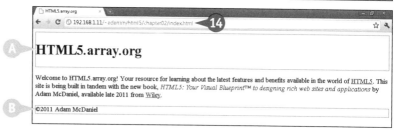

**14** Load the web page in an HTML5 web browser.

**Ⓐ** The header content appears.

**Ⓑ** The footer content appears.

**Note:** *Because the* `<header>` *and* `<footer>` *tags are displayed as CSS blocks, their boundaries extend the full length of the browser window.*

## APPLY IT

Your `<header>` and `<footer>` tag groups do not need to be the very first and last groups in `<body>`. If you want to add additional formatting throughout the entire page itself, such as to limit the overall page width, you can add an all-encompassing `<div>` tag around `<header>` and `<footer>` and then style it accordingly using standard CSS rules.

When placing your header and footer, or any other semantic layout tag, a very useful trick is to use CSS and place a little marker to remind you where a particular display block originates.

### TYPE THIS

```
header:before {
  content: "<header>";
  position: absolute;
  font-style: italic;
  color: gray;
}
```

### RESULT

The text "<header>" appears, gray and italicized, in the top-left corner of the `header` element. The `position: absolute` declaration means that it does not affect anything else in the header and is displayed independently of other content.

Note that the CSS border and "<header>" text should be used only while developing your HTML5 web page. After you are happy with the layout, proper CSS styling should replace these temporary CSS rules.

The navigation element represents a section of your web page that links to other pages, or other parts in the same page, with a series of links.

When creating navigational links, you can be very minimal and rely on CSS for all your formatting. For example, just use straight <a href> tags:

```
<nav>
  <a href='url1'>link1</a>
  <a href='url2'>link2</a>
  <a href='url3'>link3</a>
</nav>
```

Some sites overcomplicate navigational tags and turn them into an unordered list. You could do this, but then you will require additional CSS code to undo the bullet style, remove the list margin, and display everything inline.

If you simply want a series of <a href> tags to appear vertically, just like a bulleted list, assign it the display: block CSS declaration, as described in the "Apply It" on the facing page.

When first establishing the navigation, or any semantic layout element, it is a good idea to assign it a temporary CSS border declaration. This will help give you an idea of the boundaries of the navigation entries when rendered by the web browser. Later, after you are happy with the complete layout of the web page, you can remove the temporary CSS styles and apply a proper design layout.

## Declare a Navigation Layout Element

① Scroll to the <header> tag group.

② Type **<nav>**.

③ Type **</nav>**.

**Note:** In this example, the nav element is placed above the heading. This will make the CSS float property display better, when you add it later in step **6**.

④ Type **<a href='url'>link</a>** for each navigational link.

⑤ Scroll to the `<style>` tag group.

⑥ Type **header nav { border: 1px dashed black; float: right; }** to create a border.

⑦ Type **header nav a { margin: 10px; }** to set a margin.

**Note:** *If you use any other* `<nav>`.. `</nav>` *blocks in any other semantic tags, such as* `<footer>`, *the sample CSS declarations will not affect them. This example specifically targets the* `<nav>` *tag within the* `<header>` *tag.*

⑧ Save the HTML file.

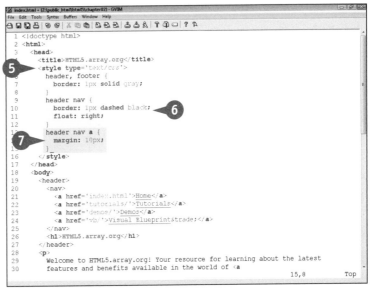

⑨ Load the web page in an HTML5 web browser.

Ⓐ The navigational list appears, aligned to the right of the `header` element block.

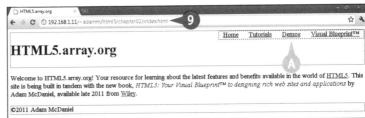

---

When using CSS, you have the freedom to reposition entire semantic tags and make significant changes to your web page's layout, all while using very little new code.

### TYPE THIS

Insert the following CSS style declarations; be sure to remove the `float: right` declaration if you used it from the example in this section:

```
header nav {
  float: left;
}
header nav a {
  display: block;
  margin: 10px;
}
```

→

### RESULT

The list now appears vertically to the left of the heading, with each link displayed with a 10 pixel margin. The main web page text flows nicely beside the `nav` element.

Note that the `header` and `nav` element borders overlap, and yet their content does not. This is a feature of CSS in which the rendering engine attempts to place objects intelligently, all while keeping content legible. Remember that the temporary borders added will be removed later, so the two element boundaries will overlap nicely.

The section and article layout elements allow you to group large amounts of display content and text content in your web page. As WHATWG conceived, one or more section blocks should appear in between the top-level header and footer element blocks, and one or more article blocks appear within a section dedicated to articles. That being said, you are free to apply sections and articles as you see fit, the point being that you understand what, within your own code, is a display section and what is a text article.

Multiple sections can be defined by assigning a CSS *class identifier* to the section. This will help you later when assigning style sheet declarations. Multiple articles can be defined with a similar class identifier for the same reason:

```
<section id='sidebar'>
  <nav>...</nav>
</section>
<section id='articles'>
  <article id='news1'>...</article>
  <article id='news2'>...</article>
  <article id='news3'>...</article>
</section>
```

Another section block could hold a secondary form of navigation on your website, as in the example in the figures below, a listing of a blog post archive by month.

## Declare Section and Article Layout Elements

**1** Scroll to one line after the </header> closing tag.

**2** Type **<section id='*articles*'>**.

**3** Type **<article>**.

**4** Insert some article content.

**5** Type **</article>**.

**6** Create a few more articles within this section.

**7** Type **</section>**.

**8** Type **<section id='*sidebar*'>** prior to the articles section.

**9** Insert secondary navigational content for this sidebar archive section.

***Note:*** *In this example, the archive text is not yet hyperlinked. The links can be added later after your layout is good.*

**10** Type **</section>**.

11 Scroll to the `<style>` tag group.

12 Type **section#*sidebar* { border: 3px dotted gray; float: right; width: 20%; }** to create a border.

13 Type **section#*articles* { border: 3px dashed black; margin: 10px; }** to create a dashed border with a margin.

14 Type **section#*articles* article { border: 2px solid gray; margin: 10px; }** to create a solid border with a margin.

15 Save the HTML file.

16 Load the web page in an HTML5 web browser.

Ⓐ The articles section appears in a dashed black border.

Ⓑ The individual articles appear in a solid gray border.

Ⓒ The sidebar section appears in dotted light gray on the right.

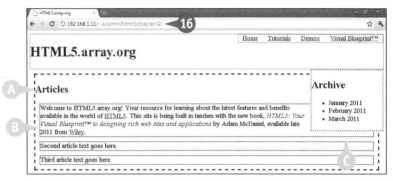

You can use CSS to alter the placement of sections, such as move the sidebar in the example shown here to the left side of the articles section. Before you can do that, the footer needs a minor amendment.

**TYPE THIS**

```
footer {
   clear: both;
}
```

**RESULT**

→ The footer will always appear at the bottom of either the articles or sidebar sections, depending on which one is longer.

**TYPE THIS**

Move the `<section id='sidebar'>` block below the `<section id='articles'>` block. Remove `float: right` from `section#sidebar` and then add this:

```
section#articles{
   float: right;
   width: 75%;
}
```

**RESULT**

→ The sidebar section appears on the left of the page, using 20% of the available width. The sidebar section appears on the right of the article section, using 75% of the available width.

Note that the `clear: both` CSS declaration must be added to the first tag that comes after the floating sections, in this case, the footer. If you had another section, such as `<section id='summary'>..</section>`, prior to the footer, you would have put your `clear` statement there instead.

A fter you have a rough layout for your web page, you can start adding in some actual content. This is done using the same tags used in previous versions of HTML: the heading and paragraph elements:

```
<h1>Heading</h1>
<p>Paragraph text</p>
...
<h2>Subheading</h2>
<p>Paragraph text</p>
...
<h3>Sub-subheading</h3>
<p>Paragraph text</p>
...
```

HTML5 does add in one new heading group semantic layout element, called <hgroup>. This enables you to group multiple heading elements together that immediately follow one another in descending order:

```
<hgroup>
   <h1>heading</h1>
   <h2>subheading</h2>
</hgroup>
<p>paragraph text</p>
...
```

You can use the heading group to alter the default margin spacing on the grouped headings, making the first and subsequent headings appear closer together.

## Declare Heading and Paragraph Layout Elements

**1** Scroll to one line after the <article> tag.

**2** Type **<h1>**.

**Note:** *In this example, the article heading is actually* <h3>. *This is because* <h1> *was used for the page title, and* <h2> *for the section title. You should use* <h1> *if this is your first heading on the page.*

**3** Insert the article title.

**4** Type **</h1>**.

**5** Type **<p>**.

**6** Insert a paragraph of text.

**7** Type **</p>**.

**8** Repeat steps **5** to **7** for the remaining paragraphs in the article.

**9** Create similar headings and paragraphs for the other articles.

**10** Type **\<hgroup\>**.

**11** Type **\<h2\>**.

**Note:** *Again, in this example, the next heading in order is* \<h4\>.

**12** Insert the optional secondary article header.

**13** Type **\</h2\>**.

**14** Type **\</hgroup\>**.

**15** Save the HTML file.

**16** Load the web page in an HTML5 web browser.

Ⓐ Here is the article's header.

Ⓑ Here is the article's secondary header.

Ⓒ Here are the article's paragraphs of text.

---

The headings shown here are way too big, and you are not yet leveraging the `hgroup` element properly. Instead, a single `hgroup`'s margin should be the same as standalone headings. You can fix this by reducing the margin and font size of the `article` heading elements and apply the margin to `<hgroup>`.

**TYPE THIS**

```
article hgroup {
  margin: 0.67em 0px;
}
article hgroup * {
  margin: 0px;
}
article h1 {
  font-size: 1em;
}
article h2 {
  font-size: 0.67em;
}
```

**RESULT**

Groups of headings appear closer together, and the heading group as a whole has a 0.67em margin, matching standalone headings. The article's primary heading is the same font size as the standard font size — which is always 1em — and the subheading is two-thirds the size.

The figure element enables you to define a container around an image, table, or code example that is used as a supporting object to complement an article. An aside element is similar to a figure, except that it is typically smaller and holds only a key quote or sentence from the article's copy. Both elements are used to draw a reader's attention to an article, punctuating a single point, or demonstrating a single example, that is described in detail by the article's main text.

```
<figure>
  [image, table, code, etc.]
</figure>
```

You can add an optional caption to a figure with a <figcaption> tag. The figcaption element is described further in Chapter 3, "Using New HTML5 User Interface Tags and Attributes."

The aside element should be used in between article paragraphs. The purpose of this is to make the aside block appear outside of the paragraph itself, having the paragraph text flow around the block:

```
<p>Paragraph text...</p>
<aside>Article quote</aside>
<p>Paragraph text continues...</p>
```

The aside element flows around the paragraph with the help of simple CSS declarations, applied by the width and float properties. In the following code, the aside block floats to the right and expands up to 25% of the available paragraph width:

```
aside { float: right; max-width: 25%; }
```

Some websites even apply a simple border, background shadow, or even a stylized double-quote image to the aside element.

## Declare Figure and Aside Layout Elements

**1** Scroll to the article's content to which you want to add a figure.

**2** Type **<figure>**.

**3** Insert an image, table, or code.

**4** Type **</figure>**.

**5** Scroll to the paragraph to which you want to add an aside.

**6** Type **<aside>**.

**7** Insert supplementary text related to the article.

**8** Type **</aside>**.

⑨ Scroll to the `<style>` tag group.

⑩ Type **aside { border: 1px solid; max-width: 20%; float: right; }** to create a border.

⑪ Type **figure { border: 1px solid; margin 2px; float: left; }** to create a border.

**Note:** *In this example, additional padding, margin, and* float: left *was added to place the figure beside the text.*

⑫ Save the HTML file.

⑬ Load the web page in an HTML5 web browser.

Ⓐ The article's figure appears within a border and small margin.

Ⓑ The article's aside text appears within a paragraph.

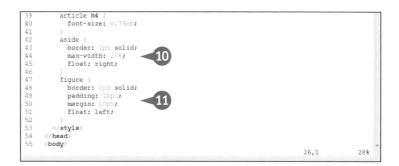

```
39      article h4 {
40         font-size: 0.75em;
41      }
42      aside {
43         border: 1px solid;
44         max-width: 20%;          ⑩
45         float: right;
46      }
47      figure {
48         border: 1px solid;
49         padding: 10px;           ⑪
50         margin: 10px;
51         float: left;
52      }
53   </style>
54   </head>
55   <body>
                                    26,1        28%
```

**HTML5.array.org**

Home    Tutorials    Demos    Visual Blueprint™

**Articles**

**Welcome to HTML5!**
Posted by Adam McDaniel on April 11, 2011

Welcome to HTML5.array.org! Your resource for learning about the latest features and benefits available in the world of HTML5. This site is being built in tandem with the new book, *HTML5: Your Visual Blueprint™ to designing rich web sites and applications* by me, Adam McDaniel, available late 2011 from Wiley.

Every few weeks this site will feature a new and interesting hack or tutorial, allowing you to keep tabs on the latest development in the world of HTML5.

New and interesting Hacks.

For the latest news and information about this site, follow Ⓑ Twitter, or sign up to this site's RSS feed.

**Archive**
- January 2011
- February 2011
- March 2011

**Article #2**
Second article text goes here.

## APPLY IT

You can apply some interesting styles to figures. This gives better guided flexibility over the old HTML 4 way of simply assigning images with the `<img>` tag alone. For example, the following CSS turns the figure image into a Polaroid-like frame.

```
Example
figure {
   border: 1px solid;
   margin: 10px;
   padding: 10px;
   padding-bottom: 50px;
   background-color: white;
}
figure img {
   border: 1px solid;
   padding: 5px;
   background-color: white;
}
```

The examples throughout this chapter have used borders to give you a rough idea as to how the semantic layout elements are being placed by your web browser. These borders, although ugly, have served their purpose, as the content in the example is now relatively populated and in the right place. It is now time to assign proper CSS styles to your semantic layout elements.

Work through one bordered block at a time, applying the style for the final page layout. In other words, do not strip everything; otherwise, you may forget where and how different layout elements interacted with each other. This can be especially true if you are using any modifying float, clear, or width properties.

When laying out your page, remember that some elements actually have preassigned values built into your web browser, such as the case with the <h1> to <h6>

heading tags, which can be overridden. Some of the CSS modifications you may want to consider applying at this stage include the following:

- Manually resize objects, via the height, width, margin, and padding properties.
- Precisely position objects, via the position property.
- Float objects, via the float and clear properties.
- Align objects, via the align property.
- Overlap objects, via the z-index property.
- Apply background colors, via the background-color property.
- Create background images, via the background-image property.

If you get lost, you can always restore the temporary CSS borders to get your bearings on the web page.

## Assign CSS Styles to Layout Elements

**Note:** *Follow these steps if you have used the temporary borders suggested as guidelines earlier in this chapter.*

① Scroll to the CSS style definitions.

② Select and delete the border declarations for the first group of CSS selectors.

③ Insert your own newly stylized declarations to this CSS selector.

④ Type /* *text* */ to insert a comment for your new CSS declaration.

⑤ Save the HTML file.

**6** Load the web page in an HTML5 web browser.

Ⓐ The new CSS style appears.

**7** Repeat steps **2** to **4** for the remaining temporary CSS borders.

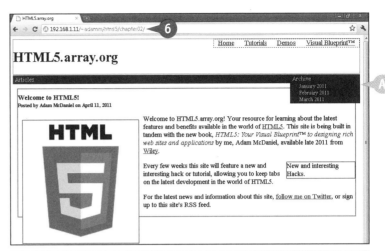

**8** Load the web page in an HTML5 web browser again.

All temporary CSS code is gone; the final CSS style is ready.

In the example shown here, CSS modifications are applied directly to the HTML page itself. This is good as a starting point, but the true strength of CSS is its capability to centralize all declarations into an external CSS file. This external file can then be referenced by every page on your website, providing a good, consistent interface.

**TRY THIS**

Cut all the CSS code within the `<style>` block and save it as a new file called base.css. Do not save the `<style>` and `</style>` tags themselves in your new file, but do remove them from your HTML file.

Insert this code into the `<head>` block, in place of the original `<style>` block:

```
<link rel='stylesheet' type='text/css' href='base.css'>
```

**RESULT**

All CSS rules stored in base.css are applied to the web page.

Pre-HTML5 web browsers will react differently to your new HTML5 code. Previous HTML specifications state that if a browser encounters a tag it does not understand, it should ignore that tag but continue processing the tag's contents. Unfortunately, this specification was implemented differently by the browser vendors.

When an HTML5 tag is viewed by a browser, regardless of its version, one of three things will happen: *1.)* The tag is recognized as an HTML5 tag. It is fully customizable by CSS. *2.)* The tag is considered an error, but a DOM node is still created. The tag is still customizable by CSS, but a `display: inline` style is implicitly applied. Or *3.)* The tag is considered an error and ignored. The JavaScript DOM also ignores the tag, resulting in no CSS support.

The first scenario happens when an HTML5 browser accesses your site. The tags are identified as "supported" and can be stylized with CSS.

The second scenario happens with most pre-HTML5 web browsers. Such browsers may not understand the new tags but can still stylize them. However, displaying them inline is wrong and must be addressed.

The third scenario describes how Internet Explorer prior to version 9 reacts to new tags. The tags are ignored, yet the content within the group is still displayed. Unfortunately, the tags themselves cannot be stylized by CSS because they do not exist in the DOM.

These two problems need to be resolved. The first solution is very simple: Just establish a `display: block` declaration for all HTML5 semantic tags.

The second problem can be solved by linking into a JavaScript project called *html5shim*. This is a third-party script tailored for Internet Explorer 8 and earlier that corrects the DOM for HTML5 code. You can find more information about html5shim at http://code.google.com/p/html5shim/.

## Provide a Fallback for Outdated Web Browsers

① Launch an older, non-HTML5 web browser.

② Type in the URL of your HTML5 web page.

The page display is distorted and incorrect.

③ Open your web page in a text editor.

**Note:** *If your CSS styles are in an external file, open that file instead.*

④ Scroll to your CSS definitions.

⑤ Type **header, footer, nav, section, article, figure, figcaption, aside { display: block; }**.

⑥ If you are using an external CSS file, save it.

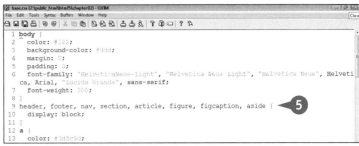

**7** Scroll to the `<head>` section of your web page.

**8** Type **<!--[if lt IE 9]>.**

**Note:** *This test ensures that the following code is loaded only for browsers earlier than Internet Explorer 9.*

**9** Type **<script src='http://html5shim.googlecode.com/svn/trunk/html5.js'></script>.**

**Note:** *You can always download this html5.js file, link to it locally, and serve it from your own web server.*

**10** Type **<![endif]-->.**

**11** Save the HTML file.

**12** Reload the web page in an older web browser.

The HTML5 semantic layout appears correctly.

**A** Internet Explorer 8 may trigger a Compatibility View pop-up.

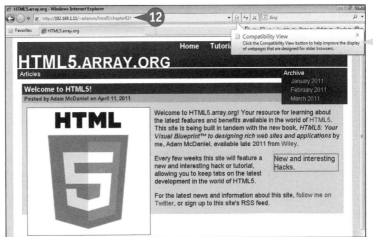

For other HTML5 tags and features, outside of the new semantic layout elements, there are implicit fallbacks for non-HTML5 browsers. This means that you do not need to rely on CSS or JavaScript trickery to at least display an appropriate warning or error message to the user.

This book describes several examples of this type of automatic fallback for complex HTML5 tags, such as the new `<canvas>` and `<video>` tags. The content within these tags will appear only on browsers that do not support the tag itself. Therefore, you can create something like this for an easy and effective fallback for browsers that do not support the Canvas or Video features of HTML5.

**Example**

```
<canvas id="animation">
We're sorry, you need an HTML5 compatible
  browser to view this HTML5 Canvas animation. Go
  to http://www.whatbrowser.org/ to download one.
</canvas>
```

**Example**

```
<video><source src="movie.webm">
We're sorry, you need an HTML5 compatible
  browser to view this WebM HTML5 movie. Go to
  http://www.whatbrowser.org/ to download one.
</video>
```

The HTML5 Canvas and Video tags are described in more detail in Chapters 10, "Drawing with the HTML5 Canvas," and 11, "Adding HTML5 Multimedia."

In an effort to promote HTML5 adoption, the W3C has created an HTML5 badge that you can place on your website. A *badge* is basically an image with supporting HTML code that promotes a specific cause or idea that you can install on your website. You can use this to show the world that your site is coded for HTML5.

Installing badges on a website is a technique that was very common in the early days of the World Wide Web; in the mid- to late 1990s, badges were often used to promote programs such as Internet Explorer 3 and Netscape Navigator 3.1, obscure social causes, cures for diseases, and so on.

Understandably, these badges got so overused and annoying that many website developers dropped them entirely.

Because the nostalgists at the W3C marketing department want to bring back badges, they have created a new logo for an HTML5 badge as an old-school throwback to those early days of the web.

You can see the new HTML5 logo and the form used to generate the HTML5 badge at www.w3.org/html/logo/.

When you configure your new HTML5 badge on the W3C's website, you have the option to display which supporting HTML5 technologies your site uses. These technologies are displayed as add-on icons to the main HTML5 badge, demonstrating your ability to support offline storage, connectivity, multimedia, enhanced graphics, device access, performance, semantics, and CSS3 styling.

## Announce HTML5 Support

**1** In a browser, type **www.w3.org/html/logo/#the-logo** and press Enter.

The W3C HTML5 Logo page loads.

**2** Click Badge Builder.

***Note:*** *If you are using an HTML5 web browser, the page actually scrolls down for you! This is a jQuery smooth-scrolling transition effect, which is explained in Chapter 8, "Using jQuery with HTML5."*

**3** Click the check boxes to customize your HTML5 badge by technology.

**4** Click Horizontal or Vertical for your badge orientation.

**Ⓐ** A preview of your badge is displayed.

**5** Highlight the badge HTML text.

**6** Right-click and click Copy.

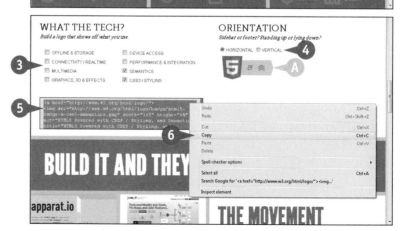

**7** Open your HTML text editor.

**8** Type **<div class='html5badge'>** to control the placement of the badge.

**9** Paste in the HTML5 badge code.

**10** Type **</div>**.

**11** Save your HTML file.

**12** Load the web page in an HTML5 web browser.

**B** The HTML5 badge appears on your web page.

**Note:** *In this example, the badge overlaps the end of the footer. This was achieved by assigning* float: right *to the* html5badge *CSS class.*

## EXTRA

Up to this point, this chapter has demonstrated only the Semantics HTML5 technology, but HTML5 is much more than that. The other HTML5 technologies are described throughout this book. After you have implemented them on your website, be sure to update your HTML5 badge!

If you have been paging ahead in this book, you have probably noticed that there are some HTML5 technologies that are not available as technology options on the HTML5 badge. This is because the badge is solely from the W3C's perspective of HTML5 technologies. Web browser vendors have been free to add their own features into their HTML5 browsers and have been advertising them as "HTML5 features," even though they are not in any official documentation.

On the other hand, one interesting technology showcased on the HTML5 badge yet is strangely unusable is called *Device Access*. As of mid-2011, no HTML5 web browsers properly support the Device API, so this book does not cover the topic. The idea behind the API is to allow the browser to access peripheral devices directly connected to your computer, such as a webcam, microphone, or smartphone over Bluetooth.

Until HTML5 is finalized in 2014, any API that has a weak adoption rate could be dropped out of the HTML5 standard entirely.

# RESIZE YOUR WEBSITE FOR MOBILE WEB BROWSERS

One lesser-known feature of CSS is its capability to alter your site's layout based on display size. This means that when your site is viewed on a mobile browser, an optimized layout for the screen real estate can appear.

Nothing is more annoying than going to a website on your favorite mobile device only to find a desktop-sized layout compressed into a tiny screen, or a layout so oversimplified and stripped down that the most useful features are crippled or absent.

There are a few different ways to apply this technique to your website. CSS allows for a `media` attribute to target a style sheet by hardware. For example, you can instruct the browser to apply base.css for all media and superimpose mobile.css for handheld devices:

```
<link rel='stylesheet' media='all'
 href='base.css'>
```

```
<link rel='stylesheet' media='handheld'
 href='mobile.css'>
```

Unfortunately, some mobile web browsers actually ignore the `handheld` property, such as iPhone and Android browsers. Instead, the most reliable way to implement this feature is to forgo the `media='handheld'` method and instead focus on absolute screen width values:

```
<link rel='stylesheet' media='screen and
 (max-width: 320px)' href='mobile.css'>
```

This loads mobile.css on screens 320 pixels or smaller. You can resize your web browser below the `max-width` threshold to experience the mobile layout on the desktop.

For iPhone and iPad users, you should also specify a `viewport` meta tag. This sets a default zoom level and specifies whether the user is allowed to zoom in or out.

## Resize Your Website for Mobile Web Browsers

**1** Scroll to the `<head>` tag group.

**2** Type **media='all'** for the default CSS.

**3** Type **<link rel='stylesheet' media= 'screen and (max-width: *value*)' href='mobile.css'>**.

**Note:** The `type='text/css'` attribute is optional and implied.

**4** Type **<meta name='viewport' content= 'width=device-width, initial-scale=1.0, user-scalable=yes'>**.

**5** Save the HTML file.

**6** Create a new file for the mobile CSS layout.

**7** Insert comments describing the change for the smaller layout.

**8** Insert the new CSS code to override the default-layout CSS code.

**9** Save the CSS file as mobile.css.

10 Open your web page in a normal browser.

The page appears normally; the mobile.css style sheet is not applied.

***Note:*** *The browser window width is above the* `max-width` *threshold set in step **3**.*

11 Narrow the browser window to below the `max-width` value.

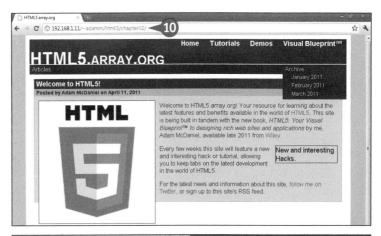

Ⓐ The mobile.css layout is applied to the desktop browser.

12 Open your web page on a mobile phone.

Ⓑ The mobile layout is applied on the phone.

***Note:*** *Most mobile phones have a maximum width of 320 pixels. Use this value as the absolute minimum value for the maximum-width detection in step **3**.*

When choosing a `max-width` value, experiment with your default site layout and slowly reduce the browser window width. As soon as the CSS layout starts to break, measure the width and use it as your threshold. You can use the broken CSS layout to identify what needs to be optimized for the smaller layout.

If you wanted to create an iPad-specific version of your website, you can create a CSS layout that specifies a `min-width` and `max-width` value range.

**Example**

```
<link rel='stylesheet' media='screen and (min-
  width: 641px) and (max-width: 800px)'
  href='ipad.css'>
```

Finally, if you are familiar with browser detection, you may be tempted to use the browser's user-agent string and categorize the device into a list of known layouts. This method is flawed because new devices are constantly coming out, and many devices misrepresent themselves. For example, the Motorola Xoom is a 10-inch tablet running Android 3.x, and its user agent identifies itself as an Android device; if your site assumes all Android devices have smartphone-sized displays, Xoom users will be left with a poorly formatted version of your website.

# DISPLAY A FIXED-METER BAR

The `meter` element, new in HTML5, enables you to display a gauge graphic to the user at any point on a web page. This is useful to display a metered bar of some absolute values to users. For example, if you were hosting a fundraiser, you could display a fundraiser goal gauge easily with `meter`. Just set the maximum and current values, and the browser will show the progress to the goal.

If the `meter` element is unsupported by the browser, the fallback display within its start and end tags will appear instead. You can use this to display a text description or a fallback image graphic:

```
<meter value='num' min='num'
 max='num'>Fallback Display</meter>
```

The `meter` element accepts several attribute values as input. At a minimum, you should set a `value` attribute as a real number between 0 and 1. If you also specify `min`

and `max` numbers, the `value` attribute must be anywhere between `min` and `max`, and the browser calculates the display as a percentage meter.

Extra numeric attributes that you can set include `low`, `high`, and `optimum`, which alter the meter's color depending on which are used. For example, using all three extra attributes, if the meter's value is between 0 and `low`, it is colored red; between `low` and `high`, yellow; and between `high` and `optimum`, green. If `optimum` is omitted, values below `low` and above `high` are yellow, and those between `low` and `high` are green. Experiment with these attributes to find the color combination that is appropriate for your meter.

The actual color theme displayed and the design of the meter graphic varies from browser to browser and by the operating system the browser is running on.

## Display a Fixed-Meter Bar

**1** Type **<meter.**

**2** Type **value='*number*'** to assign an initial meter setting.

**A** Optionally, type **min='*number*' max='*number*'** to assign a minimum and maximum range for `value`.

***Note:*** *If you omit* `min` *and* `max`*, the* `value` *must be between 0 and 1.*

**3** Type **></meter>.**

**B** Optionally, type **low='*number*'** to set a low number threshold.

**C** Optionally, type **high='*number*'** to set a high number threshold.

**D** Optionally, type **optimum='*number*'** to set a target number.

**4** Insert fallback display text or an image.

**5** Save the HTML file.

```
64        <p>
65          <meter value='50' min='0' max='100'></meter>
66        </p>
67      </article>
68    </section>
69    <footer>
70      &copy;2011 Adam McDaniel
71    </footer>
72  </div>
73  </body>
74 </html>
                                              74,1        Bot
```

```
60          attributes to find the color combination that is appropriate for
61          your meter.
62        </p>
63        <h4>Example</h4>
64        <p>
65          <meter value='50' min='0' max='100' low='25' high='75' optimum='50'>
66            Current value: 50 out of 100
67          </meter>
68        </p>
69      </article>
70    </section>
71    <footer>
72      &copy;2011 Adam McDaniel
73    </footer>
74  </div>
75  </body>
76 </html>
                                              76,1        Bot
```

48

6 Open your CSS definitions file.

7 Locate or create a CSS selector to the meter element.

8 Type **width: *value*;** to customize its width.

9 Type **height: *value*;** to customize its height.

10 Save your CSS definitions file.

11 Open your web page in an HTML5 web browser.

Ⓔ The meter gauge is displayed.

*Note:* In this example, the value is below high but close to optimum, so it is displayed in green.

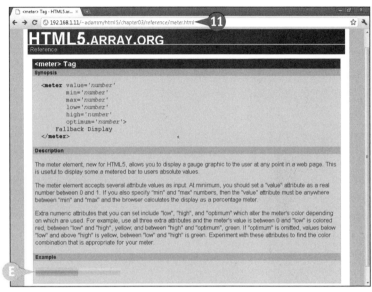

## EXTRA

You can use the CSS3 transform property, described in Chapter 5, "Enhancing Your Web Page Visually with CSS3," to rotate the meter by 90 degrees so that it displays vertically, like a thermometer gauge.

For WebKit browsers, you can override the display colors in the meter element with the following CSS selectors:

| CSS Selector | Description |
|---|---|
| meter::webkit-meter-horizontal-optimum-value | The used portion of the progress bar, when the value is optimal. |
| meter::webkit-meter-horizontal-suboptimal-value | The used portion of the progress bar, when the value is one level above or below optimal. |

For only very recent WebKit browsers, you can override the display format in the meter element by setting the CSS -webkit-appearance property to the following values:

| CSS Appearance Property Value | Description |
|---|---|
| continuous-capacity-level-indicator | Displays the meter as one continuous bar. |
| discrete-capacity-level-indicator | Displays the meter as ten thick blocks. |
| relevancy-level-indicator | Displays the meter as very thin bar slats. |
| rating-level-indicator | Displays the meter as stars. |

If -webkit-appearance is undefined or is not supported by the browser, it will fall back to the continuous-capacity-level-indicator format as the default.

# DISPLAY A MOVING PROGRESS METER

**A** progress element differs from the meter element in that its design specification says it moves to convey an in-progress task. This could be something such as downloading a file, processing a command, or any action that has a relatively short time until completed, but not instantaneously. In order to make use of this, you will need some additional JavaScript code to control the progress meter's current level.

If the progress element is unsupported by the browser, the fallback display within its start and end tags will appear instead. You can use this to display a text description or a fallback image graphic:

```
<progress value='num' max='num'>Fallback
  Display</progress>
```

The progress element accepts only two values as input; both are optional. When specified, the value attribute is a real number between 0 and max, its target. When displayed, the progress bar displays just like the meter element, showing a rendered percentage of progress.

If you do not specify the value and max attributes, the progress bar displays an animating "working" block that moves from one end of the bar to the other. This is typically deemed a waiting state, a state the user could be in if the value and max numbers have not yet been established by the device that requires measuring.

The actual color theme displayed and the design of the progress bar graphic vary from browser to browser and by the operating system the browser is running on.

## Display a Moving Progress Meter

**1** Type **<progress>**.

**2** Type **</progress>**.

**3** Save your HTML file.

**4** Load your web page in a browser.

**Ⓐ** An animated progress bar appears, moving from left to right.

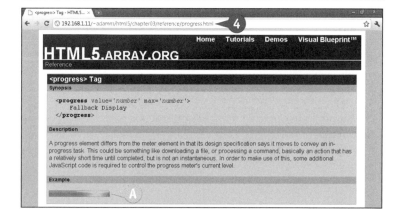

50

Ⓑ Optionally, type
**value='*number*'**.

**Note:** *If you omit* value, *a value can still be assigned in JavaScript.*

Ⓒ Optionally, type **max='*number*'**.

**Note:** *If you omit* max, *the value must be between 0 and 1, unless a new* max *number is assigned in JavaScript.*

❺ Insert fallback display text or an image.

❻ Save your HTML file.

❼ Reload your web page in a browser.

Ⓓ The progress bar appears as a solid bar, representing the percentage of value to max.

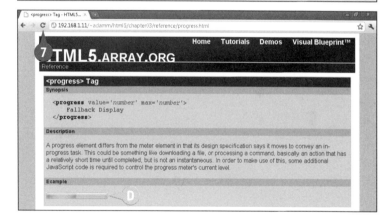

---

## APPLY IT

As mentioned, the progress bar should be tied into some sort of JavaScript process that requires measuring. To do this, you must gain access to the progress bar object in the JavaScript DOM and then manipulate the value and max variables accordingly.

In this example JavaScript code, jQuery can be used to set the progress element's attributes. As a fallback for non-HTML5 browsers, this code also sets the literal text "Progress: *value/max*" if the progress bar cannot be displayed.

**Example**
```
var value = 50, max = 100;
$('progress').attr('max', max);
$('progress').attr('value', value);
$('progress').html('Progress: '+value+'/'+max);
```

If you were to tie this into your own JavaScript code, you would need to set the max attribute once and update the value and inner HTML as your JavaScript function progresses. jQuery is described in more detail in Chapter 8, "Using jQuery with HTML5."

Chapter 2 discusses the new HTML5 semantic layout tag, `<figure>`, which enables you to define a standalone image, table, or code as a self-contained, supporting object that complements the document. Using the new `figcaption` element, you can add caption text.

Place the `<figcaption>` tag either above or below the supporting object within the `<figure>` group. Insert your caption text within:

```
<figure>
  [image, table, code, etc.]
  <figcaption>Caption Text</figcaption>
</figure>
```

Most HTML5 web browsers will not preformat `figure` or `figcaption` elements. This means that they will appear as text following an image when viewed by the browser. You should use `figure` and `figcaption` CSS selectors to add some display properties to your style sheet, such as `font`, `border`, `margin`, and `padding`.

If you do add in a `figure` or `figcaption` border, note that by default `figure` is `display:block` and will span the entire width of the page; this will look odd if the image itself is much smaller than the border. To counter this, set the `width` property on the `figure` selector to match the width of the image.

Alongside `figcaption`, you can also use an image's `title` attribute to display a short, temporary text message when the mouse cursor hovers over the image or the `alt` attribute to display a description of the image if it cannot be loaded.

## Add a Caption to a Figure

① Scroll to a `<figure>` tag block that has an image, table, or code reference.

② Type **\<figcaption>** after the image, table, or code.

③ Insert the figure's caption text.

④ Type **\</figcaption>**.

**Note:** If the figure is an image, you should add an `alt` attribute.

Ⓐ Optionally, type **alt=*'text'*** within the `<img>` tag to provide a description when the image is unavailable.

Ⓑ Optionally, type **title=*'text'*** within the `<img>` tag to provide a separate image title as a hover pop-up.

**⑤** Scroll to your CSS style definitions.

**⑥** Type **figcaption {**.

**⑦** Insert CSS declarations to customize the caption text block.

**⑧** Type **}**.

**⑨** Save the HTML file.

**⑩** Load the web page in a web browser.

**⊙** The figure's caption appears below the figure content.

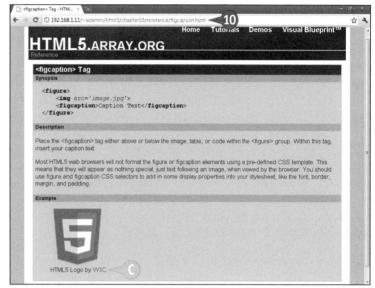

You can apply some interesting styles to figures and captions. This gives better guided flexibility over the old HTML 4 way of simply assigning images with the `<img>` tag alone.

**Example**
```
figure {
  border: 1px solid black;
  width: 128px;
}
figure, figcaption {
  padding: 5px;
}
figcaption {
  text-align: center;
  font-style: italic;
  border-top: 1px solid gray;
}
```

*HTML5 Logo by W3C*

You can highlight text in a web page, just like a highlighter pen on paper, using the new `mark` element in HTML5. This enables you to put additional new emphasis on a block of text, without using the older methods such as italicizing, bolding, or underlining:

```
<mark>text</mark>
```

Essentially, the `mark` element simply adds a yellow background color to enclosed text. The following CSS is built into all HTML5 web browsers:

```
mark {
  background-color: yellow;
}
```

Most non-HTML5 web browsers will understand `<mark>`, but you will need to explicitly assign it a CSS declaration, just

as in the preceding example. A good general guideline is to assign a value regardless; this way both newer and older HTML web browsers work fine.

In order for `mark` to be supported in Internet Explorer 8 and earlier, not only do you need to assign a CSS declaration, but you must also include the html5shim JavaScript code, as described in Chapter 2. This is because Internet Explorer does not allow CSS properties to be assigned to tags that it does not understand. The html5shim program corrects this problem.

Naturally, you can change the color by using a CSS declaration that overrides the `mark` selector. It is safe for you to redefine it on HTML5 to another background color, border color, text color, or whatever you want.

## Highlight Text

① Type **<mark>** at the start of a block of text.

② Type **</mark>** at the end of the block.

③ Save the HTML file.

④ Load the web page in an HTML5 browser.

Ⓐ The marked text appears with a highlighted background color.

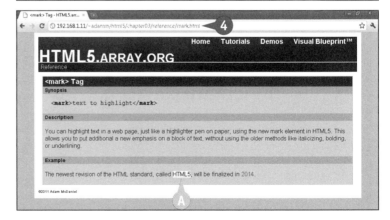

The wbr element, new in HTML5, enables you to specify a word-break opportunity so that long words can span multiple lines. This has a slightly different execution from the soft-hyphen character, &shy;, introduced in HTML 4. Whereas the <wbr> tag will just break up a long word, the &shy; code will also insert a hyphen before the line break.

When either is used, you can specify where the browser should wrap a word onto the next line of text if the word is longer than the available space on the line. Ideally, place it in between syllabic breaks. This helps the word remain legible when broken up, such as

```
Hippopoto<wbr>monstrosesquip<wbr>
 pediliophobia
```

When split across multiple lines with spacing for 30 characters, this long word would be rendered as:

```
Hippopotomonstrosesquip
pediliophobia
```

The &shy; code has the same basic implementation in your HTML code as <wbr>; however, you have the choice of using its proper code name, decimal notation (&#173;), or hexadecimal notation (&#xad;) to split up long words with a soft hyphen.

The new wbr element has already been implemented in some pre-HTML5 web browsers. For example, Firefox 3 and Internet Explorer 6 both implement correct <wbr> functionality.

## Specify Safe Line Breaks in Long Words

**1** Type **<wbr>** to break up a long word.

**Note:** Use &shy; to break up a long word with soft hyphens.

**2** Save the HTML file.

**3** Load the web page in a web browser.

Ⓐ The long word spans multiple lines.

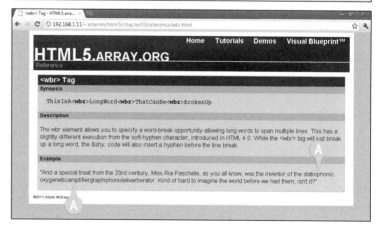

**Y**ou can configure any static text block to become editable by the user within any HTML5 web browser using the new `contenteditable` attribute. When activated, the text block will appear normal, but when it is clicked, it will transform into a form input field prepopulated with the current text.

This technique can apply to almost any text block, including sentences that are wrapped with `<span>`, paragraphs, headings, articles, and the entire body of a web page. This is possible because `contenteditable` is actually a *global attribute,* meaning it can apply to basically any tag, regardless of context:

```
<p contenteditable='true'>Editable Paragraph
   Text</p>
```

If any elements exist under a `contenteditable` block, they inherit the `contenteditable` property. If you add

`contenteditable` to `<body>`, all text blocks will be editable.

So, why make static text editable? The original purpose was to create rich text editors built as websites. Being able to see the changes in real time meant that users did not need to bother with creating text files, saving them, and then uploading them. Today, `contenteditable` is implemented on sites in such a way as to create subtle HTML form inputs.

For example, the web application Yammer (http://yammer. com) allows you to post URLs to your Yammer feed for you to comment on. When the URL is entered, Yammer retrieves the page, generates a short summary paragraph, and displays a normal form input for you to type a comment. The summary paragraph is actually editable, so you can fine-tune the auto-generated text, all while keeping the summary separate from your own comments.

## Allow the User to Edit Content

**①** Type **contenteditable='true'** into the paragraph element that you want to be editable.

**Note:** *Be careful about using* `contenteditable` *on any text block that contains a hyperlink. The link itself will become unusable, even when the text is not being edited.*

**②** Save the HTML file.

**③** Load the web page in a web browser.

The text appears as a normal paragraph.

**④** Click the paragraph text.

The paragraph becomes editable.

**Note:** *The browser displays a flashing cursor and highlights the editable block of text with a subtle border.*

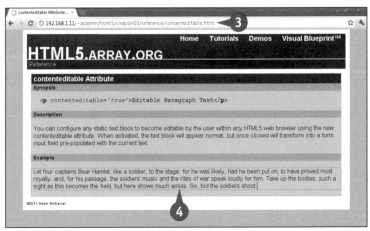

**M**ost web browsers provide a useful built-in spell-check feature available to any website that allows the user to type text. This feature is enabled when a `spellcheck` attribute is enabled on an editable text block. Note that content displayed on a site that is not editable is not spell-checked.

This technique can apply to almost any editable text block. This is possible because `spellcheck` is a new global attribute in HTML5. It is most common to see this on `input type=text` or `textarea` elements:

```
<input type='text' spellcheck='true'
 value='Spell-check text input'>
```

If any elements exist under a `spellcheck`-active block, they will inherit the `spellcheck` property. If you add

`spellcheck` to `<body>`, all form inputs and editable fields will be checked.

The spell-check feature is made possible by a built-in wordlist inside your web browser. When the browser finds a word not in this wordlist, it displays a jagged red underline that, when right-clicked, lists suggestions. An option to add the word to the wordlist is also available.

You can use any text-based element with the `spellcheck` attribute, provided that you also specify that it is editable with the `contenteditable` attribute. The wordlist used is based on the website's detected language. If you are viewing a site written in a language that you do not have a wordlist for, or if you need to spell-check in a different language, you will need to install an alternative wordlist dictionary.

### Spell-Check User Content

**1** Type **spellcheck='true'** into the input text element for which you would like to enable spell-checking.

**Note:** *Do not forget to add* `contenteditable='true'` *to spell-check editable static text blocks, such as* `<p>...</p>`.

**Note:** *Some browsers automatically spell-check* `textarea` *inputs. To disable this, simply use* `spellcheck='false'`.

**2** Save the HTML file.

**3** Load the web page in a web browser.

**4** Insert some text.

The spelling errors appear with a red underline squiggle.

**5** Right-click a spelling error.

Spelling suggestions appear in a menu.

**Ⓐ** Click a suggested word to replace the misspelled word.

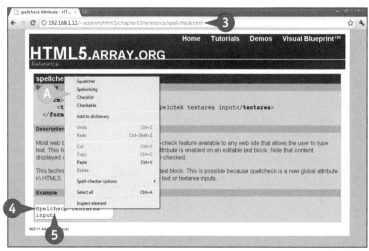

**57**

The details and summary elements enable you to display a shortened summary of a larger body, temporarily hiding the detailed content from the display. When the summary is clicked, the complete content becomes visible. For example, you can use these features to summarize an article by displaying only its first paragraph; when the article is clicked, the remaining article paragraphs will appear.

```
<details>
  <summary>Summarized content...</summary>
  Detailed content...
</details>
```

When a web browser sees this code, it knows that the content within the `<details>` tag group should be hidden by default, except for the content within the `<summary>`

group. When the summary is clicked, the complete details content is shown. Likewise, when the summary is clicked again, the details are hidden.

With the help of some simple CSS declarations, you can extend this functionality and provide information about the state of the display. The following can be used to append useful instructions for the user and make them appear clickable:

```
details summary:after { content: '(Read
  Details)' }
details.open summary:after { content: '(Hide
  Details)' }
details summary { cursor: pointer }
```

Additional information about CSS can be found in Chapter 4, "Styling with CSS3."

## Declare an Interactive Summary and Details Layout Element

**1** Scroll to the article for which you want to use the summary and details features.

**2** Type **<details>** before the first paragraph.

**Note:** Use `<details open>` if you want to display the detailed content when the page first loads.

**3** Type **</details>** after the last paragraph.

**4** Type **<summary>** within the `<details>` tag group.

**5** Insert a short summary of the article.

**6** Type **</summary>**.

**7** Scroll to the CSS declarations or create a new `<style>` tag group.

**8** Type **details summary:after { content: '*(text)*'; }** to display a queue to the user to click to read more info.

**9** Type **details.open summary:after { content: '*(text)*'; }** to display a queue to the user to click to read less info.

**10** Type **details summary { cursor: pointer; }**.

**11** Save the HTML file.

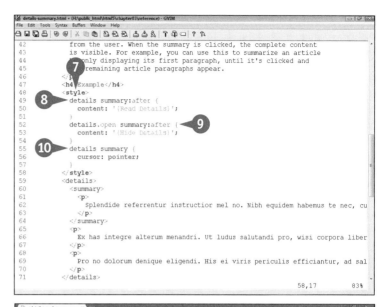

**12** Load the web page in an HTML5 web browser.

**A** Only the article summary is visible.

**13** Click the text that you added to read the details.

**B** The text changes to your hide details text.

**C** The article's details appear below the summary.

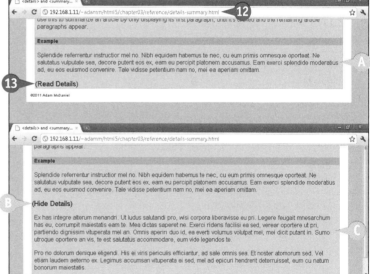

Unfortunately, as of mid-2011, no HTML5 web browsers properly support the `<details>` and `<summary>` tags. However, you can address this through a JavaScript fallback program and implement its intended functionality today. The screenshots in this section actually demonstrate one such JavaScript program.

As HTML5 browsers mature, this feature will be added, and correctly written JavaScript will yield to built-in functionality. A JavaScript example is available on this book's web page, http://html5.array.org/demos/details-summary-fallback.html.

Until you implement this type of JavaScript fallback, content within both the `details` and `summary` elements will appear at the same time, all the time.

# Introducing CSS3

Cascading Style Sheets (CSS) is a language that describes how HTML should be rendered by the web browser. CSS level 3, or more simply *CSS3*, is the third major revision of the CSS standard. CSS is maintained by the CSS Working Group (CSSWG), a collection of interested individuals and companies, but guided by the W3C.

Because most browsers have built-in standards for how HTML tags should be rendered, such as how <h1> appears in a large bold font, you can override these built-in definitions with your own CSS rules. Your CSS code is stored parallel to your HTML code, and it is possible to share one CSS file with multiple HTML files. This simplifies making cosmetic changes to an entire website as all stylization is sourced from a single file.

## What's New in CSS3

CSS3 actually started showing up in web browsers well before HTML5 was widely supported; however, today it is considered a major supporting component of the group of HTML5 technologies.

New features of CSS3 include support for multiple backgrounds, partial attribute value selectors, new pseudo-class selectors, and a new group of properties that enable you to transition, transform, animate, and stylize HTML.

## CSS Syntax

The following high-level list is an aggregated summary of CSS syntax, from CSS1 to CSS3.

### Rules

A single CSS rule typically stylizes one element a specific way, but rules are applied aggregately. This means that a single element can be targeted with multiple rules; each rule's property changes can apply and override an earlier CSS rule:

```
selector { property: value; }
```

The `selector` determines which HTML elements should be modified by the declaration, the part between the curly brackets. The `property` is the codename for the style that will be altered, and the `value` is the new style itself. The syntax for `value` differs for each property.

### Selectors

Selectors are the first part of every CSS rule. They allow you to define which elements are to be modified by the CSS declaration within the curly brackets:

```
element {...}
```

The most basic selector is to refer to an element by its tag name. This will allow you to apply your CSS declaration everywhere that <element> tag is used.

#### Selecting Elements by Class or ID

To limit your CSS declaration to only specific elements, you can refer to them either by a class or ID name:

```
element.classname {...}
element#idname {...}
```

This selector will match only elements defined as <element class='classname'> and <element id='idname'>.

#### Selecting Elements by Attributes

Elements can arbitrarily be targeted with a selector that looks only for elements with specific attributes defined, with attributes with specific values, or attributes with partial values:

```
element[attr] {...}
element[attr=value] {...}
```

These selectors will match only elements defined as <element attr='value'>. The difference is that the first example matches only if `attr` is defined; the second matches when `attr` is set to `value`.

Whereas the = operator tests for an exact value match, there are other operators that can be used to test for partial values:

| Operator | Description |
|---|---|
| ~= | Matches elements whose attribute contains `value` as a word. |
| \|= | Matches elements whose attribute matches `value` or begins with `value` followed by a dash. |
| ^= | Matches elements whose attribute begins with `value`. |
| $= | Matches elements whose attribute ends with `value`. |
| *= | Matches elements whose attribute contains `value`. |

## Selecting Elements by Pseudo-Class

Pseudo-classes are like special, built-in functions in the web browser. They help you to identify groups of elements by their placement order or pattern:

```
element:first-of-type {...}
element:last-of-type {...}
element:only-of-type {...}
element:nth-of-type(c) {...}
element:nth-last-of-type(c) {...}
```

You can use the `:*-of-type` pseudo-class to target a specific element by its ordering within its parent element. For example, if you have a large table that contains several rows, you can style odd and even rows with different background colors:

```
tr:nth-of-type(odd) { background-color: #eef; }
tr:nth-of-type(even) { background-color: #ddf; }
```

A variation of `type` is the `child` pseudo-class:

```
element:first-child {...}
element:last-child {...}
element:nth-child(c) {...}
element:nth-last-child(c) {...}
```

The `:*-child` pseudo-class targets a specific element by its ordering within its parent element, but only if the element occupies that exact position in the parent-child index.

`c` is a formula that can represent an exact type or child, alternating counts of type or child, plus an optional offset.

## Combinators

Combinators group multiple simple selectors together and produce a more complex, single selector idiom that can span multiple HTML tags. This allows you to drill down through your HTML element tree to select a specific element based on what comes before it.

### Descendent

```
selector1 selector2 {...}
```

A descendent combinator is used to match the element represented by `selector2`, whenever it exists *anywhere* underneath `selector1`'s element group.

### Child

```
selector1 > selector2 {...}
```

A child combinator is used to match the element represented by `selector2`, whenever it exists *immediately* underneath `selector1`'s parent-element group, but not deeper.

### General Sibling

```
selector1 ~ selector2 {...}
```

*General sibling*

An adjacent sibling combinator is used to match the element represented by `selector2`, whenever it follows `selector1`'s element, within the same parent-element group.

### Adjacent Sibling

```
selector1 + selector2 {...}
```

An adjacent sibling combinator is used to match the element represented by `selector2`, whenever it *immediately* follows `selector1`'s element, within the same parent-element group.

---

## Declarations

The *declaration* is a collection of one or more property/value pairs applied to the elements matched by its preceding selector.

CSS describes a collection of properties and values that are used to apply various cosmetic changes to elements. However, depending on the web browser, you may find that not every browser supports every CSS property. Therefore, you need to get creative deciding what CSS features you plan on utilizing.

## Different Engines, Nonstandard CSS3?

Depending on the web engine, some selectors, pseudo-classes, properties, and values actually do not follow the latest syntax CSS3 specifications but instead define their own, prefixed by the engine's name.

As of August 2011, the CSS3 specification is still in flux, but the browser vendors want to implement its draft specifications today and maintain the capability to support what will become the future "official" CSS3 syntax. These types of `-engine-property` names are reflective of the *current* CSS3 specification at that browser's implementation time.

Later, when CSS3 is finalized, these browsers will reimplement the feature and any new syntax changes to properties such as `transform`, `boxshadow`, and `border-image`, thus providing a way for websites to access these features on web browsers of today and tomorrow.

There is one catch. This means that if you are coding a site today, you have to implement the same CSS3 declaration three or four times, just to support all of today's browsers. Chapter 5 describes when this is the case.

You can validate any HTML5 or pre-HTML5 web browser for CSS3 support using various online tools. For CSS3, there are two different levels of validation to consider: CSS3 selector logic and CSS3 property application.

CSS3 selector logic confirms how well the browser understands the new CSS3 selectors, such as selecting an element by a partial attribute value, by its *n*th-child or *n*th-type pseudo-class, by input status, by user selection, and so on.

CSS3 property application pertains to how well the browser understands the new properties that can be applied, such as multiple background-image support, custom fonts, custom image borders, and so on.

Here are some of the online tools that you can use to validate a web browser for CSS3 support:

- The CSS3 Selectors Test — Focuses primarily on the CSS3 selector logic. It enables you to confirm that a particular selector is working properly in each web browser you

test. If you suspect that a selector is not working properly in a specific browser, test it here to confirm that.

- The Acid3 Test — A *reference rendering* test that builds a very specific image composed by HTML, CSS, and JavaScript. Most modern web browsers can pass Acid3 with ease, but it is still a good idea to verify with older browsers any failures.

- The QuirksMode.org CSS tests — Provide a very easy-to-read summary of CSS features and the available level of support. They validate selectors and declarations from both CSS2.1 and CSS3 and describe various quirks, hacks, and lesser-known tweaks to make CSS work efficiently.

Instead of testing your individual web browser, the When Can I Use... website, at http://caniuse.com, summarizes a complete list of available CSS3 features, correlated by browser support. This site is different from the QuirksMode.org CSS tests as it also compares past, present, and anticipated web browser releases, and it is frequently updated.

## Validate a Web Browser for CSS3 Support

### CSS3 Selectors Test

**1** In the browser that you want to test, type **http://tools.css3.info/ selectors-test/test.html** and press Enter.

The CSS3 Selectors Test website loads.

**A** The results of various selector tests for the browser appear.

**Note:** *Scroll down and click on any row of selector results to get more details about the actual test code involved.*

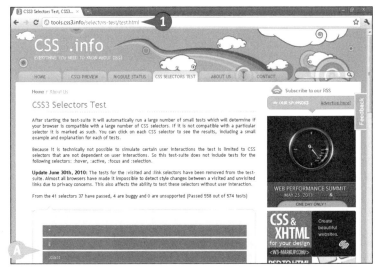

### The Acid3 Test

**1** In the browser that you want to test, type **acid3.acidtests.org** and press Enter.

The Acid3 Test website loads.

**B** This shows a successful Acid3 Test result.

**Note:** *If your browser looks any different than the This Reference Rendering link, it failed the Acid3 test.*

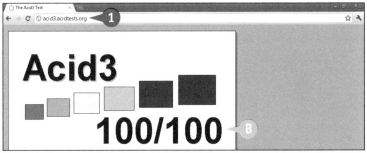

QuirksMode.org CSS Tests

**1** Type **www.quirksmode.org/css/ contents.html** and press Enter.

**2** Scroll down to the CSS3 declarations section.

*Note:* *This page also features a CSS3 selectors section, useful for comparing selector support.*

*Note:* *"Yes" indicates support and "no" complete support failure. White boxes indicate incomplete, nonstandard, or nontested support.*

**G** This shows a group of failed and nonstandard tests.

**3** Click a declaration test that is nonstandard or incomplete.

**D** This is a failed test using the standard W3C syntax.

**E** This is a successful test using the WebKit syntax.

*Note:* *Just because a QuirksMode.org test cites a WebKit, Mozilla, Opera, or Microsoft syntax, it does not guarantee support. You need to be running a version of the browser that understands the nonstandard syntax.*

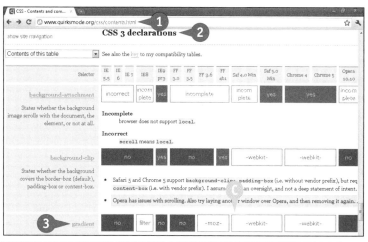

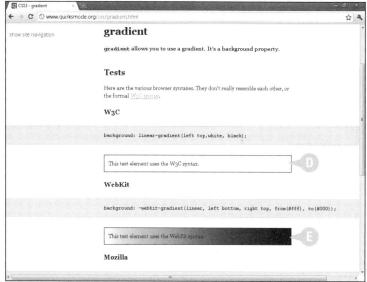

In the example in this section, the `gradient` property could be set only using the WebKit syntax for Chrome. If Firefox had been used, only the Mozilla syntax would properly display the same gradient background image. Because of this discrepancy, you actually need to specify all declaration derivatives in the same selector in order to have the same effect across supporting CSS3 web browsers.

**TYPE THIS**

```
selector {
  background: linear-gradient(top left, white,
  black);
  background: -webkit-gradient(linear, left bottom,
  right top, from(#fff), to(#000));
  background: -moz-linear-gradient(left, #fff, #000);
  filter: progid:DXImageTransform.Microsoft.gradient
  (startColorstr='#ffffff', endColorstr='#000000');
}
```

**RESULT**

The `selector` element identified will have a gradient applied as a background image for Firefox, Chrome, and Internet Explorer. Note that Internet Explorer will move only top down, and Opera is unsupported, according to the QuirksMode.org chart.

You can select any HTML element by assigning it a class or ID name and then using that name in CSS as a part of your element selector. Once selected, CSS declarations can be applied to stylize the matching HTML code:

```
element.class { ... }
element#id { ... }
```

How do you decide which method to use as your selector?

Simply put, an ID should be used only as a proper name, assigned to only one element per page. It should be a specific object or component that requires dedicated CSS rules. For example, a site logo image could be assigned an ID in HTML with `<img src='logo.jpg' id='logo'>` and be stylized in CSS via `img#logo{...}`, or just `#logo{...}`, as the *element* prefix is optional.

A class should be used as a generic name, assigned to a group of elements in any page. There can be multiple elements that share a single class name, sharing the CSS declarations assigned to that class. For example, if the header and footer share like properties, they can be created in HTML as `<header class='banner'>...</header>` and `<footer class='banner'>...</footer>`, which can be selected in CSS via `header.banner`, `footer.banner {...}`, or even just `.banner{...}`.

You can even combine the class and identifier into a single selector, further restricting matching elements. This will act like an *and* CSS conditional test: If the element has this class *and* identifier, apply the specified CSS declaration `element.class#id {...}`.

## Select an HTML Element Using Its Class or ID

**1** Open your HTML file.

**2** Type **class='*name*'** to assign a class name to a group of similar elements.

**3** Type **id='*name*'** to assign an identifier name to an individual element.

**4** Open your CSS file or scroll to the `<style>` block in your HTML file.

**5** Type ***element.name { }*** to match elements with this class name.

**6** Type ***element#name { }*** to match elements with this ID name.

**7** Type ***property: value;*** to define CSS style declarations.

All elements with this class or ID name will be stylized by these CSS declarations.

You can apply CSS declarations to HTML elements that specifically use a particular attribute within the element's HTML tag. This type of selector enables you to narrow down selection criteria and apply only CSS declarations to specific HTML code that references said element and attribute:

```
element[attr] { ... }
```

Note that this particular selector ignores the attribute's value, concentrating only on whether the attribute is defined in the original HTML page. The CSS declarations defined by this selector will be applied to every matching element and attribute in the HTML document — in other words, any reference to `<element attr='value'>`.

Do not forget, you can always combine the attribute selection component with a class or an ID name or even a class *and* an ID name. You can use this to fine-tune your CSS selection logic:

```
element[attr].class { ... }
element[attr]#id { ... }
element[attr].class#id { ... }
```

This will act like an and CSS conditional test: If the element has this attribute *and* is a member of that class or ID, or both, apply the specified CSS declarations.

Multiple attribute tests can be applied to the same element simply by repeating attributes in the selector name:

```
element[attr1][attr2] {...}.
```

If you prefer, you may even drop the element component of the selector entirely. The following will match any element that specifies a particular attribute: `[attr] {...}`.

## Select an HTML Element Using an Attribute

**1** Open your HTML file.

**2** In the element tag, type **attribute='value'** to assign an attribute to the element.

**Note:** *Remember that the value is irrelevant. Even if the HTML code is* `<element attribute>`, *it will still match the selector.*

**3** Open your CSS file or scroll to the `<style>` block in your HTML file.

**4** Type **element[attribute] { }** to match elements with this attribute.

**5** Type **property: value;** to define CSS style declarations.

All elements with this attribute will be stylized by these CSS declarations.

You can use different attribute value operators to identify HTML tags with specific attribute values. You can use this in your CSS selector logic to match on attribute values that are complete words and stylize them accordingly:

```
element[attr='value'] { ... }
element[attr~='value'] { ... }
element[attr|='value'] { ... }
```

The = operator matches elements whose attribute value *exactly* matches `value`. For example, `img[src='image.jpg']` will match only images of image.jpg. Note that other attribute values found in the selected HTML tag, such as `alt='An image'`, will be ignored by the CSS selector.

The `~=` operator matches elements whose attribute value *contains a complete word* that matches `value`. For example, `button[value~='file']` will match any `<button>`

tag with the word "file" in its `value` attribute, such as `<button value='Save file'>`.

The `|=` operator matches elements whose attribute value *exactly* matches `value` or *begins with value* immediately followed by a dash. This is typically a test used in two-character language and country code identification. For example, `p[lang|='en']` will match `<p lang='en'>` and `<p lang='en-US'>`, but not `<p lang='english'>`.

The quotes surrounding the attribute's value are not required but are a good practice. Also, double quotes can be used instead of single quotes, if you prefer.

Note that in HTML5, the attribute name is not case sensitive, but the value is case sensitive. If this were XHTML, or a future hybrid like "XHTML5," expect the name to be case sensitive as well.

## Select an HTML Element Using a Specific Attribute Value

**1** Open your HTML file.

**2** Identify an element tag with `attribute='value'` to match with the attribute-equals operator.

**3** Identify another element tag with `attribute='value'` to match with the attribute-contains-word operator.

**4** Identify a third element tag with `lang='language'` to match with the attribute-is-language-country operator.

**5** Open your CSS file or scroll to the `<style>` block in your HTML file.

**6** Type *element[attribute='value']* { } to match elements with this exact attribute value.

**7** Type *property: value;* to define CSS style declarations.

**8** Type *element[attribute~='value']* { } to match elements that contain a word in this attribute value.

**9** Type *property: value;* to define its CSS style declarations.

**10** Type *element*[lang~='*en*'] { } but match elements that use the first two language characters.

**11** Type *property: value;* to define language-specific CSS style declarations.

**12** Save your CSS and HTML files.

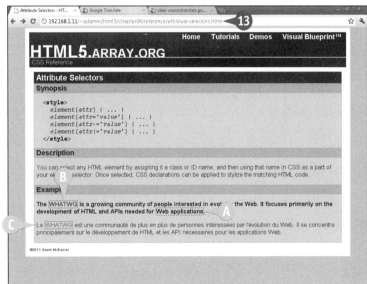

**13** View your HTML file in a web browser.

Ⓐ The element(s) matching the `attribute='value'` test are stylized.

Ⓑ The element(s) matching the `attribute~='value'` test are stylized.

Ⓒ The element(s) matching the `lang|='en'` test are stylized.

It is possible to define your own custom attributes in HTML and select them with CSS attribute selectors. This involves a new feature in HTML5 called *custom data attributes*, which enable you to define any arbitrary attribute name, as long as it is prefixed with `data-`.

**Example**
```
<img src='sunrise.jpg' data-copyright='Creative Commons'>
<style type='text/css'>
img[data-copyright='Creative Commons'] { border: 1px solid green; }
</style>
```

Note that `copyright` would not be a valid attribute, but `data-copyright` is.

CSS3 has introduced new comparison tests to identify HTML tags with partial attribute values. You can use this in your CSS selector logic to match on attribute values that are not complete words and stylize them accordingly:

```
element[attr^='value'] { ... }
element[attr$='value'] { ... }
element[attr*='value'] { ... }
```

The ^= comparison matches elements whose attribute value *begins* with `value`. For example, `object[type^='application']` will match all object elements whose MIME type begins with `application`, such as `<object type='application/x-shockwave-flash'>`.

The $= comparison matches elements whose attribute value *ends* with `value`. For example, `form[action$='.pl']` will match all forms that use a Perl CGI script, such as `<form action='submit.pl'>`.

The *= comparison matches elements whose attribute value *contains* `value`. For example, `input[name*='name']` will match all input elements whose name contains `name`, such as `<input name='firstname'>`.

The quotes surrounding the attribute value are not required but are a good practice. Also, double quotes can be used instead of single quotes, if you prefer.

The difference between this group of attribute comparison tests and those in the section "Select an HTML Element Using a Specific Attribute Value" — ~= and |= — is that these tests are not word-centric. This means that the begins-with, ends-with, and contains values do not have to be a complete word in the original HTML tag's attribute.

Note that in HTML5, the attribute name and value tests are all not case sensitive. If this were XHTML, or a future hybrid like "XHTML5," only then will the name and values be case sensitive.

## Select an HTML Element Using a Partial Attribute Value

1 Open your HTML file.

2 Identify an element tag with `attribute='value'` to use with the attribute-begins-with operator.

3 Open your CSS file or scroll to the `<style>` block in your HTML file.

4 Type *element[attribute^='value']* to match elements that begin with this attribute value.

5 Type *{ declarations }* to define its CSS style declarations.

6 Identify another element tag with `attribute='value'` to use with the attribute-ends-with operator.

7 Type *element[attribute$='value']* to match elements that end with this attribute value.

8 Type *{ declarations }* to define its CSS style declarations.

**9** Identify another element tag with *attribute*='*value*' to use with the attribute-contains operator.

**10** Type **element[attribute*='value']** to match elements that contain this attribute value.

**11** Type **{ declarations }** to define its CSS style declarations.

**12** Save your CSS and HTML files.

```
51        <h4>Example</h4>
52        <style>
53          a[href^='https://']:before {
54            content: url(lock.png);
55          }
56          a[href$='jpg'] {
57            font-style: italic;
58            font-size: 1.5em;
59          }
60   10  *[id*='bullet'] {
61            font-weight: bold;      11
62            color: red;
63          }
64        </style>
65        <p>
66          You can access our <a href='http://html5.array.org'>regular web site</a>,
67          or our <a href='https://html5.array.org'>secure web site</a>.
68        </p>
69        <p>
70          Here is a link to a picture of a <a href='tux.jpg'>penguin</a>.
71        </p>
72        <p>
73          <ul>
74            <li id='example-bullet1'>bullet 1</li>
75            <li id='example-bullet2'>bullet 2</li>
76            <li id='example-bullet3'>bullet 3</li>
77          </ul>
78        </p>
79      </article>
80    </section>
                                                60,1        89%
```

**13** View your HTML file in a web browser.

**Ⓐ** The element(s) matching the *attribute*^='*value*' test are stylized.

**Ⓑ** The element(s) matching the *attribute*$='*value*' test are stylized.

**Ⓒ** The element(s) matching the *attribute**='*value*' test are stylized.

**HTML5.ARRAY.ORG**
CSS Reference

**Attribute Selectors**
**Synopsis**

```
<style>
  element[attr] { ... }
  element[attr='value'] { ... }
  element[attr~='value'] { ... }
  element[attr|='value'] { ... }
  element[attr^='value'] { ... }
  element[attr$='value'] { ... }
  element[attr*='value'] { ... }
</style>
```

**Description**

You can select any HTML element by assigning it a class or ID name, and then using that name in CSS as a part of your element selector. Once selected, CSS declarations can be applied to stylize the matching HTML code.

**Example**

You can access our regular web site, or our 🔒secure web site. — Ⓐ

Here is a link to a picture of a *penguin*. — Ⓑ

Ⓒ
• bullet 1
• bullet 2
• bullet 3

©2011 Adam McDaniel

## EXTRA

The attribute selectors described in this section and in the section "Select an HTML Element Using a Specific Attribute Value" are fairly specialized. The examples described in both sections are just simple examples; these CSS3 attribute selectors can be used on any HTML tag with an attribute, no matter how complex.

They are most useful if you find yourself needing to stylize a specific element identified only by its attribute, and you cannot easily — or simply do not want to — modify existing HTML code to add in a unique `class` or `id` attribute.

For additional information on how these new attribute selectors work in CSS3, see the W3C page at www.w3.org/TR/css3-selectors/#attribute-selectors.

A *pseudo-class* is a predefined class that a web browser uses to match a specific type or pattern of elements. In CSS3, the list of pseudo-class names was expanded in two new areas: `type` and `child`. The `type` pseudo-class is described here; the `child` pseudo-class is discussed in the following section, "Select an HTML Element Using the Structural child Pseudo-Class."

The structural `type` pseudo-class matches a series of like elements within a shared parent:

```
element:first-of-type { ... }
element:last-of-type { ... }
element:only-of-type { ... }
element:nth-of-type(counter) { ... }
element:nth-last-of-type(counter) { ... }
```

The `:first-of-type` and `:last-of-type` selectors match the first and last elements found in a shared parent element; `:only-of-type` matches the element only if it is the only one in its parent.

For `:nth-of-type` and `:nth-last-of-type`, use *counter* to allow you to select a pattern of matching elements listed from the top down and the bottom up:

- *n* — This matches exactly the *n*th element of that type on the page, where *n* is greater than zero.
- *an* — This matches every element type whose position is divisible by *a*, where *a* is greater than zero followed by a literal n character.
- *an+b* — This matches every element type whose position is divisible by *a*, offset by *b* elements, where *a* and *b* are greater than zero, separated by literal n+ characters.

For example, `:nth-of-type(2n)` would match all even elements of the same type; `:nth-of-type(2n+1)` would match all odd elements.

## Select an HTML Element Using the Structural type Pseudo-Class

**1** Open your HTML file.

**2** Identify a series of repeating elements, such as table cells that you want to selectively modify by structural type.

**3** Open your CSS file or scroll to the `<style>` block in your HTML file.

**4** Type *element*:**first-of-type { ... }** to style *element* when it is the first of type in its parent.

**Note:** Using `tr:first-of-type` *always selects the first row of a table, and* `td:first-of-type` *always selects the first column of each row.*

**5** Type *element*:**nth-of-type( 2n )** **{ ... }** to style every second *element* when of this type.

**Note:** *All index numbers start at 1.*

**6** Type *element*:**nth-of-type( 2n+3 )** **{ ... }** to style every second *element* at least three elements from the top.

**Note:** *In this example, the offset of 3 ensures the first row, the maroon header, is ignored by the dark salmon color. Effectively, coloring starts at row #3.*

**7** Save your CSS and HTML files.

**8** View your web page in a CSS3 browser.

**A** In this example, the first elements matching the `<tr>` type are selected.

**B** The first elements matching the `<td>` type are selected.

**C** The even elements are selected.

**D** The odd elements, starting at offset #3, are selected.

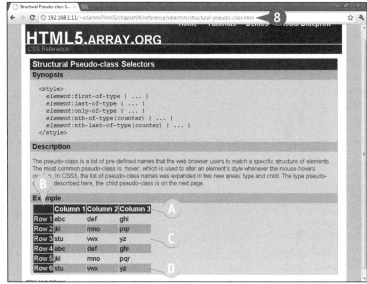

## EXTRA

There are additional pseudo-class selectors new in CSS3 related to an input element type and its current state. In all three cases, the input selector can be expanded to support attribute `type` values, such as `input[type='text']` to catch all text input elements. One of the three new input pseudo-classes could then follow, expanding the selector criteria.

**Example**
```
input:enabled { background-color: yellow; }
```

If an `input` element is flagged as enabled, this CSS rule would set its background color to yellow.

**Example**
```
input:disabled { background-color: red; }
```

If an input element is flagged as disabled, this CSS rule would set its background color to red.

**Example**
```
input:checked { background-color: green; }
```

This can be used to dynamically change an input radio button or check box based on its selected or checked status. As the input activated and deactivated, the `:checked` style is added, becoming green, and removed, becoming the color specified by its enabled or disabled CSS rule. The `:checked` pseudo-class is only supported by Opera, as of August 2011.

As mentioned earlier, a *pseudo-class* is a list of predefined names that a web browser uses to match a specific structure of elements. In CSS2, the `:first-child` pseudo-class was introduced. In CSS3, the list was expanded to allow you to match new combinations and patterns of child elements.

The structural `child` pseudo-class matches the first-level descendents of a parent element:

```
element:first-child { ... }
element:last-child { ... }
element:only-child { ... }
element:nth-child(counter) { ... }
element:nth-last-child(counter) { ... }
```

`element:first-child` matches the first element, when the element specified is the first child found underneath its parent. If a different element is the first child, the selector will ignore it. `element:last-child` does the same thing but from the parent's last element.

For `:nth-child` and `:nth-last-child`, use *counter* to select a pattern of matching elements listed from the top down and the bottom up:

- *n* — This matches exactly the *n*th child element, where *n* is greater than zero.
- *an* — This matches every child element whose position is divisible by *a*, where *a* is a number followed by a literal "n" character.
- *an+b* — This matches every child element whose position is divisible by *a*, offset by *b* elements, where *a* and *b* are numbers separated by literal "n+" characters.

For example, `:nth-child(2n)` would match all even children of the same element; `:nth-child(2n+1)` would match all odd children.

## Select an HTML Element Using the Structural child Pseudo-Class

**1** Open your HTML file.

**2** Identify a series of repeating elements, such as table cells that you want to selectively modify by structural child.

**3** Ensure that there is some diversity in the tag names on each table row.

**Note:** *In this example, the first column of each row is now* `<th></th>`, *compared to the* `<td>` *example in the previous section,* "Select an HTML Element Using the Structural type Pseudo-Class."

**4** Open your CSS file or scroll to the `<style>` block in your HTML file.

**5** Type *element:***first-child** *{ declaration }* to target every child *element* when it is the first child.

**6** Type *element:***nth-child(** *counter* **)** *{ declaration }* to target every child *element* in *counter* under its parent.

**7** Save your CSS and HTML files.

**8** View your web page in a CSS3 browser.

**A** In this example, the first `<tr>` child is selected under `<table>`.

**B** The first `<td>` child is not selected under `<tr>`!

**C** All the `nth-child`s are selected correctly.

**Note:** *In this example, the first child in `<td>`'s parent is not a `<td>`, but `<th>`. Had you used* `td:first-of-type`, *the second column would have been highlighted, which is also wrong.*

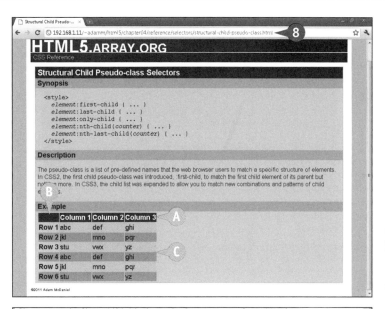

**9** In the CSS, correct the element to be the first child of its parent.

**Note:** *In this example, `<th>` is the first child, not `<td>`.*

**10** Save the file and reload your web page in the browser.

**D** The first child tag, `<th>`, of each row is properly selected and stylized.

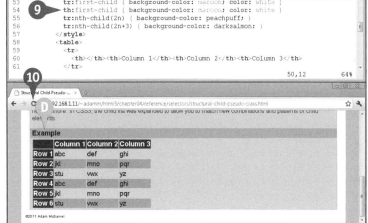

---

## EXTRA

`type` selects like elements, regardless of the existence of nonlike elements; `child` selects like elements but only when their position exactly matches the selector. Ergo, if you have `p:first-child` but the first child is a figure followed by a paragraph, nothing will match. Try swapping the `:nth-of-type` and `:nth-child` selectors, positioning elements differently, and inserting different elements. Experimenting with these two pseudo-classes is the best way to understand how they work.

There are two more minor child/parent-like tags available in CSS3: `:root` and `:empty`. The `:root` selector automatically targets the top-most level of nested HTML, the `<html>` tag itself. This allows you to specify CSS declarations prior to any other HTML tags, such as background images or colors or very low-level formatting.

The `:empty` selector targets any HTML element group that is void of any child tags. It is typically used with a tag that normally has child elements, but they are currently lacking. For example, `textarea:empty { background-color: yellow }` could be used to indicate a blank `textarea` element.

There is a new *general sibling* combinator in CSS3 that allows you to select an element when followed by a previous sibling element:

```
element1 ~ element2 { ... }
```

This will select `element2` whenever it comes after `element1` but only when `element1` and `element2` share the same parent. For example, if you have an article that begins with a heading, followed by a figure, several paragraphs and more figures, but you want the leading figure to be styled differently than the other figures, you can do something like this:

```
h1 ~ figure { style1 }
p ~ figure { style2 }
```

Do not confuse the general sibling combinator with the *child* and *adjacent sibling* combinators introduced in CSS2:

```
element1 > element2 { ... }
element1 + element2 { ... }
```

The child (>) combinator will select `element2` only when it is found directly under `element1`. If you want `element2` to be matched at any level under `element1`, use a normal descendent combinator, such as `element1 element2`.

The adjacent sibling (+) combinator will select `element2` only when it is *immediately* followed by `element1`. This is more restrictive than the general sibling (~) combinator where `element2` may come anywhere after `element1`, as long as both have the same parent element.

### Select an HTML Element by Its Sibling Element

① Open a web page with a basic structure of semantic HTML5.

**Note:** See Chapter 2, "Getting Started with HTML5 Page Layout," for more information.

② Identify sibling elements to use when searching.

③ Identify adjacent elements that you want to stylize.

④ Open your CSS file or scroll to the `<style>` block in your HTML file.

⑤ Type **sibling1 ~ element { ... }** to stylize `element` whenever it comes after `sibling1`.

Ⓐ Optionally, type **sibling2 ~ element { ... }** to stylize `element` whenever it comes after `sibling2`.

⑥ Save your CSS and HTML files.

**7** View your web page in a CSS3 browser.

**B** In this example, both elements that come after *sibling1* are stylized with a background color and centered in their boxes.

**C** In this example, the element that comes after *sibling2* is stylized with a rounded border.

**Note:** *The* border-radius *property is introduced in Chapter 5.*

**8** Return to your HTML file.

**D** In this example, the second <figure> comes after both <h5> and <p> in the same parent; therefore, it receives both general sibling styles.

## APPLY IT

The *element1* and *element2* selectors described in this section do not need to be simple HTML elements and can test for more than two. You can combine any of the earlier CSS selection rules, such as the class, ID, or attribute selectors, and add new combinators to further restrict matching elements.

```
Example
<style>
article#leadstory > h1.title ~ figure.picture {
  border: 2px solid black;
  margin: 2px;
}
</style>
<article id='leadstory'>
  <h1 class='title'>2014: HTML5 Now Finalized!</h1>
  <figure class='picture'><img src='webdevelopers.png'>
    <figcaption>Web developers embrace HTML5, but many questions remain.</figcaption>
  </figure>
</article>
```

Only the figure class picture, when followed by heading class title, under article ID leadstory will receive the changed border and margin properties.

# SELECT HTML ELEMENTS USING A NEGATING PSEUDO-CLASS

You can use the new *negating* pseudo-class selector to match all elements that do not match the supplied argument. Effectively, you are changing "select everything that matches element" into "select everything *except* this matching element."

To limit the scope of what you want to stylize, append :not(*selector*) after an initial selector:

*selector1*:not(*selector2*) { ... }

Simply put, this will select all elements that match *selector1* but do not match *selector2*.

Actually, the preceding synopsis is overly simplified. You can combine any of the CSS selector types on either side of :not, such as the class, ID, or attribute selectors, to further restrict matching elements.

Be careful about specifying the leading selector with :not. Using it as a descendent combinator with a space, for example, will produce a selector that has a very different meaning than the earlier example code:

*parent* :not(*selector*) { ... }

Effectively, the earlier example literally means, "This element matches *selector1* but does not match *selector2*." This second example means, "This element has a parent element that matches *parent* selector, and it itself does not match *selector*."

Generally speaking, always give :not a matching selector, and if you use it as a descendent combinator, also give it a parent selector, like this:

*parent* *selector1*:not(*selector2*) { ... }

## Select HTML Elements Using a Negating Pseudo-Class

① Open your CSS file or scroll to the <style> block in your HTML file.

Ⓐ Optionally, insert a parent selector to limit the descendent scope of the negating pseudo-class selector.

② Type **selector1:not(selector2)** to create a negating pseudo-class selector.

Ⓑ These elements match *selector1*.

Ⓒ This element matches *selector2*.

③ Save your HTML or CSS file.

④ View your web page in a CSS3 browser.

Ⓓ Elements that match *selector1* but not *selector2* are stylized.

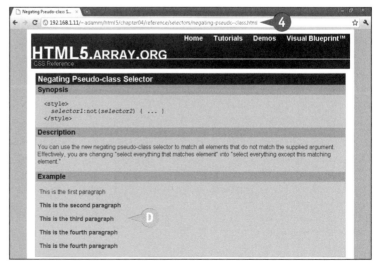

You can alter the user-selection highlight — what the user sees when selecting text — using new CSS3 pseudo-elements called `::selection` and `::-moz-selection`. The first syntax is understood by Chrome and Safari and Opera 9.5. The second syntax is supported by Firefox 3.6 and later.

No additional arguments or elements can be specified in the selector, but the CSS declaration is limited to only color-based CSS stylizing. Therefore, background images, borders, font, or text-based stylizing will be ignored:

```
::selection {
  background-color: #f00;
  color: #fff;
```

```
}
::-moz-selection {
  background-color: #f00;
  color: #fff;
}
```

In these example CSS rules, the background is changed to red, and the text color to white. Note that the two syntax methods are separate CSS rules.

Note the actual properties that you can modify are very limited: just `background-color` and `color`. Any other properties will be ignored. Also, you cannot use a descendent combinator; changes happen pagewide.

## Select HTML Elements by User Selection

1. Open your CSS file or scroll to the `<style>` block in your HTML file.

2. Type **::selection {**.

3. Insert `background-color` and `color` CSS declarations to set the highlight colors.

4. Type **}**.

5. Type **::-moz-selection { ... }** and repeat step **3** within the brackets.

6. Save your CSS or HTML file.

7. View your web page in a CSS3 browser.

8. Click and drag, highlighting text.

   The highlight colors match the new CSS rule.

In CSS3, three new properties were added to give you better control over background images repeating size, origin area, and clip area. Also, you can now layer multiple background images on top of each other:

```
selector {
  background-image: url(imagefile), ...;
  background-size: sizetype, ...;
  background-origin: boxtype, ...;
  background-clip: boxtype, ...;
}
```

The `background-size` property enables you to control the absolute size of a background image. The `sizetype` value can be a height and width as either an absolute size or percentage or two possible keywords: `cover`, which scales the image to the smallest size to fit in a content area, and `contain`, which scales it to the largest size to fit in a content area.

The `background-origin` property controls where a background should begin. The `boxtype` value can be one of these keywords: `padding-box`, `border-box`, or `content-box`. When set, the background will originate inside the padding, border, or content margins.

`background-clip` controls where to limit an element background. Its `boxtype` value options are the same as `background-origin`. When set, the background will not grow outside of the padding, border, or content margins.

It is possible to specify all background values, including the new CSS3 properties, in a single `background` property declaration, but only if you are using one background image: `background: color position size repeat origin clip attachment image;`.

## Change an Element's Background Image

① Open your CSS file or scroll to the `<style>` block in your HTML file.

② Identify an element by its selector.

③ Type **background-image: url( file );** to set a background image.

Ⓐ Optionally, type **, url( file )** to set any additional background images.

Ⓑ Optionally, type **background-size: repeattype;**.

**Note:** When using absolute values, the CSS unit px is recommended.

**Note:** When using relative percent values, `100%` represents the parent element's height and width.

**Note:** `auto` can be used to maintain scale if only one of height or width is specified.

Ⓒ Optionally, type **, repeattype** to configure any additional background images.

**Note:** If multiple `background-image`s are specified but not enough optional properties, the previous, or default, property value is reused.

D Optionally, type **background-clip: boxtype;** and **-webkit-background-clip: boxtype;** and define additional boxtypes per background image.

**Note:** WebKit browsers require their own prefixed property name.

E Optionally, type **background-origin: boxtype;** and define additional boxtypes per background image.

4 Save the file.

5 View your web page in a CSS3 web browser.

F The first background image originates in the background-origin box.

G The second background image is resized according to background-size.

H The image stops at the background-clip box.

**Note:** Try setting background-size to cover or contain and resize the browser window to see how the keywords manipulate the background image size.

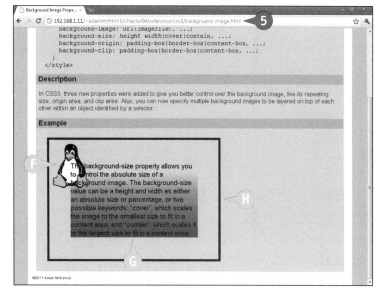

No longer are you limited to so-called *web safe fonts,* the short list of fonts built into browsers and defined in HTML 4.01. CSS3 adds support for custom fonts. You can actually import your own TrueType (TTF), OpenType (OTF), and Embedded OpenType (EOT) font files into your web page:

```
@font-face {
  font-family: MyFont;
  src: url(myfont.ttf), url(myfont.eot);
}
selector { font-family: MyFont; }
```

`@font-face` uses a selector-like syntax that you can use and reuse, once for each new custom font. The `font-family` property assigns a proper name to the font and is used later when assigning the font with a CSS rule.

The files referenced by the `src` property must be stored on your web server. They will be downloaded by the web browser and installed onto the browsing session. Multiple fonts are allowed by `src` because different browsers support different formats. For example, Internet Explorer supports only EOT and Chrome-only TTF.

If you have a font file in only one format, you can convert it using a site called *Font Squirrel,* at www.fontsquirrel. com, with the @font-face Kit Generator. It can convert one font into several different formats and provides sample HTML and CSS files demonstrating your new font. This CSS code, dubbed *The New Bulletproof @font-face Syntax,* was developed by Font Squirrel to work around several quirks and support as many browsers as possible. You can use the generator at www.fontsquirrel.com/fontface/generator and learn about the Bulletproof Syntax at www.fontsquirrel. com/blog/the-new-bulletproof-font-face-syntax.

## Customize an Element's Font

**1** Open your CSS file or scroll to the `<style>` block in your HTML file.

**2** Type **@font-face {**.

**3** Type **font-family: *name*;**.

**Note:** *The* `font-family` *name requires single or double quotes if it contains a space.*

**4** Type **}**.

**5** Type **src: url(*font*.ttf)** to define the TTF font source.

**6** Type **, url(*font*.eot);** to define the EOT font source.

**Note:** *Additional fonts can be defined. At a minimum, you should specify TTF and EOT versions.*

**7** Type *selector {* to define where to apply your custom font.

**8** Type **font-family:** *name;* to include your custom font.

**Ⓐ** Optionally, type *, fallback* as a web-safe fallback.

***Note:*** *One or more standard web-safe fonts can still be used for browsers that do not support custom fonts.*

**9** Add any additional font formatting required by the text.

**10** Type **}**.

**11** Save the file.

**12** View your web page in a CSS3 web browser.

**Ⓑ** The custom font appears in the matching `selector` block.

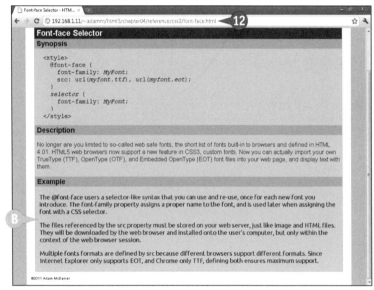

---

## APPLY IT

You can provide bold and italicized versions of fonts as separate `@font-face` CSS rules, along with the `font-style` and `font-weight` properties.

**TYPE THIS**

```
@font-face {
  font-family: MyFont;
  src: url(myfont-bold.ttf);
  font-weight: bold;
}
@font-face {
  font-family: MyFont;
  src: url(myfont-italic.ttf);
  font-style: italic;
}
h1 { font-family: MyFont }
p { font-family: MyFont }
aside { font-family: MyFont; font-style: italic }
```

**RESULT**

Two additional fonts are loaded, adding bold and italic variants of the existing MyFont family. The `<h1>` headings default to the bold `MyFont` — the `font-weight` is not specified because it is inherited — `<p>` paragraphs display the normal `MyFont`, and `<aside>` text is displayed in the italic version of `MyFont`.

You can format any element's text, such as an `<h1>` heading, a `<p>` paragraph, or a `<figcaption>` caption, to alter how it is rendered by the browser. This goes beyond simply modifying the font; you can change text overflow and line-wrapping characteristics and even draw an outline and shadow under the text:

```
selector {
  text-overflow: clip|ellipsis;
  overflow: hidden;
  white-space: nowrap;
}
```

This hides any text that would otherwise wrap in a width-restricted element. The `clip` option simply cuts off the text, and `ellipsis` displays three periods, or . . ., just before the text is cut off. You can make the hidden text visible again by using the `:hover` pseudo-class on the original selector:

```
selector:hover {
  text-overflow: inherit;
  overflow: visible;
  white-space: inherit;
}
```

HTML5 browser support is good for this feature, except for Firefox 4. It does not understand the ellipsis `text-overflow` character, instead defaulting to `clip` mode.

## Format Text Overflow inside an Element

① Type **selector** to select the block of text that will be restricted.

Ⓐ Optionally, type **width: *width*; border: *border*;** to force a smaller line width and a border to see the boundary.

② Type **text-overflow: ellipsis;**.

③ Type **overflow: hidden;**.

④ Type **white-space: nowrap;**.

⑤ Type **selector:hover** to restylize the selected block when the mouse cursor hovers over it.

⑥ Type **text-overflow: inherit;** to restore the default overflow from the parent object.

⑦ Type **overflow: visible;** to display the overflow content.

⑧ Type **white-space: inherit;** to restore the default whitespace from the parent object.

**9** View your web page in a CSS3 web browser.

**B** In this example, the text block is restricted to one line, and the overflow is hidden.

**C** The ellipsis character appears where the text was cut off.

**Note:** *If you used* `text-overflow: clip`, *or Firefox 4, nothing will appear.*

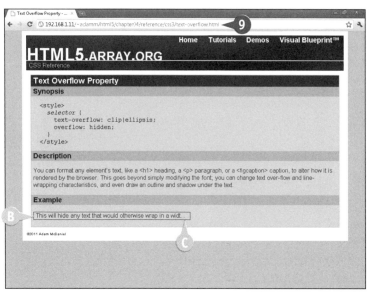

**10** Hover your mouse cursor over the text block.

The entire text block appears.

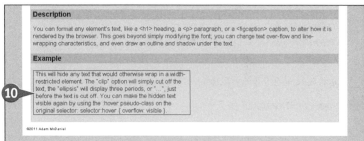

You can also configure new CSS3 features called `column-count` and `text-shadow`. `column-count` splits a text block into multiple columns and displays the text top down and right to left, newspaper-style.

**TYPE THIS**

```
selector {
  column-count: 3;
}
```

**RESULT**

The element identified by `selector` is divided into three columns. The text flows evenly into all three in order, just like columns in a newspaper.

`text-shadow` adds a background-shadow effect behind the selected text block.

**TYPE THIS**

```
selector {
  text-shadow: xpos
  ypos blur color;
}
```

**RESULT**

The element identified by `selector` is copied, shifted down and to the right by `xpos` and `ypos`, and then colored to make it look like a three-dimensional shadow.

It was not that long ago when HTML developers had to use images and tables just to produce seamless rounded borders. Thanks to CSS3, you can now modify any element that supports the `border` property and render rounded borders with `border-radius`.

The `border-width`, `border-style`, and `border-color` properties, or the `border` shorthand property, must first be applied before you can set the `border-radius` property.

Because this feature has only recently been standardized in CSS3, the actual property name varies depending on the web browser engine version. Older WebKit browsers such as Chrome and Safari use the `-webkit-` prefix, and older Mozilla browsers such as Firefox use the `-moz-` prefix. Newer versions of these browsers, plus Opera and Internet Explorer 9, use no special prefix:

```
border: width style color;
border-radius: radius;
-moz-border-radius: radius;
-webkit-browser-radius: radius;
```

The `radius` value can represent one to four values of length. When all four values are defined, they refer to the `top-left`, `top-right`, `bottom-right`, and `bottom-left` radius values. Less than four will apply a radius to symmetrical corners.

If you wanted to, you could also specify a single rounded corner in the property name, such as `border-top-left-radius`, `-moz-border-radius-topleft`, and `-webkit-browser-top-left-radius`. Note the inconsistent use of `topleft` and `top-left`. Only one value for `radius` is accepted with this format.

## Round Border Corners

**1** In an HTML file, type **<element class='round-border'>**.

**2** Insert any content that should appear in the rounded border.

**3** Type **</element>**.

**4** Save your HTML file.

**5** In your CSS file or in a `<style>` block, type **element.round-border {** to apply rounded borders by class name.

**6** Type **border: size style color;** to set a CSS1-style border as a fallback.

**7** Type **}**.

**Note:** In this example, the height and width are hard-coded to make the effect appear better in the screenshot.

8 Type **border-radius:** *radius;* to set the border radius in Opera and Internet Explorer 9.

9 Type **-moz-border-radius:** *radius;* to set the border radius in Firefox.

10 Type **-webkit-border-radius:** *radius;* to set the border radius in Chrome and Safari.

***Note:*** *It is recommended that you measure radius in pixels using* px.

11 Save your CSS file.

12 View your HTML file in a web browser.

Ⓐ The rounded border appears.

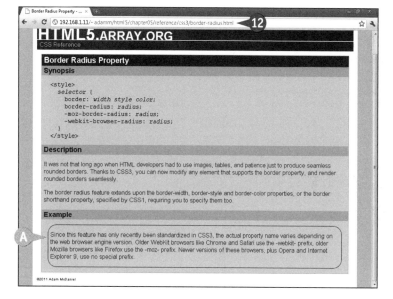

## APPLY IT

A slight modification of the aforementioned `border-radius` syntax will enable you to create a rounded border that uses two different radiuses. This can be used to create an ellipse.

**TYPE THIS**

```
div.oval {
  border: 1px solid black;
  border-radius: 500px / 200px;
  -moz-border-radius: 500px / 200px;
  -webkit-border-radius: 500px / 200px;
  width: 500px;
  height: 200px;
}
```

**RESULT**

The CSS rule forces a `<div class='oval'>` tag to 500 pixels wide, 200 pixels high. The values between the slash assigned to the various `border-radius` properties represent the inner-horizontal and inner-vertical radiuses for each corner.

Be careful as this syntax may confuse older browsers.

You can easily add a shadow effect to any element with the `box-shadow` property in CSS3. This effect requires at least two values, the relative X and Y positions, but accepts up to five values to fine-tune the shadow application:

`box-shadow: xpos ypos blur spread color, ...;`

*xpos* and *ypos* are relative coordinates to indicate where the shadow should be placed. Positive integers indicate that the shadow is placed to the right of, and below, the shadowed element. *blur* represents the size to which a blur effect will be added. For example, a setting of 10px indicates that the shadow is blurred from *color* to transparency for 10 pixels, straddling the shadow's perimeter. *spread* allows for a general increase of the shadow's height and width. *color* defines the base color of the shadow. If omitted, the shadow defaults to black.

Multiple `box-shadow` effects can be applied simply by adding a comma and then another prototype group.

Most recent HTML5 web browsers do honor the `box-shadow` property name. Older browsers such as Chrome 9 and earlier, Safari 3, and Firefox 3.5 instead use their own derivative property name. Therefore, also specify `-moz-box-shadow` and `-webkit-box-shadow` to support these browsers. These properties accept the same prototype as the standard `box-shadow`:

`-moz-box-shadow: xpos ypos blur spread color, ...;`
`-webkit-box-shadow: xpos ypos blur spread color, ...;`

## Add a Shadow Effect

**1** In an HTML file, type **<element class='shadow'>**.

**2** Insert any content that should appear in the `box-shadow` block.

**3** Type **</element>**.

**4** Save your HTML file.

**5** In your CSS file, type **element. shadow {** to apply a shadow by class name.

**Ⓐ** Optionally, add a border to make the shadow effect stand out.

**6** Type **box-shadow: xpos ypos blur spread color;** to set a blurry and complex shadow effect that renders relative to the parent object.

**Note:** A shadow with negative xpos and ypos values will appear above and to the left of the parent object.

**7** Type **}**.

**Note:** In this example, the parent's margin is increased to make the effect appear better in the screenshot.

Ⓑ Optionally, repeat *, xpos ypos blur spread color* to create additional shadow effects.

**Note:** *In this example, the 0px 0px position means that there is no shadow offset, but the spread is increased, displaying a fuzzy, centered, and white margin underneath the selected element.*

**Note:** *If the blur, spread, or color values are undefined, they will default to 0px, 0px, and black, respectively.*

⑧ Duplicate the `box-shadow` values for **-moz-box-shadow** and **-webkit-box-shadow**.

⑨ Save your CSS file.

⑩ View your HTML file in a web browser.

Ⓒ In this example, a black box shadow appears below and to the right of the object.

Ⓓ In this example, a white box shadow appears centered underneath the object.

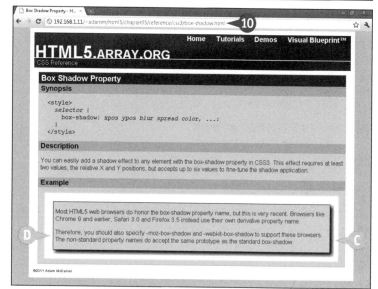

---

## APPLY IT

The `box-shadow` property allows for an extra optional keyword, `inset`, in its value. When used, the shadow's direction moves inward, toward the center of the shadowed element. This allows you to create the illusion of sunken depth, as opposed to hover depth.

**TYPE THIS**

```
-webkit-box-shadow: 5px 5px 10px black inset;
-moz-box-shadow: 5px 5px 10px black inset;
box-shadow: 5px 5px 5px gray inset;
```

**RESULT**

Most HTML5 web browsers do honor the
Chrome 9 and earlier, Safari 3.0 and Fir

Therefore, you should also specify -moz
The non-standard property names do ac

The `inset` keyword may be used either at the beginning or the end of the `box-shadow` value string.

You can set an element's visual opacity, also known as *transparency* in CSS3, using the `opacity` property. When set, the selected element will become translucent, according to the nonnegative real number value between 0 and 1. In other words, a value of 0 is completely transparent, 1 is completely visible, and any decimal number in between will achieve a see-through effect.

Older versions of Internet Explorer, versions 4 to 8 to be precise, support a similar feature through an *alpha filter*. Its value is a two-digit percentage, so if you set `opacity` to 0.75, you should also set `filter` to

`alpha(opacity=75)`. Note that Internet Explorer 9 does understand the new `opacity` property:

```
selector {
    opacity: value;
    filter: alpha(opacity=value);
}
```

Once applied, anything under the selected elements will become visible through the CSS layers. For the most part, this will be just a background image or color, but through `z-index` layering, you can actually make other elements visible underneath a transparent element.

## Change an Element's Opacity

**1** In an HTML file, type **<element class='translucent'>**.

**2** Insert any content that should appear in the translucent block.

**3** Type **</element>**.

**4** Save your HTML file.

**5** In your CSS file, type **.translucent {** to apply an opacity value by class name.

**6** Type **opacity: value;** to render the block partially translucent.

**(A)** Optionally, type **filter: alpha(opacity=value);** to support Internet Explorer 4 to 8.

**7** Type **}**.

**8** Apply a background image or color to the translucent class.

**9** Apply a background size to the parent object of the translucent class.

**Note:** *In this example, the parent and target margins are increased to make the effect stand out better in the screenshot.*

**10** Save your CSS file.

**11** View your HTML file in a web browser.

**B** The background appears partially visible to the block that has `opacity` applied.

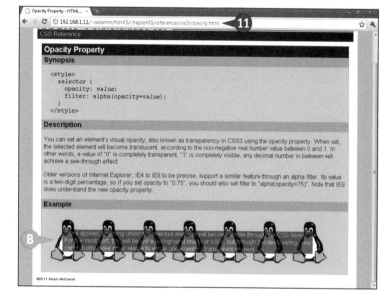

## APPLY IT

Most often, opacity is used to make the background visible, but by layering elements with the `position` and `z-index` properties, you can actually make content appear visible underneath the translucent element.

**TYPE THIS**

```
div.fixedbelow {
  position: absolute;
  z-index: 0;
  background-color: white;
}
div.translucent {
  z-index: 1;
}
```

In your HTML file, add `<div class='fixedbelow'><img src='image'></div>` above the `<div class='translucent'></div>` block.

**RESULT**

The `fixedbelow` class block is rendered below the `translucent` class block. A part of the red appears through the class that used opacity.

You can create custom borders around elements with the help of image templates and CSS3's new `border-image` property. Web browsers that support this feature dynamically map your template image to correctly stretch and shrink its edges to match the selected object, but leave the corners intact:

```
border-image: source slice repeat;
border-width: width;
```

The *source* value should be in the form of `url(imagefile)` to load the border template image. The *slice* value can be one to four numbers or percentages, representing the inward offsets from the source image, dividing it into nine segments: four corners, four edges, and a middle block.

When sized correctly, `border-image` attempts to use exactly one segment for each corner, and, depending on the value for the *repeat* option, either repeats or stretches the edges to fill the object border. `border-width` allows you to specify the width of the border around the element.

Note that Opera, Mozilla, and WebKit browsers have their own property names but accept the same value list. As a result, you need to define your `border-image` definition three more times:

```
-o-border-image: source slice repeat;
-moz-border-image: source slice repeat;
-webkit-border-image: source slice repeat;
```

## Apply an Image As an Element Border

**1** In a graphics-editing program, create a template border image, divided into nine segments.

**Note:** *To make creating the template easier, select a constant segment length and width, such as 30 x 30, and set the template's overall size to three times that, 90 x 90.*

**Ⓐ** The template's corners are all the same size.

**Ⓑ** The template's edges will be rendered with one variable axis length, perpendicular to a static width.

**2** In an HTML file, type *<element class='border-image'>*.

**3** Insert any content that should appear in the `border-image` block.

**4** Type *</element>*.

**5** Save your HTML file.

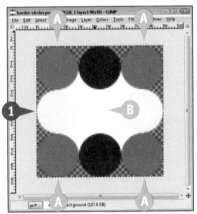

**6** In your CSS file, type *element.border-image {* to apply a border image template by class name.

**7** Type **border-image: url(*imagefile*) *slice*;** to set the source by filename and set the template's slice depth value.

**8** Repeat step **7** using the WebKit, Mozilla, and Opera prefixes.

**9** Type **border-width: *width*;** and reuse the slice value(s) from step **7** as pixels.

**10** Type **}**.

**11** Save your CSS file.

**12** View your HTML file in a web browser.

 **⦿** The template's corners appear the same in the bordered object.

 **⦿** The template's edges appear stretched to fit in the height and width of the bordered object.

**13** Type **repeat** in all `border-image` property values. Reload the page.

 **⦿** The edges appear as they did in the template but are duplicated to stretch to the height and width of the object.

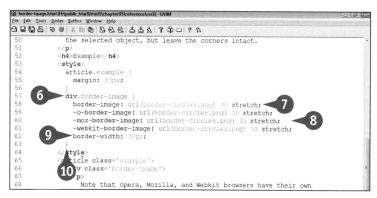

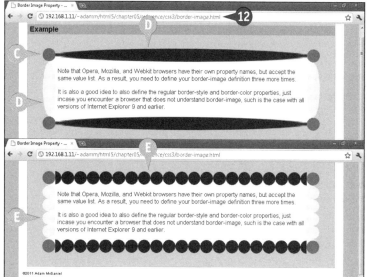

## EXTRA

There seems to be confusion over the correct syntax for `border-image`. In the CSS3 specification, two additional groups of dimensions, a `width` and `outset`, are supposed to be allowed. However, because all three dimensions can accept one to four values, the completed syntax can suddenly get very crowded.

To help with this, CSS3 says that you can specify all values as standalone properties.

**Example**

```
border-image-source: source;
border-image-slice: slice;
border-image-width: width;
border-image-outset: outset;
border-image-repeat: repeat;
```

The problem here is that no browser understands these standalone properties.

The solution? Keep your border image as simple as possible. Try to keep all corners and edges symmetrical; otherwise you will limit end-user support, at least until CSS3 and the HTML5 web browsers standardize and accept these new standalone properties.

# Customize a Scroll Bar with Images

**Y**ou can create a custom scroll bar on any display block that has the `overflow` property set. This can be used to replace the bland scroll bar that is built into the browser's operating system. This feature is supported in only the desktop WebKit browsers Chrome and Safari; WebKit introduced the feature, and it is not yet included in CSS3:

```
selector { overflow: auto; display: block;
  width: windowwidth; height: windowheight; };
::-webkit-scrollbar { width: scrollbarwidth;
  height: scrollbarheight; };
```

*windowwidth* and *windowheight* are length values indicating the size of the scrollable window that you want to create. *scrollbarwidth* and *scrollbarheight* represent the maximum width of the vertical scroll bar and maximum height of the horizontal scroll bar. Now you can start defining the style of the main scroll bar components: the buttons with `::-webkit-scrollbar-button`, the movable bar with `::-webkit-scrollbar-thumb`, and the bar's track with `::-webkit-scrollbar-track` and `::-webkit-scrollbar-track-piece`.

The scroll bar style selectors accept additional pseudo-classes that define the style of scroll bar subcomponents. For example, you can extend `::-webkit-scrollbar-button` by adding `:vertical` or `:horizontal` into the selector to stylize the scroll bar axis differently; then create another rule and add `:increment` or `:decrement` to stylize the direction buttons differently. This will allow you to produce unique directional buttons.

Creating the scroll bar first requires you to define the basic CSS structure, rather than apply the images now. Therefore, it is easier to begin with basic CSS `border` and `background-color` properties to help you understand how the selectors function and add images later.

---

## Customize a Scroll Bar with Images

### Create a Custom Scroll Bar Framework

**1** In your HTML file, type **<element class='scrollbar'>**.

**2** Insert HTML code to be scrolled with your custom scroll bar.

**3** Type **</element>**.

**4** Save your HTML file.

**5** In your CSS rules file or in a <style> block, type **element.scrollbar { overflow: auto; width: *width*; height: *height*; }** to initialize the scroll bar.

*Note: Reuse this selector for the remaining steps.*

*Note: The* `display: block` *declaration is implied by all <div> tags. If you want to scroll a different tag group, you may need to add it in.*

*Note: The* `overflow` *property also accepts the value* `scroll`, *which configures the scroll bars to be displayed regardless of text size.*

**6** Type **selector::-webkit-scrollbar { width: *width*; height: *height*; }** to assign scroll bar height and width to the horizontal and vertical axis.

**⑦** Type *selector*::**-webkit-scrollbar-button { ... }** to stylize all buttons.

**Note:** *Specifying* `height` *here will only affect the vertical axis buttons; and* `width` *only the horizontal axis buttons.*

**⑧** Type *selector*::**-webkit-scrollbar-thumb { ... }** to stylize the movable thumb bar.

**⑨** Type *selector*::**-webkit-scrollbar-track { ... }** to stylize the bar's available track.

**⑩** Save your CSS file.

**⑪** View your HTML file in a web browser.

**Ⓐ** The custom scroll bar buttons appear.

**Ⓑ** The custom scroll bar thumb bar appears.

**Ⓒ** The custom scroll bar track appears.

**Note:** *Replace* `::-webkit-scrollbar-track` *with* `::-webkit-scrollbar-track-piece` *only when you want to style the incrementing and decrementing track portions separately.*

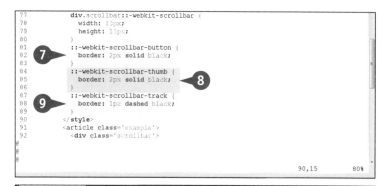

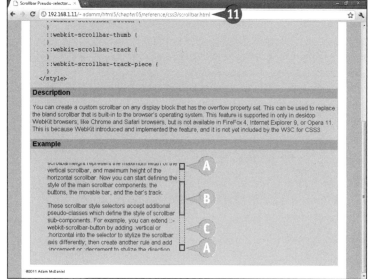

---

continued ➤

Now that you have a working scroll bar with just borders, you can start to create images for the buttons and the track piece. To begin, mock up your scroll bar in a graphics editor as a static image and then chop it into button, track, and track-piece image files.

Because the track and thumb piece length can be variable, depending on the dimensions of the window and amount of text, you must use the `border-image` CSS3 property. This will stretch the images to fit within the scroll bar component area.

The buttons' size will be static. In this case, you can simply use multiple `background-image` files layered on top of each other — one for the background and another for an arrow image — and placed precisely with `background-position`.

You should note that so far the `::-webkit-scrollbar` selectors have not been prefixed by any type of CSS descendent selector. This means that anything on the web page that is scrollable, including the browser window itself, will have the same scroll bar theme. You can create multiple scroll bar themes by prefixing all `::-webkit-scrollbar` CSS rules with a parent selector class. However, both selectors must be side by side; do not insert a space as required by normal descendent combinators:

```
.scroller1::-webkit-scrollbar-button { /*
   theme1 */ }
.scroller1::-webkit-scrollbar-track  { /*
   theme1 */ }
.scroller2::-webkit-scrollbar-button { /*
   theme2 */ }
.scroller2::-webkit-scrollbar-track  { /*
   theme2 */ }
```

## Customize a Scroll Bar with Images (continued)

### Add Images to the Scroll Bar

⑫ Edit *selector*`::-webkit-scrollbar-button` to stylize all buttons with a nonrepeating background image.

⑬ Type *selector***::-webkit-scrollbar-button:vertical:increment { ... }** to stylize the vertical increment button.

⑭ Repeat step **13** for the decrement button.

**Note:** If you used `overflow: scroll` in step 5, you will also need to stylize the horizontal increment and decrement buttons, and later, the horizontal track and thumb images.

⑮ In an image editor, create a vertical scroll bar thumb bar image, ensuring that its width matches the `::-webkit-scrollbar` width defined in step **6**.

⑯ Create a vertical scroll bar track with the same width.

Ⓐ The edging depth will remain fixed, specified in `border-width` and `border-image` later in steps **18** and **19**.

**Note:** In this example, the fixed boundary of both images is exactly one pixel.

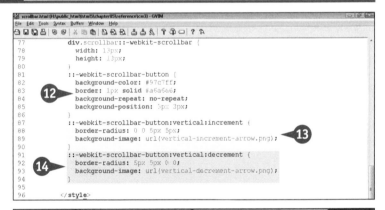

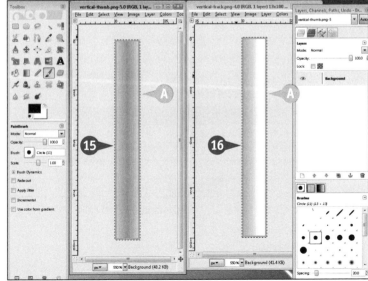

**17** Type *selector***::-webkit-scrollbar-thumb:vertical { }** to stylize a specific thumb bar.

**18** Type **-webkit-border-image:** *source width height***;**.

*Note: Because only WebKit browsers can have a customized scroll bar, only* -webkit-border-image *is required.*

**19** Type **border-width:** *width height***;** to match step **16**'s border-image widths, using px units!

**20** Repeat steps **17** to **19** for the ::-webkit-scrollbar-track:vertical border image.

*Note: If you used* overflow: scroll *in step 5, you will also need to assign the horizontal track and thumb border images.*

**21** Save your CSS file.

**22** View your HTML file in a web browser.

**B** The custom scroll bar button images appear.

**C** The custom scroll bar thumb bar image appears.

**D** The custom scroll bar track image appears.

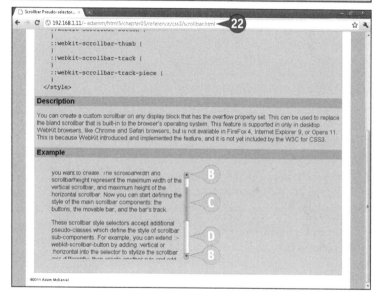

## EXTRA

The pseudo-classes :hover and :active can be also be used to create new CSS rules, one at a time, onto any of the scroll bar style selectors. You can highlight that a component is movable by changing its color when the cursor is over it and then changing the color again when the component is actively in use.

Internet Explorer supports only changing scroll bar colors. This is done by simply assigning one of the following CSS properties a color: scrollbar-arrow-color, scrollbar-base-color, scrollbar-darkshadow-color, scrollbar-face-color, scrollbar-highlight-color, scrollbar-shadow-color, or scrollbar-track-color.

It is relatively safe to mix the two methods together in the same CSS source. Just remember that Internet Explorer does not understand the overlay property, so only the textarea element and the page body can be modified.

# APPLY A COLOR GRADIENT

You can assign a linear color gradient in CSS3 that renders one side of an object in one color, shifting across the color spectrum to the other side of the object and the second color. `linear-gradient` is applied to the `background-image` property:

```
background-image: linear-gradient( start,
  color1 percent, color2 percent, ... );
```

*start* defines a pair of coordinate numbers, or simple words, that specify where the color gradient will begin. Words such as `top left, top, top right, left, right, bottom left, bottom,` and `right` indicate that the gradient progresses from the specified location to the opposite side or corner. You can even specify degrees; for example, `-90deg` is equivalent to `top`. Specify one or more *color percent* values to assign a color gradient, separating each with a comma. *color* can be represented as any CSS color name, RGB, HSL, or hex value. *percent*

defines at what point along the gradient path the color is fullest, and is actually optional; when omitted, the browser will evenly space all colors across the gradient path.

Because CSS3 has not finalized the `linear-gradient` syntax, each web browser vendor has implemented the feature using its own specific value name. To implement this, essentially you define the `background-image` property multiple times:

```
background-image: -moz-linear-gradient( ...
  );
background-image: -webkit-linear-gradient(
  ... );
```

WebKit and Mozilla browsers have the best support for this feature. As of August 2011, Opera and Internet Explorer are planning to add in support. You may specify their anticipated values today as `-o-linear-gradient` and `-ms-linear-gradient`.

## Apply a Color Gradient

**1** In your CSS file, create a selector for an object to which you want to apply a gradient.

**2** Type **background-image: linear-gradient( );**.

**Note:** *In this example, the parent margin and target width, height, and border are modified to make the effect stand out better in the screenshot.*

**3** Type **top left,** to start the gradient in the top-left corner of the element.

**Note:** *You can fine-tune where the gradient starts by entering in a degree value, such as* 30deg.

**4** Insert a series of colors that will appear in the gradient, separated by commas.

**A** Optionally, type **value%** for any colors to assign them a specific percentage point along the gradient path.

**Note:** *If unspecified,* 0% *and* 100% *is implied for the first and last colors. All colors in between are divided evenly in between these start and end values.*

**5** Repeat steps **2** to **4** and if preferred, the optional bullet for the Opera, Microsoft, Mozilla, and WebKit linear gradient prefixes.

**6** Save your CSS file.

**7** View your Web page in a WebKit browser such as Chrome or Safari.

**B** In this example, the first color appears at the top left.

**C** The second color appears at 30%.

**D** The third color appears at 70%.

**E** The third color continues to the end of the linear gradient path.

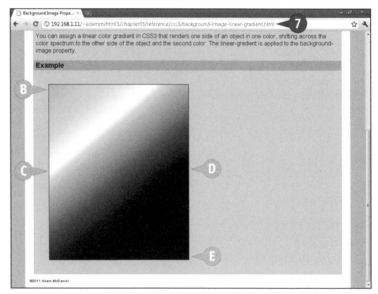

---

## EXTRA

Prior to Chrome 10, earlier versions of WebKit implemented gradients using a very different syntax.

**Example**
```
background-image: -webkit-gradient(
linear, xstart ystart, xend yend,
  color-stop(percent, color)
);
```

The main difference is `linear` as an argument, along with ending coordinates and a `color-stop` function. It is possible to specify `-webkit-gradient` and `-webkit-linear-gradient` in the same CSS rule.

Because Chrome browsers are automatically upgraded, there are not many users with earlier versions; you can safely ignore this legacy syntax.

A radial gradient version is also available, also not yet accepted by the W3C and requiring similar name variants. It follows a similar structure to `linear-gradient` but requires some additional information, such as a degree value for the starting coordinates, along with a behavioral size constant argument.

For more information, see Mozilla's CSS3 Documentation site at https://developer.mozilla.org/en/CSS/-moz-radial-gradient.

Ou can transform any type of block object in CSS3 using the new `transform` property allowing you to scale, skew, rotate, and translate objects:

```
.scale { transform: scale( xpercent, ypercent
 ) }
.skew { transform: skew( xdegrees, ydegrees )
 }
.rotate { transform: rotate( degrees ) }
.translate { transform: translate( xpos, ypos
 ) }
```

The `scale` function is relatively simple. It will resize an object into a new width and height using `xpercent` and `ypercent` as a decimal value between 0 to 1. If only one value is defined, the browser scales the object proportionally.

The `skew` function changes the 2D perspective of the object by slanting it left or right by `xdegrees` and up or down by

`ydegrees`. You may specify only one value here, in which case only the x-axis is skewed. Alternatively, you can use `skewx(xdegrees)` or `skewy(ydegrees)` to specifically target an axis.

The `rotate` function rotates an object on its center pivot point by `degrees` value.

The `translate` function actually moves an object by `xpos` and `ypos` pixels away from its original position. Alternatively, you can use `translatex(xpos)` or `translatey(ypos)` to specifically target only one direction.

All four major HTML5 web browser engines require their own specific prefix for the `transition` property. This is once again because the W3C has not yet finalized the syntax for the `transform` property, and as such it may change sometime in the future.

## Transform Object Dimensions

**1** In an HTML file, type **<element class='scale'>**.

**2** Insert any content that should appear in the `scale` transformation block.

**3** Type **</element>**.

**4** Repeat steps **1** to **3** for the `skew`, `rotate`, and `translate` blocks.

**5** Save your HTML file.

**6** In your CSS file, type **.scale { transform: scale( value ); }** to scale an object by class name.

**7** Type **.skew { transform: skew( xdegrees, ydegrees ); }** to skew an object by class name.

**8** Type **.rotate { transform: rotate ( degrees ); }** to rotate an object by class name.

**9** Type **.translate { transform: translate ( xpos, ypos ); }** to move an object by class name.

**Note:** *Transformations work only on* `block` *and* `inline-block` *display objects, not on* `inline` *or* `list` *display objects.*

**10** Repeat steps **6** to **9** for the Opera, Internet Explorer, Mozilla, and WebKit prefixed property names.

**11** Execute multiple arguments through specific x and y functions for `-ms-transform` only.

**Note:** *This is necessary because Internet Explorer 9 has issues with using multiple argument transforms.*

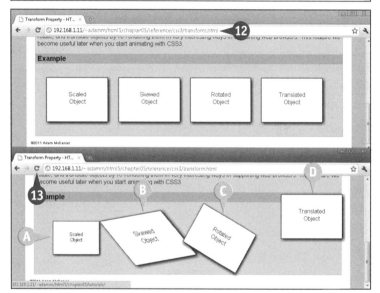

```
69      .scale {
70          transform: scale( 0.75 );
71          -o-transform: scale( 0.75 );
72          -ms-transform: scale( 0.75 );
73          -moz-transform: scale( 0.75 );
74          -webkit-transform: scale( 0.75 );
75      }
76      .skew {
77          transform: skew( 40deg, -10deg );
78          -o-transform: skew( 40deg, -10deg );
79          -ms-transform: skewx( 40deg ) skewy( -10deg );
80          -moz-transform: skew( 40deg, -10deg );
81          -webkit-transform: skew( 40deg, -10deg );
82      }
83      .rotate {
84          transform: rotate( 30deg );
85          -o-transform: rotate( 30deg );
86          -ms-transform: rotate( 30deg );
87          -moz-transform: rotate( 30deg );
88          -webkit-transform: rotate( 30deg );
89      }
90      .tranlate {
91          transform: translate( 50px, -50px );
92          -o-transform: translate( 50px, -50px );
93          -ms-transform: translatex( 50px ) translatey( -50px );
94          -moz-transform: translate( 50px, -50px );
95          -webkit-transform: translate( 50px, -50px );
```

**12** View your HTML file in a web browser.

The original object layout appears.

**13** Save your CSS file and reload the page.

**A** In this example, the first object has been resized.

**B** The second object has been skewed.

**C** The third object has been rotated.

**D** The fourth object has been moved.

## EXTRA

The `scale`, `rotate`, `skew` functions all use the center of the object as the origin point. You can change this with `-browser-transform-origin: x y`. The values for x and y can be coordinate numbers or literal text, such as `top left`, `left`, and `bottom right`.

To combine transformations, all functions must be specified on a single browser-specific transform CSS value. Unfortunately, this can create very long and cumbersome CSS rules.

When the W3C finalizes CSS3, every browser should simply understand `transform`, and as such, the number of total declarations will shrink to a fraction of what is required today.

```
transform: rotate( 10deg ) translate(100px,
    10px);
-o-transform: rotate( 10deg ) translate(100px,
    10px);
-ms-transform: rotate( 10deg ) translate(100px)
    translate(10px);
-moz-transform: rotate( 10deg ) translate(100px,
    10px);
-webkit-transform: rotate( 10deg )
    translate(100px, 10px);
```

Transitions are a very easy way to create simple object-morphing animations as it changes from one style into another, using nothing but CSS. To do this, you must define a CSS rule with transition and an initial *property* value:

```
selector {
  transition: property, duration, timing,
  delay;
  property: value1;
}
```

Then, for mouse-based transitions, use :hover on the second CSS rule and set the ending *property* value:

```
selector:hover { property: value2; }.
```

The transition property's first value states the actual CSS property to be transitioned and its starting *property* value. *duration* is the number of seconds that should

be spent during the transition effect on that property. At a minimum, you need only these first two values to get a working transition effect. The optional *timing* and *delay* values control the animation rate and the number of seconds before the transition process starts. The website http://cssglue.com/cubic contains a very useful tool that enables you to visualize different *timing* rates.

Because CSS3 has not finalized the transition syntax, each web browser vendor has implemented the feature using its own specific value name in the first selector:

```
-o-transition: property, duration, timing,
  delay;
-moz-transition: property, duration, timing,
  delay;
-webkit-transition: property, duration,
  timing, delay;
```

## Transition between Styles

**1** In an HTML file, type **<element class='transition'>**.

**2** Insert any content that should appear in the transition block.

**3** Type **</element>**.

**4** Save your HTML file.

**5** In your CSS file, type **element.transition { to apply a transition animation by class name.

**6** Type **transition-property: *property*;** to select which property changeover to animate.

**7** Type **transition-duration: *seconds*;** to define how long to animate the transition effect.

**8** Repeat steps **6** and **7** using the WebKit, Mozilla, and Opera prefixes.

**Note:** *As of version 9, Internet Explorer does not yet support transitions.*

**9** Type ***property*: *value*;** to set the initial display value of the transitional property.

**10** Type **}**.

⑪ Type *element.transition***:hover {** to define the mouse-over transitional style.

⑫ Type *property***:** *value***;** to set the final display value of the transitional property.

**Note:** *If you add any properties to this* :hover *rule, the transitional effect will not apply. Instead, the object will abruptly change, applying that untransitioned property's value, at the start of the transition cycle.*

⑬ Type **}**.

⑭ Save your CSS file.

⑮ View your HTML file in a web browser.

⑯ Move your mouse cursor over the transitional object.

Ⓐ The object begins to morph into the new style.

Ⓑ The object is displayed as the target style.

⑰ Move your mouse cursor off the object.

The object morphs back to its initial style.

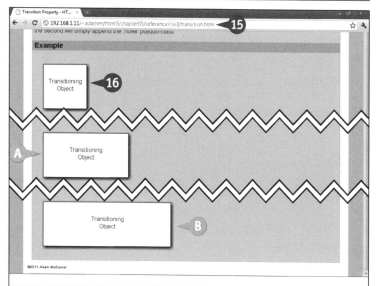

## APPLY IT

The transition property syntax is capable of supporting only one property changeover. However, if you have multiple properties to change in a single event, you can use the longhand transition syntax.

| TYPE THIS | | RESULT |
|---|---|---|
| ```transition-property: property1, property2, ...;transition-duration: duration1, duration2, ...;transition-timing-function: timing1, timing2, ...;transition-delay: delay1, delay2, ...;``` |  | Multiple properties can now be transitioned to, all at once. Similarly, different durations, timing functions, and delays can be applied to the additional property changes. If you specify only one *duration*, *timing*, or *delay* value, the same value is used for all properties being transitioned. |

# CREATE SIMPLE ANIMATIONS

O ne of the highly anticipated features of CSS3 is its capability to create simple animations without any JavaScript. A new group of animation properties and a selector expand on the idea of transitions, described in the previous section. To begin, compose a CSS rule that matches what you would like to animate:

```
selector {
  -webkit-animation-name: name;
  -webkit-animation-direction: direction;
  -webkit-animation-duration: duration;
  -webkit-animation-iteration-count: count;
  property: value1;
}
```

The name value is an identifier used to link the selected element to the @-webkit-keyframes rule. The

direction value, which defaults to normal, can be changed to alternate, causing the animation to move forward and backward every two cycles. The duration value describes the number of seconds that one animation cycle must complete in. The count value indicates the number of animation cycles that should be executed. @-webkit-keyframes states the property's value at a percentage of each cycle, for this animation name:

```
@-webkit-keyframes name {
  percent1 { property: value2; ... }
  percent2 { property: value3; ... }
  ...
}
```

The same name value used in -webkit-animation-name is specified after @-webkit-keyframes.

## Create Simple Animations

**1** In an HTML file, type **<element class='animate'>**.

**2** Insert any content that should be animated in the element tag block.

**3** Type **</element>**.

**4** Save your HTML file.

**5** In your CSS file, type **element. animate { }** to create the animation style.

**6** Type **-webkit-animation-name: name;**.

**Ⓐ** Optionally, type **-webkit-animation-direction: direction;**.

**7** Type **-webkit-animation-duration: seconds;**.

**Ⓑ** Optionally, type **-webkit-animation-iteration-count: count;**.

**Note:** You can use the keyword infinite to indicate that the animation continues indefinitely.

**8** Insert the initial state of the animating CSS selector.

```
80          </style>
81          <article class='example'>
82      1     <div class='animate'>
83              <p>Animating Object</p>      2
84      3     </div>
85          </article>
86        </article>
87      </section>
88      <footer>
89        &copy;2011 Adam McDaniel
90      </footer>
91    </div>
92  </body>
                                        80,15        98%
```

```
animation.html (H:\public_html\html5\chapter05\reference\css3) - GVIM
File  Edit  Tools  Syntax  Buffers  Window  Help
63          article.example {
64            margin: 30px 0px;
65          }
66          article.example div {
67            left: 100px;
68            width: 300px;
69            display: inline-block;
70            height: 6em;
71            border: 1px solid black;
72            margin-left: 3%;
73            box-shadow: 3px 3px 10px 0px black;
74            background-color: white;
75          }
76          article.example div p {
77            text-align: center;
78            margin: 2.5em 0;      6
79          }
80      5  div.animate {
81            -webkit-animation-name: jumpy;
82            -webkit-animation-direction: normal;      Ⓐ
83      7     -webkit-animation-duration: 4;
84            -webkit-animation-iteration-count: infinite;  Ⓑ
85            border: 1px solid black;
86            box-shadow: 3px 3px 10px 0px black;
87          }
88        </style>
89        <article class='exa    8  >
90          <div class='animat
91            <p>Animating Object</p>
92          </div>
                                        88,15        87%
```

102

**9** Type **@-webkit-keyframes** *name* **{ }** to create the animation procedure for *name*.

**10** Type *percent* **{** *declarations* **}** to assign CSS at this percentage of the animation cycle.

**Note:** *percent may use the keywords* from *and* to *as shortcuts to 0% and 100%.*

**11** Repeat step **10** for the other animation keyframes.

**12** Save your CSS file.

**13** View your HTML file in a web browser.

**C** The first keyframe appears.

**D** The object transitions to the second, third, and fourth keyframes.

**E** In this example, the object transitions back to the first keyframe and then repeats the cycle.

**Note:** *The cycle repeats depending on the optional* animation-iteration-count. *If none is defined, only one cycle is performed.*

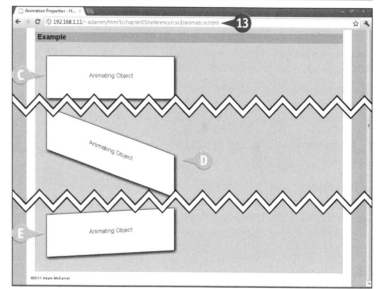

## EXTRA

Optionally, some additional attributes are available to fine-tune your animation selector:

```
-webkit-animation-delay: delay;
-webkit-animation-timing-function: timing;
-webkit-animation-play-state: state;
```

The delay value is the number of seconds after the animation trigger is made — the selector matched an object — until the animation cycle begins. The timing value indicates the animation rate at which the cycles are executed. Both values are very similar to the delay and timing values described in the section "Transition between Styles." The state value enables you to set whether the animation is currently playing or not. You can set the initial play state to off, or paused, and it will not start running when the page loads. Only when this value is set to running, which is the default, will the animation play. Typically, you could create a JavaScript play/pause button that controls the CSS3 animation play state by changing this property's value.

continued

It is possible to extend the CSS3 animations by layering multiple keyframe scripts on top of one animating object. This type of concurrency even offers independent control of the other animation properties.

To add concurrent animations, all you need to do is define a new @-webkit-keyframes *name* and append that new *name* onto -webkit-animation-name by separating the names with commas. Then simply add new values onto the other animation properties, separating them with commas. Note that if an animation property does not have enough values specified, that property's last value is repeated for the remaining animations that are applied to the object.

The example on the previous page starts the animation immediately after the web page first loads. It is possible to use the :hover pseudo-class to trigger the animation when the user has the mouse cursor over the animating object.

To do this, establish an original *selector* that sets the initial styles of the animating object but not the animation properties. Because *selector*:hover inherits *selector* and defines the animation properties, the keyframes will animate only when hovering. When the user's mouse cursor leaves the object, the initial style is restored:

```
selector {
  property: value1;
}
selector:hover {
  -webkit-animation-name: name, ...;
  -webkit-animation-duration: duration, ...;
}
```

## Create Simple Animations (continued)

**14** In your CSS file, create a new @-webkit-keyframes procedure with a different *name*.

**15** Type , *name* as a second value into -webkit-animation-name.

**16** Insert secondary values for the other animation properties.

**Note:** If you use two animation keyframes but do not define enough values into an animation property, its existing value is used for the secondary keyframe cycle.

**17** Type *.animate:hover { }* to create the animating style with the mouse event trigger.

**18** Move the animation properties from the .*animate* selector into .*animate*:hover.

**19** Save your CSS file.

```
97    }
98    @-webkit-keyframes rounder {
99      from {
100       border-radius: 0px;
101     }
102     to {
103       border-radius: 50px;
104     }
105   }
106   div.animate {
107     -webkit-animation-name: jumpy, rounder;
108     -webkit-animation-direction: normal, alternate;
109     -webkit-animation-duration: 4s, 1s;
110     -webkit-animation-iteration-count: infinite;
111     border: 1px solid black;
112     box-shadow: 3px 3px 10px 0px bl
113   }
114   </style>
115   <article class='example'>
                                        114,15      87%
```

```
animation.html [H:\public_html\html5\chapter05\reference\css3] - GVIM
File  Edit  Tools  Syntax  Buffers  Window  Help

88    }
89      75% {
90        -webkit-transform: skewy( -20deg );
91        -webkit-transform-origin: bottom left;
92      }
93      100% {
94        -webkit-transform: skewy( 0deg );
95        -webkit-transform-origin: bottom left;
96      }
97    }
98    @-webkit-keyframes rounder {
99      from {
100       border-radius: 0px;
101     }
102     to {
103       border-radius: 50px;
104     }
105   }
106   div.animate {
107     border: 1px solid black;
108     box-shadow: 3px 3px 10px 0px black;
109   }
110   div.animate:hover {
111     -webkit-animation-name: jumpy, rounder;
112     -webkit-animation-direction: normal, alternate;
113     -webkit-animation-duration: 4s, 1s;
114     -webkit-animation-iteration-count: infinite;
115   }
116   </style>
117   <article class='example'>
                                        116,15      87%
```

**20** View your HTML file in a web browser.

**A** The `animate` class is applied, but there is no movement.

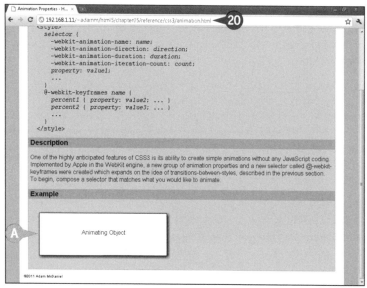

**21** Hover your mouse cursor over the object.

**B** The animation cycle begins, with two independent keyframes active.

**22** Move your mouse cursor away from the object.

The object returns to its default CSS state.

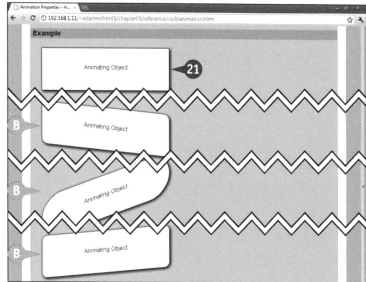

## EXTRA

If you need something more complex than `:hover`, JavaScript can be deployed to configure detailed playback timing. Simply set the object to `-webkit-animation-play-state: paused` in the CSS file and change it to `playing` in JavaScript when you want the animation to launch.

This feature was designed and implemented by the WebKit developers directly, which is why its property names all have the `-webkit-` prefix. Fortunately, the W3C has adopted the standard as a working draft. Hopefully, within the next few years, it will be accepted as standard CSS3 functionality by the W3C and implemented across all major web browsers.

Mozilla has already added CSS animations into Firefox 5; you can try it by duplicating all WebKit animation properties and keyframes declarations with the `-moz-` prefix.

# Introducing the Flexible Box Model

The Flexible Box Model is a module of the draft CSS3 specification, and by extension, HTML5. It enables you to organize web page data into multiple rows or columns as a new `display: box` object.

Because this is still a draft feature, its specifications could still change. This is why not all browsers support this feature, and those that do require a special prefix to all flexible box properties. As of August 2011, only WebKit browsers such as Safari, Chrome, and Firefox support the Flexible Box Model working draft specification dated July 23, 2009.

## Purpose

The Flexible Box Model makes it easier to construct one-dimensional data — one row with multiple columns or one column with multiple rows — than HTML tables, and it provides additional flexibility when ordering and stylizing the data in your CSS rules.

## Implementation

To implement the Flexible Box Model, you will need a parent block object, such as a `<div>` tag group, which holds a series of child objects, such as paragraphs, tables, images, or even other boxes.

### HTML Structure

To create a flexible box, you must start with a parent object that contains multiple child objects of any type; each child object becomes a box cell. Assign the parent a CSS ID or class name:

```
<div class='box-parent'>
  <div>child1</div>
  <p>child2</p>
  <table><tr><td>child3</td></tr></table>
  <figure><img src='child4.jpg'></figure>
</div>
```

### Display Property

Set the new box `display` property on the parent object:

```
div.box-parent { display: box; display: -moz-box;
  display: -webkit-box; }
```

Do not forget the `-moz-` and `-webkit-` derivatives. They must be set here and on all other `box*` property names.

### Direction

You can set the directional axis of the flexible box by setting the `box-orient` property:

```
div.box-parent > child { box-orient: axis; }
```

The `axis` value can be `horizontal`, `vertical`, or `inherit`. If unspecified, `horizontal` is the default.

### Flexibility

Individual box-child objects can have a *flex ratio* value applied. This instructs the browser how to calculate the size each box-child object should expand to. When all the box-child objects have a `box-flex` value, an individual child can expand or shrink relative to the sum of the other `box-flex` siblings:

```
div.box-parent > child { box-flex: ratio; }
```

If a box-child's `box-flex` ratio is unspecified, the default is 0 (zero), or the smallest size possible. So, if you assign a single box-child a value of 1, it will expand to 100% of the available width; two box-children set to 1 would each take up 50% of the available width, and so on.

## Placement

You can control the horizontal placement of box-child objects by assigning a `box-pack` value to the box-parent object:

```
div.box-parent { box-pack: packing; }
```

The *packing* value can be set to `start`, `end`, `center`, or `justify`, which will force all the box-child objects to the left, right, middle, or averaged placement, respectively.

You can control the vertical placement of box-child objects with the `box-align` value:

```
div.box-parent { box-align: alignment; }
```

The *alignment* value can be set to `start`, `end`, `center`, `baseline`, or `stretch`.

## Display Order

You can modify the display order of the box-child objects with the help of `box-direction`, which is set on the box-parent, or `box-ordinal-group`, which is set on individual box-children. If unspecified, the box-children are rendered in the same order as they exist in the HTML code:

```
div.box-parent { box-direction: direction; }
```

Possible values for *direction* are `normal`, `reverse`, and `inherit`.

The `box-ordinal-group` property enables you to assign arbitrary numbers to box-child objects directly, which act as a primary sorting variable. Child objects that share the same `box-ordinal-group` number fall back to HTML ordering:

```
div.box-parent > child { box-ordinal-group: number; }
```

For `box-ordinal-group` sorting to take effect, all box-children require a *number*.

## Supported Web Browsers

The Flexible Box Model is supported as of Firefox 3.0, and all versions of Chrome and Safari, including their mobile counterparts, such as the Android and iOS browsers. For each of the box-related properties and values, you will need to prefix `-webkit-` and `-moz-` to activate the Flexible Box Model on these browsers.

Support is expected to be added into Internet Explorer 10, which will likely require an `-ms-` prefix.

As for Opera 11.50, support is unavailable and not expected anytime soon.

## Alternatives to the Flexible Box Model

Depending on what your goals are, the Flexible Box Model may not be sufficient for your application. There are a few alternatives that you can consider.

### Tables

Tables have been the venerable rendering standard since HTML 3. If you have a complex two-dimensional structure with multiple rows and columns, tables remain the best resource to use.

The Flexible Box Model can handle multiple rows and columns, but only by nesting multiple boxes within each other. The precise cell alignment of row and column boundaries

throughout the body of the nested box objects will be lost, making the end result rather ugly.

If a clean row and column alignment is required, use a regular HTML table.

### Multi-Column Layouts

CSS3 columns are similar to the Flexible Box Model, but the idea of box-children is not used. Instead, child objects are displayed vertically in a series of two or more columns, spanning horizontally. The effect is exactly like columns in a newspaper.

Columns are described later in this chapter.

# CREATE A HORIZONTAL FLEXIBLE BOX MODEL

To create a horizontal Flexible Box Model, you must first create a parent object in HTML and then assign that object new CSS3 tags to indicate that it is a box and that it flows horizontally:

```
display: box;
display: -moz-box;
display: -webkit-box;
box-orient: horizontal;
-moz-box-orient: horizontal;
-webkit-box-orient: horizontal;
```

The `display` property is assigned a new value, aptly named `box`. This activates the box properties described throughout this chapter. There are no HTML5 tags that imply the `display: box` declaration automatically, so you must specify it whenever you want to use the Flexible Box Model.

The `box-orient` property controls the axis the box-children are displayed on. If unspecified, the box is displayed horizontally.

Note that because the Flexible Box Model is a CSS3 feature still in development, there are engine-specific prefixes that are required in order to activate it. This includes the Mozilla and WebKit prefixes. For all other browsers, content will appear normally, like vertical block objects.

A flexible box typically spans the entire width of its parent object or the browser window itself. The height of a horizontal box is set by the height of the largest box-child. You can use the `height` and `width` properties on the box-parent object.

## Create a Horizontal Flexible Box Model

**1** In an HTML file, type *<element class='horizontal-box'>*.

**2** Insert any content blocks that should appear in the horizontal flexible box block.

**3** Type *</element>*.

**4** Save your HTML file.

**5** Open your CSS file or scroll to the `<style>` block in your HTML file.

**6** Type *element.horizontal-box {* to apply the horizontal flexible box by class name.

**7** Type *display: box;*.

**8** Type *box-orient: horizontal;*.

**9** Repeat steps **7** and **8** with the Mozilla and WebKit flexible box prefixes.

**10** Type *}*.

Ⓐ Optionally, type **border: 2px dashed black;** to display a dashed border around the Flexible Box Model.

Ⓑ Optionally, type *element.horizontal-box > * { border: 2px solid black; }* to display a solid border around the flexible box-children.

⑪ Save your CSS file.

⑫ View your HTML file in a web browser.

The Flexible Box Model appears, spanning the available width.

Ⓒ The Flexible Box Model child objects appear.

Ⓓ This is the overall space the box-parent object uses.

**Note:** Apply width and height *properties to the parent and child box objects to set absolute sizes.*

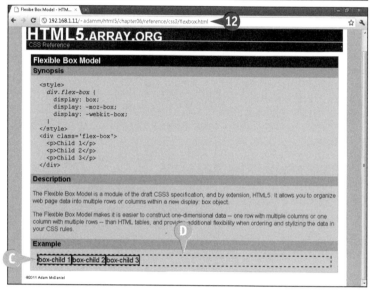

## APPLY IT

In WebKit, the width of a horizontal box automatically spans to be 100%. This contradicts with Mozilla where its width spans to the minimum required by the box-children. This can adversely affect placement of content before and after the flexible box.

### TYPE THIS

```
<style>
div#box {
  display: box;
  box-orient: horizontal;
  border: 2px solid black;
}
</style>
Content prior to the flexible box...
<div id='box1'>
  <p>Paragraph 1</p><p>Paragraph 2</
p><p>Paragraph 3</p>
</div>
...followed by content after the flexible box.
```

### RESULT

→

In Chrome and Safari, the page appears like this:

Content prior to the flexible box...
box-child 1 box-child 2 box-child 3
...followed by content after the flexible box.

However in Firefox 4, the page appears like this:

Content prior to the flexible box... box-child 1 box-child 2 box-child 3 ...followed by flexible box.

To avoid this problem, make sure content that precedes and follows a flexible box is wrapped in a block display element, such as a <div> or <p> tag group.

To create a vertical Flexible Box Model, you must first create a parent object in HTML and then assign that object new CSS3 tags to indicate that it is a box and that it flows vertically:

```
display: box;
display: -moz-box;
display: -webkit-box;
box-orient: vertical;
-webkit-box-orient: vertical;
-moz-box-orient: vertical;
```

A vertical flexible box requires the same display: box declarations as its horizontal counterpart.

The box-orient property controls the axis that the Flexible Box Model displays its children on. If you are nesting vertical boxes together, you can also set the value of subboxes to inherit.

Note that because the Flexible Box Model is a CSS3 feature still in development, there are engine-specific prefixes that are required in order to activate it.

A vertical flexible box typically spans the entire width of its parent object, which could be the browser window itself. The height of a vertical box is set by the total height of all box-children. You can use the height and width properties to change the flexible box dimensions on the box-parent object.

Note that in the March 22, 2011, working draft, the W3C renamed display: box to display: flexbox; however, no browsers implement this new naming convention yet. Browsers are expected to be backward compatible, at least with the -moz-box and -webkit-box values.

## Create a Vertical Flexible Box Model

**1** In an HTML file, type **<element class='vertical-box'>**.

**2** Insert any content blocks that should appear in the vertical flexible box block.

**3** Type **</element>**.

**4** Save your HTML file.

**5** Open your CSS file or scroll to the <style> block in your HTML file.

**6** Type **element.vertical-box {** to apply the vertical flexible box by class name.

**7** Type **display: box;**.

**8** Type **box-orient: vertical;**.

**9** Repeat steps **7** and **8** for the Mozilla and WebKit flexible box prefixes.

**10** Type **}**.

**A** Optionally, type **border: 2px dashed black;**.

**B** Optionally, type *element.vertical-box > * { border: 2px solid black; }*.

**11** Save your CSS file.

**12** View your HTML file in a web browser.

The Flexible Box Model appears, spanning the available width.

**C** The Flexible Box Model child objects appear.

*Note:* *Block objects, such as the box-child <div> tags in this example, automatically span to the maximum width.*

*Note:* *Apply* width *and* height *properties to the parent and child box objects to set absolute sizes.*

```
83          -moz-box-orient: vertical;
84          -webkit-box-orient: vertical;
85       border: 2px dashed black;
86       }
87    div.vertical-box > * {
88       border: 2px solid black;
89       }
90    </style>
```

Flexible Box Model - HTML...
← → C  ☉ 192.168.1.11/~adamm/html5/chapter06/reference/css3/flexbox.html

**Flexible Box Model**

**Synopsis**

```
<style>
  div.flex-box {
    display: box;
    display: -moz-box;
    display: -webkit-box;
  }
</style>
<div class='flex-box'>
  <p>Child 1</p>
  <p>Child 2</p>
  <p>Child 3</p>
</div>
```

**Description**

The Flexible Box Model is a module of the draft CSS3 specification, and by extension, HTML5. It allows you to organize web page data into multiple rows or columns within a new display: box object.

The Flexible Box Model makes it is easier to construct one-dimensional data — one row with multiple columns or one column with multiple rows — than HTML tables, and provides additional flexibility when ordering and stylizing the data in your CSS rules.

**Example**

box-child 1
box-child 2
box-child 3

©2011 Adam McDaniel

---

## APPLY IT

Horizontal and vertical boxes can be nested together to provide an effect similar to tables in HTML.

**TYPE THIS**

```
<style>
  div.vertical-box { display: box; box-orient:
  vertical; }
  div.horizontal-box { display: box; box-
  orient: horizontal; }
  div.parent-box > * { border: 1px solid
  black; margin: 2px 2px 0 0; }
</style>
<div class='vertical-box'>
  <div class='horizontal-box parent-box'>
    <div>child 1,1</div><div>child 1,2</
  div><div>child 1,3</div>
  </div>
  <div class='horizontal-box parent-box'>
    <div>child 2,1</div><div>child 2,2</
  div><div>child 2,3</div>
  </div>
</div>
```

Do not forget to include the -moz- and -webkit- flexible box prefixes.

For precise alignment, use a normal HTML table.

**RESULT**

| box-child 1,1 | box-child 1,2 | box-child 1,3 |
| box-child 2,1 | box-child 2,2 | box-child 2,3 |

A two-row, three-column table appears, constructed by nesting two horizontal boxes in a vertical box. This example is overly simplistic. What would happen if a single box-child contains more characters than its siblings?

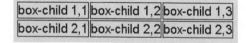

| box-child 1,1 | box-child 1,2 | box-child 1,3 |
| box-child 2,1 ..... | box-child 2,2 | box-child 2,3 |

# STRETCH AND SHRINK OBJECTS IN A FLEXIBLE BOX

**Y**ou can control the size of child objects within a flexible box with the `box-flex` property. When this is set on a box-child object, the child will have a higher- or lower-size priority, when compared to the other children in the flexible box object:

```
box-flex: ratio;
-moz-box-flex: ratio;
-webkit-box-flex: ratio;
```

The `ratio` value can be any positive number, but it is pretty rare to require any value higher than 2. Effectively, `0` makes the box-child as small as possible, or not flexible, and the highest `ratio` number stretches the box-child to be as large as possible, or the most flexible. All ratios are relative, so any number between 1 and the highest number

is treated as a partial stretch, proportionate to the other ratios and number of children currently in that box.

To calculate the width of an individual box-child object, the browser takes the overall width of the box — or height if it is a vertical box model — multiplies by the box-child object's `box-flex` ratio, and then divides by the total ratios of all the children. For example, if a flexible box is 600px wide and has three box-children with `box-flex` ratios of 1, 2, and 0, the first child will be $600 \times 1 \div 3 = 200px$, the second $600 \times 2 \div 3 = 400px$, and the third $600 \times 0 \div 3 = 0px$. Naturally, this is only a rough calculation as the contents of each child can affect the overall width; thus forcing a child to `box-flex: 0` will display larger than 0px wide. Essentially, the first child is half the width as the second, whereas the third is as small as possible.

## Stretch and Shrink Objects in a Flexible Box

**1** Create a horizontal or vertical Flexible Box Model object in your HTML and CSS files.

**2** Type *div.horizontal-box > :nth-child(n) {* to target the parent box's *n*th child object.

**3** Type **box-flex: 1;** to set the parent box's *n*th child object flex ratio to 1.

**4** Repeat step **3** for the Mozilla and WebKit flexible box prefixes.

**5** Type **}**.

**6** Save your CSS file.

**7** View your HTML file in a web browser.

**Ⓐ** In this example, the *n*th box-child expands to the full width because it is the only child object with a `box-flex` value.

**Ⓑ** The box-children with no `box-flex` value do not expand beyond the size forced by their content.

112

**8** Repeat steps **2** to **5** on a different box-child, and increase the `box-flex` value to 2.

```
90        div.horizontal-box > :nth-child(1) {
91            box-flex: 1;
92            -moz-box-flex: 1;
93            -webkit-box-flex: 1;
94        }
95        div.horizontal-box > :nth-child(2) {
96            box-flex: 2;
97            -moz-box-flex: 2;
98            -webkit-box-flex: 2;
99        }
100    </style>
```

**8**

**9** Save your CSS file.

**10** Reload your page in the web browser.

**C** In this example, this box-child has the largest width because it has the largest ratio.

**D** This box-child with the smaller ratio expands to a smaller width.

```
□ Flexible Box Model - HTM... ×
← → C ① 192.168.1.11/~adamm/html5/chapter06/reference/css3/flexbox.html              ☆ ⚙

HTML5.ARRAY.ORG
10 Reference

Flexible Box Model
Synopsis

<style>
    div.flex-box {
        display: box;
        display: -moz-box;
        display: -webkit-box;
    }
</style>
<div class='flex-box'>
    <p>Child 1</p>
    <p>Child 2</p>
    <p>Child 3</p>
</div>

Description

The Flexible Box Model is a module of the draft CSS3 specification, and by extension, HTML5. It allows you to organize
web page data into multiple rows or columns within a new display: box object.

The Flexible Box Model makes it easier to construct one-dimensional data -- one row with multiple columns or one
column with multiple rows -- than HTML tables, and provides additional flexibility when ordering and stylizing the data in
your CSS rules.

Example

box-child 1                         box-child 2                              box-child 3

©2011 Adam McDaniel
```

**D**    **C**

---

**EXTRA**

The `box-flex-group` property was a part of the July 23, 2009, Flexible Box Model working draft specification but has since been dropped in the more recent March 22, 2011, working specification.

It is important to be aware of `box-flex-group` if you encounter it described on HTML5 or CSS3 websites, but avoid it yourself, at least until the specification is standardized, sometime by 2014:

```
box-flex-group: number;
-moz-box-flex-group: number;
-webkit-box-flex-group: number;
```

Grouping box-children by `box-flex-group` will subdivide the length of flexible space, in which the width of like box-children will be calculated based on the total ratios of children within the same group. Any space left over will then be allocated to the next `box-flex-group` of children, and so on.

This method of calculation seemed overkill for the specification, which is why it was dropped from CSS3.

Y ou can pack box-children together on one side of the horizontal axis of the Flexible Box Model. This will enable you to force child objects to appear on the left, right, centered, or justified across the forced width of a flexible box.

The term *forced width* refers to setting the `min-width` or `width` properties of the box-parent object to be larger than the *natural width,* or the width produced solely by the box-children. Forced width implies whitespace within the Flexible Box Model, and packing involves placement within that whitespace.

Note that horizontally packing objects is pointless if you employ the `box-flex` property to stretch one or more box-children to the entire width of a flexible box:

```
box-pack: packing;
-moz-box-pack: packing;
-webkit-box-pack: packing;
```

The *packing* value can be set to one of four keywords:

- `start` — Aligns all box-children to the left.
- `end` — Aligns all box-children to the right.
- `center` — Aligns all box-children to the middle, horizontally.
- `justify` — Forces the first and last box-children to be placed on the left and right and all other box-children to average spacing in between them.

Note that in the March 22, 2011, working draft, the W3C renamed `box-pack` to `flex-pack`; however, no browsers implement this new naming convention yet. Browsers are expected to be backward compatible, at least with the `-moz-box-pack` and `-webkit-box-pack` properties.

## Horizontally Pack Objects within a Flexible Box

**1** Create a horizontal or vertical Flexible Box Model object in your HTML and CSS files.

**A** Optionally, add borders around each of the box-children to help you to visualize their position and size.

**B** Optionally, type **width: *value*;** on the parent so that the children can expand.

**2** Type **box-pack: *type*;** to set the horizontal packing of the box-children.

**3** Repeat step **2** for the Mozilla and WebKit prefixes.

**4** Save your CSS file.

**5** View your HTML file in a web browser.

The box-children are forced to horizontally pack with the `box-pack` property value.

```
78   div.horizontal-box {
79       display: box;
80       display: -moz-box;
81       display: -webkit-box;
82       box-orient: horizontal;
83       -moz-box-orient: horizontal;
84       -webkit-box-orient: horizontal;
85       border: 2px dashed black;
86       width: 100%;
87       box-pack: justify;
88       -moz-box-pack: justify;
89       -webkit-box-pack: justify;
90   }
91   div.horizontal-box > * {
92       border: 2px solid black;
93   }
94   </style>
```

HTML5.ARRAY.ORG
CSS Reference

**Flexible Box Model**

**Synopsis**

```
<style>
  div.flex-box {
    display: box;
    display: -moz-box;
    display: -webkit-box;
  }
</style>
<div class='flex-box'>
  <p>Child 1</p>
  <p>Child 2</p>
  <p>Child 3</p>
</div>
```

**Description**

The Flexible Box Model is a module of the draft CSS3 specification, and by extension, HTML5. It allows you to organize web page data into multiple rows or columns within a new display: box object.

The Flexible Box Model makes it is easier to construct one-dimensional data -- one row with multiple columns or one column with multiple rows -- than HTML tables, and provides additional flexibility when ordering and stylizing the data in your CSS rules.

**Example**

box-child 1                    box-child 2                    box-child 3

©2011 Adam McDaniel

You can align box-children together on one side of the vertical axis of the Flexible Box Model. This will enable you to force child objects to appear on the top, bottom, middle, baseline, or stretched across the forced height of a flexible box.

As mentioned earlier, the term *forced height* refers to setting the `min-height` or `height` properties of the box-parent object to be larger than the *natural height*, or the height produced solely by the box-children. Forced height implies whitespace within the Flexible Box Model, and vertical alignment involves placement within that whitespace:

```
box-align: alignment;
-moz-box-align: alignment;
-webkit-box-align: alignment;
```

The `alignment` value can be set to one of five keywords:

- `start` — Aligns all box-children to the top.
- `end` — Aligns all box-children to the bottom.
- `center` — Aligns all box-children to the middle, vertically.
- `stretch` — Forces the height of all box-children to span the height of the box.
- `baseline` — Aligns all box-children along their baselines, as in normal text. This is equivalent to using `display: inline` on the box-children directly, while maintaining other flexible box properties.

Note that in the March 22, 2011, working draft, the W3C renamed `box-align` to `flex-align`; however, no browsers implement this new naming convention yet. Browsers are expected to be backward compatible, at least with the `-moz-box-align` and `-webkit-box-align` properties.

## Vertically Align Objects within a Flexible Box

① Create a horizontal or vertical Flexible Box Model object in your HTML and CSS files.

Ⓐ Optionally, add borders around each of the box-children to help you to visualize their position and size.

Ⓑ Optionally, type **height: *value*;** on the parent so that the children can expand.

② Type **box-align: *type*;** to set the vertical alignment of the box-children.

③ Repeat step **2** for the Mozilla and WebKit prefixes.

④ Save your CSS file.

⑤ View your HTML file in a web browser.

The box-children are forced to vertically align with the `box-align` property value.

**Note:** *This example also demonstrates* `box-pack: justify` *from the previous page, coupled with* `box-align: end`. *Experiment with the different values for these two properties.*

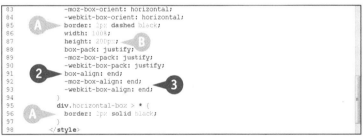

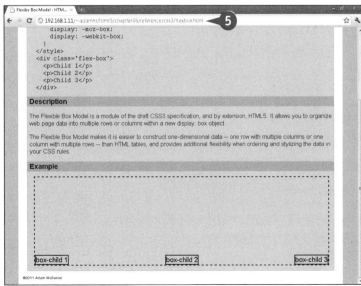

# REORDER OBJECTS IN A FLEXIBLE BOX

You can change the display order of objects within a flexible box without changing the order of the objects in the HTML source code. This is done by setting the `box-ordinal-group` property to one or more box-children:

```
box-ordinal-group: number;
-moz-box-ordinal-group: number;
-webkit-box-ordinal-group: number;
```

A lower `box-ordinal-group` value means that the child should be displayed earlier in the box display order, and a higher value means later. If multiple children share the same value, as a group they appear in the value's position, but their individual order is decided by their HTML ordering. All children have a default `box-ordinal-group` property value of 1, meaning that they are all members of the first ordinal group, unless explicitly set otherwise. Note that a value of 0 (zero) indicates a box-child should be hidden

entirely from the flexible box. 0 can be arbitrarily set to hide any box-child, even if other children do not have a `box-ordinal-group` value. For example, if you have a horizontal flexible box of five children assigned the values of 5, 4, 0, 2, and 1, the children will be displayed in reverse, and the third will be omitted entirely. If you assign them the values of 2, 2, 1, 1, and 1, the last three child objects described in the HTML will be displayed first, followed by the first two.

Note that in the March 22, 2011, working draft, the W3C renamed `box-ordinal-group` to `flex-order`; however, no browsers implement this new naming convention yet. Browsers are expected to be backward compatible, at least with the `-moz box-ordinal-group` and `-webkit-box-ordinal-group` properties.

## Reorder Objects in a Flexible Box

1 Create a horizontal or vertical Flexible Box Model object in your HTML and CSS files.

**Note:** *In this example, the number of box-children was increased to better demonstrate this feature.*

2 Type *parent* > **:nth-child(*n*) {** to set the parent box's *n*th child object.

3 Type **box-ordinal-group: 2;** to set the child object's `ordinal-group` to 2.

**Note:** *Remember that by default all box-children are implicitly set with* `box-ordinal-group: 1`.

4 Repeat step **3**'s value for the Mozilla and WebKit flexible box prefixes.

5 Type **}**.

6 Save your CSS file.

7 View your HTML file in a web browser.

Ⓐ In this example, the *n*th box-child is displayed at the start of the flexible box, displacing the other objects, because its `box-ordinal-group` is set to 1.

The remaining box-children share their `box-ordinal-group` value, displaying in the same order as their HTML code.

**8** Repeat steps **2** to **5** on a different box-child, and set the `box-ordinal-group` value to 0 to make it not be displayed.

**9** Save your CSS file.

```
83        -moz-box-orient: horizontal;
84        -webkit-box-orient: horizontal;
85        border: 2px dashed black;
86      }
87      div.horizontal-box > * {
88        border: 2px solid black;
89      }
90      div.horizontal-box > :nth-child(1) {
91        box-ordinal-group: 2;
92        -moz-box-ordinal-group: 2;
93        -webkit-box-ordinal-group: 2;
94      }
95      div.horizontal-box > :nth-child(4) {
96        box-ordinal-group: 0;
97        -moz-box-ordinal-group: 0;
98        -webkit-box-ordinal-group: 0;
99      }
100    </style>
101    <article class='example'>
102      <div class='horizontal-box'>
103        <div>box-child 1</div>
104        <div>box-child 2</div>
105        <div>box-child 3</div>
106        <div>box-child 4</div>
107        <div>box-child 5</div>
108      </div>
109    </article>
110    </article>
111  </section>
112  <footer>
```

**10** Reload your web page.

In this example, the box-child with a `box-ordinal-group: 0` is now gone.

**HTML5**.ARRAY.ORG
Reference

**Flexible Box Model**

**Synopsis**

```
<style>
  div.flex-box {
    display: box;
    display: -moz-box;
    display: -webkit-box;
  }
</style>
<div class='flex-box'>
  <p>Child 1</p>
  <p>Child 2</p>
  <p>Child 3</p>
</div>
```

**Description**

The Flexible Box Model is a module of the draft CSS3 specification, and by extension, HTML5. It allows you to organize web page data into multiple rows or columns within a new display: box object.

The Flexible Box Model makes it easier to construct one-dimensional data -- one row with multiple columns or one column with multiple rows -- than HTML tables, and provides additional flexibility when ordering and stylizing the data in your CSS rules.

**Example**

box-child 2 | box-child 3 | box-child 5 | box-child 1

©2011 Adam McDaniel

---

## EXTRA

A simpler way to reverse the ordering of flexible box children is to set the `box-direction` property.

**Example**
```
div#box {
  box-direction: reverse;
  -moz-box-direction: reverse;
  -webkit-box-direction: reverse;
}
```

The ordering of box-children, and by extension whether a child is displayed or not — in fact, any CSS declaration — can be controlled in JavaScript. For example, using jQuery's `css()` function, you can manipulate any property and assign it a new value. Be sure to also change the Mozilla and WebKit properties in additional `css()` function calls and to import the jQuery library as described in Chapter 8, "Using jQuery with HTML5."

The multi-column layout is a module of the draft CSS3 specification, and by extension, HTML5. It enables you to organize web page data into multiple columns of variable height and width, depending on how much content there is to display.

Because this is still a draft feature, its specifications could change. This is why not all browsers support this feature, and those that do require a special prefix to all flexible box properties, as per their time of implementation. As of August 2011, only Safari, Chrome, and Firefox support the multi-column layout working draft specification dated December 17, 2009. A newer specification was released on April 12, 2011, to address minor clarification issues in the original draft.

For browsers that do not yet support multi-column layouts, content is displayed normally, like a top-to-bottom series of objects, so there is an inherent level of backward compatibility. What these browsers do lose is the special column formatting that a multi-column layout provides.

## Purpose

The multi-column layout makes it is easier to read large amounts of text, and it enables better use of space, just like columns in a newspaper. This newspaper-column style format has been used in print for centuries, and now the layout style can easily be transferred to web pages with very little code change.

## Implementation

To implement a multi-column layout, you will need a parent block object, such as a `<div>` tag group. Anything found within it, such as paragraphs, tables, and images, are automatically rendered like columns in a newspaper.

### HTML Structure

To create a multi-column layout, you must start with a parent object, which holds any number of child objects of any type. The parent object needs to be selectable by CSS later, so assign its element an ID or class name to make it easier to match:

```
<div class='multi-column'>
  <h1>...content...</h1>
  <p>...content...</p>
  <aside>...content...</aside>
  <figure><img src='content.jpg'></figure>
  <p>...content...</p>
  ...
</div>
```

### Column Count

You can set the preferred number of columns to appear in a text block with `column-count`:

```
div.multi-column {
  column-count: number;
  -moz-column-count: number;
  -webkit-column-count: number;
}
```

Normally, a multi-column layout's height is dictated by the height of the text divided by the number of columns. If you force the parent object's height to be artificially high, the number of `column-count` columns will still be created, but the text will not fill into it properly, leaving whitespace in the multi-column layout.

### Column Width

The horizontal column width can be controlled with `column-width`. When set, it dictates the minimum width of individual columns:

```
div.multi-column {
  column-width: size;
  -moz-column-width: size;
  -webkit-column-width: size;
}
```

If `column-count` is set too high on smaller screens, it can squish the columns together, making the content rather hard to read. The `column-width` property allows you to set the smallest width allowed, overriding the `column-count` variable to a smaller number if necessary.

### Column Gap

The gap in between the columns is configurable using the `column-gap` property:

```
div.multi-column {
  column-gap: size;
  -moz-column-gap: size;
  -webkit-column-gap: size;
}
```

### Column Ruler

You can display a subtle ruler in between each column with `column-rule`. It will appear as a line with a customizable width, style, and color. In fact, its syntax is exactly the same as the CSS `border` property:

```
div.multi-column {
  column-rule: width style color;
  -moz-column-rule: width style color;
  -webkit-column-rule: width style color;
}
```

### Horizontal Column Span

If you need to bisect a multi-column layout and have an element span the entire width, you can do that with `column-span`:

```
div.multi-column > child {
  column-span: none|all;
  -moz-column-span: none|all;
  -webkit-column-span: none|all;
}
```

If unspecified, the default value is `none`, which means that the child block appears normally within a column's width. If you use the value `all`, it will effectively end any previous content's column layout, span the entire width of all columns, and then start a new column layout.

The multi-column layout is supported as of Firefox 3.5 and all versions of Chrome and Safari, including their mobile counterparts, such as the Android and iOS browsers.

Support has been added into Internet Explorer 10 and Opera 11.1; however, these versions do not require any special prefix and follow the April 12, 2011, W3C working draft standard.

# CREATE A MULTI-COLUMN LAYOUT

You can create a multi-column layout rather easily in CSS3. Simply configuring the `column-count` property, and its Mozilla and WebKit equivalents, in an HMTL element block will cause any content to automatically format itself into narrow vertical columns in your web browser, just like text columns in a newspaper:

```
selector {
  column-count: number;
  -moz-column-count: number;
```

```
  -webkit-column-count: number;
}
```

Individual children have no control over the height of the multi-column layout. Instead, the layout height is extended only by the total height of the children divided by the number of columns.

Anything can be displayed as content within a multi-column layout. This includes Flexible Box Models, tables, or even another multi-column layout.

## Create a Multi-Column Layout

1. In an HTML file, type **<element class='multi-column'>**.

2. Insert any content that should appear in the multi-column layout block.

3. Type **</element>**.

4. Save your HTML file.

5. Open your CSS file or scroll to the `<style>` block in your HTML file.

6. Type **element.multi-column {** to apply the multi-column layout by class name.

7. Type **column-count: *number*;** to define the number of columns the layout will have.

8. Repeat step **7** with the Mozilla and WebKit prefixes.

9. Type **}**.

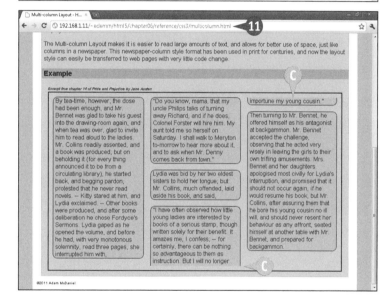

Ⓐ Optionally, type **border: 2px solid black; padding: 10px;** to display a solid border around the multi-column layout and add some padding.

Ⓑ Optionally, type *element.multi-column* > * { border: 1px solid black; border-radius: 10px; background-color: lightgray; } to display a rounded border and background color around the multi-column layout children.

⑩ Save your CSS file.

⑪ View your HTML file in a web browser.

The multi-column layout appears in a solid border.

The multi-column layout child objects appear with rounded borders and a background color.

Ⓒ Paragraphs that continue beyond the column height boundary abruptly stop and continue at the top of the next column.

**Note:** *In this example, each paragraph has rounded borders, but the borders do not round when the paragraph is broken up by a new column.*

---

**EXTRA**

There are some extended multi-column layout properties that you can use but are not required. This includes `column-width`, which sets the minimum width that a column should be rendered as, and `column-gap`, which sets the width in between the columns.

**Example**
```
div.multi-column {
  column-width: size;
  -moz-column-width: size;
  -webkit-column-width: size;
}
```

Before you set a `column-width` value, slowly resize your browser window, making it narrower. You will see how the browser attempts to maintain `column-count` columns, despite text readability. When you find the smallest width where text is still legible, set that width to `column-width`.

**Y**ou can customize your multi-column layout further by adding a simple ruler border and extend the gap width in between each column:

```
selector {
    column-rule: width style color;
    -moz-column-rule: width style color;
    -webkit-column-rule: width style color;
    column-gap: size;
    -moz-column-gap: size;
    -webkit-column-gap: size;
}
```

The *width* value refers to the width of the column ruler line. The *style* value refers to the style of the line, which can be solid, dashed, or dotted. The *color* value can be any valid CSS color notation.

If column-gap's *size* is unspecified, the default size is 1em. The unit *em* refers to multiples of the current font size. In most browsers, the default font size is 12 points, or one-sixth of an inch. The em unit automatically resizes itself if the users modify their font size; as such, column-gap increases as the font increases.

## Add a Ruler and Gap in between Columns

**1** Scroll to your multi-column layout parent CSS selector.

**2** Type **column-rule: *width style color*;** to specify the ruler display properties in between each column.

**3** Type **column-gap *size*;** to specify the margin gap in between each column.

④ Repeat steps **2** and **3** with the Mozilla and WebKit flexible box prefixes.

⑤ Save your CSS file.

```
70     div.multi-column {
71         column-count: 3;
72         -moz-column-count: 3;
73         -webkit-column-count: 3;
74         border: 2px solid black;
75         padding: 10px;
76         column-rule: 3px dashed red;
77 ④ ── -moz-column-rule: 3px dashed red;
78         -webkit-column-rule: 3px dashed red;
79         column-gap: 2em;
80 ④ ── -moz-column-gap: 2em;
81         -webkit-column-gap: 2em;
82     }
```

⑥ View your HTML file in a web browser.

Ⓐ A custom ruler is configured in between each column.

Ⓑ A custom gap is configured in between each column.

*Note: The gap affected the overall placement of the paragraphs. In this example, the cutoff of the fourth paragraph to the third column has moved.*

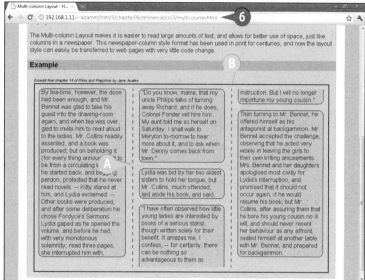

The `column-rule` property can be split up into separate property declarations. This follows the same CSS practice of allowing multivalue properties to be set via specific property names, just like `display`, `border`, `margin`, and `padding`.

**Example**
```
column-rule-width: width;
-moz-column-rule-width: width;
-webkit-column-rule-width: width;
column-rule-style: style;
-moz-column-rule-style: style;
-webkit-column-rule-style: style;
column-rule-color: color;
-moz-column-rule-color: color;
-webkit-column-rule-color: color;
```

To further the look of a newspaper on your web page, you can span objects horizontally across columns to display headlines, bylines, and figures that cover the entire width of the columns:

```
selector > child {
  column-span: none|all;
  -moz-column-span: none|all;
  -webkit-column-span: none|all;
}
```

The value for `column-span` can be only one of two keywords: `none`, which is the default, or `all`, which is the entire width.

Whatever you are spanning horizontally must be a `display: block` object such as a paragraph, heading, or other semantic tag group. Despite its name, do not use the `<span>` tag because it displays inline. If you are unsure, you can always force an element to be displayed as a block object.

For example, to span an image across all columns, you would do something like this:

```
div.multi-column > img {
  column-span: all;
  -moz-column-span: all;
  -webkit-column-span: all;
  display: block;
}
```

## Span Objects Horizontally across Columns

**1** Create a multi-column layout HTML and CSS code.

**2** Identify spanning text blocks to begin a new multi-column layout.

**Note:** *If you have several different elements that you want to span, you may want to consider creating a new class, such as* `<element class='column-span'>`.

**3** Open your CSS file or scroll to the `<style>` block in your HTML file.

**4** Type *div.multi-column > element* **{** to select anything with the class under the parent selector.

**5** Type **column-span: all;** to activate the column-spanning property.

**6** Type **}**.

⑦ Repeat step **5** with the Mozilla and WebKit flexible box prefixes.

⑧ Insert any additional formatting properties for the `multi-column` class.

⑨ Save your CSS file.

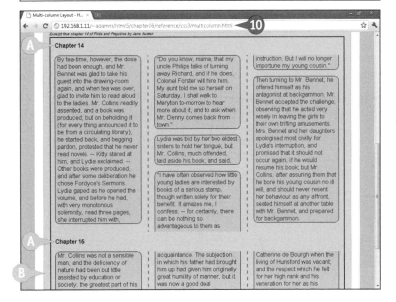

⑩ View your HTML file in a web browser.

Ⓐ In this example, the headings span across the multi-column layout.

Ⓑ The text after the second `column-span: all` creates a new multi-column layout.

---

**EXTRA**

The current multi-column layout specification stipulates that `column-span` can be only an all-or-nothing type of property. This means that it can span the entire multi-column width or none at all. Therefore, for example, it is impossible to configure an object to span only two of three columns.

Up to this point, this chapter has discussed a multi-column layout that may seem overkill for basic website design. There is a shortcut property available, `columns`, which sets `column-width` and `column-count` at once:

```
div.multi-column {
  columns: 200px 3;
  -webkit-columns: 200px 3;
}
```

Depending on the amount of text contained within `<div class='multi-column'>`, this example will span three columns, but only if the browser width is greater than $3 \times 200$ px plus the `column-gap`. If it is less, one or more columns will be removed, maintaining the per-column width.

**Y**ou can use the *number input type* to restrict input fields to numeric values only. Supported web browsers will inhibit any nonnumeric data from being submitted. You can set a minimum and maximum number range and an interval. If a number is outside of the specified range or is not divisible by the stepping value, it will be rejected with a pop-up message.

```
<input type='number' name='field'
 value='number' min='number' max='number'
 step='number'>
```

The `type='number'` attribute value activates the number-specific input options of the user's web browser, if supported. Additional `input` element attributes, such as `name` and `value`, have the same meaning and functionality

common in HTML forms. Any combination of the `min`, `max`, and `step` attributes can be optionally applied. `step` specifies the interval size of valid numbers, starting at 0, unless `min` is specified.

When the number input type is activated, a pair of up and down buttons will appear beside the input field.

The number input type feature is supported by all recent releases of Chrome and Opera. For older and other web browsers, the number input type falls back to a text input type. For this reason, do not rely on the web browser to error-correct your numeral form inputs! Proper error-correction and validation must also occur on the server-side CGI script that receives the submitted form.

## Create a Number Input Type

① Open an HTML file and locate the `<form>` tag group to which you want to add a number input type.

② Type **<input type='number' name='*field*'**.

Ⓐ Optionally, type **value='*number*'** to assign a default number value.

Ⓑ Optionally, type **min='*number*' max='*number*' step='*number*'** to specify an allowable number range and stepping period.

③ Type **>**.

④ Save your HTML file.

⑤ Open your HTML file in a web browser.

The number input field appears.

⑥ Clicking either arrow button or using your scroll wheel will increment and decrement the number field.

Ⓒ Optionally, type a number beyond the range of the minimum or maximum and submit the form.

Ⓓ A rejection message appears.

**Note:** *The nonnumeric characters are automatically purged from numeric fields when you submit the form.*

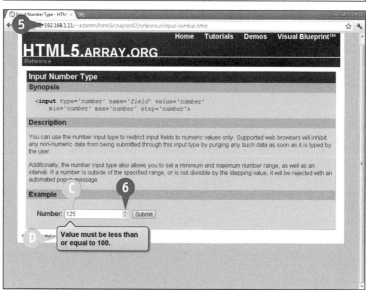

You can use the *telephone input type* to accept into an input field telephone numbers and characters such as +, -, and a space. When a web form requires a phone number for an input field, it is relatively simple for desktop users to simply type in a phone number, but on mobile web browsers, there is no point in displaying a full-sized virtual keyboard; instead, only a numeric keypad with the telephone-related characters appears.

```
<input type='tel' name='field'
  value='telephone'>
```

The `type='tel'` attribute value activates the telephone-specific input options of the user's web browser, if supported. Additional `input` element attributes, such as `name` and `value`, have the same meaning and functionality common in HTML forms.

Because newer HTML5 desktop web browsers do not pay special attention to the telephone input type itself, they treat it as a normal text input type, just like pre-HTML5 browsers. Therefore, it is relatively safe to deploy this on your website today. No special sanitization or value restriction is done by the browser, mobile or desktop — meaning do not assume that the data entered by the user is an actual phone number.

If you want to restrict the value to syntax that looks like a phone number, see the section "Restrict Input Values Using Pattern Matching" later in this chapter. Be careful implementing this, as telephone number syntax varies worldwide. However, if your form requires a North American telephone number, adding the attribute `pattern='[0-9]{3}-[0-9]{3}-[0-9]{4}'` is acceptable.

This feature is supported by all recent releases of iOS Safari and the Android browser.

## Create a Telephone Input Type

**1** Open an HTML file and locate the `<form>` tag group to which you want to add a telephone input type.

**2** Type **<input type='tel' name='*field*'**.

**Ⓐ** Optionally, type **value='*telephone*'** to assign a default telephone number.

**3** Type **>**.

**4** Save your HTML file.

**5** Open your HTML file in a mobile web browser.

**6** Touch the field to bring up the virtual keyboard.

The keyboard appears like a telephone keypad.

*Note: When this input type is viewed on a desktop browser, nothing special happens.*

Y ou can use the *email input type* to restrict input fields to values formatted like email addresses only. Supported web browsers will reject values that are not formatted with an @ sign and a specific domain name with a TLD (top-level domain), such as *user@domain*.com — or to be precise, values that do not follow RFC5322. Note this feature makes no effort to verify that the user owns the email address provided or whether it is even real.

```
<input type='email' name='field'
 value='email' multiple>
```

The `type='email'` attribute value activates the email-specific input options of the user's web browser. Additional `input` element attributes, such as `name` and `value`, have the same meaning and functionality common in HTML forms. In addition, the optional `multiple` attribute can be used to allow the user to insert multiple email addresses, separated by a comma.

The email input type is executed differently on some mobile web browsers, such as iOS Safari and Firefox Mobile. These browsers display a keyboard optimized for entering in email information, making it easier to access common email-related characters, such as @ and ".com." Note that both browsers do not check for RFC5322 validation and may allow any value to be submitted.

Email address validation is supported by all recent releases of Chrome, Firefox, and Opera. For older and other web browsers, the email input type falls back to a text input type. For this reason, do not rely on the web browser to error-correct your email form inputs! Proper error-correction and validation must also occur on the server-side CGI script that receives the submitted form.

## Create an Email Input Type

1 Open an HTML file and locate the `<form>` tag group to which you want to add an email input type.

2 Type **<input type='email' name='*field*'**.

Ⓐ Optionally, type **value='*email*'** to assign a default email value.

Ⓑ Optionally, type **multiple**.

3 Type **>**.

4 Save your HTML file.

5 Open your HTML file in a web browser.

6 Type in an invalid email address.

7 Submit the form.

Ⓒ A message appears, saying that the address is formatted incorrectly.

**Note:** *Chrome does not permit additional spacing around an email address. With* `multiple`, *this includes spacing around the comma. Firefox and Opera ignore any additional spacing.*

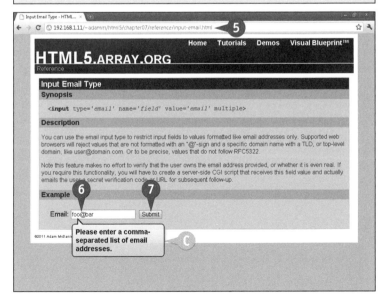

**Y**ou can use the *URL input type,* new in HTML5, to restrict input fields to values formatted like an absolute HTTP or HTTPS Internet address prefix. Supported web browsers will reject values that are not formatted with a proper prefix, but the address itself is not verified to determine whether it is real.

```
<input type='url' name='field' value='url'>
```

The `type='url'` attribute value activates the URL-specific input options of the user's web browser, if supported. Additional `input` element attributes, such as `name` and `value`, have the same meaning and functionality common in HTML forms. If you assign `value='url'` to prepopulate the input field, the URL should be formatted with a proper prefix, such as `http://www.mydomain.com`, but if not it will still be inserted into the form. As such, unless the user edits the value, the form input will be rejected.

Additionally, the URL input type provides hints to some mobile web browsers such as iOS Safari to display a keyboard optimized for entering in URL information. This makes it easier for the user to access common URL-related characters, such as a period, /, and ".com." Note that Mobile Safari does not do the URL-formatting test and may allow any information to be submitted.

This feature is supported by all recent releases of Chrome, Firefox, Opera, and iOS Safari. For older and other web browsers, the URL input type falls back to a text input type. For this reason, do not rely on the web browser to error-correct your URL form inputs! Proper error-correction and validation must also occur on the server-side CGI script that receives the submitted form.

## Create a URL Input Type

1 Open an HTML file and locate the `<form>` tag group to which you want to add a URL input type.

2 Type **<input type='url' name='*field*'**.

Ⓐ Optionally, type **value='*url*'** to assign a default URL value.

**Note:** *Even if you do not have a default URL, setting* `value='http://'` *will encourage users to type in the rest of the address with the proper prefix.*

3 Type **>**.

4 Save your HTML file.

5 Open your HTML file in a web browser.

6 Type an incomplete or badly formatted URL.

7 Submit the form.

Ⓑ A pop-up message appears, requesting a valid URL address.

8 Open your HTML file in a mobile browser, such as iOS Safari. Touch in the URL field.

Ⓒ The keyboard changes to display the /, period, and ".com" keys.

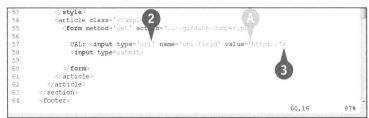

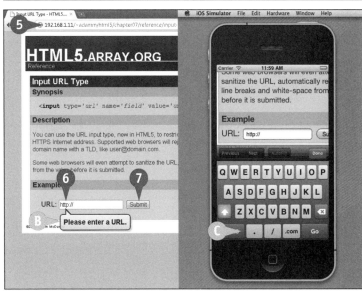

**Y**ou can use the *search input type,* new in HTML5, to create an input field designed to support a search query. Supported web browsers will apply additional user interface elements to make the query prompt more functional:

```
<input type='search' name='field'
 value='query'>
```

The `type='search'` attribute value activates the search-specific input options of the user's web browser, if supported. Additional `input` element attributes, such as `name` and `value`, have the same meaning and functionality common in HTML forms.

At a fundamental level, the search input type simply acts like a text input type, except for some very minor user interface changes. Specifically, in Chrome, an *X* appears to the right of the text field; clicking it will clear the search query. In addition, in Mac OS X Safari, the search field appears rounded so that it is consistent with the user interface of other Apple products, such as iTunes.

The search input type feature is supported by all recent releases of Safari, Chrome, Firefox, and Opera. For older and other web browsers, the search input type falls back to a text input type.

## Create a Search Input Type

**1** Open an HTML file and locate the `<form>` tag group to which you want to add a search input type.

**2** Type **<input type='search' name='field'**.

**Ⓐ** Optionally, type **value='query'** to assign a default query value.

**3** Type **>**.

**4** Save your HTML file.

**5** Open your HTML file in a web browser.

**6** Start typing in a search query.

**Ⓑ** In Chrome and Safari, an *X* appears, allowing you to clear your search field.

**Note:** *Safari also rounds the edges of input search fields.*

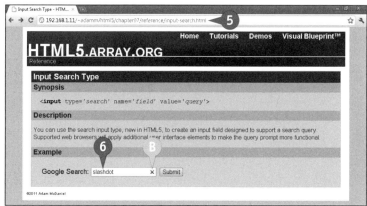

You can use the new `required` input attribute to force the user to supply a value in any input field. Supported web browsers will pop up a simple message saying that the field is required if the user attempts to submit a blank value:

```
<input ... required>
```

The `required` attribute, when applied to an input element, activates the require-input feature in the user's web browser, if supported.

One unfortunate problem with the require-input feature is that if multiple fields are required and missing a value, only the first one will receive the pop-up notification error. The user will need to correct the first problem and submit the form again before being notified of the second error.

To sidestep this issue, simply make it clear which fields are actually required by labeling them in the HTML form differently, as in the following:

```
First name (required): <input type='text'
  name='firstname' required>
Last name (required): <input type='text'
  name='lastname' required>
Address: <input type='text' name='address'>
```

The require-input feature is supported by all recent releases of Chrome, Firefox, and Opera. For older and other web browsers, the `required` attribute is ignored. For this reason, do not rely on the web browser to error-correct your required form inputs! Proper error-correction and validation must also occur on the server-side CGI script that receives the submitted form.

## Require a Value in an Input Field

① Open an HTML file and locate the `<input>` tag in which you want to require a value.

② Type **required** as a new attribute for the `input` element.

*Note: You may use* `required='on'`*; however, the value itself is irrelevant.*

③ Save the HTML file.

④ Open your HTML file in a web browser.

⑤ Click the Submit button, ignoring the required field.

Ⓐ A pop-up message appears over the required field that was ignored.

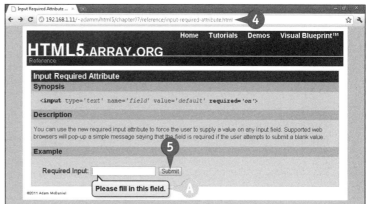

You can use the `placeholder` input attribute to insert a one-line text string into any text-based input field. When the form loads, supported web browsers will display this string in the input area with gray text and automatically clear it when the user attempts to type in a value. This is useful to provide a subtle description or formatting hints that the user is expected to follow in order to submit your form:

```
<input type='text' ... placeholder='text'>
```

The `type` attribute can be a text-based input type, such as `text`, `telephone`, `url`, `email`, and `search`. The `placeholder` attribute value appears as gray text in the input field itself, if supported. When the user clicks in the field, the placeholder text disappears, allowing the user to type.

Because the placeholder text can be used to advise the user how to format an input value, you may want to combine it with the `pattern` attribute, described later in this chapter in the section "Restrict Input Values Using Pattern Matching." This enables you to instruct the user how to format an answer and provides a way to enforce correctly formatted answers.

For example, a company warranty form may require a 15-digit product serial number like this:

```
Product Serial number (required):
<input type='text' name='serialnum'
 placeholder='Enter all 15 digits'
 pattern='[0-9]{15}' required='on'>
```

The placeholder feature is supported by all recent releases of Safari, Chrome, Firefox, and Opera. For older and other web browsers, the `placeholder` attribute is ignored, and the text field is rendered empty.

## Set a Placeholder for an Input Field

1. Open an HTML file and locate the text-based `<input>` tag in which you want to put a placeholder.

2. Type **placeholder='*text*'** as a new attribute for the `input` element.

3. Save the HTML file.

4. Open your HTML file in a web browser.

Ⓐ The placeholder text appears in the form input field.

5. Type something into the text field.

The placeholder text disappears.

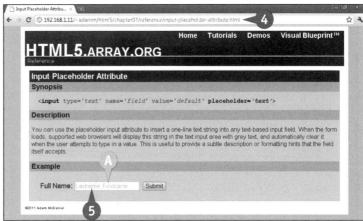

**Y**ou can use the `autofocus` input attribute to automatically move the user's cursor, or insertion point, directly to any input field as soon as the web page loads. This is useful to direct the user to input fields that are required to be populated early after the page loads, such as a username field:

```
<input ... autofocus>
```

The `autofocus` attribute activates the auto-focus feature in the user's web browser, if supported. The attribute does not require a value — in fact, its value can be anything; the browser only looks for the attribute name to enable the feature. This means that you could use the value `on` if it makes better sense to you; however, even if you set `autofocus=off`, it will still be enabled! The browser pays no attention to this attribute's value.

The auto-focus feature is supported by all recent releases of Safari, Chrome, Firefox, and Opera. For older and other web browsers, the `autofocus` attribute is ignored. Fortunately, this feature can easily be implemented using a little fallback JavaScript with jQuery. For example, after you load the jQuery library as described in Chapter 8, "Using jQuery with HTML5," the following code will auto-focus `input` elements with the `autofocus` attribute defined, even if the attribute is not natively understood:

```
<script type='text/javascript'>
  $(function(){
    $("input[autofocus]").focus();
  });
</script>
```

## Auto-Focus on an Input Field

**1** Open an HTML file and locate the `<input>` tag on which you want to auto-focus.

**2** Type **autofocus** as a new attribute for the `input` element.

***Note:*** *Remember, the value itself is irrelevant; you could use* `autofocus=on` *to make the end result clear.*

**3** Save the HTML file.

**4** Open your HTML file in a web browser.

**Ⓐ** The text `input` element automatically has focus; the insertion point cursor flashes ready for input.

***Note:*** *If multiple input elements are set to auto-focus, in Firefox the first input receives the focus and the cursor, but in Chrome, Safari, and Opera, it is the last input.*

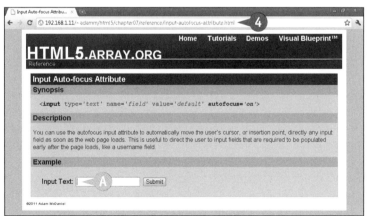

You can use the `autocomplete` input attribute to instruct the browser how it should remember the values in a form after it is submitted. When the form loads again, supported web browsers will present a pull-down list showing all previous values after the user types the first character that matches a previously used value. This feature is enabled by default, but should be disabled for security text fields, such as usernames and Q&A authentication.

You can disable it on your website by applying `autocomplete='off'` to a form tag:

```
<form ... autocomplete='off'>
<input type='text' ... >
</form>
```

Or set `autocomplete='off'` on individual `input` elements; no values will be cached, nor will a pull-down list appear:

```
<form ... >
<input type='text' ... autocomplete='off'>
</form>
```

There is a strange quirk here you should be aware of. If you leave auto-complete enabled on a form and then later decide to disable it, you must actually deactivate the attribute on the form *and* the input elements! `autocomplete='off'` on the form will disable any *new* values from being cached, but *previously* cached values will still appear in `input` element pull-down lists. If your website is not yet deployed, you only need to disable auto-complete on the form.

## Disable Auto-Completion of Input Text

**1** Open an HTML file and locate the `<form>` tag group in which you want to disable auto-completion.

**Note:** *Auto-complete is on by default on all forms and text input types.*

**2** Type **autocomplete='off'** within an `<input>` tag to disable auto-completion only on this element.

**Note:** *In this example, two input fields are used, one with auto-completion enabled and one disabled.*

**3** Save the HTML file.

**4** Open your HTML file in a web browser.

**5** Insert and submit text into the fields.

**6** Reload the form.

**7** Insert the beginning characters again.

**A** A pull-down list appears of the completed value only in the enabled field.

Optionally, in the code, type **autocomplete='off'** in the `<form>` tag to disable auto-complete in the entire form.

No new auto-completion values will be cached.

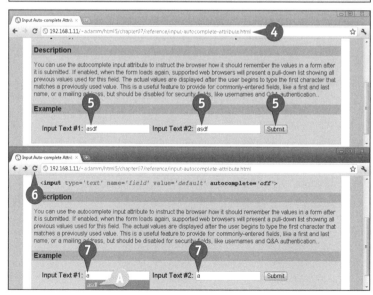

The Google Chrome web browser supports a speech input feature, which enables the user to transcribe voice data into text input values. Although this is not currently a part of any official HTML5 specification, you can add the attribute `x-webkit-speech` to text-based form inputs to activate it:

`<input type='text' ... x-webkit-speech>`

Unlike what the name implies, this feature is not supported by any other WebKit browsers.

The `type` attribute can be a text-based input type, such as `text`, `number`, `telephone`, and `search`. This is limited because `x-webkit-speech` is accessible only within simple text or number attributes and will not work on the URL, email, or date input type elements.

This feature is supported in Chrome 11 and later. All other browsers simply ignore the special attribute, thus causing no compatibility issues if you add this feature to your website.

The new Google Speech API actually performs the voice-to-text conversion. This means that the speech input feature's algorithm and code is not found locally on the user's web browser but is accessible only over the Internet and kept proprietary by Google's licensing and copyright.

In fact, as of August 2011, the Google Speech API is not yet publicly documented. However, some enterprising users have identified its interface code in Chrome and have produced simple third-party programs to interact with it. A useful blog post by Mike Pultz on March 2011, at http://mikepultz.com/2011/03/accessing-google-speech-api-chrome-11/, demonstrates a simple program that interfaces with the API outside of Chrome, by uploading a FLAC sound file to a Google web service.

## Using Speech Input

1. Open an HTML file and locate the text-based `<input>` tag for which you want to use speech input.

2. Type **x-webkit-speech** as a new attribute for the `input` element.

3. Save the HTML file.

4. Open the HTML file in Chrome 11 or later.

5. Click the microphone icon.

*Note: If you do not have a microphone installed on your computer, an icon may not appear.*

6. Speak into your microphone.

Ⓐ The input monitor moves as the microphone and browser records your voice.

Ⓑ The Google Speech API will attempt to convert your voice into text for the input field.

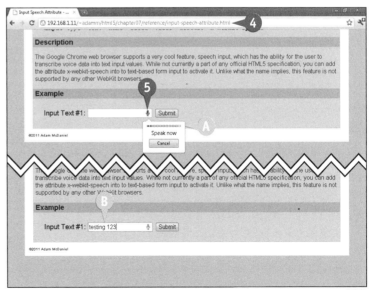

**I**f you have a text input field that supports text input and you want to provide a subtle list of suggested values, you can create a drop-down list of suggestions that will appear immediately under the form input as the user starts typing.:

```
<input type='text' ... list='listid'>
<datalist id='listid'>
  <option label='label1' value='value1'>
  <option label='label2' value='value2'>
  ...
</datalist>
```

The `type` attribute can be a text-based input type, such as `text`, `telephone`, `email`, and `search`. In the `input` element, add a new attribute, `list`, and assign it an identifier. The `datalist` element must have a matching `id` attribute value, binding the `datalist`'s options to

that `input` element. Within `datalist`, define a series of `option` elements with `label` and `value` attributes; `label` will appear in the drop-down list, and `value` will be used when the form is submitted.

When the drop-down list is rendered, the content that appears depends on the browser. In Opera, both the `label` and `value` attributes appear on the list; in Firefox, only the `label` attribute appears. As such, the text will be filtered on both attributes in Opera and only on one in Firefox.

Other web browsers ignore the `list` attribute and `<datalist>` tag. The `input` element will act like a normal text field. Therefore, implementing this feature today is relatively safe; however, read the Extra for an important footnote about Safari.

## Create a Drop-Down List for Text Input Suggestions

**1** Open an HTML file and locate the text-based `<input>` tag to which you want to add a suggestion list.

**2** Type **list='listid'**.

**3** Type **<datalist id='listid'>**.

**4** Type **</datalist>**.

**Note:** Multiple `<input>` tags can share the same `<datalist>` tag group.

**Note:** The `<datalist>` group can appear anywhere within the body of your web page. It does not need to reside within the `<form>` tag group or near the targeted `<input>` tag.

**5** Type **<option label='*label*' value='*value*'>** to define a single suggested input option.

**6** Repeat step **5** for any additional suggested text options.

**7** Save the HTML file.

**8** Open your HTML file in Opera.

**9** Start typing text in a text input field.

**A** A drop-down list of suggested text input values and labels appears.

**10** Click a suggestion to insert the value in the input field.

**Note:** *If you simply continue typing a unique value, all suggested text options will disappear.*

**11** Open your HTML file in Firefox.

**12** Start typing text in a text input field.

**B** A drop-down list of suggested text labels appears.

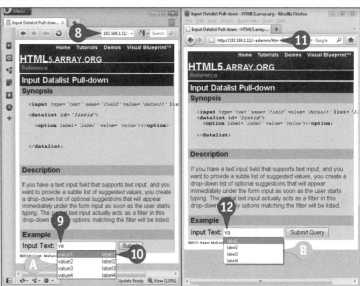

Safari versions prior to 5.1 may experience major problems with the suggested drop-down list feature. The browser will simply stop rendering any HTML content after the `<datalist>` tag group!

This bug is caused by unclosed `<option>` tags found within `<datalist>`. Simply closing the `<option>` tag allows Safari to render the web page:

```
<datalist id='listid'>
  <option label='label1' value='value1'></option>
```

```
  <option label='label2' value='value2'></option>
  ...
</datalist>
```

Naturally, the actual drop-down list feature will still not work, as Safari itself does not support it, but at least the rest of the page will be rendered correctly. The HTML5 specification does not specify whether the `<option>` tag requires a closing tag. Fortunately, the other browsers that do support this feature will continue to work.

You can use the `pattern` matching attribute, new in HTML5, to restrict input fields to values that follow a custom formatting pattern that you define. This is useful if you need to ensure that the user submits correctly formatted values; otherwise, the browser displays a message to the user and stops the form submission process:

```
<input type='text' ... pattern='pattern'
  title='title'>
```

The `type` attribute can be a text-based input type, such as `text`, `number`, `telephone`, and `search`. The *pattern* variable represents a *regular expression* syntax that defines the format of acceptable values that can be submitted by the user. A regular expression allows you to restrict values to very specific, finely tuned formats. Because different programming languages have different regular expression syntaxes, HTML5 follows the JavaScript pattern syntax. The *title* variable is a plain-text explanation of what the regular expression

represents. It will be displayed to the user as a pop-up bubble if the user's value does not match *pattern*.

There is not enough space here to fully describe the JavaScript pattern semantics, but there are some excellent websites available. One such resource is the JavaScript Programmer's Guide to Regular Expressions, www.javascriptkit.com/javatutors/redev.shtml. This tutorial covers JavaScript declarations, patterns, flags, and methods; note that only the patterns' syntax applies to this HTML5 feature.

Input pattern matching is supported by all recent releases of Chrome, Firefox, and Opera. For older and other web browsers, the `pattern` attribute is simply ignored. For this reason, do not rely on the web browser to error-correct your restricted form inputs! Proper error-correction and validation must also occur on the server-side CGI script that receives the submitted form.

## Restrict Input Values Using Pattern Matching

1 Open an HTML file and locate the text-based `<input>` tag for which you want to restrict input.

2 Type **pattern='*pattern*'** to define a restrictive regular expression pattern.

**Note:** *In this example, the pattern used, `[A-Z]{3}`, represents exactly three characters, suitable for an ISO 3166-1 three-character country code.*

3 Save your HTML file.

4 Open your HTML file in a web browser.

5 Insert an incorrect value in the restricted text field.

6 Submit the form.

The form submission is aborted.

Ⓐ A pop-up appears, displaying a generic text message requesting the required format.

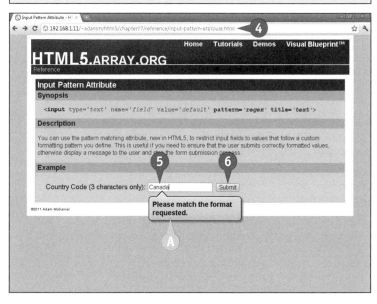

7️⃣ Return to your HTML file.

8️⃣ Type **title='*title*'** to supply a simple explanation of the pattern.

9️⃣ Save your HTML file.

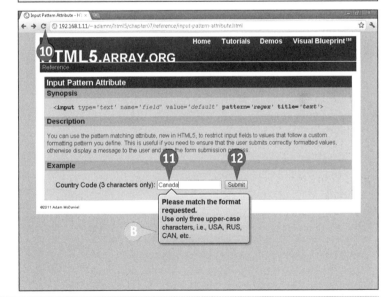

🔟 Reload your HTML file in a browser.

⓫ Again, insert an incorrect value in the restricted text field.

⓬ Submit the form.

The form submission is stopped.

Ⓑ A pop-up appears, displaying the text from the `title` attribute.

**EXTRA**

Be careful about mixing the `pattern` attribute with input types other than `text` in Opera: Although Opera 11 will honor `type='text'` `pattern='*pattern*'` attributes, using `type='tel'` `pattern='*pattern*'` to enforce a specific telephone number format will cause the pattern-matching validation to be ignored! This is because Opera supports pattern matching only on free-text fields, whereas other browsers support it on restricted text fields as well.

In addition, the browsers that do not support the `pattern` attribute, such as Internet Explorer and Safari, do understand the `title` attribute. This will allow your plain-text explanation of the regular expression to appear in a subtle pop-up message when the users hover their mouse cursor over the input field.

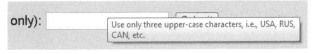

# CREATE A DATE INPUT TYPE

You can use the *date input type,* new in HTML5, to restrict input fields to values formatted like a date string:

`<input type='date' name='field' value='date'>`

The `type='date'` attribute value activates the date-specific input options of the user's web browser, if supported. If you assign `value='date'` to prepopulate the input field, the date format should match the `yyyy-mm-dd` format.

Other date-related input types are also available in HTML5: `month`, `week`, `time`, `datetime`, and `datetime-local`. The `type='month'` and `type='week'` input types are similar to `type='date'` in idea, except that they follow a `yyyy-mm` and `yyyy-Www` format. To clarify, the week syntax is four year digits, followed by a literal `w` and then two week digits, such as `2011-W24`.

Time can also be represented here and optionally appended to `date`. The time follows the 24-hour format `hh:mm:ss.mmm`. When accepted for input here, the user may optionally omit the lesser time units, such as seconds and milliseconds, and only specify a time like `13:54`.

The date input type feature is supported by all recent releases of Safari, Chrome, and Opera. However, as of Chrome 13 and Safari 5.1, support for the date input type is very weak. Opera provides the best level of support today. For all older and other web browsers, the date input type falls back to a text input type.

Because not many browsers support the date input type, there are several third-party JavaScript fallbacks that can easily be employed. jQuery UI provides a Datepicker function that can be used as a fallback; you can download it from http://jqueryui.com/demos/datepicker.

## Create a Date Input Type

**Use the HTML5 Date Input Type**

1. Open an HTML file and locate the `<form>` tag group to which you want to add a date input type.

2. Type **<input type='date' name='field'>**.

   Optionally, type **value='date'** to assign a default date value.

3. Save your HTML file.

4. Open your HTML file in Opera.

5. Click the date field.

   Ⓐ The date pop-up appears.

6. Click a date or the Today button to fill in the date input field.

7. Open your HTML file in Chrome.

8. Click the up arrow.

   Ⓑ The date is increased one day from today.

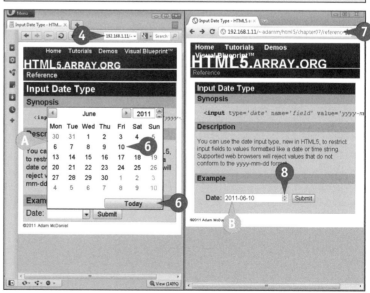

**Use a Date Input Fallback Script**

⑨ Import the jQuery UI library, including its CSS and JavaScript code.

⑩ Type **$(function() { $("#datepicker").datepicker() } );** to initialize the Datepicker in JavaScript.

⑪ Type **id='datepicker'** on the date `input` element to identify it for the jQuery UI.

⑫ Save your HTML file.

⑬ Open your HTML file in Chrome or Firefox.

⑭ Click the date field.

Ⓒ The jQuery UI Datepicker appears.

⑮ Select a date.

The selected date is written to the date field.

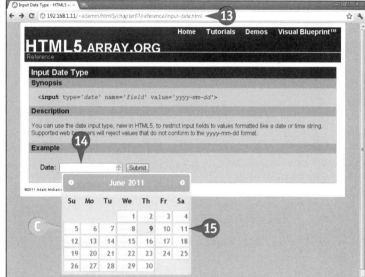

When you select a jQuery UI Datepicker date, the format is $dd/mm/yy$, which conflicts with the HTML5 format. To standardize this, add the following line after `$("#datepicker").datepicker()`:

```
$("#datepicker").datepicker("option","dateFormat","yy-mm-dd");
```

Note, in the jQuery UI, $yy$ expands the year in four digits.

After you have a working native HTML5 date picker and a working JavaScript date picker as a fallback, you will need to inhibit the JavaScript fallback if the HTML5 method is properly supported; otherwise, the UI layouts can conflict with each other!

To solve this problem, you can use a JavaScript library called Modernizr, downloadable from www.modernizr.com. This library can detect whether individual features are supported and allow for a fallback process to execute.

Ensure that the jQuery, jQuery UI, and Modernizr libraries are all imported, as described in Chapter 8.

```
<script>
  $(function() {
    if ( ! Modernizr.inputtypes.date )
      $("#datepicker").datepicker();
  });
</script>
```

**Y**ou can use the *range input type,* new in HTML5, to create a sliding input field. Supported web browsers will display a slider bar and a thumb piece that can be moved left and right. The value of the `input` element changes depending on the position of the thumb piece:

```
<input type='range' name='field'
value='number' min='number' max='number'
step='number'>
```

Because the range input type is effectively a slider version of the number input type, it also supports the same optional `min`, `max`, and `step` attributes. If absent, `min` defaults to 0, `max` is 100, and step is 1. The `value` attribute automatically defaults to one-half of `max` minus `min`, or 50.

In WebKit browsers, you can customize the slider CSS itself. This is done by disabling the `-webkit-appearance` property and then applying your own CSS declarations to the `input` element directly:

```
input[type='range'] {
  -webkit-appearance: none;
  property: value;
  ...
}
```

To modify the movable thumb piece, duplicate this format and append `::-webkit-slider-thumb` to the selector.

The range input type feature is supported by all recent releases of Safari, Chrome, and Opera. For older and other web browsers, the range input type falls back to a text input type.

## Create a Range Input Type

① Open an HTML file and locate a `<form>` tag group to which you want to add a range input type.

② Type **<input type='range' name='*field*'**.

Ⓐ Optionally, type **value='*number*'** to assign a default number value.

Ⓑ Optionally, type **min='*number*' max='*number*'** to assign allowable minimum and maximum number values.

Optionally, type **step='*number*'** to assign a number interval rate.

**Note:** *If undefined,* min *is 0,* max *is 100,* step *is 1, and* value *is 50% of the range.*

③ Type **>**.

④ Save your HTML file.

⑤ Open your HTML file in a web browser.

Ⓒ The range `input` element appears.

**Note:** *The slider UI changes depending on the operating system and web browser the page is loaded under.*

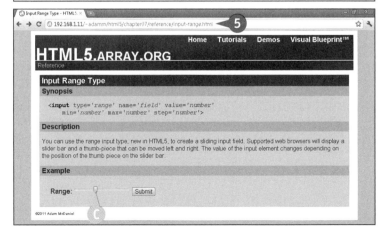

142

**6** Open your CSS file or scroll to the `<style>` block in your HTML file.

**7** Type **input[type='range'] { -webkit-appearance: none;** *property*: *value*; **... }** to customize the slider bar in WebKit browsers.

**8** Type **input[type='range']::-webkit-slider-thumb { -webkit-appearance: none;** *property*: *value*; **... }** to customize the slider thumb piece in WebKit browsers.

**9** Save your CSS file.

**10** Reload your HTML file in Chrome or Safari.

● The range `input` element appears, with the custom CSS layout.

*Note:* *Some browsers, such as Firefox, do not understand the* webkit *property names but will understand your CSS selector in step* **7**. *Because Firefox will fall back to a text input type, it will also apply the non-*webkit *CSS properties!*

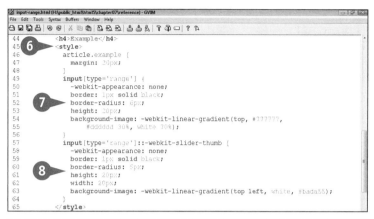

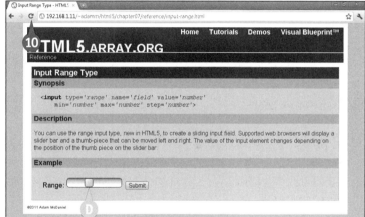

You may find it useful to display actual number values beside the range slider. This can easily be accomplished with jQuery code that listens for changes on the input element, reads the current value, and inserts it in an `<output>` tag group after the slider UI display.

**TYPE THIS**

Ensure that the jQuery library is imported, as described in Chapter 8.

```
<input type='range' id='range1'><output
 id='range1'></output>
<script>
  $("input#range1").change(function(){
    $("output#range1").html( $(this).val() );
  });
</script>
```

**RESULT**

→ The current value is displayed in the output element immediately after the range slider. It updates as the user moves the slider left and right.

Note that the CSS ID `range1` was used to link the input and output elements in jQuery. If you have multiple input range elements on the same page, pair each with its own output element through a unique identifier they can share.

# CREATE A COLOR INPUT TYPE

**Y**ou can use the *color input type,* new in HTML5, to display a color selection input field on supported web browsers. The actual color selection user interface differs between web browsers, but the idea is to allow the user to visually select a color via a color wheel or square and then translate that value into a standard HTML color code:

```
<input type='color' name='field'
 value='color'>
```

The `type='color'` attribute value activates the search-specific input options of the user's web browser, if supported. Additional `input` element attributes, such as `name` and `value`, have the same meaning and functionality common in HTML forms. If you assign `value='color'` to

prepopulate the input field, the color should be in `#rrggbb` hexadecimal color format.

Because not many browsers support the color input type, there are several third-party JavaScript fallbacks that can easily be employed. One of these is a jQuery plug-in called *ColorPicker,* available at www.eyecon.ro/colorpicker/.

The color input type feature is supported only by recent releases of Opera. For older and other web browsers, the color input type falls back to a text input type. For this reason, do not rely on the web browser to error-correct your color form inputs! Proper error-correction and validation must also occur on the server-side CGI script that receives the submitted form.

## Create a Color Input Type

### Use the HTML5 Color Input Type

①  Open an HTML file and locate the `<form>` tag group to which you want to add a color input type.

②  Type **<input type='color' name='*field*'>**.

Optionally, type **value='#rrggbb'** to assign a default color value.

③  Save your HTML file.

④  Open your HTML file in Opera.

⑤  Click the color input field.

A basic color selector appears.

Ⓐ  Optionally, click a basic color to update the input field.

⑥  Click the Other button.

Ⓑ  A more complex color selector appears.

⑦  Click a color.

⑧  Click OK.

The selected color is displayed in the color field.

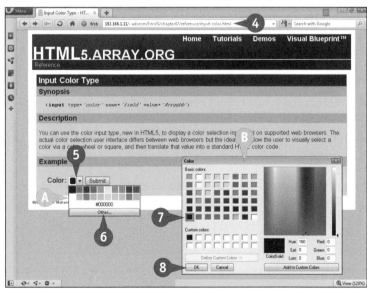

144

**Use a Color Input Fallback Script**

**9** Import the jQuery library.

*Note: See Chapter 8 for more information on jQuery.*

**10** Import the ColorPicker plug-in library.

**11** Type **$(function() { $("#colorpicker"). ColorPicker( { ... } );** to initialize the ColorPicker plug-in in JavaScript.

**12** Type **id='colorpicker'** on the date `input` element to identify it for the jQuery UI.

**13** Save your HTML file.

**14** Open your HTML file in Chrome or Firefox.

**15** Click the color field.

● The jQuery UI ColorPicker appears.

**16** Select a color.

**17** Click the Close button.

The selected color's value is written to the text field.

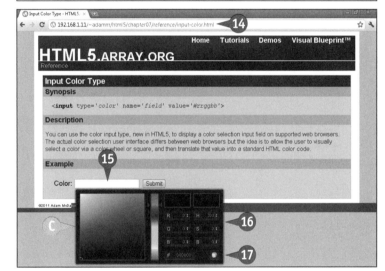

## APPLY IT

After you have a working native HTML5 color picker and a working jQuery color picker as a fallback, you will need to inhibit the JavaScript fallback if the HTML5 method is properly supported; otherwise, the UI layouts can conflict with each other!

To solve this problem, you can use a JavaScript library called Modernizr, downloadable from www.modernizr.com. This library can detect whether individual features are supported and allow for a fallback process to execute.

### TYPE THIS

Ensure that the Modernizr library source is imported.
```
<script>
  $(function() {
    if ( ! Modernizr.inputtypes.color ) {
      // Initialize ColorPicker plug-in
      // as described in step 12.
    }
  });
</script>
```

### RESULT

Modernizr detects whether the color input type is supported by the user's web browser. If it is not, the jQuery ColorPicker plug-in is allowed to initialize.

In HTML 4.01 and earlier, all `input` elements needed to be within a `form` element group. In HTML5, it is now possible to store these `input` elements outside of the form group, provided that you specify a `form` attribute in the `input` element to link the two together:

```
<form ... id='formid'>
</form>
<input ... name='input1' form='formid'>
```

The same `formid` value must be applied to the `id` attribute on the `form` element and the `form` attribute on the `input` element.

Note that an `input` element that appears within a form block may also be assigned to a different form using this method. So, why exactly was the external `input` elements feature added to HTML5? The short answer is obvious:

so that form `input` elements no longer needed to reside within the `form` tag group. But when would that happen?

If you are working on a web page that needs to generate fields dynamically in JavaScript, you may encounter a situation in which form `input` elements appearing "over here" need to supply data to a form that begins "over there," and vice versa. With this feature, you can be sure you do not create any orphaned input elements.

The linked input field feature is supported by all recent releases of Chrome, Firefox, and Opera. For older and other web browsers, the external `input` elements will be ignored, which could significantly break form functionality until these browsers are updated. Because support is not widely available and no proper fallback can be easily implemented, be careful if choosing to implement this feature.

## Link an Input Field to a Specific Form

**1** Open an HTML file and locate the `<form>` tag group to which you want to add a linked input field.

**2** Type **id='*formid*'**.

**3** Create a form `input` element outside of the `<form>` block.

**4** Type **form='*formid*'** to link this `input` element to the form block.

**5** Save your HTML file.

```
49        }
50        </style>
51        <article class='example'>
52
53          <form method='get' action='../cgi/data-dumper.pl' id='myform'>
54            Text #1: <input type='text' name='text-field1'>
55            <input type=submit>
56          </form>
57
58        </article>
59      </article>
60    </section>
61    <footer>
62      &copy;2011 Adam McDaniel
63    </footer>
```

input-linked-form.html (H:\public_html\html5\chapter07\reference) - GVIM
File  Edit  Tools  Syntax  Buffers  Window  Help

```
35 &lt;/form&gt;
36 &lt;input type='text' name='field' value='value' <span class='bold'>form='formid'</span
   >&gt;</code></pre>
37        <h4>Description</h4>
38        <p>
39          In HTML 4.01 and earlier, all input elements needed to be within
40          a form element group. In HTML5, it is now possible to store these
41          input elements outside of the form group, provided that you
42          specify a form attribute in the input element to link the two
43          together.
44        </p>
45        <h4>Example</h4>
46        <style>
47          article.example {
48            margin: 20px;
49          }
50        </style>
51        <article class='example'>
52
53          <form method='get' action='../cgi/data-dumper.pl' id='myform'>
54            Text #1: <input type='t     name='text-field1'>
55            <input type=submit>
56          </form>
57
58          Text #2: <input type='text' name='text-field2' form='myform'>
59
60        </article>
61      </article>
62    </section>
63    <footer>
                                                        60,17            87%
```

**6** Open your HTML file in a web browser.

The external `input` element appears normally.

**7** Interact with the `input` elements.

**8** Click the Submit button.

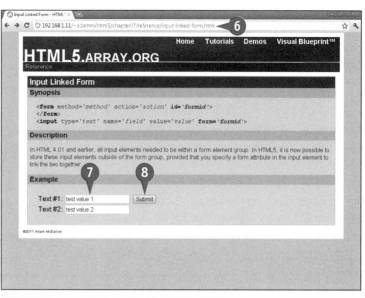

**A** The normal `input` element's value appears.

**Note:** *The CGI script in this example simply dumps the CGI object received using Perl's* `Data::Dumper` *module.*

**B** The linked `input` element's value appears.

**Note:** *If you perform this test on a browser that does not support linked* `input` *elements, such as Internet Explorer or Safari, the second linked element will not be sent to the CGI script.*

## APPLY IT

It is possible to share `input` elements in different forms. In the following example, you can pull unassociated text inputs directly into a form being submitted with jQuery.

```
Text: <input type='text' name='text'
 id='shared'>
<form ... id='myform1'>
  Text (myform1): <input type='text'
 name='text-form1'>
  <input type=submit>
</form>
<form ... id='myform2'>
  Text (myform2): <input type='text'
 name='text-form2'>
  <input type=submit>
```

```
</form>
<script>
  $('form').submit(function(){
    var form = this;
    $('input#shared').each(function(){
      $(this).clone().appendTo(form);
    });
  });
</script>
```

This example has the added benefit of being backward compatible with pre-HTML5 web browsers and HTML5 browsers that do not support the linked-input field feature.

# Introducing jQuery

**A**lthough it is not a part of any W3C or WHATWG specification, jQuery performs an important role as a contributor to HTML5's adoption: It makes common and complex JavaScript tasks much easier to implement. By simplifying large portions of code into two or three lines, jQuery automates some of the little tricks and quirks required to execute complex tasks across most common web browsers.

jQuery provides the fastest, easiest, and most efficient way to produce a sexy HTML5 experience. Think of it like this: jQuery is to HTML5 as the automatic transmission is to a freeway.

Some argue that although jQuery helps you implement JavaScript, it does not help you learn it. Such is the case if you encounter a problem that is not handled by jQuery; you are stuck, whereas a true JavaScript hacker would have no trouble coding a solution. This is completely true. In fact, the "language shortcuts" jQuery uses seem very un-JavaScript-like, even to mid-level JavaScript developers, which actually hinders its adoption!

Although this book does not focus on JavaScript directly, this chapter does introduce you to a few of these language shortcuts and shows you how they can play an important role in the HTML5 world. In order for you to proceed, it is assumed that you have at least a moderate knowledge of JavaScript, just as you should already have with HTML 4.01.

## Loading jQuery

To use jQuery, you can either download and install the JavaScript library or use a link to a hosted copy.

### Download and Install

Download the latest version of jQuery from the jQuery Project, www.jquery.com, and save the library alongside your HTML files on your web server. If you cannot download it, you may link to an externally hosted copy. You have the option of selecting the development format or the minimized production format. See the section "Download jQuery" for more information.

## jQuery Library

jQuery is fairly specific about when and how its functionality can be executed. For the most part, all you need to remember is the jQuery global function and the document-ready setup process.

### The jQuery Global Function

jQuery provides a global function with a very unorthodox name, `$` — just a dollar sign. This is automatically used as a shortcut to provide easy access to the `jQuery()` global function.

### The Document-Ready Setup

Before you can execute any jQuery function or method, one of two things must happen in each web page: Your jQuery code must be defined after all HTML code that it will manage, or you must delay the execution of your jQuery code until after the document has finished loading.

The latter is preferred because this makes the placement of your code independent of the HTML. The document-ready method calls a function when the document is finished loading; therefore, all your jQuery-specific code runs inside of this handler function:

```
$(document).ready(function(){
    ...
});
```

Because this document-ready code is rather long and very common, you can use a shortcut:

```
$(function(){
    ...
};
```

Note that you do not need an individual `$(function(){...});` wrapper for each jQuery call, but you do need at least one to house every jQuery call that is executed after the page loads. Local functions are exempt, as long as they are called from somewhere within this document-ready block.

If you happen to forget this wrapper and your jQuery and JavaScript code is defined prior to the HTML it is manipulating, jQuery simply will not run!

## Select HTML Elements

jQuery is designed to let you select the HTML element or elements that you are interested in and then execute a method on them to manipulate them. The selection process uses a syntax very similar to CSS.

### CSS-Style Selectors

jQuery uses selectors that closely follow CSS. The method that follows will be applied to all matching HTML elements:

```
$('p').method();
$('div.classname').method();
$('section#idname').method();
$('input[attr=value]').method();
```

There is a subset of non-CSS-style pseudo-class selectors available, such as `$(':checkbox')`, `$(':button')`, and `$(':contains()')`, which are not valid in CSS3 but are valid within jQuery.

### Object Selectors

Some methods require that you select the entire document or window object in order to proceed. You can do so by specifying the object variable in the selector function and then calling your method:

```
$(document).method();
$(window).method();
$(this).method();
```

The `$(this)` object selector is unique as it is only applicable inside a function handle of another method. Effectively, `$(this)` is a shortcut to the parent object that triggered the original selector match.

## Applying jQuery Methods

After you have a `$(selector)` established, you can begin calling jQuery methods.

### Calling Methods

jQuery has methods that enable you to manipulate the DOM of all HTML elements that match `$(selector)`. For example, you can add a CSS class, manipulate HTML element attributes, change entire HTML blocks, and even make an HTML block dynamically disappear with an animation:

```
$(selector).addClass(classname);
$(selector).attr(key, value);
$(selector).html(code);
$(selector).hide();
```

Other methods register for action events and define handler functions when the action is performed by the user on the selector defined.

### Chaining Methods

Most jQuery methods actually return a jQuery object of the same type as the original `$(selector)`. This means that you can chain multiple methods together in a single command with a single selector:

```
$(selector).method1().method2().method3();
```

Note that depending on the method used, the contents of the jQuery object may be slightly different than the original selector. This is true for methods that manipulate the selected object list itself:

```
$('input:checkbox').css('background-color', 'red').
  find(':checked').css('color', 'green');
```

In this example, all input check boxes are selected, and a `background-color: red` CSS declaration is applied to them. Then, of those that were modified, `find()` filters out the ones that are checked from the initial selector, allowing `css()` to set `color: green` only to them.

In order to use jQuery on your website, you can download it from its home page at www.jquery.com or use a CDN (content delivery network) hosted copy of the software. The CDN method is described on the next page and does not require you to download anything.

If you prefer to have a local copy, you can proceed with the procedure described here.

jQuery is available for download in two release formats: a minimized production format and an full-sized development format. The production format is useful if you have used jQuery before or are more interested in speed and efficiently loading the library on a production website.

The examples in this book use the development format because this version is most useful for understanding how jQuery works, especially later on when you use the Chrome Inspector.

The download process itself is not like a typical program that you download online. Instead, the jQuery source is displayed right in the web browser; you need to save the page as a file on your hard drive and then transfer that file to your web server. After it is downloaded, you can load jquery.js into your website.

jQuery also provides hundreds of third-party plug-in libraries that allow for specialized functionality. These plug-ins are available at the jQuery Project Plug-ins page http://plugins. jquery.com, and they follow the same basic download and install process described here and in the following section.

Although most of these third-party plug-ins are simple hacks, some have grown into standalone projects themselves, such as jQuery UI. Available at http://jqueryui. com, this plug-in extends jQuery by adding in themes, widgets, and even more effect animations. Note that jQuery UI's download process is different from jQuery itself: You download a Zip archive that contains the JavaScript library, CSS library, and supporting documentation and examples.

## Download jQuery

**1** In a web browser, go to the jQuery Project page at www. jquery.com.

**2** Click Development.

**Note:** When you are ready to deploy jQuery on your live website, download the Production version.

**3** Click Download jQuery.

The literal jQuery source appears in your web browser.

**4** Right-click anywhere on the page.

**5** Click Save As.

**6** Select your website directory.

**7** Click Save.

jQuery is now downloaded and ready for you to load into your website.

As mentioned earlier, if you choose to download the jQuery source code, after that, the next step is to load jquery.js into your website. If you choose to forgo downloading and use a CDN, you still need to load the jQuery source code into your website, but from the CDN's URL.

Regardless of method, the syntax to load jquery-*version*.js into your HTML code's <head> block is the same:

```
<script type='text/javascript'
    src='jquery-version.js'></script>
```

To find a list of CDN-hosted jQuery servers, go to the jQuery Project page at http://docs.jquery.com/Downloading_jQuery#CDN_Hosted_jQuery. The example below uses the code.jquery.com host, which is provided by Media Temple. Other versions available are hosted by Google and Microsoft.

So, how do you decide which method to use? Ultimately, if you have web server–hosting capabilities and the ability to upload files or are developing on your own local web server, download your own local copy. If you a producing a website that is accessible only through an online HTML editor, you will need to use the CDN copy.

Do not use the CDN method for a large-scale production website; it may slow down web page load times unnecessarily, as now you are dependent on the response time of a third party.

Do not forget, you can always switch back and forth if your needs ever change; simply delete the existing <script src='*jquery*.js'></script> code and repeat steps **1** to **4** below, based on your current requirements.

## Load jQuery

### From a Downloaded Copy

**1** Download jQuery.

**2** Open an HTML file in a text editor.

**3** Type **<script type='text/javascript' src='jquery-*version*.js'></script>** into the <head> group.

***Note:*** *For the Production version, use* jQuery-*version*.min.js.

**4** Save your HTML file.

jQuery is ready to use.

***Note:*** *Stop here. There is no need to load jQuery over CDN if you load it locally.*

### From a CDN

**1** Go to http://docs.jquery.com/ Downloading_jQuery#CDN_Hosted_ jQuery.

**2** Right-click the CDN that you want.

**3** Click Copy Link Address.

**4** Open an HTML file in a text editor.

**5** Paste the CDN URL within **<script type='text/javascript' src='*URL*'> </script>** into the <head> group.

**6** Save your HTML file.

# EXECUTE JQUERY METHODS ON ELEMENTS

After jQuery is loaded, you can execute any jQuery methods using the following syntax within a `<script type='text/javascript'>` tag group:

```
<script type='text/javascript'>
  $(selector).method(params);
  ...
</script>
```

The dollar sign is a special function exported by the jQuery library; you use it to specify a CSS-style selector that identifies an HTML object or objects. `.method(params)` indicates what you want to apply to that selector, described by the jQuery API. Multiple methods can be called in a row.

If your jQuery code comes before your selected HTML code, you can instruct jQuery to wait until the page has loaded:

```
<script type='text/javascript'>
  $(document).ready(function(){
    $(selector).method(params);
    ...
  });
</script>
```

If you look closely, the preceding wrapper uses the same jQuery preamble but with a specific selector and method: `document` indicates the root level of the DOM, the entire document; `ready()` is a method that waits for the *load* event on the selector; and `function(){...}` houses what will be executed when the event fires.

## Execute jQuery Methods on Elements

1 Open an HTML file with jQuery loaded.

2 Identify the HTML element that you want to manipulate with jQuery.

3 Go to your `<script type='text/javascript'>` block or a JavaScript file loaded after jQuery.

**Note:** *This* script *element can load a separate JavaScript file where you can place your commands. If you want to do this, add* src='myfile.js' *to the script element and open* myfile.js *in a text editor instead.*

4 Type **$(document).ready(function() {** to begin a jQuery document-is-ready block.

5 Type **});** to end the jQuery `ready()` handler function.

**6** Type **alert( $(*selector*).html() );**

**Note:** *This code simply repeats the literal HTML in an* alert() *pop-up message; this is a good test to verify that jQuery and the selector you chose are working.*

**Note:** *Code within jQuery's anonymous* function() *handlers are event based and run asynchronously from the rest of your JavaScript code.*

**7** Save your HTML and any JavaScript files.

**8** Open your HTML file in a browser.

**A** In this example, if jQuery and your selector are good, a pop-up message appears, repeating the selector's HTML code.

**Note:** *If there is an error, you can use the JavaScript console in your browser to debug it. If you are using Chrome, the Chrome Inspector can do this, as described in Chapter 9, "Inspecting and Debugging Your Website."*

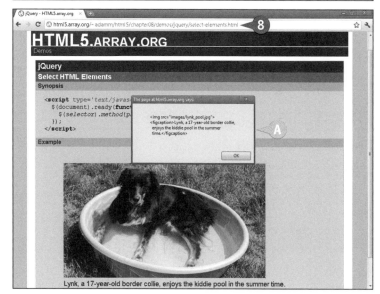

You can shorten the $(document).ready() wrapper to something a little easier to remember:

```
$(function(){
  $(selector).method(params);
  ...
});
```

As you develop jQuery source code, $(function() {...}); is what you will use most often when you want to execute jQuery code after the page has finished loading, but both it and the $(document).ready(function(){ ... }); wrapper are equivalent.

Some jQuery API methods do not require the $(*selector*) prefix, such as utility methods, which will never manipulate HTML elements directly.

```
$(function(){
  alert( "jQuery " + .fn.jquery + " is
  successfully installed" );
});
```

In this example, a pop-up message appears that executes .fn.jquery, which is an internal method that returns jQuery's version number.

# Manipulate HTML Elements via the DOM

You can manipulate and change HTML elements found in the DOM with jQuery. This enables you to dynamically change the original HTML tags and attributes rendered in the web browser after the web page actually loads.

The HTML content within selected elements can be modified using the `html()` method. Or you can inject new HTML content before HTML elements using `before()` and after using `after()`. In all three cases, you can specify the new HTML code as a parameter to the method.

You can also edit the selected HTML elements by adding or changing individual attributes. Use `attr()` to get or set values or `removeAttr()` to remove an attribute.

Finally, you can remove selected HTML elements using `detach()`. This will purge the selected element and all its descendents from your web page.

Note that the plural "selected elements" was used to describe these HTML manipulation methods. Remember, the jQuery selector uses a CSS-style selector syntax and behavior, meaning that the method used on the selector is applied to all possible elements that match. Therefore, if you want to manipulate only one HTML element, make sure that its selector is specific enough, such as by using a CSS `#id` with an HTML `id` attribute.

A complete list of all manipulation methods provided by the jQuery API can be found at the jQuery API Reference page at http://api.jquery.com/category/manipulation/.

## Manipulate HTML Elements via the DOM

**1** Open an HTML file with jQuery loaded.

**2** Identify the HTML element that you want to manipulate with jQuery.

**3** Go to your `<script type='text/javascript'>` block or a JavaScript file loaded after jQuery.

**4** Type **$(function() { } );** if not yet defined.

**Note:** If you already have a handler function block or a `$(document).ready()` block, there is no need to create another one.

**5** Type **$(selector).after(.**

**6** Insert the new HTML code that will replace the code currently found within all elements that match selector.

**7** Type **);** to close off the `html` method.

**8** Type **$(selector).html( newcode );** to change the selected elements' contents.

**Note:** New HTML elements can instantly be used as selectors. In this example, the `<figcaption>` tag group that was added with `after()` is being modified slightly with `html()`.

```
45    });
46    &lt;/script&gt;
47    </code></pre>
48         <h5>Example</h5>
49         <style>
50            article.example {
51              margin: 20px;
52            }
53         </style>
54         <script type='text/javascript'>        3
55         $(function(){                            4
56
57            });
58         </script>
59         <article class='example'>
60           <figure id='lynk-pool' class='picture'>
61             <img src='images/lynk_pool.jpg'>
62             <figcaption>Lynk, a 17-year-old border collie,
63               enjoys the kiddie pool in the summer
64               time.</figcaption>
65           </figure>
66         </article>
67       </article>
68     </section>
69     <footer>
70        &copy;2011 Adam McDaniel
71     </footer>
72     </div>
73     </body>
74   </html>
                                             58,17        Bot
```

```
54       <script type='text/javascript'>
55         $(function(){                                    5
56         $('figure#lynk-pool').after(
57           "<figure id='sad-dogs' class='picture'>" +
58           "<img src='images/sad_dogs.jpg'>" +           6
59           "<figcaption>The dogs are do not like being cooped up inside." +
60           "</figcaption></figure>"
61         );                                               7
62         $('figure#sad-dogs figcaption').html("Fire, Evil-lyn and Aero are " +   8
63           "sick of being cooped up inside when it's raining.");
64         });
65       </script>
```

**9** Type **$(*selector*).attr( *key, value*** **);** to add or modify an attribute in all HTML elements that match *selector*.

**Note:** *Use* removeAttr(*key*) *to remove an attribute from the selected elements.*

**10** Type **$(*selector*).detach();** to remove all HTML elements that match *selector*.

**11** Save your HTML and any JavaScript files.

**12** Open your HTML file in a browser.

New HTML code is injected into the document.

**A** In this example, the contents of an HTML element are modified using html().

**B** The attribute of an HTML element is modified using attr().

An HTML element specified by detach() is purged entirely.

You may think that there is not much benefit to dynamically changing a web page immediately after it is loaded. Why not just simply modify the original HTML source code to the final result directly, rather than modify it with jQuery?

The "trick" shown in the example in this section was performed in jQuery because, as is shown in the next section, "Customize Browser Events with jQuery," there are other jQuery components that can be used to identify when a change like this should happen, and

potentially what the final result will be, based on JavaScript events and logic.

For example, you can use jQuery to make it so that when a user clicks button A, the page performs change B. This makes a lot more sense from a user-interface standpoint than simply performing change B as soon as the page loads.

Therefore, customize browser events in jQuery so that you can manipulate the DOM as the user interacts with your website.

One of jQuery's strengths is its capability to modify browser activity based on *what* event you are interested in, rather than *how* to monitor the event and override it, as in the traditional JavaScript process.

There are three components required when customizing a browser event in jQuery: What is the object, what will the user do to that object, and what process occurs when the user does it.

The first component is easy; that is the standard $(*selector*) you have used earlier. The second component is the event method itself. Here are some of the most common browser events you can customize:

- click(), dblclick() — When the user clicks or double-clicks an object.

- hover() — When the user hovers over an object. Note that this event takes two handler functions, representing when the user hovers in and hovers out.
- focus(), blur() — When the user selects and deselects a form element.
- submit() — When the user submits a form.
- keypress() — When the user presses a key.
- keydown(), keyup() — Divides a keypress event into separate key-down and key-up events.

The third component is the handler function within which an event object needs to be retrieved: function(*event*) { ... }. This helps you identify additional specifics about the event itself.

A full list of jQuery API events, including the low-level bind() method that provides the most flexibility, can be found at http://api.jquery.com/category/events/.

## Customize Browser Events with jQuery

**1** Open an HTML file with jQuery loaded.

**2** Identify the HTML element that you want to manipulate with jQuery.

**3** Go to your <script type='text/javscript'> block or a JavaScript file loaded after jQuery.

**4** Go to a $(function(){ } jQuery block or create one if it does not yet exist.

**5** Type **$(*selector*).*event*(function(event){** to create a selector and *event* listener and begin the handler function.

**Note:** *In this example, a simple* click *event is used. See the jQuery API documentation for all event methods.*

**6** Verify that the selector you chose will identify the correct target elements.

**7** Insert the code that will execute when the event occurs.

**8** Type **});**.

*Note: Built-in browser events will still execute after your event handler function finishes.*

Optionally, type **event. preventDefault();** to inhibit any built-in browser event activities on this event.

*Note: Inhibiting the normal event in this way is very useful on hyperlinks or submit form events. It enables you to cancel the normal click process and perform alternative functionality.*

*Note: In this example, nothing normally happens when the user simply clicks an* img *element, so* event. preventDefault() *has no effect.*

**9** Save your HTML and any JavaScript files.

**10** Open your HTML file in a browser.

**11** Trigger the event on an object identified by the selector.

The registered event handler function runs.

## APPLY IT

The contents of the event object differ based on what is actually clicked. One way to determine what a jQuery event contains when an event occurs is to use the `console.log()` function.

Note that this is not a jQuery function, nor standard JavaScript. It is provided by some JavaScript debuggers such as the Chrome Inspector and Firebug. It allows you to not only log an arbitrary variable or text, but also browse complex structures, such as your event object.

**TYPE THIS**

```
$('.clickme')(function(event){
  console.log(event);
});
```

**RESULT**

Click the paragraph to trigger the event and open the JavaScript console. In Chrome, click 🔧 → Tools → JavaScript Console. Alternatively, in Firefox, you can install Firebug (www.getfirebug.com) and click 🐞 to open the console.

Click ▶ to browse the event object in the JavaScript console window.

# HIDE AND SHOW CONTENT WITH jQUERY

You can add special effects to your web page with jQuery, the simplest being `hide()` and `show()`, both of which will do as advertised, but with an optional *duration* parameter that produces a transition effect to dynamically make the content disappear and reappear in the browser. These effects, along with `animate()`, `fade()`, and `slide()`, launch when the user triggers an event such as a button click, mouse hover, or a keypress.

So, to tie the display of one element to the event of another, you will need to first customize the browser event on the first event selector, as described in the preceding section, and then in the event handler function call the effect method on a target selector, or what you want to manipulate.

For example, you can easily control the display of a `<element id='content'>...</element>` block by creating two span tags and registering a `click` event handler on them:

```
<span id='hide-content'>Hide Content</span>
<span id='show-content'>Show Content</span>
<script type='text/javascript'>
$('span#hide-content').click(function()){
   $('#content').hide(500)
});
$('span#show-content').click(function()){
   $('#content').show(500)
});
</script>
```

A complete list of all transition effects and display methods can be found at http://api.jquery.com/category/effects/.

## Hide and Show Content with jQuery

**1** In your HTML file, type **<span id='*action-content*' class='fake-link'>*Action Text*</span>** to create jQuery "links" that hide and show content.

**Note:** *The* `fake-link` *class makes any nonhyperlink element appear like a clickable link to the user. Use the CSS rule* `.fake-link { text-decoration: underline; cursor: pointer; color: blue }`.

**2** Type **id='*content*'** in a block that will be hidden and displayed.

**3** Go to your `<script type='text/javascript'>` block or a JavaScript file loaded after jQuery.

**4** Type **$('span#hide-*content*').click(function(event)){ $(#*content*).hide( 500 ) });.**

**5** Type **$('span#show-*content*').click(function(event)){ $(#*content*).show( 500 ) });.**

**Note:** *If you have multiple objects you want to hide and show, repeat steps 1 to 5 but replace* content *with a unique identifier.*

**6** Save your HTML or JavaScript files.

**7** Open your HTML file in a browser.

**8** Click the `hide-content` object.

Ⓐ The content block animates as it disappears.

**9** Click the `show-content` object.

Ⓑ The content block reappears.

**Note:** *The* `click()` *event can be tied to any HTML object, such as a paragraph, image, or table. Furthermore, any type of event can be used to trigger the effect, such as* `dblclick()`, `hover()`, *or even a specific keyboard letter.*

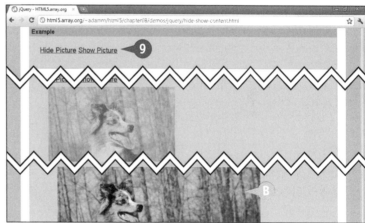

## APPLY IT

If you want to set an element to be hidden when the page first loads, simply set `display: none` to its CSS rule.

The *duration* argument used in this example was 500 milliseconds, or one-half second. It can be a number or literally the text `fast` or `slow`, which indicates 200ms and 600ms, respectively.

`toggle()` can be used to combine `hide()` and `show()` into a single event object and flip between display states.

### TYPE THIS

```
<span id='toggle-content'>Toggle Content</a>
<script type='text/javascript'>
$(function(){
  $('span#toggle-content').click(function(event)){
    $('#content').toggle(500);
  });
});
</script>
```

### RESULT

→ Clicking the fake link once will hide the content block, and again will show it.

# Add and Remove CSS Classes on Elements with jQuery

It is possible for you to dynamically add or remove CSS styles on elements through established class names. This is done by manipulating the `class` attribute on selected elements. Essentially, if you create an HTML tag such as `<element>`, you can dynamically convert it into `<element class='classname'>` and then back to `<element>`, all through jQuery. This process is similar to adding or removing attributes, as described earlier in this chapter, but different as a single class attribute can have multiple values.

There are four jQuery methods that you can use to manipulate an element's class:

```
$(selector).addClass(classname);
$(selector).removeClass(classname);
$(selector).hasClass(classname);
if ($(selector).hasClass(classname)) { ... }
```

`addClass()` simply adds `classname` into all elements that match `selector`, and `removeClass()` removes `classname`. The `hasClass()` method returns a Boolean that is true if `classname` is currently a member of `selector` elements; otherwise, it returns false. The `toggleClass()` method actually combines all three CSS methods into one: It checks if `classname` is present, adds `classname` if missing, and removes it if present.

Note that these methods work only when `classname` is already established as a CSS rule with an *element-less* class selector; a selector with no element name preceding the period:

```
<style type='text/css'>
  .classname { property: value; }
</style>
```

## Add and Remove CSS Classes on Elements with jQuery

1. Open an HTML file with jQuery loaded or a JavaScript file loaded after jQuery.

2. Use `.classname` as the parent selector to define the CSS class styles.

3. Go to a `$(function(){ }` jQuery block or create one if it does not yet exist.

4. Listen for browser events you can use to add and remove the CSS manipulation code.

5. Type `$(selector).addClass( classname );`.

6. Type `$(selector).removeClass( classname );`.

7. Create a function that runs when the page loads and when a class is modified.

8. Type `if ( $(selector).hasClass ( classname ) ) {`.

9. Insert code that runs when the class is present.

10. Type `}`.

Ⓐ Optionally, type `else { ... }` and insert code that runs when the class is absent.

11. Save your HTML or JavaScript files.

**12** Load your HTML file in a web browser.

**13** Trigger the event that will call the `addClass()` method.

The CSS class is applied.

**B** The `hasClass()` code modifies the display content.

**14** Trigger the event that will call the `removeClass()` method.

The CSS class is removed.

**C** The `hasClass()` code modifies the display content.

## EXTRA

If you are more interested in controlling the CSS declarations on an element directly, use the method `css()` to get or set individual properties and their values. This manipulates the `style` attribute in any HTML element that matches your `$(selector)`:

```
$(selector).css(property); // Get value
$(selector).css(property, value); // Set value
$(selector).css(property, ""); // Remove value
```

This first line returns the current value of the `property` applied to the first element that matches `selector`. Naturally, this getter can only read the first element

because properties are element specific; so make sure that your selector is specific enough!

The second line sets the CSS `property` to `value` on all elements that match `selector`. Unlike the getter, this setter will work on all elements that match `selector`.

The third line removes `property` from all selected elements, via an empty `value`. Note that this will work only if the element actually has the property assigned to its `style` attribute. If an element received a property through a CSS class or ID, this method cannot remove it, but you can still override it with the setter.

**Y**ou may have a requirement that an element link needs to send additional data to JavaScript, beyond the typical `id` and `class` attribute selectors and standard element attributes. Such is the case if you have multiple objects, each registered to the same browser click event handler function, but additional "parameters" need to be passed into that handler function.

This can be done by specifying arbitrary `data-*` attributes in your HTML elements, which are user-defined attributes exempt from HTML5 validation checking. In the jQuery handler function that receives the event, you can retrieve the attribute's value with `$(this).attr('data-*')`.

Imagine a series of buttons that all run the same JavaScript function `run_program()`, but each button runs the

function with a different parameter. You can create the series of buttons with the same class and then set the `data-var` attribute to the unique value for each button:

```
<button class='run-program' data-
    var='0'>Off</button>
<button class='run-program' data-var='1'>On:
    1</button>
<button class='run-program' data-var='2'>On:
    2</button>
<button class='run-program' data-var='3'>On:
    3</button>
```

jQuery can register a `click` event on the `button.run-program` selector, allowing you to monitor all four buttons at once. When the user clicks one, retrieve the custom attribute value within the function handler with `$(this).attr('data-var')`.

## Send Custom HTML Attribute Data into jQuery

**1** Open an HTML file with jQuery loaded.

**2** Type **<button class='run-program' data-var='value'>Button Text</button>**.

**Note:** *Any element can be used with* `data-*`, *such as an* <a> *or* <img> *tag. In this example,* <button> *is most appropriate as it signifies that something will happen on-screen.*

**3** Repeat step **2**, using a different value for the `data-var` attribute, for each element.

**4** Go to your `<script type='text/javascript'>` block or a JavaScript file loaded after jQuery.

**5** Scroll to a JavaScript `$(function() {...});` group or create one if it does not yet exist.

**6** Type **$('button.run-program').click(function(){** to register for a `click` event on all the elements.

**7** Type **var data = $(this).attr('data-var');** to retrieve the custom data attribute value.

**8** Type **});**.

**9** Use the *data* variable wherever it is required by your function code.

**10** Save your HTML and any JavaScript files.

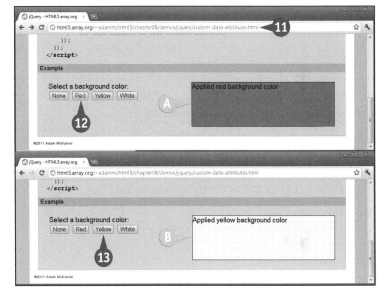

**11** Load your HTML file in a web browser.

**12** Click a button.

**Note:** *In this example, the* click *method and event is used because it is the primary event fired by the* button *element.*

**A** The event handler and function run with that button's custom attribute value.

**13** Click another button.

**B** The same event handler and function run again, but this time with a different attribute value.

This example demonstrates that custom data can be stored in HTML and flow into JavaScript.

Another good use case for this feature is the pop-up window function, window.open(). This example sets the pop-up window's URL, width, and height in HTML and executes it in JavaScript:

```
<a class='popup' data-url='popup.html' data-width='400' data-height='200'>Open Popup Window</a>
<script>
$('a#popup').click(function(event){
  window.open($(this).attr('data-url'), 'popup', 'width='+$(this).attr('data-width') + ',height=' +
  $(this).attr('data-height'));
  event.preventDefault();
});
</script>
```

# USING SCROLLING TRANSITIONS WITH jQUERY

If your website uses any `<a href='#topic'> Go To Topic</a>` hash links tied to `<h1 id= 'topic'>Topic Content</h1>` markers on the same page, you can use jQuery and a plug-in called *ScrollTo* to provide a smooth-scrolling animation process.

Before you begin, your first option is to link directly to the jQuery ScrollTo plug-in from your web page, as described earlier in the chapter with the CDN method of jQuery itself, using http://flesler-plugins.googlecode.com/files/jquery.scrollTo-1.4.2.js.

Your second option is to download the plug-in file, place it on your web server, and load it directly:

```
<script src='jquery.scrollTo-1.4.2.js'></script>
```

After the file is imported, you can call the ScrollTo plug-in anywhere within jQuery, typically from within an overridden click event function handler, using the following code:

```
$(selector).scrollTo(target, duration, settings);
```

You can omit the `(selector)` component and just use `$.scrollTo()` to scroll the entire web page. *target* is the DOM object you want to scroll to, *duration* is the time the animation will take get there, and *settings* is an optional option map of configuration options.

Additional information about the jQuery ScrollTo plug-in, including the complete list of settings, can be found at http://flesler.blogspot.com/2007/10/jqueryscrollto.html.

## Using Scrolling Transitions with jQuery

1. Download the jQuery ScrollTo plug-in from http://flesler-plugins.googlecode.com/files/jquery.scrollTo-1.4.2-min.js.

**Note:** *This URL downloads the minimized version of the plug-in. If you want to study how the plug-in works, remove "-min" from the address.*

**Note:** *Your alternative is to link directly to the plug-in, as mentioned earlier.*

2. Open an HTML file with jQuery loaded.

3. Type `<script type='text/javascript' src='plugin.js'></script>` to load the plug-in in the `<head>` block, after jQuery itself is loaded.

4. Type `<nav id='top'></nav>` to create a navigation layout.

5. Type `<a href='#topic1>First Topic</a>` to create a topic hash link.

6. Type `id='topic1'` where you want the first topic link to scroll to.

7. Type `<nav><a href='#top'>Back to Top</a></nav>` to create a navigation hash link.

8. Repeat steps **5** to **7** for all other topic hash links.

9 Go to your `<script type='text/javscript'>` block or a JavaScript file loaded after jQuery.

10 Scroll to a JavaScript `$(function(){...});` group or create one if it does not yet exist.

11 Type **$('a[href^=#]'). click(function(){ });** to register for a `click` event on the hash links.

12 Type **event.preventDefault();**.

13 Type **$.scrollTo( this.hash,** *duration* **);** to activate the ScrollTo plug-in.

14 Save your HTML or JavaScript file.

15 Load your HTML file in a web browser.

16 Click one of the navigational links.

The page visibly scrolls down as it moves to the selected topic.

17 Click the link that returns you to the navigation links.

The page visibly scrolls back up as it moves to the navigation.

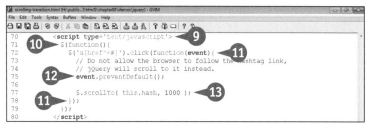

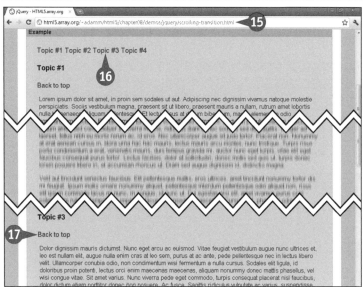

## APPLY IT

It is possible to customize the animation's speed at different points of the routine. This is done by specifying an `easing` option into `$.scrollTo()` and importing a second plug-in, called *jQuery Easing*.

Note that if you do not use the Easing plug-in, you can still use the `easing` option here, but the only types available are `linear` and the default, `swing`.

### TYPE THIS

Download and load jQuery Easing from http://gsgd.co.uk/sandbox/jquery/easing/jquery.easing.1.3.js into your website and then specify the easing option in the `$.scrollTo` function:

```
$.scrollTo(this.hash, 1000, {
  easing: 'easeInOutQuad'
});
```

### RESULT

The animation moves more smoothly, starting out slowly, gaining speed, and then ending slowly as it approaches its target link.

Additional information about the jQuery Easing plug-in, as well as a complete list of easing types available, can be found at http://gsgd.co.uk/sandbox/jquery/easing/.

Google Chrome has a built-in development tool called the *Chrome Inspector*. You can use it to examine the HTML elements in a web page; review what resources — or files, cookies, and databases — are active; follow network activity; break and step through JavaScript code; understand a timeline of events; profile the CPU usage; and audit overall web page performance.

This chapter focuses on the Chrome Inspector's most common tasks — reviewing and changing HTML and CSS code and debugging JavaScript code.

The complete features list and documentation for the Chrome Inspector can be found online at Google Chrome Development Tools, http://code.google.com/chrome/devtools/docs/overview.html.

If you are not using Google Chrome, there are equivalents available for other major web browsers:

- Firebug is a free and open-sourced HTML and JavaScript debugger for Firefox — and one of the more advanced and mature third-party applications in its class. For other browsers, Firebug Lite is also available. You can download either version at Firebug's website, http://getfirebug.com.

- Safari has the Web Inspector, an identical clone of the Chrome Inspector. In fact, both inspectors are provided by WebKit; therefore, everything in this chapter also applies to Safari. To use the Web Inspector, you must first enable the Develop menu: Open Safari Preferences, click the Advanced tab, and enable Show Develop Menu in Menu Bar.

- Internet Explorer 9 features the Developer Toolbar, which is very similar to the Chrome Inspector but lacks some features. However, it can validate your website on Internet Explorer 7 and 8, without needing either version installed. Access it by pressing F12.

- Opera's Dragonfly shares much of the same layout, shortcuts, and user interface as the Chrome Inspector. It looks cleaner and has a few extra features.

## Launch the Chrome Inspector

1. Open the Google Chrome web browser.

2. Click the wrench menu button.

3. Click Tools.

4. Click Developer Tools.

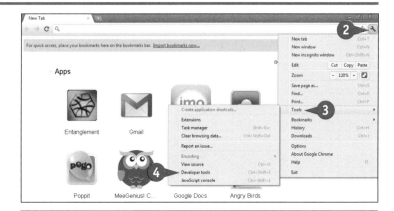

The Chrome Inspector opens at the bottom of the browser.

Ⓐ Various components of the inspector appear as buttons.

5. Click the Undock Inspector button.

The Chrome Inspector becomes a separate window.

**6** Click the Dock Inspector button.

The Chrome Inspector returns to the browser window.

**7** Click the Close Inspector button.

The Chrome Inspector closes. The browser window returns to normal.

## EXTRA

There are several hotkeys and shortcuts that you can use to launch the Chrome Inspector and other tools useful in developing web pages.

| Keyboard Shortcut | Description |
|---|---|
| Shift+Ctrl+I | Launches the inspector. |
| Shift+Ctrl+J | Launches the inspector's JavaScript Console panel. |
| Shift+Ctrl+C | Examines an element in the inspector. (See the following section for more information.) |
| Ctrl+U | Views the web page source code (separate from the inspector). |

After the inspector is launched, there are several other keyboard shortcuts that you can use in the program.

| Keyboard Shortcut | Description |
|---|---|
| ? | Brings up Help. |
| Ctrl+] | Moves to the next panel. |
| Ctrl+[ | Moves to the previous panel. |
| Esc | Toggles the JavaScript console. |
| Ctrl+F | Focuses on the search box. |
| Ctrl+G | Finds the next search. |
| Shift+Ctrl+G | Finds the previous search. |

If you are using Chrome on the Mac, replace Shift with Option and Ctrl with ⌘.

# EXAMINE ELEMENTS' STRUCTURE AND LAYOUT

The Chrome Inspector enables you to examine a web page's elements' structure with its Elements panel. This panel can be launched multiple ways: You can right-click a rendered HTML element, you can open up the inspector with the Chrome menu, or press one of the keyboard shortcuts described in the preceding section, "Launch the Chrome Inspector."

When examining an element, it is possible to highlight the rendered HTML block and the source code tree at the same time by using the Examine Element keyboard shortcut or the 🔍 button in the inspector itself. This is a very useful way to follow how a web page is built, all the way from the highest-level <html> root down to the deepest table cell, paragraph, or image.

CSS elements appear along the right side of the Elements panel. The order CSS declarations appear in this panel indicates where the CSS was applied, by filename. It even shows you where any earlier CSS declarations got overridden by later ones. Selecting the Computed Style option enables you to see a complete list of what was declared, and the Show Inherited check box expands the completed list to see what Chrome itself is implicitly assigning.

The following section, "Modify HTML and CSS Code in Real Time," shows you how to use this Examine Elements feature to actually modify the source code in real time and apply changes to the rendered HTML without needing to reload the web page.

## Examine Elements' Structure and Layout

① Open the web page in Google Chrome.

② Right-click the first HTML element that you want to examine.

③ Click Inspect Element.

**Note:** You can also press Ctrl+Alt+C (or Shift+⌘+C on Mac OS X) to launch the Inspect Element mode.

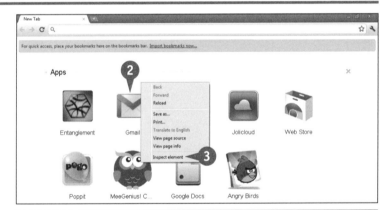

The Chrome Inspector appears with the Elements panel selected.

Ⓐ The object is highlighted in the browser, with its tag name and dimensions.

Ⓑ The HTML element code is highlighted in the inspector.

Ⓒ Optionally, click ▶ to expand any collapsed HTML source code.

Ⓓ The element's applied CSS code is displayed.

④ Hover your mouse cursor across the different HTML nodes.

🅔 The hovered element's rendered HTML block is highlighted above.

🅕 Optionally, click the hierarchal list of elements to browse to a parent DOM node.

⑤ Click the magnifying glass button to select an element on the page to inspect.

⑥ Click a highlighted HTML block.

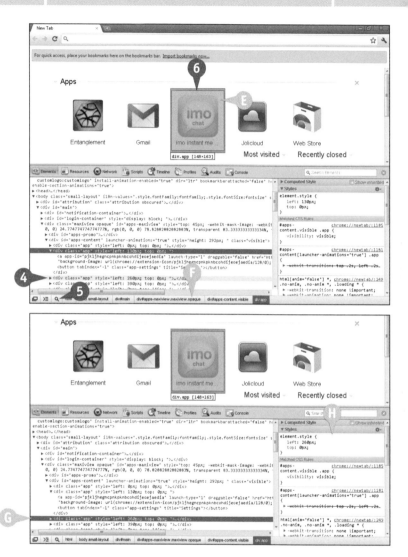

🅖 The inspector's Elements panel moves and highlights that specific element's HTML node.

🅗 That element's applied CSS declarations appear on the right.

---

**EXTRA**

The Elements panel enables you to browse the entire HTML tree as a visual representation of the document object model (DOM). Anything used to construct this page in the HTML source code is visible, even inline JavaScript and CSS. You can examine the CSS more closely on the right side of this panel, and the JavaScript in the Scripts panel, which is described later in this chapter in the section "Examine JavaScript Code."

The Elements panel has its own set of keyboard and mouse shortcuts.

| Shortcut | Description |
|---|---|
| Up/Down | Navigates. |
| Right/Left | Expands/collapses a node. |
| Double-click a tag | Expands a node. |
| Return or double-click an attribute | Edits an attribute. |

One of the strengths of the Chrome Inspector is its capability to modify HTML and CSS code in real time, without the requirement of reloading the web page or even modifying the original HTML files directly. This gives you the opportunity to experience and develop HTML and CSS in a whole new way, using a cause-and-effect relationship. For example, if an element is not appearing in the right place in the browser window, adjust its `left`, `top`, and `position` property values in the inspector and watch it move accordingly.

The one thing that the Chrome Inspector cannot do is save your changes to the original HTML file. This feature is designed to do simple one-off changes and to examine how the rendering changes. You still need your HTML text editor

to save any of your inspector-guided changes, and you need to upload them to your web server.

The actual modification is done by simply double-clicking an HTML element node in the inspector and typing in a new value. CSS properties and values can be modified in a similar way, and you can temporarily disable any CSS declaration simply by unchecking it; this helps you to better understand any CSS inheritance problems or override any unwanted CSS behavior introduced by the web browser itself.

Naturally, modifying source code and seeing it in real time is great if Chrome is your users' only web browser, but it is likely not. Do not forget to save your changes and test them in other HTML5 web browsers, too; you may not have the same inspectorlike tools available, but at least you can get most of your HTML development debugged here in Chrome!

## Modify HTML and CSS Code in Real Time

**1** Inspect the HTML element that you want to modify in the Chrome Inspector.

**Note:** *See the preceding section for more information.*

**2** Right-click the element's tag name in the Elements panel.

**3** Click Edit As HTML.

The tag name becomes editable in the Inspector.

**4** Modify the tag name or attribute and click outside of the edit box.

**Ⓐ** The HTML change is reflected in the main web browser window.

**Note:** *If you are simply editing existing tags or text blocks, you can double-click what you want to modify, make your change, and press Enter to apply it in the window.*

**5** Double-click a CSS rule in the CSS pane to modify it.

**Note:** *Modifying a rule within the* `element.style { }` *CSS pane is like editing the HTML element's* `style` *attribute directly.*

The CSS property or value becomes editable in the inspector.

⑥ Type in a property name.

⑦ Press Tab to edit the property value.

⑧ Type in a new property name or value and press Enter.

**Note:** *Pressing tab again will allow you to edit the next CSS property down, and so on.*

Ⓑ The CSS change is reflected in the main web browser window.

⑨ Hover over a CSS rule.

Ⓒ A check box will appear.

**Note:** *If there are multiple CSS declarations in this rule, multiple check boxes will appear.*

⑩ Uncheck a check box to temporarily disable a CSS rule.

That particular declaration is disabled, and the original CSS re-renders based on what is still available.

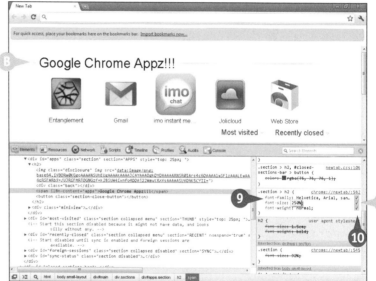

## APPLY IT

You can add a CSS class into an HTML element and see the effect right away in the Chrome Inspector.

### TYPE THIS

1. Inspect an HTML element that you want to modify.
2. If the element does not yet have a `class` attribute, type it in along with a value. If it already has a class, double-click its `class` attribute value to edit it.

```
<div class="back"></div>
<span class="link" i18n-content=
<button class="section-close-but-
</h2>
```

3. Insert the new class name. If you want to keep the existing class intact, leave a space between names.

### RESULT

The Chrome Inspector applies the new CSS class to the HTML element in real time.

Google Chrome Appz!!!

You can use the same trick, modifying CSS in your HTML code in real time, on the `style` attribute as well.

Y ou can use the Chrome Inspector to examine the JavaScript code of any website. You can do so by using the Scripts panel found in the inspector window. When you examine your JavaScript code, it is also possible to review any errors and warnings produced by executing the JavaScript code and then reference back to the code where the error occurred. This is done by using the JavaScript Console panel, a subcomponent of the Chrome Inspector.

This console will also allow you to execute arbitrary JavaScript code, and use it to interact with the DOM components and the elements in your website.

Some websites use JavaScript optimizers and minimizers to make code download and execution more efficient for the web browser. This is done by removing comments, unnecessary whitespace, and line feeds and by reducing

variables and local function names to the absolute minimum number of characters required to maintain uniqueness. Unfortunately, this makes it extremely difficult for a human to read the source code, as the code now reads like JavaScript gibberish.

To counter this problem, the Chrome Inspector has a code *Pretty-Print* feature that enables you to reorganize optimized and minimized JavaScript into human-readable code. It adds a line feed after each statement, adds appropriate spacing within statements, and even applies proper indenting based on nesting brackets. However, it cannot restore the original comments or variable and function names. So you will be forced to use your imagination a little, but now you can step through the source code as it is executed, a process which is described later in this chapter in the section "Step through JavaScript Code."

## Examine JavaScript Code

**1** With the website open, launch the Chrome Inspector.

**2** Click Scripts.

**3** Click the filename pull-down.

A list of all active JavaScript files is presented.

**Ⓐ** Optionally, select a different JavaScript file to see its source code.

**Note:** *All active Chrome extensions will also appear in this list. If you have too many extensions installed and cannot find the right JavaScript file, they will be disabled when you load a new Chrome window in Incognito mode (Shift+Ctrl+N). Restart at step **1** with the new Incognito browser.*

**Note:** *JavaScript code that has been minimized will appear in very few lines, very compressed, and hard to read.*

**Ⓑ** Optionally, click the Pretty Print button if the code is unreadable.

**Note:** *The Pretty-Print Code feature is available only in Chrome 13 and later.*

The JavaScript code is now readable.

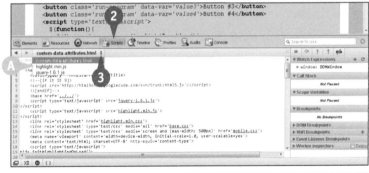

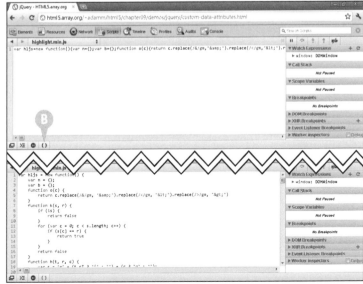

④ Click Console to see if there were any errors executing the code.

The JavaScript Console panel appears.

⊙ JavaScript error, warning, and log messages appear.

⑤ Click the filename associated with a warning or error message.

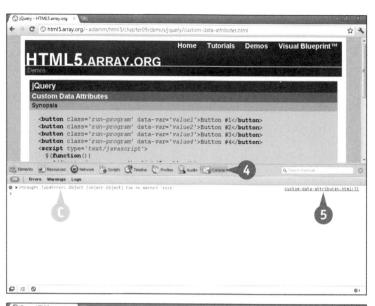

⊙ The Resources panel opens, displaying the offending line of code and a detailed warning or error message.

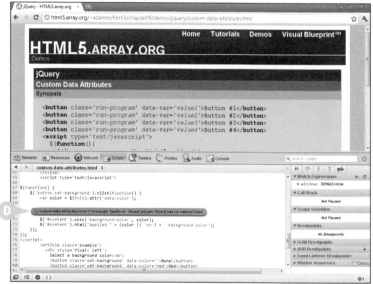

The Chrome Inspector's Resources panel describes everything that was downloaded on a website, whereas the Elements and Scripts panels describe everything that was used for rendering the web page. To fix a warning or error message in JavaScript, you will have to edit and reexecute the source code anyway — which cannot happen in either the Resources or Scripts panels — and reload the web page. Therefore, edit your original JavaScript code, fix the error, and reload; the

inspector's JavaScript Console panel will tell you if the problem is fixed.

The true strength of the Scripts panel is its capability to set up JavaScript breakpoints, add watch expressions, examine variables, and review the call stack. Or in other words, it is used to examine and control the real-time execution of your JavaScript code. The remainder of this chapter focuses on these tasks.

# Add a JavaScript Breakpoint

As you examine a JavaScript source code file, you may be able to gain only limited insight into its purpose and process by reading the code; you may need to be able to execute it and watch the process unfold. The best way to do this is to set up a JavaScript breakpoint in the Chrome Inspector.

If you have used a debugger in any native application environment before, the process is essentially the same, except much simpler. The JavaScript debugger is built right into the interpreter and browser, and there is no compiler involved; therefore, you can quickly execute, intervene, monitor, and manipulate JavaScript code in your program.

The first step is to configure a line of the JavaScript code as a breakpoint. This line, when the browser reaches it

while executing your code, will pause your program and grant you control over what the interpreter knows about all variables, functions, and the call stack. From here, you can abort execution or step through it line by line, function by function. With the code paused, you can even review and change the values of variables and arbitrarily execute new functions, thus applying the manipulated results into your existing code once execution is resumed.

This is a vital technique if you have a bug in your JavaScript code. Even if you do not know where the bug is or what is causing it, breakpoints allow you to intervene in the execution, examine the situation, and choose to continue execution to the next breakpoint, continue unhindered, or stop execution entirely.

## Add a JavaScript Breakpoint

① View your JavaScript code in the Scripts panel.

② Click the line number of a JavaScript code line to set a breakpoint there.

Ⓐ Optionally, click the Reload button to reload the web page and restart execution.

**Note:** *Reloading is only required if the code executes only on page load. If your breakpoint is in an area of event-driven code, you can simply interact with the web page normally.*

Ⓑ The breakpoint pauses code execution.

**Note:** *All interaction with the main web browser window is suspended.*

Ⓒ The Call Stack pane shows which functions are currently active.

Ⓓ The Scope Variables pane displays the active local and global variables and current values.

③ Click ▶ to expand JavaScript objects and see their structure.

Ⓔ Optionally, double-click a variable to edit its value; press Enter to save it.

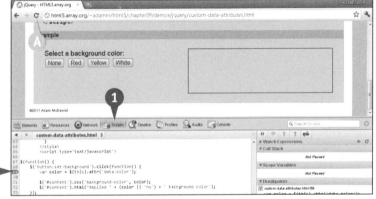

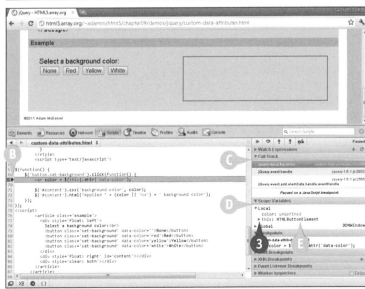

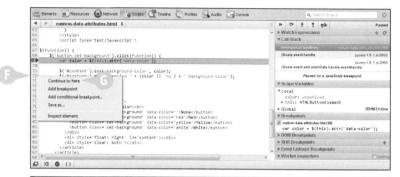

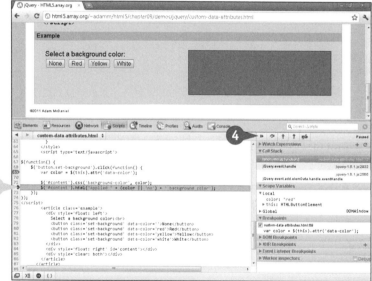

Ⓕ Optionally, right-click a line number later in the code order.

Ⓖ Optionally, click Continue to Here to create a one-time-use breakpoint.

Ⓗ With the optional steps, code execution continues up until the temporary breakpoint.

④ Click the Continue button (or press F8) to continue the code-execution process.

The code execution continues to the next breakpoint, or if none is found, browser control is restored.

If you have a large number of breakpoints, you can disable and reenable them all by clicking ⟦⟧. You can remove a breakpoint entirely simply by clicking its line number or by right-clicking it in the Breakpoint pane and selecting Remove Breakpoint. As of Chrome 13, the only way to remove all breakpoints is to close the browser tab.

Additional breakpoint types are also available:

- Conditional breakpoints — Set a conditional expression on a line that must return true to pause code execution. This is useful when dealing with `for()` and `while()` loops or repeating functions. Right-click a line number and select Add Conditional Breakpoint.

- DOM breakpoints — Set a breakpoint on an HTML element whenever its DOM is mutated by JavaScript code. Simply inspect an HTML element in the Elements panel, right-click, and select Break on Subtree Modifications, Break on Attribute Modifications, or Break on Node Removal to set a DOM breakpoint.

- Event listener breakpoints — Set a breakpoint whenever an event is triggered, such as an activity triggered by a keyboard, mouse, or other browser interaction on the website.

After the code execution is suspended by a breakpoint, you can step through subsequent lines of code in the inspector and watch the results unfold in the browser as each line is executed. There are three different levels of "stepping" that you can use in the Chrome Inspector, each of which dictates where the debugger's attention moves to with respect to the new functions it encounters:

- (Step Over) — This instructs the debugger to proceed until the next line of code, but if it encounters a new function, to "step over" it by executing it all in one step. The end result is the execution is paused at the next line of code in the current block, or when the current function ends, at the next line of the parent function block.

- (Step Into) — This instructs the debugger to proceed until the next line of code, but if it encounters a new function, to "step into" it and open its source code in the Scripts panel, increasing the call stack. When the function block ends, control is passed to its parent function block.

- (Step Out) — This instructs the debugger to finish executing the current function and to pause when control is passed to its parent function in the call stack.

Although the three step methods will eventually lead to the end of the program, Step Into will take the longest possible path of pauses, and Step Out will take the shortest path, relative to where you set your breakpoint.

## Step through JavaScript Code

1. Establish a JavaScript breakpoint and suspend code execution.

2. Click the Step Over button (or press F10) to step over to the next line of code in this block.

A. Only the next line of code is executed.

**Note:** *The Call Stack and Scope Variables panes on the right may change, based on the code that was just executed.*

3. Click the Step Into button (or press F11) to step into the next line of code to be executed.

B. The debugger moves to the "next line of code" as indicated by the step-into command.

**Note:** *In this example, the debugger jumped into a jQuery method. Now the jQuery code can be followed.*

C. Optionally, continue clicking the Step Into button (or pressing F11) to follow deeper into the JavaScript code.

4. Click the Step Out button (or press Shift+F11) to step out of the current function and into its calling block.

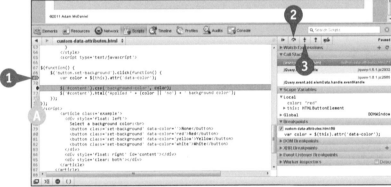

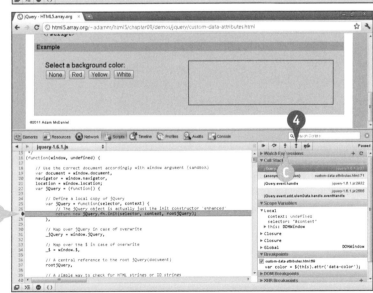

The debugger moves to the calling function from step **3**; now the results of the statement can be applied to your local and global variables.

**Note:** *If there are no other items in the call stack, execution finishes and control is passed to the browser window.*

⑤ Click a function in the Call Stack pane.

ⓔ The source code changes to see where the execution point is from the perspective of that function.

⑥ Click the Continue button (or press F8) to continue the code execution process.

The code execution continues to the next breakpoint, or if none is found, browser control is restored.

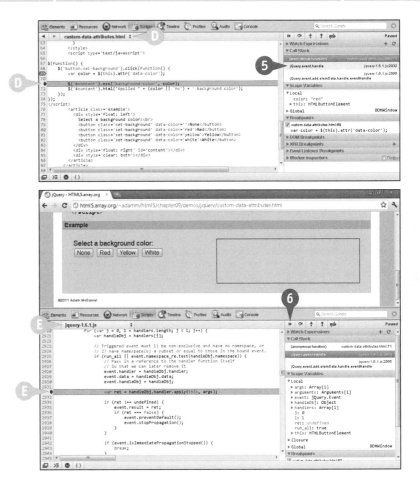

Deciding which step command to use depends on where the code is that you are interested in. Pay attention to the Call Stack and Scope Variables panes so that you can get your bearings in an unfamiliar program.

Think of the stepping process like this:

- Step Over — Repeatedly clicking ⌐ will execute code in the current block or, if exhausted, move to its parent function block and execute code there.

- Step Into — Repeatedly clicking ⌐ will execute code in the current block and follow all subfunctions until exhausted, then move to the parent, and so on.

- Step Out — Repeatedly clicking ⌐ will complete the current function and return to its parent.

In other words, Step Into is useful if you want to explore new functions, and Step Out is useful if you have traversed too deep into your code and want to instantly move up the stack.

Remember, if you proceed past the code line you are interested in or cannot locate it, you can always reload the browser and restart the debugger or create a new breakpoint at a more appropriate location.

# ADD A WATCH EXPRESSION

**W**ith a watch expression, you can create a JavaScript-like statement inside the Chrome Inspector itself and actually watch it change as you step through the code. This can be extremely useful if a function is being executed with the wrong input variable, when the variable itself changes as each line of code is executed, and you want to monitor the function and how the input variable is calculated. Effectively, a watch expression is exactly like reexecuting the same line of code every time the main execution process pauses and examining the results.

This may seem like a convoluted use case right now, but as you explore and begin to debug jQuery, watch expressions

will become a valuable tool. This is especially true if you are dealing with interactive content, and you want to examine the cause-and-effect relationship between using your website and JavaScript's perspective of your actions.

The simplest-possible watch expression could be just a standard variable name; this is just like monitoring the Scope Variables list, but this list can get rather large. Watching a variable you are interested in means that it will always be at the top of the Watch Expressions pane, making it easier to find and monitor.

## Add a Watch Expression

**1** Establish a JavaScript breakpoint and suspend code execution.

**2** Click ▶ to expand the Watch Expressions pane, if it is collapsed.

**3** Click the Add button to add a new watch expression.

**4** Type a JavaScript variable, function, or statement and press Enter.

**A** The watch expressions execute at this stage of the paused program.

**5** Repeat steps **3** and **4** for any other watch points.

**6** If the expression returns an object, click ▶ to view its contents.

**7** Click the Step Over button to step through your program.

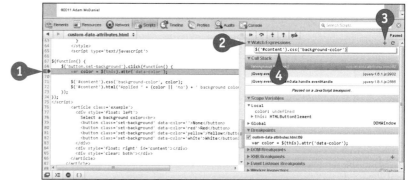

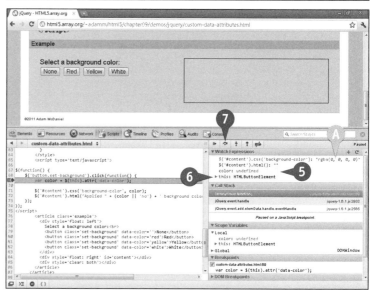

**B** The watch expressions are reevaluated, updating their output each time the main program pauses.

**8** Click the Continue button to let your program finish.

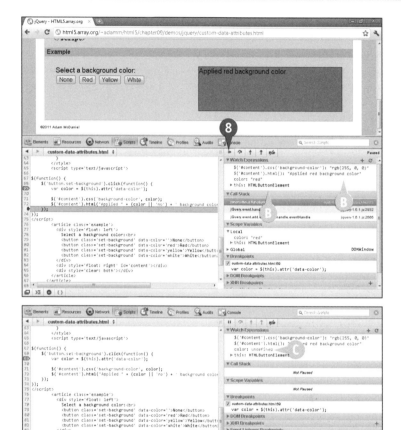

**C** Some watch expressions become undefined.

*Note: A watch can become undefined if was established as a local variable at the breakpoint but is no longer in scope. If you restart your program and break again, its new value will be restored to this pane.*

If you are interested only in a simple variable or want to examine an object or a function's contents, the Chrome Inspector has a very useful trick to view almost any data type at a glance.

Simply hover your cursor over an evaluated function, variable, or object in the Scripts pane. A pop-up will appear that shows you exactly what the variable or object holds or, in the case of a function, its source code, without your having to create a watch expression or step into the code itself.

The HTML5 canvas grants you a very fine level of control over the individual pixels on your web page. The canvas can be used to create just about anything using JavaScript: custom UI elements, image manipulation, animations, and custom keyboard and mouse interfaces. In addition to the other new HTML5 features and the JavaScript DOM (document object model), the canvas integrates seamlessly with video files, audio clips, and touchscreen events, alongside venerable keyboard and mouse activity. Essentially, you now have access to nearly all the tools that developers in Flash or traditional system and game platforms have been using for years.

It is no secret that the canvas was borne out of the frustrations with the Adobe Flash plug-in. Although Flash served its purpose well enough — introduced many years ago because web developers were pushing the boundaries of HTML and JavaScript too far — opponents argue that it had security problems, was CPU intensive, was inefficient, and lacked proper touchscreen support. This restricted its deployment and adoption, especially on mobile devices such as phones and tablets.

As the Canvas API is still relatively new and under active development, its overall performance varies between browsers and implementations. It does not yet exceed the performance of Flash under certain tests according to independent third parties; however, its potential as a Flash-killer is certainly looming.

## Browser Support

The canvas is available in all the latest builds of the popular web browsers. That being said, the overall implementation level and performance capabilities do differ. Generally speaking, Chrome and Firefox provide some of the best overall level of JavaScript engine speed and animation capabilities, followed by Opera and Safari. Internet Explorer 9 is the first release from Microsoft that supports the Canvas API, and its overall capabilities are very good.

Currently, the only market share of users that may not have canvas support are Internet Explorer 6 to 8 legacy users. There are two *polyfills,* or programs that provide newer compatibility to older browsers, available for these legacy users:

- ExplorerCanvas (http://excanvas.sourceforge.net) is a JavaScript program that uses Microsoft's *vector markup language* (VML) to emulate the Canvas API. Note that VML has not been updated since 1998, so it lacks some of the features the Canvas API supports, such as drawing text, but you should at least be able to display basic canvas shapes and animations. Note that this chapter uses jQuery's `$(function(){...});` to wrap the Canvas API, which appears incompatible with ExplorerCanvas. Instead, use `<body onload='init()'>` and create an `init()` function that calls the Canvas API. See the ExplorerCanvas examples directory for more information.

- Google Chrome Frame (www.google.com/chromeframe) was introduced in Chapter 1, "Introducing HTML5." This program actually exports the entire Chrome-rendering engine as an Internet Explorer plug-in. It provides the best level of canvas support for legacy users, but it does require a program to be locally installed on the user's computer.

## The Canvas API

The Canvas API is currently under development by WHATWG. Its latest specification document can be found at the WHATWG page at www.whatwg.org/specs/web-apps/current-work/multipage/the-canvas-element.html.

### The canvas Element

A canvas can be created using the `canvas` element, new for HTML5, at any point within the `<body>` tag group on your web page:

```
<canvas id='identifier' height='500'
  width='500'>Fallback Content</canvas>
```

The `id` attribute enables you to easily locate this particular `canvas` element in JavaScript. Its value can be anything you want, as long as it is unique among all elements.

It is important to note that these `height` and `width` attributes are not the same as the CSS `height` and `width` properties. These attributes set the total number of pixels in the canvas, whereas the CSS properties set the total display area that the canvas allocates and scales the pixels accordingly. You should never need to set the CSS `height` and `width` properties on a `canvas` element.

If you ever need to read or change these `height` and `width` attribute values, use the `canvas.height` and `canvas.width`, or `context.canvas.height` and `context.canvas.width`, JavaScript variables.

## JavaScript Initialization

Your canvas must be initialized in JavaScript in order to draw on it. This involves locating the `canvas` element in the DOM and then retrieving the drawing context object using `canvas.getContext()`. This object provides the core of the actual canvas API methods and attributes:

```
<script type='text/javascript'>
  var canvas = document.getElementById(identifier);
  if (canvas.getContext) {
    var context = canvas.getContext(type);
    // Use context object to draw on the canvas
  }
</script>
```

Alternatively, if you are using jQuery, you can replace `document.getElementById(identifier)` with `$('canvas#identifier')[0]`.

The conditional test on `canvas.getContext` verifies that the browser actually supports the canvas element. If it does not, the `canvas.getContext` test will return false, and the contents within the `<canvas>...</canvas>` tag group will be displayed as a fallback.

All the methods and attributes described below use either the `canvas` or `context` objects.

### Methods

- `context = canvas.getContext(type)` — Loads a canvas context API from the `canvas` object.
- `url = canvas.toDataURL(mimetype)` — Allows you to export a drawn canvas as an image URL. The `mimetype` argument can be `image/png`, `image/jpg`, or `image/gif`; however, the PNG format is the most widely supported.
- `canvas.toBlob(callback, mimetype)` — Allows you to export the drawn canvas image as a *blob* object, itself being arbitrary data that can be passed through one of the FileSystem APIs. These APIs are not discussed at length in this book but are summarized in Chapter 13, "Storing Data Using a Client-Side Database." Note that this newer method is not yet supported by any HTML5 web browsers, as of Firefox 5 and Chrome 13.

### Attributes

- `canvas.width` — Gets or sets the canvas width in display pixels.
- `canvas.height` — Gets or sets the canvas height in display pixels.

## The 2D Context API

When you run `canvas.getContext(type)`, there is only one API currently available: `2d`. This will enable you to access the `canvas` element's pixels as a two-dimensional drawing plane.

### Drawing on the Canvas

There are two main drawing processes available in the Canvas API: stroke and fill. A *stroke* involves drawing a line or a border with a specific thickness and color along a path, shape, or text.

A *fill* involves flooding the area within a closed shape or text with a color. The color that can be used for either process can be a solid color, a linear gradient, a radial gradient, or an image pattern.

Both a stroke and fill allow specific Canvas API attributes to configure their behavior. When such an attribute changes, it applies itself to all future calls to the drawing methods, until it is changed to something else. These are the global attributes, fill attributes, and stroke attributes and are all detailed here.

continued ▶

```
context.strokeStyle = 'blue';
context.fillStyle = 'red';
context.fillRect(10, 20, 50, 100);
context.fillStyle = 'black';
context.fillRect(20, 30, 100, 100);
context.strokeRect(0, 0, 200, 100);
```

In this code example, `context.strokeStyle` and `context.fillStyle` are attributes that affect the `context.strokeRect()` and `context.fillRect()` drawing methods. First, one red rectangle is created at (10, 20) that is 50 pixels wide and 100 tall; then a black rectangle is created at (20, 30) and 100 pixels wide and tall. Finally, a blue rectangle border is created at (0, 0) and 200 pixels wide and 100 tall.

So, in this code example, the drawing configuration changes three times. The blue `strokeStyle` applies to all stroke methods that follow it, and the red `fillStyle` applies to all fill methods that follow it. Because `fillStyle` changes to black midway through, it changed the behavior of all fill methods that follow.

## Context State

The *context state* is the current drawing configuration of all global, text, fill, and stroke attributes, plus the current plane transformation method settings. Because the drawing environment and behavior can change drastically whenever the drawing configuration changes, two methods are used to manage temporary state changes.

### Methods

- `context.save()` — Saves the current values for all global, text, fill, and stroke attributes plus plane transformation settings into a stack array.
- `context.restore()` — Restores all global, text, fill, and stroke attributes plus plane transformation settings to the latest state stored in the stack and removes that configuration from the array.

This implementation may seem strange at first, but subsequent sections in this chapter help its purpose become evident. Essentially, think of it like this: If you ever need to modify the current drawing configuration, run `context.save()` first; when you are done with the modified configuration, run `context.restore()`. This works particularly well in functions that perform one specific canvas task using a temporarily modified drawing configuration.

### Global Attributes

- `context.globalAlpha` — Sets an overall level of opacity for every drawing function in the canvas to follow. Its supported range is a decimal number from 0, which is completely transparent, to 1, which is completely visible.
- `context.globalCompositeOperation` — Configures how semitransparent drawing methods blend into already-drawn objects. Although this is not often used, you can find the list of options in the WHATWG Canvas API specification.
- `context.canvas` — A reference to the original `canvas` object that was used during `canvas.getContext('2d')`.

## Plane Transformations

The context drawing plane, known mathematically as a *flat Cartesian surface,* can be altered and changed on the fly. The changes applied by any of these methods can be backed up using `context.save()` and restored using `context.restore()`.

### Methods

- `context.scale(x, y)` — This enables you to alter the plane by scaling it. The default state is 1x and 1y. You can scale it by locking its aspect ratio with $x = y$, increasing the horizontal width with $x > y$, and increasing the vertical scale with $x < y$, and you can mirror it with $-x = y$ or $x = -y$.
- `context.translate(x, y)` — Normally, the (0, 0) origin is in the top-left corner of the plane. Run this function to reposition the origin to any new location point.

- `context.rotate(angle)` — Rotates the x- and y-axes by pivoting on the origin point.
- `context.transform(a, b, c, d, e, f)` — Performs an identity matrix transformation to skew the plane's display. This can be used to emulate a perspective in the canvas drawing.
- `context.setTransform(a, b, c, d, e, f)` — Just like `context.transform()`, except that this method resets the identity matrix to the default and then applies the transformation change.

## Drawing Shapes

Simple shape drawing in the canvas is limited to squares and rectangles. Although this is not a very complicated process, it is useful for creating simple four-sided shapes without resorting to paths, which themselves are better suited for complex shapes. All three methods use $(x,y)$ as the top-left point and grow $w$ pixels wide and $h$ pixels down.

### Methods

- `context.fillRect(x, y, w, h)` — Draws a solid rectangle or square.
- `context.strokeRect(x, y, w, h)` — Draws a rectangular or square line.
- `context.clearRect(x, y, w, h)` — Erases a solid rectangle or square from the canvas display. Basically, it is like drawing a transparent shape to make the website content under the canvas visible.

### Attributes

The `fillStyle`, `shadowBlur`, `shadowColor`, `shadowOffsetX`, and `shadowOffsetY` attributes described later in this section in the "Color and Style" subsection apply to the `fillRect()` method. Additionally, the `strokeStyle`, `lineCap`, `lineJoin`, `lineWidth`, and `miterLimit` attributes, also described in "Color and Style," apply to the `strokeRect()` method.

## Drawing Paths

Complex and irregular shapes can be drawn as canvas paths. A *path* is an invisible line that builds the shape's structure by moving an "invisible ink" pen from point to point. That shape can be filled or stroked, which actually draws it to the screen.

### Methods

- `context.beginPath()` — Starts a new path by clearing out any previously established path points.
- `context.rect(x, y, w, h)` — Creates a rectangular path.

- `context.moveTo(x, y)` — Moves the pen to a new point.
- `context.lineTo(x, y)` — Creates a line from the current pen location to the specified point.
- `context.arc(x, y, radius, startAngle, endAngle, clockwise)` — Creates an arc using the specified point as the center. `radius` determines how big the arc is, and `startAngle` and `endAngle` determine where the arc begins and ends. The clockwise Boolean, if true, states that the pen moves clockwise from `startAngle` to `endAngle`, or, if false, the pen moves counterclockwise from `startAngle` to `endAngle`.
- `context.arcTo(x1, y1, x2, y2, radius)` — Creates an arc of `radius` size that joins two tangent lines, the first defined by the current location to $(x1,y1)$, the second defined by $(x1,y1)$ to $(x2,y2)$.
- `context.quadraticCurveTo(cpx, cpy, x, y)` — Creates an elongated arc that moves from the current pen location to $(x,y)$, using control points $(cpx,cpy)$ to influence its curve.
- `context.bezierCurveTo(cp1x, cp1y, cp2x, cp2y, x, y)` — Creates a double-elongated curve, also known as a *Bézier curve,* from the current pen location to $(x,y)$. It uses two pairs of control points to influence the curve at two locations along the path.
- `context.closePath()` — Creates a straight line from the current pen location to the first point in the path.
- `context.fill()` — Draws the path area with the `fillStyle` color.
- `context.stroke()` — Draws a border along the path area with the `strokeStyle` color.
- `context.drawSystemFocusRing(element)` — Draws a native system focus ring around the current path, only if the `element` specified has focus.
- `context.drawCustomFocusRing(element)` — Returns true if the specified `element` has focus. Then you can draw your own focus ring using the path and `stroke()` or `fill()`.
- `context.scrollPathIntoView()` — If the canvas exceeds the overall browser screen size, this method will scroll the path into the viewable display area.
- `context.clip()` — Constrains the drawable clipping area with the current path.
- `context.isPointInPath(x, y)` — Allows you to verify whether point $(x,y)$ exists at any location along the current path line.

continued

## Attributes

The `fillStyle`, `shadowBlur`, `shadowColor`, `shadowOffsetX`, and `shadowOffsetY` attributes described later in this section in the "Color and Style" subsection apply to the `fill()` method. Additionally, the `strokeStyle`, `lineCap`, `lineJoin`, `lineWidth`, and `miterLimit` attributes, also described in "Color and Style," apply to the `stroke()` method.

## Text Drawing Methods

The text drawing methods allow you to place a single line of text, using a single font configuration, anywhere in the canvas. Any midway changes within the text string to the location, such as line wrapping, or font, such as bold and italic, must be handled by a new call to a text drawing method.

## Methods

- `context.fillText(text, x, y, maxWidth)` — Draws *text* in the current `font` at $(x,y)$ using a solid `fillStyle` setting. An optional *maxWidth* size determines how much text should actually be drawn.

- `context.strokeText(text, x, y, maxWidth)` — Draws *text* in the current `font` at $(x,y)$ using a lined-border `strokeStyle` setting. An optional *maxWidth* size determines how much text should actually be drawn.

- `metrics = context.measureText(text)` — Measures *text* in the current `font` to determine the width it would occupy without actually drawing it.

## Attributes

The following attributes can be used to control how various draw functions execute. Each attribute value can be stored and retrieved in the drawing stack using `save()` and `restore()`:

- `context.font` — Sets the current font using a syntax that matches the CSS `font` property.

- `context.textAlign` — Sets the horizontal text alignment with values like `start`, `end`, `left`, `right`, or `center`.

- `context.textBaseLine` — Sets the vertical alignment of the $(x,y)$ point to the height of the text itself. Values accepted are `top`, `hanging`, `alphabetic`, `ideographic`, or `bottom`.

- `metrics.width` — The `context.measureText()` method returns a `metrics` object. This object has one property, `width`, which can be used to retrieve the measured text's width.

The `fillStyle`, `shadowBlur`, `shadowColor`, `shadowOffsetX`, and `shadowOffsetY` attributes described later in this section in the "Color and Style" subsection apply to the `fillText()` method. Additionally, the `strokeStyle`, `lineCap`, `lineJoin`, `lineWidth`, and `miterLimit` attributes, also described in "Color and Style," apply to the `strokeText()` method.

## Direct Pixel Manipulation

Direct pixel manipulation implies the ability to create a blank `ImageData` object or convert an existing canvas display into an `ImageData` object, giving yourself the ability to query and manipulate exact pixel values.

## Methods

- `imagedata = context.createImageData(w, h)` — Creates a new `ImageData` object of the specified *w* width and *h* height.

- `imagedata = context.createImageData(imagedata)` — Creates a copy of an existing `ImageData` object.

- `imagedata = context.getImageData(x, y, w, h)` — Creates a new `ImageData` object sourced from the canvas itself.

- `context.putImageData(imagedata, dx, dy)` — Allows you to inject an `ImageData` object into the canvas at $(dx, dy)$.

- `context.putImageData(imagedata, dx, dy, dirtyX, dirtyY, dirtyW, dirtyH)` — Allows you to inject an `ImageData` object into the canvas at $(dx, dy)$ but also to specify a rectangular dirty clipping region relative to the `ImageData` object. Therefore, only the content within the clipping region will be drawn to the canvas.

## Attributes

- `imagedata.width` — The width of the `ImageData` object.

- `imagedata.height` — The height of the `ImageData` object.

- `imagedata.data[]` — An array of numbers, called the `CanvasPixelArray`, representing the red, green, blue, and alpha channel values for every pixel in `ImageData`. Because there are four channels per pixel, the total size of `imagedata.data[]` is the total pixels times four.

- `imagedata.data.length` — The total length of `CanvasPixelArray`. Dividing by four gets the total number of pixels in the `ImageData` object.

## Color and Style

Each time that you draw on the canvas, you have the option to use a solid color, gradient, or pattern. This is done by assigning either a color string or style object to the `fillStyle` or `strokeStyle` attribute. Most often, a solid color is all that is required, so specifying a color string that follows a CSS-like color syntax — such as `red`, `#ff0000`, or `rgb(255,0,0)` — into either attribute is the quickest way to add colors to your canvas.

## Methods

The following methods are used to create complex styles:

- *gradient* = context.createLinearGradient(*x0*, *y0*, *x1*, *y1*) — Creates a linear gradient that contains gradient colors that change from (*x0*,*y0*) to (*x1*,*y1*). The output of this function is a gradient object that first must receive at least two `addColorStop()` calls before it is assigned to `fillStyle` or `strokeStyle`.

- *gradient* = context.createRadialGradient(*x0*, *y0*, *r0*, *x1*, *y1*, *r1*) — Creates a radial gradient that contains gradient colors that change from (*x0*,*y0*) and a radius of *r0*, outward to (*x1*,*y1*) and a radius of *r1*. The output of this function is a gradient object that first must receive at least two `addColorStop()` calls before it is assigned to `fillStyle` or `strokeStyle`.

- *gradient*.addColorStop(*offset*, *color*) — Adds a specific color stop at an offset location to the *gradient* object. The *offset* value must be a decimal number between 0 and 1, and the *color* value follows the same CSS-like color syntax.

- *pattern* = context.createPattern (*image*, *repetition*) — Allows you to assign a specific image object as a repeating or scaling pattern.

## Fill Attributes

The following fill attributes are used when you call the fill-related methods: `fill()`, `fillRect()`, or `fillText()`:

- `context.fillStyle` — Accepts a color string, gradient object, or pattern object to which it specifies the fill color, gradient, or pattern used by the fill-related methods. If unspecified, the fill color is black.

- `context.shadowOffsetX`, `context.shadowOffsetY` — Accepts an integer value to specify where a shadow should be placed beside a fill object created by one of these methods. If unspecified, there is no shadow.

- `context.shadowBlur` — Accepts an integer value to specify how quickly the shadow's edges blur away. If unspecified, the shadow has no blur effect.

- `context.shadowColor` — Accepts a CSS-like color string to specify the color of the shadow itself. If unspecified, black is used.

## Stroke Attributes

The following stroke attributes are used when you call the stroke-related methods: `stroke()`, `strokeRect()`, or `strokeText()`:

- `context.strokeStyle` — Accepts a color string, gradient object, or pattern object to which it specifies the line color, gradient, or pattern used by the stroke-related methods. If unspecified, the line color is black.

- `context.lineCap` — Specifies how the ends of open lines will be capped. Options include `butt`, `round`, and `square`.

- `context.lineJoin` — Specifies how the corners of line paths will be filled in when two lines meet at different angles. Options include `bevel`, `round`, and `miter`.

- `context.lineWidth` — Sets the stroked line width in pixels.

- `context.miterLimit` — If `context.lineJoin` is set to `miter`, a limit of the miter length can be applied.

**B**efore you can begin drawing on the canvas, you must declare a canvas element, along with its identifier and dimensions. This process serves three purposes. First, it allows you easy access to the element in JavaScript. Second, it enables you to define the canvas pixel area size using the height and width properties. Third, it enables you to define fallback content that will be displayed on non-Canvas API web browsers:

```
<canvas id='surface' width='500'
 height='500'>
  <img src='static-image.jpg'>
</canvas>
```

The id attribute is optional, but it does make locating this particular canvas element easier, especially if you have multiple canvases on the same page. If you know the absolute height and width values, specify them now; otherwise, you may use rough values as placeholders and modify them in JavaScript later. The content within the canvas tag group represents any fallback method that you have available. This can be a static image showing what the user will be seeing, a Flash version of the drawing or animation, or perhaps a simple text message that prints, "Your browser does not support the HTML5 Canvas API."

After you have your canvas element defined, you can use JavaScript to locate the canvas in the DOM, access the 2D canvas API, and start to apply shapes, lines, text, colors, gradients, images, and animations.

## Declare a canvas Element

**①** Open an HTML file with jQuery loaded.

**②** Type **<canvas id='*surface*' width='*500*' height='*300*'>** to set a canvas element 500 pixels wide by 300 pixels tall.

**③** Insert some fallback content for when canvas support is unavailable.

**④** Type **</canvas>**.

**⑤** Go to your <script type='text/ javascript'> block or a JavaScript file loaded after jQuery.

**⑥** Scroll to a JavaScript $(function() {...}); group or create one if it does not yet exist.

**⑦** Type **var canvas = $('canvas#*surface*') [0];** to access the canvas element with id='surface' using jQuery.

***Note:*** *If you are not using jQuery, you skip step **6** and replace step **7** with* var canvas = document. getElementById('surface');. *Be sure to specify your JavaScript after the* <canvas> *tag or in a* document.onload = function(){{ ... }}; *function.*

**⑧** Type **if (canvas.getContext) { }** to verify that the canvas object has the getContext function.

**9** Type **var context = canvas. getContext('2d');** to access the two-dimensional canvas context of functions.

**Note:** 2d *is the only context currently available in the Canvas API.*

**Note:** *In this example, the rest of the code is described throughout this chapter. It is just shown here to make the canvas look like something when you view it.*

**10** Save your JavaScript and HTML files.

**11** Load your HTML file in an HTML5 web browser.

The Canvas API sample text and border appear.

**12** Load your HTML file in a non-HTML5 web browser.

The non–Canvas API fallback content appears.

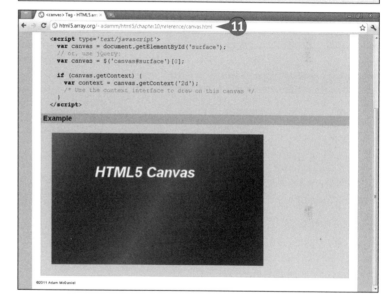

## APPLY IT

It is possible to declare a canvas that acts just like a dynamic background image.

**TYPE THIS**

```
<style type='text/css'>
  body{ margin:0; padding:0 }
  canvas#surface{ position:fixed; z-index:-1 }
</style>
<script type='text/javascript'>
  function onWindowResize() {
    context.canvas.width = window.innerWidth;
    context.canvas.height = window.innerHeight;
    // (Re)draw canvas contents
  }
  $(window).resize(onWindowResize);
  onWindowResize();
</script>
```

**RESULT**

When the page first loads, onWindowResize() is registered as a resize event handler. This ensures that if the user resizes the browser, the canvas is adjusted to match the current settings. Because the function also runs at load time, the canvas width and height match the displayable browser dimensions right away. The CSS rules here simply set the canvas to run underneath the actual website content, just like a background image.

If you ever need to resize an existing canvas object, do not modify the CSS width and height properties. This will cause your canvas to scale by forcing the same number of pixels to appear in a larger or smaller area.

The simplest, and only, shape you can draw on the canvas natively is a rectangle. This may seem like a very restrictive statement, but the canvas rectangle is not designed to be just a simple shape; it provides you with a way to set a solid background color across the entire canvas plane, draw a box or border around a selected area, or erase part or all of the drawing area.

For more complex shapes, everything from lines, to triangles, stars, circles, hearts, bears, cars, and people, you must use a canvas path, as described in the next section, "Draw Paths on the Canvas."

There are three types of rectangles that you can draw on the canvas:

- Clear rectangle — `clearRect(x, y, w, h)` — This erases whatever was previously drawn in the canvas and exposes underlying HTML elements.
- Fill rectangle — `fillRect(x, y, w, h)` — This draws a solid rectangle using the current `fillStyle` setting.
- Stroke rectangle — `strokeRect(x, y, w, h)` — This draws a rectangular border using the current `lineWidth` and `strokeStyle` settings.

`fillStyle` and `strokeStyle` define the color styling to draw with. In their simplest form, they use CSS-style values, such as `#ff0000`, `rgb(255,0,0)`, or color keywords like `red`. These properties are explained in the sections "Using Solid Color on the Canvas" and "Using Linear Gradient Colors on the Canvas" later in this chapter. If you do not specify them here, the default color is black.

## Draw Basic Rectangles on the Canvas

① Open an HTML or JavaScript file with a canvas and 2D context variables loaded.

**Note:** In this example, and for the rest of the chapter, the `canvas` element's size is 700 x 500 pixels.

② Type **context.fillStyle = '#FF8000';** to set the current fill style color to orange.

**Note:** The `fillStyle` attribute is described later in the section "Using Solid Color on the Canvas."

③ Type **context.fillRect(50, 50, 300, 200);** to fill a 300 x 200 rectangle at (50, 50) with the fill color.

④ Type **context.strokeStyle = '#0000FF';** to set the current stroke style color to blue.

**Note:** The `strokeStyle` attribute is described later in the section "Using Solid Color on the Canvas."

⑤ Type **context.strokeRect(100, 100, 300, 200);** to draw a 300 x 100 rectangle at (100, 100) with the stroke color.

⑥ Type **context.clearRect(*75, 75, 100, 100*);** to erase a 100 x 100 square at (75, 75).

⑦ Save your HTML or JavaScript file.

⑧ Load your HTML file in an HTML5 web browser.

The canvas methods render a drawing in the canvas element.

Ⓐ In this example, a yellow rectangle is drawn.

Ⓑ A blue rectangle is drawn.

Ⓒ A clear square erases part of the blue and yellow rectangles.

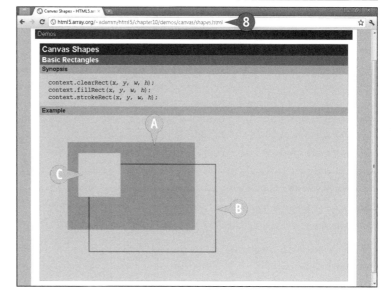

```
47        <script type="text/javascript">
48          $(function(){
49            var canvas = $('canvas#surface')[0];
50            if (canvas.getContext) {
51              var context = canvas.getContext('2d');
52
53              context.fillStyle = '#FF0000';
54              context.fillRect(50, 50, 300, 200);
55
56              context.strokeStyle = '#0000FF';
57              context.strokeRect(100, 100, 300, 200);
58
59              context.clearRect(75, 75, 100, 100);
60            }
61          });
62        </script>
```

---

The default background color of a canvas is actually transparent. This makes other elements, such as the web page `<body>` tag, that do have a CSS `background-image` or `background-color` property to show up through the canvas drawing area. This is useful as the content you draw will appear to float above the background under it.

If you choose, you can apply a specific background color to the canvas. This can happen as soon as you have received its 2D context object. Use the attributes `context.canvas.width` and `context.canvas.height` to get the width and height of the `canvas` element.

**TYPE THIS**

```
context.fillStyle = '#FF00FF';
context.fillRect(0, 0, context.canvas.width,
  context.canvas.height);
```

**RESULT**

A purple rectangle is drawn encompassing the entire size of the `canvas` element.

The `fillStyle` property is discussed later in this chapter.

# DRAW PATHS ON THE CANVAS

**C**omplex and irregular shapes can be drawn as canvas *paths,* generated by placing an "invisible ink" pen at a specific location and defining straight lines, arcs, or curves to build a shape. That shape can be filled or stroked, which draws it to screen.

All paths must begin with `beginPath()`. This removes all points established by any earlier paths. Note that previously drawn paths will remain on the canvas; this function just removes any of the analogous invisible ink.

Path-generation methods allow you to control your invisible ink pen:

- `moveTo(x, y)` — This moves the pen to a specific location in the canvas. This is useful as the first method in a new path to define where you want the path to begin.
- `lineTo(x, y)` — This creates a straight line path between the current pen location and the specified coordinates.

- `rect(x, y, w, h)` — This creates a rectangular path, just like calling one `moveTo` and four `lineTo` methods.
- `arc(x, y, radius, startAngle, endAngle, drawClockwise)` — This creates an arc or circle centered at *x* and *y*. The angles are measured in radians, and the path can be drawn clockwise or counterclockwise.
- `bezierCurveTo(cp1x, cp1y, cp2x, cp2y, x, y)` — This draws a parametric Bézier curve to create smooth and fluid lines that gravitate toward two pairs of control points and influence the path's curve, from the current position to *x* and *y*.
- `quadraticCurveTo(cpx, cpy, x, y)` — This draws a quadratic curve from the current position to *x* and *y*. The control point influences the middle of the path's curve.

When the path shape is complete, close and fill the path with a specific color with `fill()` or draw a line along the path with `stroke()`.

## Draw Paths on the Canvas

**1** Open an HTML or JavaScript file with a canvas and 2D context variables loaded.

**2** Type **context.beginPath();** to start a new path.

**3** Type **context.moveTo(x, y);** to move the path "pen" to a specific point.

**4** Type **context.lineTo(x, y);** to draw a line from the previous point to (x, y).

**A** Optionally, repeat steps **3** and **4** to draw additional lines.

**5** Type **context.rect(x, y, height, width);** to add a standalone rectangle segment to the path.

**6** Type **context.arc(x, y, radius, Math.PI, 2*Math.PI, true);** to create an arc drawing, centered at (x, y) moving clockwise from π to 2π.

**Note:** *Be sure to use* `Math.PI` *and not* `Math.Pi`.

**7** Type **context.stroke();** to draw a line along the path.

**8** Type **context.beginPath();** to erase the previous path.

**9** Type **context.moveTo(0, 500);**.

**10** Type **context.bezierCurveTo(0, 0, 250, 500, 500, 500);** to create a Bézier curve from the previous point to (500, 500), gravitating toward control points (0, 0) and (250, 500).

**Note:** *The quadratic curve is the same basic idea as a Bézier curve, except there is only one control point.*

**11** Type **context.fill();** to fill the path.

**12** Save your HTML or JavaScript files.

**13** Load your HTML file in an HTML5 web browser.

**B** In this example, the straight line paths are drawn.

**C** The rectangular line path is drawn.

**D** The arc path is drawn.

**E** This is the curved Bézier path, filled in.

**Note:** *The rectangle created a whole new path segment, as it implies* moveTo().

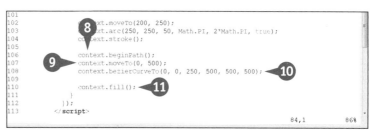

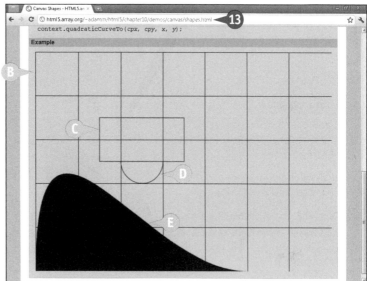

## APPLY IT

After drawing with stroke() or fill(), you can create a new path with beginPath(). However, if you draw your path and then add more points to it without declaring a new path, all earlier points will remain active for any subsequent drawing methods and will be drawn twice.

Sometimes, when drawing a line along a path, you may want the entire path shape to be unbroken. Call closePath() to add a new path line back to the very first point and then call stroke().

**TYPE THIS**

```
context.beginPath();
context.arc(50, 20, 25, Math.PI, 0, true);
context.stroke();
context.beginPath();
context.arc(50, 60, 25, Math.PI, 0, true);
context.closePath();
context.stroke();
```

→

**RESULT**

Two semicircles are created. The first one starts from $\pi$ to zero radians, or 180° to 0°. The second uses the same arc path, but closePath() adds a straight line back to the start of the arc.

Note that closePath() is implied if you use fill(). Experiment with this example by changing coordinates, removing the additional beginPath()s, and by changing stroke() to fill().

**D**rawing canvas text combines the capabilities of CSS fonts with the fill and stroke procedures described earlier in this chapter. Essentially, your font is defined using the same syntax as the CSS font property; this includes the ability to take advantage of @font-face, new in CSS3 and described in Chapter 4, "Styling with CSS3." The text itself creates a path that can either be filled or stroked.

Start by specifying the font the text will be drawn as:

```
context.font = 'font-style font-variant
  font-weight font-size font-family';
```

All font values are order specific, although not all are required. At a minimum, you must specify *font-size* and *font-family* values to properly set a canvas font. All values use the same syntax as their CSS equivalents.

You may optionally control the text alignment, relative to the point where text will be drawn, using the context.textAlign and context.textBaseline attributes. Possible values for the former are start, end, left, right, and center. Possible values for the latter are top, hanging, middle, alphabetic, ideographic, and bottom. See the WHATWG page at www.whatwg.org/specs/web-apps/current-work/multipage/the-canvas-element.html#dom-context-2d-textbaseline for an explanation.

After your font properties are all defined, you can call fillText() or strokeText() to actually draw the text to the canvas using the current fillStyle and strokeStyle attribute settings, described earlier in this chapter:

```
context.fillText(text, x, y);
context.strokeText(text, x, y);
```

## Draw Text on the Canvas

**1** Open an HTML or JavaScript file with a canvas and 2D context loaded.

**A** Optionally, type **context.save();** before you change the font or text attributes, if you want to restore the previous values.

**2** Type **context.font = 'size "Times New Roman",serif';** to define the font size and a font family name, plus a fallback generic font family name.

**Note:** *As there are spaces in this example's font name, only that name is wrapped in quotes.*

**Note:** *There are no spaces between the comma-separated font names.*

**B** Optionally, type **bold** to use a bold font weight.

**C** Optionally, type **italic** to use an italic font style.

**D** Optionally, type **small-caps** to use a small-capped font variant.

**Note:** *Because the font style, variant, and weight all use unique keywords, they could be specified in any order preceding the font size and font family.*

E) Optionally, type **context.textAlign = 'center';** and **context.textBaseline = 'middle';** to center the text on the (x, y) point.

3) Type **context.fillText(*text*, *x*, *y*);** to draw filled text at (*x*, *y*).

4) Type **context.strokeText(*text*, *x*, *y*);** for stroked text at (*x*, *y*).

F) Optionally, type **context.restore();** if you used save() earlier to restore the attribute values.

5) Save your HTML or JavaScript file.

6) Load your HTML file in an HTML5 web browser.

*Note: In this example, and for the rest of the chapter, a grid layout is used to better show you the origin point, the x- and y-axes, and the placement of objects.*

G) The text is drawn with fillText().

H) The text is drawn with strokeText().

I) This is the point used to position the text, centered by the textAlign and textBaseline modifications.

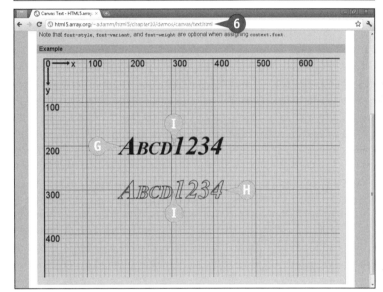

## APPLY IT

If you want to use precise text placement in the canvas, such as drawing multiple text strings after each other, you need to know the overall width of the text string in the selected font prior to actually writing it to the screen. This can be done with the measureText(*text*) method, which returns a metrics object.

The pixel width of the font can be accessed using metrics.width.

### TYPE THIS

```
var todayStr = 'Today is';
var dateStr = new Date();
context.textBaseline = 'top';
context.font = 'italic 30px arial';
var todayStrMetrics = context.measureText(todayStr);
context.fillText(todayStr, 0, 0);
context.font = 'bold 40px arial';
context.fillText(dateStr, todayStrMetrics.width, 0);
```

### RESULT

The measureText() method calculates the width of the first string and uses the width in the placement of the next string. This way, the text "Today is" appears in a normal 30px font followed by the date in a bold 40px font.

You can customize what color is used when drawing on the canvas. Earlier sections of this chapter have shown shapes, paths, and text drawn in black, which is the default if the `fillStyle` and `strokeStyle` attributes are undefined.

```
context.fillStyle = 'color';
context.strokeStyle = 'color';
```

The `color` value can be one of four string formats:

- `#RRGGBB` — Specifies an RGB color in three pairs of hexadecimal numbers, from `00` for no color to `FF` for maximum color, depending on position. For example, `#FF8000` is maximum red, half green, and no blue, which appears orange.
- `rgb(rrr,bbb,ggg)` — Specifies an RGB color, very similar to `#RRGGBB`, except the values are decimal numbers from 0 to 255. For example, `rgb(255,128,0)`

is orange. The format `rgba()` adds an alpha transparency value: a decimal number from 0 to 1.

- `hsl(hue,saturation,lightness)` — Specifies an HSL color by providing its hue, saturation, and lightness values. `hue` is a decimal number from 0 to 255, and `saturation` and `lightness` are percentage numbers. For example, `hsl(32,100%,50%)` is orange. The format `hsla()` adds an alpha transparency value, just like `rgba()`.
- `colorname` — Allows you to specify a literal color name from a predetermined list, such as `black`, `white`, `orange`, `fuchsia`, `olive`, `chocolate`, `hotpink`, and `khaki`. For a complete list, see the W3C page at www.w3.org/TR/css3-color/#svg-color.

When either style attribute is defined, use `fill()`, `fillRect()`, `fillText()`, `stroke()`, `strokeRect()`, and `strokeText()` to create colorful canvas objects.

## Using Solid Color on the Canvas

1 Open an HTML or JavaScript file with a canvas and 2D context variables loaded.

2 Type **context.save()** to back up the current attribute settings.

3 Type **context.strokeStyle = '#BADA55';** to set the stroke style to a dark yellow-green color.

4 Type **context.fillStyle = 'rgba(0,128,128,0.5)';** to set the fill style to teal at 50% transparency.

5 Draw some canvas objects, such as shapes, paths, or text strings.

6 Save your HTML or JavaScript file.

7 Load your HTML file in an HTML5 web browser.

Ⓐ In this example, a dark yellow-green line is drawn for stroked shapes.

Ⓑ A teal color is drawn for filled shapes.

**Note:** *Because the teal is 50% transparent, you can see items previously drawn underneath it.*

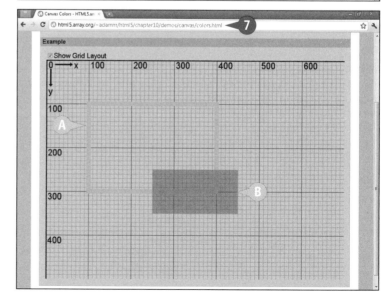

**8** Go back to your HTML or JavaScript file.

**9** Type **context.restore();** to restore the strokeStyle and fillStyle values to what they were before context.save() was called.

**10** Continue drawing more stroked or filled paths, rectangles, or text strings.

**11** Save your HTML or JavaScript file.

**12** Load your HTML file in an HTML5 web browser.

**C** The stroked and filled shapes created after context. restore() revert to the previous strokeStyle and fillStyle settings.

**Note:** As strokeStyle or fillStyle both were not defined prior to context.save(), they both reverted to black.

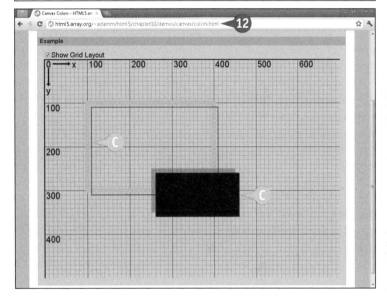

---

You can use a shadow fill to simulate depth on any shape or text, regardless of filling it with a solid color or stroking it with a lined border.

**Example**
```
context.shadowColor = 'color';
context.shadowOffsetX = number;
context.shadowOffsetY = number;
context.shadowBlur = number;
```

The syntax for shadowColor's color value is the same as described above for the fill and stroke styles:

#RRGGBB, rgb(rrr, bbb, ggg), hsl(hue, saturation, lightness), or colorname.

Essentially, whatever is being drawn will be mirrored at coordinates offset by shadowOffsetX and shadowOffsetY. The edges will then be blurred to transparency using the length of shadowBlur.

The shadow fill can be stored and reverted, just like the other fill and stroke styles, using context.save() and context.restore().

**Y**ou may use linear gradient colors in place of a solid stroke or fill color. This allows you to add interesting multicolored effects on a single canvas object that blend from one color into another.

To create a gradient, you must first call `createLinear Gradient()` and specify the coordinates for where the first color begins (*x0, y0*) and the last color ends (*x1, y1*):

```
var gradient = context.
 createLinearGradient(x0, y0, x1, y1);
```

The *gradient* object created must then be assigned color-stop offsets. An offset determines where along the (*x0, y0*) to (*x1, y1*) path that a specific color will be strongest:

```
gradient.addColorStop(offset, 'color1');
gradient.addColorStop(offset, 'color2');
```

For each `gradient.addColorStop()` call, the *offset* variable must be a unique decimal number within 0 and 1.

If *offset* is 0, its color is applied to the (*x0, y0*) point and everywhere before it on the path. The *offset* of 1 color is applied to the (*x1, y1*) point and everywhere after it. All other color offsets in between 0 and 1 will appear at their relative offset location between (*x0, y0*) and (*x1, y1*).

Assign the *gradient* object to `fillStyle` or `strokeStyle`. This will draw it to the canvas when you use `fill()`, `fillRect()`, `fillText()`, `stroke()`, `strokeRect()`, or `strokeText()`:

```
context.fillStyle = gradient;
context.strokeStyle = gradient;
```

The canvas location where this gradient is drawn determines which portions of the color blend actually appear. The gradient will remain active until `fillStyle` or `strokeStyle` are changed.

## Using Linear Gradient Colors on the Canvas

**1** Open an HTML or JavaScript file with a canvas and 2D context variables loaded.

**2** Type **var *gradient* = context. createLinearGradient(*100, 100, 400, 400*);** to define a gradient that moves diagonally from (100, 100) to (400, 400).

***Note:*** *If you want a horizontal gradient, set the first and third parameters to the same x-axis value; for a vertical gradient, set the second and fourth parameters to the same y-axis value.*

**3** Type ***gradient*.addColorStop(0,*'red'*);** to use red at offset 0.

**A** Optionally, type ***gradient*.addColorStop (*0.5,'white'*);** to use white at offset 0.5, which is effectively at (250, 250) in the `createLinearGradient()` path.

**4** Type ***gradient*.addColorStop(1,*'blue'*);** to use blue at offset 1.

***Note:*** *You can continue adding new colors at different offsets between 0 and 1.*

**5** Type **context.save()** to back up the current attribute settings.

**6** Type **context.style = gradient;** to assign the linear gradient as the stroke or fill style.

**7** Use a stroke- or fill-related method to draw with the linear gradient.

**8** Type **context.restore();** to restore your previous attribute settings from the save point, thus removing the gradient from the drawing style.

**9** Save your HTML or JavaScript file.

**10** Load your HTML file in an HTML5 web browser.

The objects are drawn with the linear gradient as their painted colors, relative to the linear gradient path.

**B** This is the point where the linear gradient begins.

**C** This is the point where the linear gradient ends.

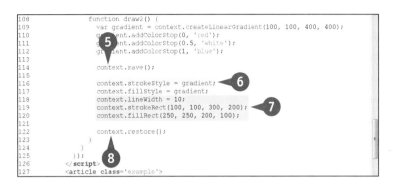

```
108    function draw2() {
109        var gradient = context.createLinearGradient(100, 100, 400, 400);
110        gradient.addColorStop(0, 'red');
111        gradient.addColorStop(0.5, 'white');
112        gradient.addColorStop(1, 'blue');
113
114        context.save();
115
116        context.strokeStyle = gradient;
117        context.fillStyle = gradient;
118        context.lineWidth = 10;
119        context.strokeRect(100, 100, 300, 200);
120        context.fillRect(250, 250, 200, 100);
121
122        context.restore();
123    }
124    }
125    });
126    </script>
127    <article class='example'>
```

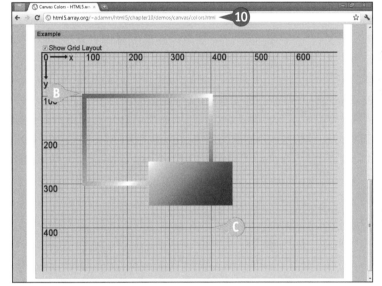

## EXTRA

Calling `gradient.addColorStop()` once does not make a gradient;, it only makes a solid color, regardless of the `offset` value. Only when you have multiple `gradient.addColorStop()` calls, each with a unique offset between 0 and 1, will a color gradient be constructed.

In addition, you do not need to use 0 and 1; any two partial values will suffice. In the previous example, had you only assigned two color stops to 0.5 and 0.75, the perceived path would shrink to (250, 250) and (300, 300).

It is possible to create a gradient that fades into transparency. This is done by using `rgba` (`red,green,blue,0`) as a `gradient.addColorStop()` color. The three color channel

values should match your canvas background color or image as closely as possible. So, if your background is solid black or an image that is mostly black, use `rgba(0,0,0,0)`.

For example, the following color stops create a gradient that moves from red to transparent-white:

```
gradient.addColorStop(0, 'red');
gradient.addColorStop(1, 'rgba(255,255,255,0)');
```

Note this technique also works on radial gradients, as described in the next section, "Using Radial Gradient Colors on the Canvas."

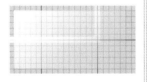

197

# USING RADIAL GRADIENT COLORS ON THE CANVAS

An alternative to the linear gradient is the radial gradient. This allows you to add interesting multicolored effects on a single canvas object that actually blend seamlessly from one color into another, but in a circular fashion — outgoing from a specific point and incoming into another specific point.

To create a gradient, you must first call `createRadialGradient()` and specify the absolute coordinates for where the first color begins $(x0, y0)$, the radius outward as $r0$, and where the last color ends $(x1, y1)$, plus its radius, $r1$:

```
var gradient = context.createRadialGradient
  (x0, y0, r0, x1, y1, r1);
```

The `gradient` object created must then be assigned color-stop offsets. An offset determines where along the radial path a specific color will be strongest:

```
gradient.addColorStop(offset, 'color1');
gradient.addColorStop(offset, 'color2');
```

For each `gradient.addColorStop()` call, the `offset` variable must be a unique decimal number between 0 and 1. If `offset` is 0, its color is applied to the $(x0, y0)$ point and everywhere before $r0$. If `offset` is 1, its color is applied to the $(x1, y1)$ point and everywhere after $r1$. All color offsets in between will appear relationally between the two circles.

Assign the `gradient` object to `fillStyle` or `strokeStyle`. This will draw it to the canvas when you use `fill()`, `fillRect()`, `fillText()`, `stroke()`, `strokeRect()`, or `strokeText()`. The gradient will remain active until `fillStyle` or `strokeStyle` are changed.

## Using Radial Gradient Colors on the Canvas

**1** Open an HTML or JavaScript file with a canvas and 2D context variables loaded.

**2** Type **var gradient = context. createRadialGradient(250, 250, 50, 250, 250, 200);** to define a gradient that starts at (250, 250) and changes colors from a 50 pixel radius up to a 200 pixel radius.

**3** Type **gradient.addColorStop(0,'red');** to use red at offset 0.

**Ⓐ** Optionally, type **gradient. addColorStop(0.5,'white');** to use white at offset 0.5.

**4** Type **gradient.addColorStop(1,'blue');** to use blue at offset 1.

**Note:** *You can continue adding new colors at different offsets between 0 and 1.*

**Note:** *You do not need to use 0 and 1 for the first two offset values, but you do need at least two `addColorStop()`s with different offsets and colors.*

**5** Type **context.save()** to back up the current attribute settings.

**6** Type **context.*style* = gradient;** to assign the radial gradient as the fill or stroke style.

**7** Use a fill- or stroke-related method to draw with the radial gradient.

**8** Type **context.restore();** to restore your previous attribute settings from the save point, thus removing the gradient from the drawing style.

**9** Save your HTML or JavaScript file.

**10** Load your HTML file in an HTML5 web browser.

The objects are drawn with the radial gradient as their painted colors, relative to the linear gradient path.

Ⓑ This is the area before the linear gradient begins. In this example, it is a 50 pixel radius from the start point at (250, 250).

Ⓒ This is the area where the linear gradient ends. In this example, it is a 200 pixel radius from the same start point.

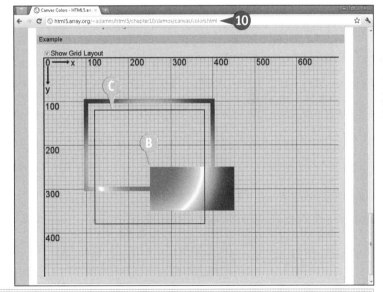

## EXTRA

By setting a radial gradient with different $(x0,y0)$ and $(x1,y1)$ points and adjusting the values so that $x1$ progresses from $x0$ to $x0+r0$, or $y1$ progresses from $y0$ to $y0+r0$, you can create some very interesting radial gradient effects.

For example, the following three images demonstrate three different states: when $x0=y0=x1=y1$ and $r0>r1$; when $x1$ starts to increase toward $x0+r0$; and when $x1$ moves beyond $x0+r0$:

# DRAW AN IMAGE ON THE CANVAS

You can draw an image onto any point in the canvas using drawImage(). This provides a convenient way to import image files stored on your web server into the canvas:

```
var image = document.getElementById(imageID);
context.drawImage(image, destX, destY);
```

*imageID* identifies for the image in HTML, as in <img src='image.jpg' id='*imageID*'>. drawImage()'s *destX* and *destY* values indicate the point in the canvas where the image will appear.

Alternatively, if the image resource is not available as an HTML img element, you may download it dynamically using a new Image() object's src attribute. This requires you to listen for the object's load event, which tells you the resource has been downloaded and can be displayed:

```
var image = new Image();
image.src = 'image.jpg';
image.onload = function() {
   context.drawImage(image, destX, destY);
};
```

If, after the canvas initially draws the image, you happen to reassign image.src to a new file, the image.onload function expression will run again and draw the new image. This will overwrite the existing image; however, if the new image is a smaller size, parts of the older image will remain visible. If this proves to be a problem, you can call clearRect() with the previous image's dimensions before drawImage().

## Draw an Image on the Canvas

**1** Open an HTML or JavaScript file with a canvas and 2D context variables loaded.

**2** Type **var image = new Image();** to create the image object.

**3** Type **image.src = '*image.jpg*';** to specify the image file that you want to draw on the canvas.

**4** Type **image.onload = function(){ };** to specify an anonymous function expression on the load event.

**5** Type **context. drawImage(image, x, y);** to draw the top left of the image at the point (x, y) after it has been downloaded from the web server.

**6** Save your HTML or JavaScript file.

**7** Load your HTML file in an HTML5 web browser.

**A** The image is drawn on the canvas, with the top left of the image at the point (x, y) specified.

```
58        function draw1() {
59            var image = new Image();
60
61            image.src = 'images/laika_jump.jpg';
62            image.onload = function() {
63                context.drawImage(image, 100, 10 );
64            };
65        }
66    }
67    });
68    </script>
```

## APPLY IT

It is possible to send all images through an alpha-channel transparency filter, called `globalAlpha`. Simply assign to it a decimal value between 0, for completely transparent, to 1, for completely visible before drawing your image.

Actually, this `globalAlpha` attribute applies itself to all drawing methods, not just `drawImage()`. Therefore, it is a good idea to call `save()` to back up the current setting, which if left untouched is 1, make the change and draw the image, and then call `restore()` to restore the saved setting.

### TYPE THIS

```
image.onload = function() {
  context.save();
  context.globalAlpha = 0.5;
  context.drawImage(image, 100, 100);
  context.restore();
};
```

### RESULT

The current attribute settings are backed up, and then the image is drawn at the point (100, 100) with 50% transparency; anything under the image remains visible. The modified `globalAlpha` value is then reset to its previous setting.

In addition, the `globalCompositeOperation` attribute can be used to customize how the canvas merges semitransparent object colors in with the existing canvas content. Most of the time, the default setting of `source-over` is sufficient, but if you want to customize it, an explanation of the options can be found at the WHATWG page at www.whatwg.org/specs/web-apps/current-work/#dom-context-2d-globalcompositeoperation.

# SCALE A CANVAS IMAGE

You can scale an image before drawing it into the canvas using a similar procedure to the one described in the section "Draw an Image on the Canvas," except this time, you must specify two more parameters to the `drawImage()` method, a destination width and height:

```
context.drawImage(image, destX, destY, destW,
  destH);
```

*destX*, *destY*, *destW*, and *destH* specify the destination region of the canvas you are copying to. If *destW* and *destH* do not match the image's original width and height, it will be scaled when drawn onto the canvas.

## Scale a Canvas Image

**1** Perform steps **1** to **4** from the section "Draw an Image on the Canvas."

**2** Type **context. drawImage(image, *100*, *10*, *500*, *700*)** to draw an image at (100, 10) and scale it to 500 pixels wide and 700 pixels high.

**3** Save your HTML or JavaScript file.

```
84      <h5>Example</h5>
85      <style>
86        article.example {
87          margin: 10px;
88        }
89      </style>
90      <script type="text/javascript">
91        $(function(){
92          var canvas = $('canvas#surface')[1];
93          if (canvas.getContext) {
94            var context = canvas.getContext('2d');
95
96            drawGridLayout(context);
97            draw2();
98
99            function draw2() {
100             var image = new Image();
101
102             image.src = 'images/laika_jump.jpg';
103             image.onload = function() {
104               context.drawImage(image, 100, 10, 500, 700 );
105             };
106           }
107         }
108       });
109     </script>
110     <article class='example'>
111       <input type=checkbox id='showgrid' checked>Show Grid Layout
112       <canvas id='surface' width='700' height='500'>
113         Your browser does not support the HTML5 canvas.
```

**4** Load your HTML file in an HTML5 web browser.

**Ⓐ** The scaled image is drawn on the canvas.

You can crop an image before drawing it into the canvas using a similar procedure to the one described in the section "Draw an Image on the Canvas," except this time you must specify four more parameters to the drawImage() method:

```
context.drawImage(image, srcX, srcY, srcW,
  srcH, destX, destY, destW, destH);
```

srcX, srcY, srcW, and srcH specify the region of the source image that you are copying from. Likewise, destX, destY, destW, and destH specify the region of the canvas you are copying to. If srcW and srcH do not equal destW and destH, the cropped image will also be scaled.

## Crop a Canvas Image

**1** Perform steps **1** to **4** from the section "Draw an Image on the Canvas."

**2** Type **context. drawImage(image, *srcX*, *srcY*, *srcW*, *srcH*, *destX*, *destY*, *destW*, *destH*)** to crop and scale an image.

**3** Save your HTML or JavaScript file.

**4** Load your HTML file in an HTML5 web browser.

**A** The cropped image is drawn on the canvas.

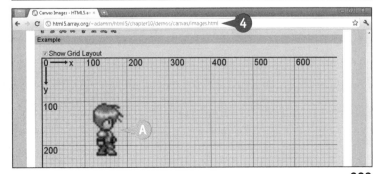

The HTML5 canvas gives you direct access to individual pixels. You can use this to query individual pixels for red, green, blue, and alpha channel values. This process is done by retrieving a static snapshot of the canvas as an image creating the image's data array:

```
var image = context.getImageData(x,y,w,h);
```

This method will take a rectangular picture of the canvas element and store it in an ImageData object. This object provides three properties: height, width, and data. The data property is actually an array that contains a massive list of numbers, four for each pixel, that describe the pixel's color channels:

```
for (var x = 0; x < image.width; x++){
  for (var y = 0; y < image.height; y++){
    var index = (y*image.width+x)*4;
    var red   = image.data[index+0];
    var green = image.data[index+1];
    var blue  = image.data[index+2];
    var alpha = image.data[index+3];
    // The pixel at (x,y) holds
  rgba(red,green,blue,alpha)
  }
}
```

For each pass of the two for loops, x and y will contain the point whose pixel is currently being queried. The index variable indicates where in image.data[] that this pixel's colors are found. Finally, the four channels' values are found in image.data[index] to image.data[index+3].

## Query Individual Canvas Pixels

**1** Open an HTML or JavaScript file with a canvas and 2D context variables loaded.

**2** Draw something on the canvas.

**3** Type **var image = context. getImageData(**srcX , srcY, srcW, srcH**);** to take a snapshot of the canvas as an image data array.

**4** Type **for (var x = 0; x < image.width; x++) { }** to scan through each x-axis pixel.

**5** Type **for (var y = 0; y < image.height; y++) { }** to scan through each y-axis pixel.

**6** Type **var index = (y*image. width+x)*4;** to access the base index of each individual pixel.

**7** Type **var red = image.data[index+0];** to access the red channel value.

**8** Type **var green = image.data[index+1];** for the green channel value.

**9** Type **var blue = image.data[index+2];** for the blue channel value.

**10** Type **var alpha = image.data[index+3];** for the alpha channel value.

**11** Process the x, y, red, green, blue, and alpha variables in a pixel-query function.

**Note:** *In this example, the* magnifyPixel() *function draws a 20 x 20 rectangle in the pixel's color beside the sample canvas image. The rectangle is placed at the same (x, y) coordinates of the pixel, relative to the rectangle size. The effect is that the image sampled by* getImageData() *appears magnified.*

**12** Save your HTML or JavaScript files.

**13** Load your HTML file in an HTML5 web browser.

**A** This is the area sampled by getImageData().

**B** This shows the results of the function that processes the pixel colors within the sample area.

## APPLY IT

When you can query the canvas's individual pixel colors, it is very easy to build something to manipulate them. Often this is done by creating an image filter that uses logic to calculate a new color and updating the same index position of the *image*.data[] array. Once complete, run putImageData() to update the canvas.

### TYPE THIS

```
var image = context.getImageData(0,0,100,100);
for (var i = 0; i < image.data.length; i += 4) {
  var sum = image.data[i] + image.data[i+1] +
  image.data[i+2];
  image.data[i] = image.data[i+1] = image.
  data[i+2] = sum/3;
  image.data[i] += 150;
  image.data[i+1] += 75;
}
context.putImageData(image,0,0);
```

### RESULT

For each pixel, the value of the three color channels are added together, averaged, and synchronized. This converts the image into black and white. Next, 150 is added to red and 75 to green, which inserts a brown that converts the image into a crude sepia tone.

Finally, putImageData() writes the sepia image data directly onto the canvas element at (0, 0).

The putImageData() method accepts three different parameter formats, exactly like drawImage().

# TRACK MOUSE ACTIVITY ON THE CANVAS

Tracking mouse activity on the canvas allows your users to interact with your canvas drawing. This process involves registering event listener functions on mouse event activity. Your canvas JavaScript can identify what the user clicked and update the display accordingly:

```
canvas.addEventListener(eventType,
  onEventFunction, false);
```

Note that the `canvas` object is used here, not `context`; the event listener registration is predicated on the actual `canvas` element, not the Canvas API. You can now supply `eventType`, `onEventFunction`, and a Boolean, which almost always is false: This indicates that events bubble up the DOM starting at the `canvas` element, which is most appropriate in a mouse-activity context.

The following mouse events can be used as `eventType` to specify the function's target action:

- `click`, `dblclick` — Standard click and double-click actions; mutually exclusive on the same target.
- `mousedown`, `mouseup` — The click-hold and click-release actions. Use these if you want to fine-tune a click into two events.
- `mouseover`, `mouseout` — When the user's mouse cursor hovers over the target and when it leaves.
- `mousemove` — The mouse cursor is moved within the target. Useful for hover and drag-and-drop applications: `mousedown` and `mousemove` as the drag and `mouseup` as the drop.
- `mousewheel` — When the user's scroll wheel is used by the user while hovering over the target.

The `mousedown`, `mousemove`, and `mouseup` events can be used together to fine-tune the control you have over complex mouse interactions, such as drag and drop.

## Track Mouse Activity on the Canvas

### Listen for Mouse Events

**1** Open an HTML or JavaScript file with a canvas and 2D context variables loaded.

**2** Type **canvas.addEventListener ('mousedown',** *onMouseDown*, **false);** to declare the `mousedown` event handler.

**3** Type **function** *onMouseDown* **(event) { }.**

**4** Type **if ( event.button == 0 ) { }** to identify only to primary button clicks.

**5** Type **canvas.addEventListener ('mousemove',** *onMouseMove*, **false );** to declare the `mousemove` event handler.

**6** Type **canvas.addEventListener ('mouseup',** *onMouseUp*, **false);** to declare the `mouseup` event handler.

**Note:** *These event registrations are within the* `mousedown` *function because they must only respond when the mouse is "down-then-moving" and "down-then-up."*

**7** Create functions for the `mousedown` and `mouseup` events.

**8** Type **canvas.removeEventListener** (*eventType*, *function*, **false**)**;** to unregister the `mousemove` and `mouseup` events after the user releases the initial `mousedown` button.

Ⓐ The functions removed must match the functions that were added.

```
55        var tux = new Image();
56        tux.src = "images/tux.jpg";
57        tux.onload = function() {
58          var zoom = 40;
59
60          context.clearRect(0, 0, context.canvas.width, context.canvas.height);
61          context.drawImage(tux, 0, 0);
62
63          canvas.addEventListener('mousedown', onMouseDown, false);
64
65          function onMouseDown(event) {
66            event.preventDefault();
67            if ( event.button == 0 ) {
68              canvas.addEventListener('mousemove', onMouseMove, false);
69              canvas.addEventListener('mouseup', onMouseUp, false);
70            }
71          }
72
73          function onMouseMove(event) {
74          }
75
76          function onMouseUp(event) {
77            canvas.removeEventListener('mousemove', onMouseMove, false);
78            canvas.removeEventListener('mouseup', onMouseUp, false);
79          }
80
81          function magnifyImage(srcX, srcY) {
82            var image = context.getImageData(srcX, srcY, zoom, zoom);
83            for ( var x = 0; x < image.width; x++ ) {
84              for ( var y = 0; y < image.height; y++ ) {
                                                              55,17        50%
```

**9** Add canvas functionality that occurs when the mouse button is initially pressed down.

**10** Add canvas functionality that occurs when the mouse button is released.

**Note:** *In this example, the* `no-cursor` *class assigns* `cursor: none`. *This allows the canvas to display its own mouse cursor, but only while the mouse is pressed down.*

**Note:** *If you want to know where the user clicked and released the mouse button, you must detect its offset position in the canvas. This is described on the next page.*

```
68          function onMouseDown(event) {
69            event.preventDefault();
70            if ( event.button == 0 ) {
71              canvas.addEventListener('mousemove', onMouseMove, false);
72              canvas.addEventListener('mouseup', onMouseUp, false);
73              $('canvas').addClass('no-cursor');
74            }
75          }
76
77          function onMouseMove(event) {
78          }
79
80          function onMouseUp(event) {
81            canvas.removeEventListener('mousemove', onMouseMove, false);
82            canvas.removeEventListener('mouseup', onMouseUp, false);
83            $('canvas').removeClass('no-cursor');
84          }
85
```

## EXTRA

Unregistering the events during `mouseup` ensures that the browser will not send unrelated mouse activity to your midworkflow listener functions. Remember that the mouse workflow always begins with `mousedown`, may contain multiple `mousemoves`, and always ends with a single `mouseup`. In the example here, the code in step 4 was used to restrict the type of initiating mouse activity that launches this workflow, which is completed by the code in step 8.

If you are interested in scroll wheel actions, they are a little more difficult to respond to. The delta scroll

resolution — the amount of scroll wheel change in a mouse event — is drastically different between browsers and operating systems. Specifically, the delta value on Safari on Mac OS X is ≈20,000 per mouse event, Chrome in Windows is ≈900, and Internet Explorer 9 in Windows is ≈1,400 — and Opera in Windows is ≈120 and on Linux is ≈80, but also has reversed up/down delta direction!

Adomas Paltanavicius wrote a very good article, available at www.adomas.org/javascript-mouse-wheel/, that tries to make sense of this problem. The article is a little outdated, but it still applies today to the HTML5 canvas.

continued ▶ 207

When an event launches your *onEventFunction*, an event object parameter is provided that details the contextual information associated with the mouse event. As such, the event object contains several properties that allow you to identify exactly where and what the user clicked:

- event.screenX, event.screenY — The click location relative to the user's monitor.
- event.clientX, event.clientY — The click location relative to the user's browser window.
- event.pageX, event.pageY — The click location relative to the web page.
- event.offsetX, event.offsetY — The click location relative to the target element.
- event.ctrlKey, event.shiftKey, event.altKey, event.metaKey — Booleans that specify whether the Ctrl, Shift, Alt, or meta (⌥ or ⌘) keys were pressed in tandem with the mouse button.

- event.button — An integer indicating which mouse button was pressed: 0 for primary, 1 for middle, 2 for secondary.

In the context of a canvas click, the location you will be interested in is event.offsetX and event.offsetY. These properties will always indicate where the user clicked relative to the top-left origin point of the canvas itself, regardless of where the canvas element appears in the browser window.

Unfortunately, not all browsers provide event.offsetX and event.offsetY, so they require you to calculate this yourself by subtracting the canvas element's offset location by event.pageX and event.pageY. What complicates things is that the process to determine an element's offset location also differs by browser. Fortunately, jQuery's offset() method can be used to easily identify the canvas element's offset, which helps you calculate event.offsetX and event.offsetY as a fallback.

## Track Mouse Activity on the Canvas (continued)

### Identify Where the User Clicked

**11** Type **canvasOffset = $( 'canvas#surface' ).offset();**.

**Note:** *jQuery's* offset() *method runs on page load and window resize, but the actual offset calculation (in step 13) must be repeated for each mouse event.*

**12** Type **var x = event.offsetX** and **var y = event.offsetY** to get the event's coordinates relative to the canvas element.

**13** Type **|| event.pageX - canvasOffset.left;** and **|| event.pageY - canvasOffset.top;** as fallback calculations for the offsetX and offsetY values.

**14** Add functionality that occurs when the mouse moves while pressed down.

**Note:** *Duplicate steps 12 and 13 in the* onMouseDown *and* onMouseUp *functions if required.*

**A** In this example, onMouseDown and onMouseMove perform the same canvas functionality. This is why the former calls the latter.

```
72         canvas.addEventListener('mouseup', onMouseUp, false);
73         $('canvas').addClass('no-cursor');
74       }
75     }
76
77     var canvasOffset = $('canvas#surface').offset();
78     window.addEventListener('resize', function() {
79       canvasOffset = $('canvas#surface').offset();
80     }, false);
81
82     function onMouseMove(event) {
83       var x = event.offsetX || event.pageX - canvasOffset.left;
84       var y = event.offsetY || event.pageY - canvasOffset.top;
85
86
87     function onMouseUp(event) {
```

```
68     function onMouseDown(event) {
69       event.preventDefault();
70       if ( event.button == 0 ) {
71         canvas.addEventListener('mousemove', onMouseMove, false);
72         canvas.addEventListener('mouseup', onMouseUp, false);
73         $('canvas').addClass('no-cursor');
74         onMouseMove(event);
75       }
76     }
77
78     var canvasOffset = $('canvas#surface').offset();
79     window.addEventListener('resize', function() {
80       canvasOffset = $('canvas#surface').offset();
81     }, false);
82
83     function onMouseMove(event) {
84       var x = event.offsetX || event.pageX - canvasOffset.left;
85       var y = event.offsetY || event.pageY - canvasOffset.top;
86
87       // Adjust (x,y) to the top-left corner of the zoom-box. This
88       // centers the zoom-box at the user's click point.
89       x -= ~~(zoom/2);
90       y -= ~~(zoom/2);
91
92       context.clearRect(0, 0, context.canvas.width,
93           context.canvas.height);
94       context.drawImage(tux, 0, 0);
95       magnifyImage(x, y, 40, 40);
96     }
97
```

```
92,1                                    51%
```

**15** Save your HTML or JavaScript file.

**16** Load your HTML file in an HTML5 web browser.

The canvas image's default state is drawn on the browser: Nothing has been clicked.

**17** Click once on the canvas image.

Ⓑ The canvas responds to the `mousedown` and `mouseup` events.

**18** Click and drag across the canvas image.

Ⓒ The canvas responds to the `mousedown` and `mousemove` events.

**Note:** *In this example, the magnified image updates as the mouse cursor drags across the original image.*

**19** Let go of the mouse button.

The canvas responds to the `mouseup` event. Subsequent `mousemove` and `mouseup` events over the canvas are ignored.

## EXTRA

Be aware of touch-sensitive mobile devices with HTML5 browsers — specifically, the Android and iOS tablets and phones. Although they do trigger `mouseclick`, `mousedown`, and `mouseup` events, there are no `mouseover`, `mousemove`, or `mouseout` events. This will make developing touch and drag a little different — and hovering impossible. Instead, these browsers implement `touchstart`, `touchmove`, and `touchend`, with a slightly more complicated event object structure that is required to add multitouch support.

The term *multitouch* refers to multiple touch events that are tracked independently, like multiple mouse pointers. This provides new functionality gestures, like

pinch-to-zoom, and double- or triple-finger scrolling. You can technically provide this functionality on your website for your mobile phone and tablet users, but this requires you to monitor events simultaneously and calculate relative distances and movement between each finger within the touchable area.

A blog post by Ross Boucher provides a very good example of a *single touch*-to-mouse event shim, available at http://ross.posterous.com/2008/08/19/iphone-touch-events-in-javascript/. He demonstrates how to translate `touchstart` and `touchmove` events into `mousedown` and `mousemove` activity. The post focuses on the iPhone platform but transfers seamlessly to the Android.

The *origin,* the name for the point at (0, 0), is in the top-left corner of the canvas element. Whereas this works well enough if you are just starting out drawing on the canvas — increase x to go right, increase y to go down — it does make things a little more difficult to understand if you have multiple objects to draw together as a group, especially if that group is positioned at multiple relative locations on the canvas.

In fact, this will become a major problem when you start working with canvas animations. Imagine that you have a group of shapes that make up a character in a game, and the character moves from right to left on the screen. You could calculate the absolute x and y coordinates for all points to build the character, at every location along the

character's travel path, but this is too much work and prone to errors.

To help with this problem, you can translate the location of the origin to a new point on the canvas. Then when you draw your character, you do not need to calculate the position of the head, body, arms, and legs separately; you just code it once, relative to the origin, and simply move the origin around when you want to move the character.

```
context.translate(x,y);
```

When you draw your objects, you can simply leave the origin at its new location or move it back to the top left. Either way works; it does not matter — that is, unless you are animating and need to constantly save and restore the baseline coordinates in a stack array, as described below.

## Translate the X- and Y-Axes

**1** Open an HTML or JavaScript file with a canvas and 2D context variables loaded.

*Note: In this example, a grid layout is drawn in the canvas to demonstrate the location of the (0, 0) origin and the size and layout of the drawing area.*

**2** Draw a shape at coordinates (100, 100).

**3** Save your HTML or JavaScript file.

**4** Load your HTML file in an HTML5 web browser.

**A** The (0, 0) point appears in the top-left corner of the canvas element.

**B** The shape is placed at the point (100, 100).

*Note: In this example, arcs will automatically center on the point used.*

**5** Go back to your HTML or JavaScript file.

**6** Type **context.translate(x, y);** before calling any drawing methods, moving the origin to the coordinates (x, y).

**7** Save your HTML or JavaScript file.

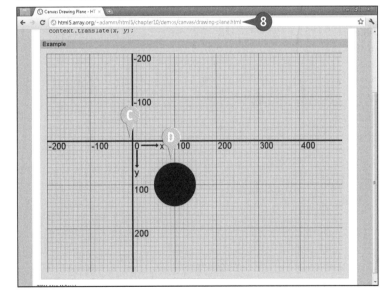

**8** Load your HTML file in an HTML5 web browser.

**C** The origin has moved to the new location.

**D** The shape created at (100, 100) is offset by the origin point change.

You can translate the origin as many times as required while drawing on the canvas. This is particularly useful if you have a complex object, such as a person, that you want to move across the screen. Rather than redraw each individual component, draw it once relative to (0, 0) and then move the origin point where you want the character to move.

Fortunately, the methods `save()` and `restore()` can be used to save a backup of the current drawing settings

and then restore them all when done. Multiple backups can be stored and retrieved in a LIFO (last in, first out) order.

Unfortunately, there is no way to retrieve what the current translate point is. So be careful when nesting multiple context saves and restores; make sure that you have the same number of each. It can get very confusing, and you may get lost in case you miss a `restore()` somewhere in the middle of your program.

You can rotate the entire canvas two-dimensional drawing plane, which makes drawing objects at a specific angle much easier as the number line the x- and y-axes follow is actually altered. For example, rotating a 100 x 100 canvas by 45° will move point (0, 100) from the far right, to the near bottom-right corner; point (50, 50) moves from the exact center to the middle of the left-side border.

Regardless of whether you need to rotate a shape 180°, 45°, or 1°, do not spend your time calculating the shape's absolute coordinates rotated at an angle; just rotate the axes themselves.

All rotations occur around the origin point. Therefore, unless you first use `translate()`, your rotation will pivot around the top left of the canvas. The rotation direction itself moves clockwise and must be specified in radians:

```
context.translate(x,y);
context.rotate(radians);
```

If you prefer to work in degrees and cannot remember how to specify radians from your high school trigonometry days, note that 1° is equal to $\pi/180$, or written in JavaScript, `Math.PI/180`. Therefore, 90° is `90*Math.PI/180`, which can be simplified to `Math.PI/2`.

The `save()` and `restore()` methods apply to the `rotate()` method, too. It is usually a good idea to run `save()` just before you manipulate the drawing plane and then run `restore()` when you are done.

## Rotate the X- and Y-Axes

**1** Open an HTML or JavaScript file with a canvas and 2D context variables loaded.

**2** Type **context.translate( context. canvas.width/2, context.canvas. height/2);** to move the origin point to the center of the canvas.

**Note:** *Rotating always pivots around the origin point.*

**3** Draw a shape at coordinates (100, 100).

**4** Save your HTML or JavaScript file.

**5** Load your HTML file in an HTML5 web browser.

**Ⓐ** The origin appears in the center of the `canvas` element.

**Ⓑ** The shape appears relative to the origin.

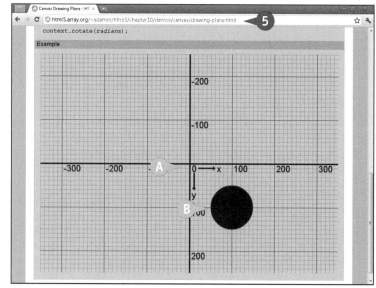

**6** Go back to your HTML or JavaScript file.

**7** Type **context.rotate(*radians*);** before calling any drawing methods to rotate the xy plane clockwise.

**Note:** *Math.PI/6 in radians is 30°.*

**8** Save your HTML or JavaScript file.

**9** Load your HTML file in an HTML5 web browser.

**C** The axes are rotated clockwise by the radian amount specified.

**D** The shape created is also rotated, pivoting on the origin point.

```
81      if (canvas.getContext) {
82          var context = canvas.getContext('2d');
83
84          context.translate(context.canvas.width/2, context.canvas.height/2);
85          context.rotate(Math.PI/6);
86          drawGridLayout(context);
87
88          context.beginPath();
```

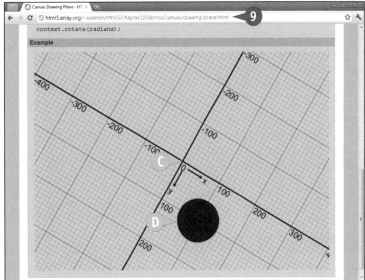

---

## APPLY IT

The JavaScript `Math` object contains a multitude of functions for working with angles and performing trigonometric operations. `Math.atan2(y,x)` returns the angle of direction of any point.

**TYPE THIS**

```
context.rotate(Math.atan2(100,200));
```

→

**RESULT**

The canvas plane is rotated as the x-axis crosses through the point (200, 100), an angle of roughly 0.46364 radians, or about 26.5°. Note that `Math.atan2()` first requires the y coordinate and then x, unlike most functions.

If you are more familiar with degrees than radians, you can follow this conversion chart to help you identify a radian representation for commonly used angles that is simpler than `degrees*Math.PI/180`.

| Degrees | Radians | Degrees | Radians |
|---------|---------|---------|---------|
| 0 | 0 | 90 | Math.PI/2 |
| 30 | Math.PI/6 | 180 | Math.PI |
| 45 | Math.PI/4 | 270 | 3*Math.PI/2 |
| 60 | Math.PI/3 | 360 | 2*Math.PI |

**B**efore you can begin creating animations on the canvas, it is important to understand the correct way to time your animations in HTML5 web browsers.

Prior to HTML5, JavaScript animations relied on the `setTimeout()` and `setInterval()` functions. These allowed you to create asynchronous pseudo-threads — not true process threads, which are discussed in Chapter 16, "Running Secondary JavaScript Threads Using Web Workers" — that split the JavaScript flow. One problem was that they were active regardless of the browser's current visible state: If you opened a website with an active animation in one tab and then navigated to another tab, the animation would still be active in the CPU, calculating and updating a hidden browser window. Furthermore, exact timing was never precise, and a consistently smooth frame rate was nearly impossible.

Mozilla developed a solution, `mozRequestAnimation Frame()`. This allows the JavaScript to notify the web browser to say, "I have something to animate," and the web browser can coordinate the animation frame with the UI refresh rate. The end result is smoother animations that automatically pause when the browser's display is hidden on-screen.

WebKit has also jumped on board with this idea, creating `webkitRequestAnimationFrame()`.

Because this is not yet an official API specification — there is no `requestAnimationFrame()` function — you will need to create a JavaScript shim to call the correct function per browser. This will check which browser-specific function is available and runs accordingly or automatically falls back to the legacy functionality — in this case, `setTimeout()`.

This shim technique comes courtesy of a blog post by Google employee Paul Irish at http://paulirish.com/2011/ requestanimationframe-for-smart-animating/. It is important to note that this new function is not canvas specific. You can use it for any type of JavaScript animation in any web browser.

## Create Animations on the Canvas

### Build an Animation Frame Shim

1. In a JavaScript file, type **window. requestAnimFrame = (function(){** to declare the shim function as `requestAnimFrame()`.

2. Type **})();** to close the shim function.

3. Type **return window. requestAnimationFrame ||.**

*Note: By stating the anticipated name for the function first, your shim will automatically default to it when the implementation is standardized and web browsers have it implemented.*

4. Type **window. webkitRequestAnimationFrame ||.**

5. Type **window. mozRequestAnimationFrame ||.**

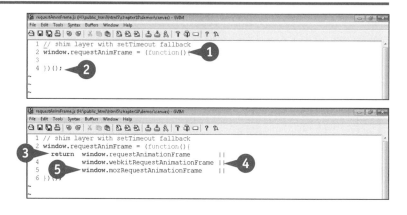

**6** Type **window.
oRequestAnimationFrame ||.**

**7** Type **window.
msRequestAnimationFrame ||.**

**Note:** *These Opera and Microsoft versions of* requestAnimationFrame() *may not exist today, but they may in the future before the specification is finalized.*

**8** Type **function(callback, element)
{ };.**

**Note:** *Because* setTimeout *accepts a timeout parameter, it must be called inside an anonymous function that manages the callback and a minimal timeout value.*

**9** Type **window.setTimeout(callback,
1000/60);** to fall back to the legacy function.

**Note:** *The timeout value used is 16.67 milliseconds. This is roughly the fastest value that legacy browsers can support without overloading the CPU.*

**10** Save your JavaScript shim file as requestAnimFrame.js.

```
1 // shim layer with setTimeout fallback
2 window.requestAnimFrame = (function(){
3   return  window.requestAnimationFrame      ||
4           window.webkitRequestAnimationFrame ||
5           window.mozRequestAnimationFrame    ||
6           window.oRequestAnimationFrame      ||
7           window.msRequestAnimationFrame     ||
8 })();
```

```
1 // shim layer with setTimeout fallback
2 window.requestAnimFrame = (function(){
3   return  window.requestAnimationFrame      ||
4           window.webkitRequestAnimationFrame ||
5           window.mozRequestAnimationFrame    ||
6           window.oRequestAnimationFrame      ||
7           window.msRequestAnimationFrame     ||
8           function(/* function */ callback, /* DOMElement */ element){
9               window.setTimeout(callback, 1000 / 60);
10          };
11 })();
```

Although requestAnimationFrame() assumes that you want the absolute fastest animation frame rate available, basically 60fps, its implementation supersedes the original setTimeout() and setInterval() functionality in which a very small delay could be used to hit a number that was close enough to a full frame rate.

Now that the frame-rate problem is solved, at least for some browsers, the original purpose of setTimeout() and setInterval() got ignored. These functions provided a simple way to set up an arbitrary delay before executing an asynchronous function.

So how can you restore the convenience of this delay, yet take advantage of the requestAnimationFrame() features? You can do so with the help of Joe Lambert's extension to Paul Irish's

shim, which you can view at the GitHub Gist page at https://gist.github.com/1002116/.

Highlight Joe's requestInterval.js and requestTimeout.js code — the functions requestInterval(), clearRequestInterval(), requestTimeout(), and clearRequestTimeout() — and copy and paste it into your requestAnimFrame.js.

Joe gives some background to his design in his blog post "A better setTimeout()/setInterval()" on his web page at http://blog.joelambert.co.uk/2011/06/01/a-better-settimeoutsetinterval/.

The implementation is exactly the same as the venerable setTimeout(), clearTimeout(), setInterval(), and clearInterval().

continued

Now that you can create fast and efficient animation frames, thanks to Paul Irish's `requestAnimFrame()` shim described on the previous page, you can now apply movement into your canvas drawing.

Basic animations consist of four distinct stages:

1 Draw the initial frame — This creates the initial setup of the canvas "scene" using all the techniques described throughout this chapter. Here you may also run any precalculation and initialization routines that will make the second stage run more efficiently.

2 Calculate the next frame — In order to achieve smooth animations, you must not spend any more time calculating the next frame than you have to. Here you calculate the changed objects' positions, prepare any new images for display, and process any user interaction events.

3 Clear the current frame — Depending on how the current and next frame differ, you may need to clear any objects or drawing relics if their presence interferes with the overall animation effect. Try to avoid running `clearRect()` on the entire canvas plane, as this could slow down the next stage.

4 Draw the next frame — You can now update the canvas plane with the second stage's calculations. You should try to recycle as much of the previous frame as possible by not redrawing objects that have not changed in this frame. Again, to achieve the fastest frame rate possible, spend as little time here as necessary.

After the cycle is complete, you can choose to continue the animation process by looping back to the second step, calculation, repeating the animation process indefinitely. Or you can simply let your JavaScript program finish naturally; end your animation by leaving the final frame active on the canvas.

## Create Animations on the Canvas (continued)

### Loop an Animation Function

① Open an HTML file with a `canvas` element declared.

② Type **<script type='text/javascript' src='requestAnimFrame.js'></script>** to import the frame-animation shim.

③ Go to a `<script type='text/ javascript'>` block or a JavaScript file loaded after the Animation Frame shim with a canvas and 2D context variables loaded.

④ Insert JavaScript code that runs once and initializes the canvas animation as stage 1.

⑤ Type **function *animateObject()* {** to define the animation loop.

⑥ Type **calculateObject();** to run stage 2 and store its results in global variables.

⑦ Type **clearObject();** to erase the object's previous frame position for stage 3.

**Note:** For efficiency, ensure that `clearObject()` only clears the "changing" object area of the canvas and avoid clearing the entire canvas plane if possible.

**8** Type **drawObject();** to draw the object's new frame for stage 4.

**9** Type **requestAnimFrame ( animateObject );** to create a controlled infinite animation loop inside of *animateObject()*.

**Note:** *This will create the fastest-possible animation speed. To slow it down, use* requestTimeout(*animateObject*, 50) *to delay each frame by at least 50 ms.*

**10** Type **animateObject();** back in stage 1 to launch the animation loop.

**11** Save your JavaScript or HTML files.

**12** Load your HTML file in an HTML5 web browser.

**A** The animation process loop launches.

**13** Open the Task Manager or Activity Monitor.

**B** This shows the overall animation CPU load.

**Note:** *Minimize your web browser. The CPU load will drop as the animation process is frozen. Had you used* setTimeout(), *the animation CPU would have started higher and remain high even while minimized.*

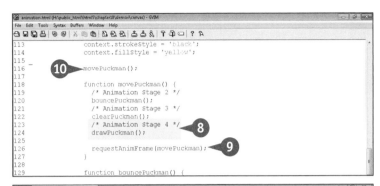

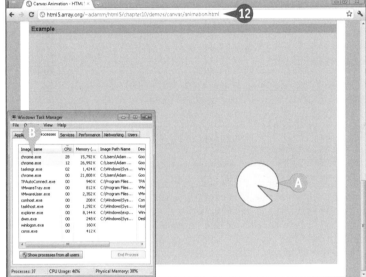

## EXTRA

The clear stage 3 comes after the calculate stage 2 to reduce any potential flickering; however, the calculate stage may produce new $x$ and $y$ values that are of no use to the clear stage. Therefore, the calculate stage must first back up $x$ and $y$ so that the clear stage knows where to work.

You can create concurrent animation loops running at different rates by duplicating steps 5 to 10 here with different function names. You can then use a different delay in step 9 to create independently moving animation objects. Note, however, that if the independent loops control of the same object, they will need to share the same stage 3 and stage 4 processes.

For example, in this "Puckman" animation, you can make the character object bounce across the screen at one frame rate but open and close his mouth at a slightly faster frame rate. Because the entire character is redrawn after either a move or chomp frame change, both loops call clearObject() and drawObject(). In turn, these functions know how to handle a move or chomp frame change by accessing the calculated values for both animations.

The completed Puckman example can be viewed at http://html5.array.org/demos/canvas/animation.html.

# Introducing HTML5 Audio and Video

HTML5 audio and video provide the means for you to deploy rich content on your website without requiring any third-party plug-in. Support is already available not only in HTML5 web browsers, but also in many of today's mobile devices. This means that with very little effort you can post movies and music online for your users to view or listen to on nearly any modern platform or device.

The complete HTML5 video specification can be found on the WHATWG page at www.whatwg.org/specs/web-apps/current-work/multipage/the-video-element.html.

## HTML5 Video and Flash Video

Prior to HTML5, Adobe Flash was the standard platform for delivering rich multimedia content online, partly thanks to the rise of websites like YouTube. Although Flash required a third-party plug-in, developing animations and content was relatively easy, and its capability to play video right in the browser was unmatched.

However, citing reliability, security, and performance problems with the Flash cross-platform development environment, web browser developers started to weigh the pros and cons of using Flash, especially on mobile devices. They found that better battery life, hardware-based video decoding, and vector graphic animations could all be offered by the browser directly, using the standards developed under the HTML5 banner.

An essay written by Steve Jobs in April 2010 sums up Apple's decision to drop Flash on the iPhone and develop HTML5 and is available at Apple's web page www.apple.com/hotnews/thoughts-on-flash/.

## <video>...</video>

The `<video>` tag group defines where in a web page that a video object will appear. There are two ways to define the video source content. First, a single movie file can be used in the `src` attribute, described here. The second involves moving the `src` attribute into the `<source>` tag, as described later in this section in the subsection "<source>."

```
<video src='moviefile.format' attributes>
   Fallback content
</video>
```

The contents within the `<video>` tag group will be used as fallback content for browsers that do not support the HTML5 `video` element. This can be a Flash-based movie playback program, a static image of the movie, or even a hyperlink to download the video file.

The following optional attributes can be specified within the `<video>` tag itself:

- `src='file'` — Specifies the movie file to play. Cannot be used in tandem with the `<source>` tag.

- `width='value'`, `height='value'` — Set an initial width and height of the `video` element prior to playing. Also, they will scale the video while playing. These are strongly recommended because the website layout will shift around when preload or playback starts as the element is adjusted to the movie's actual dimensions.

- `poster='image'` — Sets an image to appear within the `video` element prior to playback, akin to a movie poster. Note that `poster` is mostly useful if `preload='none'`; when `preload` is active, the first frame automatically becomes the poster image.

- preload='*state*' — Controls how the movie file will download into the web browser when the page first loads. Values for *state* are none, which suggests that no predownload should occur; metadata, which suggests that the video dimensions, first frame, track list, audio channels, and duration are downloaded automatically; and auto, which suggests that the movie download can begin as soon as possible. Note that the suggestions indicated by this attribute are merely that; there is no requirement for a web browser to follow them.

- autoplay — A Boolean attribute that states the movie may automatically play when enough data has been downloaded to buffer playback without stopping. Automatically sets preload='auto'. Again, this may be ignored by some web browsers, such as those found on mobile devices.

- controls — A Boolean attribute that indicates the web browser can use its built-in user-interface overlay to control video playback and volume control. Do not use this if you plan on providing your own video interface controls.

- loop — A Boolean to restart the video when it reaches the end of playback.

- muted — A Boolean to mute the volume by default when playback starts.

## <audio>...</audio>

The <audio> tag group defines where in a web page an audio object will appear. As with the video element, there are two ways to define the audio source content, in the element itself or with the <source> tag, described later in "<source>":

```
<audio src='soundfile.format' attributes>
   Fallback content
</audio>
```

The contents within the <audio> tag group will be used as fallback content for browsers that do not support the HTML5 audio element. This can be a Flash-based sound playback program or a hyperlink to download the audio file.

The following optional attributes can be specified within the <audio> tag:

- src='*file*' — Specifies the sound file to play. Cannot be used in tandem with the <source> tag.

- preload, autoplay, controls, and loop — These attributes have the same functionality as described in the "<video>...</video>" subsection.

## <source>

The <source> tag can be used within either the <video> or <audio> tag groups. It replaces the single-file src attribute, allowing you to specify multiple source files along with a MIME type and codec. The browser can then make an informed decision as to which file format it understands best without having to download each file:

```
<video attributes>
   <source src='moviefile.format1' type='mimetype1'>
   <source src='moviefile.format2' type='mimetype2'>
   <source src='moviefile.format3' type='mimetype3'>
   Fallback content
</video>
```

This is the most ideal way to specify video and audio in HTML5 as not all web browsers understand every major format. However, it is more work to produce because the same file needs to be converted up to three formats.

# Understanding Audio and Video Formats

The audio and video data that is stored within sound and movie files are produced, stored, and retrieved using different multimedia formats. However, the word *format* is an oversimplification: The proper way to identify a sound and movie file is by its container and its codecs.

## Containers and Codecs

A *container* is like an envelope for the audio and video found within sound and movie files. It determines how many audio and video data streams are stored and how they can be retrieved. The data stream itself is compressed using either an audio or video codec. The container typically determines the media file's extension.

### Movie Containers

A movie container usually houses one video data stream and one or more audio data streams:

- The OGG (*.ogv) movie container is a freely usable container format that can technically house any type of codec; however, it is most commonly used with Theora for video and Vorbis for audio.

- The WebM (*.webm) movie container is also a freely usable container format, but this version was only first released by Google in May 2010 as an efficient way to deliver HTML5 video. Despite its age, it is one of the better-supported formats among HTML5 web browsers. It uses the VP8 video codec and Vorbis audio codec.

- The MP4 (*.mp4) movie container, also known as MPEG-4 Part 14, is the latest version of MPEG video and audio files developed since 1988. Although not a free container, it tends to support other nonfree codecs, such as H.264, MP3, and AAC.

### Video Codecs

The *video codec* determines how visual data is compressed and decompressed in a movie container. Usually, only one video codec data stream exists in a container:

- Theora is a freely usable video codec designed for the OGG container. It is designed to offer a free and comparable alternative to the MPEG video formats.

- VP8 is also a freely usable video codec, released alongside the WebM container. It was originally developed and patented by On2 Technologies, and Google released the specification under the Creative Commons license after its purchase of On2.

- H.264 is the video codec most often used in MP4 movie containers. It offers excellent compression and is the standard on Blu-ray, Adobe Flash, Microsoft Silverlight, and other online streaming services such as YouTube, Hulu, and Netflix. A license is required to produce a program that can encode and decode with H.264, but no license is required to use such a program or play back a file when used on the Internet.

### Sound Containers and Audio Codecs

Often, a sound container and a sound codec are defined by the same format standard. This is the case of OGG Vorbis (*.ogg) and MPEG-1 Audio Layer III (*.mp3).

- Vorbis (*.ogg) is a freely usable audio codec designed for the OGG container and was developed as an alternative to the MPEG audio formats.

- The MP3 (*.mp3) sound container and codec is an older but more widely supported format. First popularized in 1998, it is not as efficient as most of today's audio codecs, but it remains popular, especially on mobile devices.

- The AAC (*.m4a, *.aac) sound codec is stored in the same container as MP4 but as an audio-only file. The AAC codec was produced as a successor to the MP3 format; it is more efficient and offers much better quality output. It too is encumbered by the same style of patents as the MP3 format.

- The WAV (*.wav) sound container typically holds raw and uncompressed audio streams stored as the PCM (pulse-code modulation) codec.

## HTML5 Browser Support

There are different levels of support for each video and audio file. Choosing which one to encode your multimedia presentation in is based on your target market.

### HTML5 Video Formats

Here are the main video formats — codecs, plus containers in parentheses — supported by the major HTML5 web browsers.

| Browser Version | Theora (OGG) | VP8 (WebM) | H.264 (MP4) |
|---|---|---|---|
| Chrome | 3.0+ | 6.0+ | No* |
| Firefox | 3.5+ | 4.0+ | No |
| Internet Explorer | No† | No† | 9.0+ |
| Opera | 10.5+ | 10.6+ | No |
| Safari | No‡ | No§ | 3.1+ |

### HTML5 Audio Formats

Here are the "out-of-the-box" formats supported by the major HTML5 web browsers. Because all browsers support at least Vorbis or MP3, you only really need to encode your sound files in these two formats.

| Browser Version | Vorbis | MP3 | AAC | WAV |
|---|---|---|---|---|
| Chrome | 3.0+ | 3.0+ | No* | 3.0+ |
| Chromium** | 3.0+ | No | No | 3.0+ |
| Firefox | 3.5+ | No | No | 3.5+ |
| Internet Explorer | No† | 9.0+ | No | No |
| Opera | 10.5+ | No | No | 10.5+ |
| Safari | No‡ | 3.0+ | 3.0+ | No |

+ Or later.

* Google has removed H.264/AAC support for Chrome, but Windows Chrome users can restore it with the help of the Microsoft WMP HTML5 Extension for Chrome, available at the Interoperability Bridges and Labs Center at www.interoperabilitybridges.com/wmp-extension-for-chrome.

** Chromium, the open-sourced version of Chrome that is not produced by Google, is on this list because it has a different level of support than Chrome.

† Internet Explorer can support Theora, Vorbis, and VP8 with the help of the OpenCodecs DirectShow filter, available from Xiph.org at http://xiph.org/dshow/.

‡ Safari can support Theora and Vorbis with the help of the OpenCodecs QuickTime component, available from Xiph.org at http://xiph.org/quicktime/.

§ Safari can support VP8 with the help of a WebM QuickTime component, available from Google Code at https://code.google.com/p/webm/downloads/.

**I**f you already own the rights to post a movie file online, or at least the inclination, it is quite likely that its audio and video will need to be changed into a format that is more appropriate for HTML5 web browsers. This process, called *reencoding,* involves a software program that is capable of decoding — or more simply, playing — the existing audio and video streams and then encoding the playback into a new format.

There are dozens if not hundreds of free programs available online that can do this. One program that is particularly user-friendly is called the *Miro Video Converter,* produced by the same developers who wrote Miro (www.getmiro.com), an open-sourced music and video player.

The Miro Video Converter (MVC) is available for the Windows and Mac OS X platforms. It is very easy to install and use and actually acts as a front end for one of the most powerful multimedia toolboxes available, FFmpeg.

MVC installs a copy of FFmpeg, itself an open-source program that performs the actual video and audio conversion. Essentially, MVC is a front end for FFmpeg's myriad of command-line options. If you want to produce a custom encoding process, you can always run FFmpeg from the command line.

For more information on how to interact with FFmpeg directly, you can peruse the FFmpeg Documentation web page at http://ffmpeg.org/ffmpeg-doc.html.

## Install a Movie Encoder

### Download the Miro Video Converter

**1** Go to the Miro page at www.mirovideoconverter.com.

**2** Click Download Miro Video Converter (for Windows).

**OR**

**2** Click Download MVC for Mac OS X (for Mac OS X).

**Note:** *Depending on your browser, you may be warned that this type of download can harm your computer.*

**3** Click Keep (or Save) if prompted.

The MVC installer downloads onto your computer.

Install the Miro Video Converter
in Windows

① Launch the MVC installer.

② Click Browse and select a
different installation directory,
if preferred.

③ Keep clicking Next to proceed
through the installation screens.

④ Click Close to close the installer
when completed.

MVC is now installed.

Install the Miro Video Converter
on Mac OS X

① Double-click Miro Video
Converter.

② Click and hold the Miro Video
Converter.app icon.

③ Drop the icon into the
Applications folder.

MVC is now installed.

## APPLY IT

If you want to execute FFmpeg from the command line, you must first locate the directory path to the FFmpeg
executable, depending on your operating system.

**TYPE THIS**

In a Windows Command prompt, run these commands:

```
cd "C:\Program Files\Participatory Culture
  Foundation\Miro Video Converter\ffmpeg-bin"
ffmpeg.exe -version
```

**RESULT**

The output of FFmpeg's version
information on Windows, including
compile-time libraries and configuration.

**TYPE THIS**

In a Mac OS X Terminal, run these commands:

```
cd "/Applications/Miro Video Converter.app/
  Contents/Resources"
ffmpeg -version
```

**RESULT**

The output of FFmpeg's version
information on Mac OS X, including
compile-time libraries and configuration.

After you install the Miro Video Converter (MVC) program, you can put it to work and reencode your movies for HTML5 web browsers. MVC is designed to be very user-friendly and makes it easy to convert your files to the format that you want.

MVC's pull-down menu lists several options for different formats, but for the purposes of this chapter, you should look at Theora, WebM (vp8), and MP4. These represent the top three codecs that all HTML5 browsers best support. There are additional device-specific formats in the list, but their main purpose is to adjust the size of your video for the device display.

Note that if your original video's dimensions are too big to fit in a typical web browser window, you should run your video through a device-specific encoder, such as iPad to scale it to 1024 x 768, iPhone for 640 x 480, and iPod

Touch for 480 x 320, and then convert that to Theora and WebM because it is already in MP4 format. Obviously, this is a highly inefficient way to resize a movie, but if you are just starting out with video, it can get the job done.

When you reencode the same file twice, you will get a lower-quality output from MVC or any other video-conversion program. For this reason, it is always best to work from the original source content with the highest bit rate and lowest compression. Reencoding the same file from one highly compressed format into another will introduce video noise, blurriness, and distortion.

For a listing of the actual FFmpeg command-line options used for each conversion profile, see the Participatory Culture Foundation page at https://develop.participatoryculture.org/index.php/ConversionMatrix.

## Reencode Movies with the Miro Video Converter

1 Click Start ➔ Programs ➔ Miro ➔ Miro Video Converter (or click Applications ➔ Miro Video Converter.app in Mac OS X).

The Miro Video Converter program starts.

2 Click Choose a File.

The Open dialog box appears.

3 Navigate to a movie file and select it.

4 Click Open.

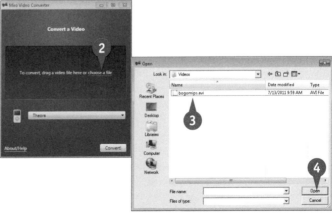

⑤ Click the Video Formats down arrow.

⑥ Click a format: Theora, WebM (vp8), or MP4.

⑦ Click Convert.

The reencoding process begins.

Ⓐ The current progress is displayed.

When completed, the output file will be saved as *movie*.theora.ogv, *movie*. webmvp8.webm, or *movie*.mp4video. mp4 in the same directory as the source.

Optionally, you can rename the output file and remove the MVC profile name, but keep the movie title and the extension name — for example, *movie*.ogv, *movie*. webm, or *movie*.mp4 extension.

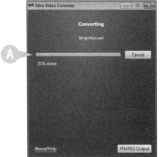

## EXTRA

If there are any problems with the reencoding of your movie, click the **FFMPEG** Output button. This will display a detailed log that summarizes any problems. One such issue that can cause your reencoding process to fail is the audio sample rate, as indicated by this error message:

```
Error while opening encoder for output stream
  #0.1 - maybe incorrect parameters such as bit_
  rate, rate, width or height
```

This means that your movie was using a sound input rate that is not acceptable by MVC and the requested format. Scroll up in the log, and you will see the input format for the audio stream:

```
Stream #0.1: Audio: libvorbis, 22050 Hz, mono,
  s16, 160 kb/s
```

The ideal audio value is **44100 Hz** or higher; anything less, such as **22050** or **8000 Hz**, could cause a failure in converting your file. This appears to be a problem only with the WebM and MP4 formats; Theora seems immune to this problem. Until this bug is fixed in MVC, resample your audio to 44100 Hz first and then pass it through MVC.

If you are still having problems, click the About/Help link and then click the Please Visit Our Get Satisfaction Page link.

After you have your movie encoded in the HTML5-friendly codecs, you are ready to place the video on your web page. You do so by using the `<video>` tag group, its optional attributes, and `<source>` tags — one for each movie file format:

```
<video height='640' width='480'
 poster='image' controls preload>
  <source src='movie.mp4' type='video/mp4;
codecs="avc1.640029,    mp4a.40.2"'>
   <source src='movie.webm' type='video/webm;
codecs="vp8, vorbis"'>
   <source src='movie.ogv' type='video/ogg;
codecs="theora, vorbis"'>
   Fallback display.
</video>
```

Although the `height` and `width` variables are not required, they are highly recommended. Otherwise, only when the video is preloading or starts playing will the element adjust to the video's actual height and width. This results in shifting the website layout to support the larger `video`

element. Because both Android and iOS Safari do not respect the `preload` or `autoplay` attributes, the `height` and `width` should be set to provide a good user experience.

Use `poster` to set an initial image; its size must match `height` and `width`. Otherwise, older versions of Chrome and Safari may fail to scale the image and could crash the browser.

Additional Boolean attributes that you can specify include `controls` for the browser to provide control buttons, `autoplay` to automatically start playing, `muted` to mute volume when played, and `loop` to repeat the playback.

The `<source>` tag's src attribute defines each file format the movie is encoded with. Its `type` attribute declares files' MIME type and codec.

The content within the `<video>` tag group is automatically used as a fallback for non-HTML5 web browsers.

## Play Movies with the HTML5 video Element

**①** In an HTML file, type **<video width='640' height='480' controls>** to create a video object 640 pixels wide by 480 tall that uses the browser's built-in controls.

**②** Insert fallback content to appear if the HTML5 `<video>` tag is not supported.

**③** Type **</video>**.

**Ⓐ** Optionally, type **preload='state'** to set a movie preload state of `auto`, `metadata`, or `none`.

**Note:** If `preload` is used without a value or if no `preload` is used at all, it defaults to `metadata`.

**Note:** If `autoplay` is used, `preload` is set to `auto`.

**Ⓑ** Optionally, type **poster='image'** to set a default image to appear before the video starts.

**Note:** Defining a poster on Safari 5 and Internet Explorer 9 will flash and then hide the poster image, caused by preloading the video. This can be fixed if you use `preload='none'`.

④ Type **<source src='*movie*.mp4'
type='video/mp4; codecs=
"avc1.640029, mp4a.40.2"'>** to
add an H.264 MP4 file.

**Note:** *iPhones and iPads prior to iOS 4.0
required the MP4 file to be the first
resource; otherwise, no video would play.*

⑤ Type **<source src='*movie*.webm'
type='video/webm; codecs="vp8,
vorbis"'>** to add a WebM (vp8) file.

⑥ Type **<source src='*movie*.ogv'
type='video/ogg; codecs="theora,
vorbis"'>** to add an Ogg Theora file.

⑦ Save your HTML file.

⑧ Load your HTML file in a web
browser.

The movie's poster image appears.

Ⓒ The movie control buttons appear.

**Note:** *The built-in control layout appears
different for each HTML5 web browser.*

⑨ Click the Play button.

The movie starts to play back.

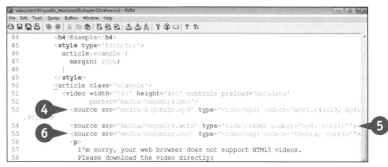

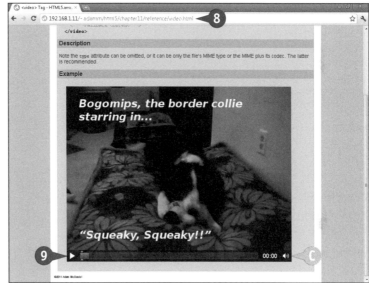

---

## EXTRA

If you originally used the iPhone MVC profile to
create your H.264 video, you should specify a different
codec value in its `<source>` tag. Replace your
`<source ... type='video/mp4'>`'s `codecs` value
with the following for the iPhone MVC profile video
file: `codecs="avc1.42E01E, mp4a.40.2"`. The
original video codec string, `avc1.640029`, describes
an H.264 high flavor video, whereas `avc1.42E01E`
describes an H.264 baseline flavor video.

Niall Kennedy wrote a very good article on his blog
that demystifies H.264 flavors, levels, and features, at
www.niallkennedy.com/blog/2010/07/h264-video.html.

For HTML5, you may assume that because different
platforms support different codecs better, you could
specify multiple `<source type='video/mp4'>` lines
and deliver a high-definition H.264 movie to desktops
and a standard-definition H.264 movie to mobile
devices. Unfortunately, this is not possible. All browsers
that support H.264 will attempt to play the first MP4
movie listed in `<source>`, regardless of the declared
codec. So, if you use the MP4 profile, the iPhone and
iPad will use more processor power than necessary to
display basically the same thing on a smaller display,
and the iPhone profile on Safari and Internet Explorer 9
will display a lower video quality.

# PLAY SOUND WITH THE HTML5 AUDIO ELEMENT

You can play sound files in HTML5 just as you can movie files. Because the structure and implementation of `<audio>` and `<video>` are so close together, collectively they are referred to as the *media elements*. There are some attributes found in `<video>` that do not apply to `<audio>`, such as `height`, `width`, and `poster`, but everything else, including ensuring that you have the proper encoding of your sound files for each web browser, is basically the same idea:

```
<audio controls preload>
  <source src='music.mp3' type='audio/mpeg'>
  <source src='music.ogg' type='audio/ogg;
 codecs="vorbis"'>
  Insert fallback content here.
</audio>
```

Additional Boolean attributes that you can specify include `controls`, for the browser to provide control buttons, `autoplay` to automatically start playing, and `loop` to repeat the playback.

The `<source>` tag represents the various file formats that the movie is encoded with. Typically, you could specify resource files for MP3, Ogg Vorbis, AAC, WMA, and WAV, with appropriate MIME type values. Note that the MP3 and Ogg Vorbis versions are sufficient to hit all HTML5 web browsers; therefore, there is no need to also create others, especially a WAV format, as its file size could be ten times larger than the others.

The content within the `<audio>` tag group is automatically used as fallback for non-HTML5 web browsers. This space can be used to launch a Flash-based audio player or to display direct download links to the audio files.

## Play Sound with the HTML5 audio Element

① In an HTML file, type **<audio controls>** to create an audio object that uses the browser's built-in controls.

② Insert fallback content to appear if the HTML5 `<audio>` tag is not supported.

③ Type **</audio>**.

Ⓐ Optionally, type `preload='state'` to set a sound file preload state of `auto`, `metadata`, or `none`.

**Note:** If `preload` is used without a value or if no `preload` is used at all, it defaults to `metadata`.

**Note:** If `autoplay` is used, `preload` is set to `auto`.

④ Type **<source src='*sound*.mp3' type='audio/mpeg'>** to add an MP3 file.

⑤ Type **<source src='*sound*.ogg' type='audio/ogg; codecs= "vorbis"'>** to add an Ogg Vorbis file.

⑥ Save your HTML file.

⑦ Load your HTML file in a web browser.

The audio resource loads.

Ⓑ The movie control buttons appear.

⑧ Click the Play button.

The sound file starts to play back.

***Note:*** *The built-in control layout appears different for each HTML5 web browser.*

---

**EXTRA**

Like `<video>`, `<audio>`'s `codecs` parameter is optional. It is recommended for the Ogg container though, as it allows you to specify different audio codecs. Although Vorbis is by far the most popular format for the majority of audio applications, such as music and sound effects, you can use Speex for storing spoken language, such as phone recordings and speeches.

Speex , available at www.speex.org, was originally developed as a free audio compression format for VoIP applications, and as such can only handle mono audio in 8, 16, and 32 kilohertz.

Speex audio files use the .spx extension, but its `audio/x-speex` MIME type is not a part of HTML5. Therefore, you must use its Ogg container MIME type, `audio/ogg`, plus the correct `codec` parameter in your HTML5 web page's `<source>` tag:

```
<source src='mylecture.spx' type='audio/ogg;
  codec="speex"'>
```

As of August 2011, the actual level of browser support for Speex is not great. In fact, only Opera 11.5 supports Speex natively. But if you want to test it out, you will likely experience as much as 40% better compression than Ogg Vorbis.

It may seem pointless to make the `controls` attribute optional in the `<audio>` and `<video>` tags. When omitted, no playback buttons will appear in the web browser. This is actually intentional, as you can still control the playback of either element using some simple JavaScript methods and event listeners.

This moves control over the playback experience from the user to the website itself. Your goal as a web developer should be to only trigger playback when it is appropriate, such as during an HTML5 Canvas game or when chaining playback of multiple video files together.

Before you begin, you must locate the `audio` or `video` element in the JavaScript DOM. The easiest way to do this is to assign the element an `id` attribute and then use `document.getElementById()` to interface with the media object:

```
var video = document.
  getElementById('mymovie');
video.load();
video.play();
```

This simple example has essentially re-created the `autoplay` attribute. The `load()` method will initiate the download of the most appropriate resource, which is required if `preload='none'` or `preload='metadata'`. The `play()` method will trigger the process that starts playback only after enough data has been downloaded. You need to call `load()` only once, but you can call `play()` as many times as you want to play the file. To pause playback, use `pause()`.

The `load()` and `play()` methods run asynchronously through event broadcasters and listeners. They coordinate using the `readyState` property, which stores the current state of the resource download.

## Control Audio and Video Playback with JavaScript

**1** Open an HTML file with jQuery loaded and a `<video>` or `<audio>` tag defined.

**2** Type **<script type='javascript'>**.

**3** Type **var *media* = document.getElement ById('*mymedia*');** to interface with the audio or video element's object.

**4** Type **</script>**.

**5** Type **id='*mymedia*'** to assign the same identifier to the media object used in step **3**.

**6** Type **<button id='play'>*Play*</button>** to create a play button.

**Note:** *In this example, the Play button is used for both starting and pausing playback. Unicode characters represent the play and pause symbols.*

**7** Type **_media_.load();** to begin downloading the video or audio resource.

**8** Type **$('button#play').click(function(){** to tie the play button's `click` event to a function handler.

**9** Type **_media_.play();** to trigger playback.

**10** Type **});**.

⑪ Add a listener function for the `timeupdate` event, triggered when the current time position changes.

⑫ Add a listener function for the `durationchange` event, triggered when the media duration is known.

⑬ Type **~~(this.currentTime)** and **~~(this.duration)** to retrieve the current time and duration in whole seconds.

Ⓐ Optionally, display and update a progress slider and output timestamp with step **13**'s values.

⑭ Save your HTML or JavaScript files.

⑮ Load your HTML file in an HTML5 web browser.

The media file loads without built-in controls.

Ⓑ The custom controls appear.

⑯ Click the play button.

Ⓒ The input gauge and output timestamp change as the media plays.

**Note:** *If you left the* `controls` *attribute active, you would see that the built-in controls and the JavaScript controls are synchronized.*

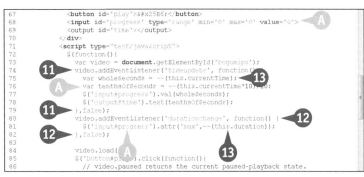

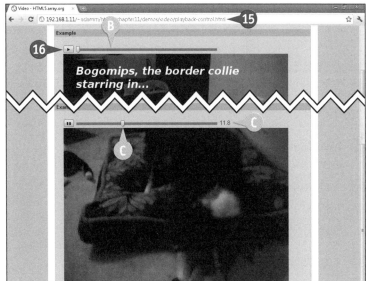

## APPLY IT

The `currentTime` and `duration` properties store timestamps measured in seconds but with 10-15 digits after the decimal point. Because the example here is concerned only with using the seconds value as whole numbers, `~~(number)` is used as a very efficient way to round down and is much faster than `Math.floor()`.

Regarding the playback itself, you may set `currentTime` directly to change the current playback position.

### TYPE THIS

```
$('input#progress').mousedown(function(){video.
  pause()});
$('input#progress').mouseup(function(){video.
  play()});
$('input#progress').change(function(){
  video.currentTime = $(this).val();
  $('output#time').text($(this).val());
});
```

### RESULT

 Clicking the input gauge pauses the video, and sliding the gauge moves `currentTime`, changing the video display in real time. Releasing the gauge restarts video playback at the new `currentTime`.

If you are not satisfied with the built-in player controls offered by your HTML5 web browser and you have no interest in creating your own controls and JavaScript code, you may be interested in a program called *VideoJS*. Produced as an add-on JavaScript program, it not only provides a way for you to create custom video playback controls using nothing but CSS, but also provides a built-in fallback to non-HTML5 browsers to launch a Flash-based video player.

VideoJS requires you to add additional code around your existing `<video>` tag group. This includes wrapping it in a master `<div class='video-js-box'></div>` block and requires you to add some additional class names to the `<video>` tag itself.

If `<video>` is not supported, VideoJS allows for a Flash Video player fallback that must be placed within the `<video>` tag group as a new `<object>` block. If both Flash and HTML5 are not supported by the browser, an additional text block inside of `<object>` can be used to provide video download instructions as a second-level fallback.

To download VideoJS, go to http://videojs.com and click the Download link on the right. You will receive a zip archive that contains the library. Unzip the archive to extract the video.js and video-js.css files and save them into your website directory.

After that, you can begin adding VideoJS to your website.

## Embed a Movie Player with VideoJS

**1** Open an HTML file with a `<video>` element.

**2** Type **`<script type='text/javascript' src='video.js'></script>`** to import the VideoJS library.

**3** Type **`<link rel='stylesheet' type='text/css' media='screen' href='video-js.css'>`** to import the VideoJS CSS.

**4** Type **VideoJS.setupAllWhen Ready();** to activate VideoJS.

**5** Type **`<div class='video-js-box'>`** and **`</div>`** around the `<video>` tag group.

**6** Type **class='video-js'** into the `<video>` tag itself.

**A** Optionally, type **`<object class='vjs-flash-fallback' type='application/x-shockwave-flash' data='`*flashplayer.swf*`'>`** to use a Flash player fallback.

**Note:** *You can use the direct link to Flowplayer, shown in the example. See www.flowplayer.org.*

**B** Optionally, add any additional `<param>` tags required by the Flash player.

⑦ Insert within the `<object>` tag group any fallback content for users who have no HTML5 video and no Flash support.

**Note:** *Simply duplicate the resources specified in your video's `<source>` tags as hyperlinks.*

**Note:** *If you did not use a Flash player fallback, insert step **7**'s code directly under the `<video>` tag group.*

⑧ Save your HTML file.

⑨ Load your HTML file in a web browser.

Ⓒ The new VideoJS control interface appears in the video element, replacing the browser's built-in controls.

**Note:** *Chrome 13 and earlier appears to have problems loading VideoJS movies if the MP4/H.264 format is the first `<source>` referenced. Fortunately, Chrome 14 is not affected by this bug.*

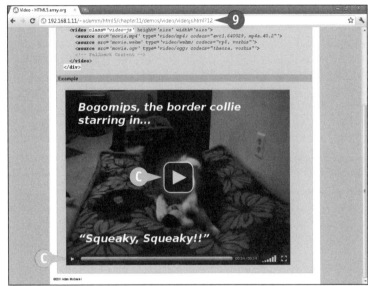

## EXTRA

The VideoJS instructions state the second-level failover block in step 7 should be after the `<video>` block, within `<div class='video-js-box'>`, and use the class `vjs-no-video`. However, due to a bug in how VideoJS hides this failover content, I recommend that you insert the second-level failover within the `<object>` tag, as shown in the example here.

Included in the VideoJS download Zip archive is a `skins` subdirectory. These are samples that you can use to get an idea of how to create your own custom HTML5 video skin.

To install the demo skins, copy the `skins` directory onto your website and type this in after step 3's `<link ...` `href='video-js.css'>`:

```
<link rel='stylesheet' type='text/css'
  media='screen' href='skins/hu.css'>
<link rel='stylesheet' type='text/css'
  media='screen' href='skins/tube.css'>
<link rel='stylesheet' type='text/css'
  href='skins/vim.css' media='screen'>
```

Next, to activate one of the skins — only one can be active at a time — modify step 5 and add one of the new class names: `hu-css`, `hu-tube`, or `hu-vim`:

```
<div class='video-js-box hu-css'>...</div>
```

Save and reload your web page in the browser. VideoJS's `hu-css` theme is applied to your `video` element.

The mouse has always been one of the easiest user interface tools to learn how to use; you just point and click. Unfortunately, some mouse interaction also has been one of the hardest features to support directly in JavaScript, such as identifying what the user is pointing at and which button was clicked. For a long time, websites were forced to instruct the browser as to what the user could click, where it was, and what it did. Anything that did not involve a single left click was overly complicated and inconsistent across browsers.

Eventually, direct mouse detection and control was offered in 2000 with the W3C DOM Level 2 `MouseEvent` object, but not all browsers adopted it properly. This led to cross-browser code complexity and confusion. With every new generation of browsers released, these mouse-related problems are slowly going away, but one mouse-centric staple that was never properly established was the drag-and-drop interface. Operating systems have been using it as early as 1988, but this was off-limits to website developers who did not want to invest in a lot of `MouseEvent` work.

Browsers themselves implemented built-in drag-and-drop features several years ago, such as how dragging an image onto a desktop produces a copy of the image file or how dragging a link onto the tab bar produces a new tab. But websites themselves could not interact directly with the desktop or even provide their own OS-like user interface of icons, trash cans, and what not — that is, they could not until WHATWG included in the HTML5 specification additional attributes and events specifically designed for sites to support drag and drop natively within the web browser itself. Today, websites can allow users to drag and drop one object into any other object, trigger custom-tailored JavaScript commands, and even interact with the desktop, such as when downloading and uploading files.

## Browser Support

The actual web browser support for native HTML5 drag and drop differs, especially among HTML5 web browsers themselves.

### Desktop Browsers

Currently, most of the major HTML5 web browsers support the new HTML5 drag-and-drop attributes and events, except for Opera 11.50.

While Opera is working on the issue, one developer has produced an article that demonstrates a way to emulate drag and drop with the `mousedown`, `mousemove`, and `mouseup` events. Moving beyond the HTML5 specification, the article also explains how accessible rich Internet applications (ARIA) support can be added. Essentially, ARIA allows for users with reduced mobility to navigate a mouse-centric interface using only the keyboard or another device. You can read about Opera's drag-and-drop example with ARIA support at the Dev.Opera page at http://dev.opera.com/articles/view/accessible-drag-and-drop/.

The Opera example does work in other HTML5 web browsers, but again, it does not follow the official HTML5 drag-and-drop specification.

### Mobile Browsers

The whole point-and-click paradigm introduced by the mouse falls apart quickly on mobile devices. There is no mouse, only a touchscreen, so some user interface aspects provided by the mouse are lost. Although touch does open up new user interface doors, some are closed, such as hovering and the scroll wheel.

What is interesting, though, is that you might assume that drag and drop would survive in the mobile realm. The mousedown, mousemove, mouseup events translate perfectly into the touchstart, touchmove, and touchend events. Therefore, HTML5 native drag-and-drop support should be here, yet support is nonexistent in today's HTML5-aware mobile web browsers.

Perhaps one day support will be added. But what is most perplexing is that the HTML5 Test, at www.html5test.com, reports that *some* support exists: The built-in browsers tested on iOS 4.4.3 and Android 3.1 both report support for drag-and-drop *events* but no support for drag-and-drop *attributes,* yet both are required. Strange, but true.

## Identify Draggable Elements

Elements that you intend to be clicked and dragged must be identified as *draggable*, using the draggable attribute. Simply set its value to true:

```
<element draggable='true'>...</element>
```

When this is set, HTML5 web browsers will fire off additional browser events that you can use in JavaScript to follow the drag-and-drop process. This attribute causes no visual change to the element; that must be handled by CSS. For example, you can indicate to the user that an element is draggable by changing the mouse cursor displayed over the element:

```
[draggable=true] { cursor: move; }
```

The img element and hyperlinks have draggable='true' implicitly set; however, this particular CSS selector will not match them. For clear HTML code, set the draggable attribute on every element that you intend to allow the user to drag and set the CSS to show the user it is possible to drag.

All of your draggable elements should be registered listeners for the dragstart and dragend events, described later in this section in the subsection "Browser Event Workflow."

## Identify Drop Zone Elements

There are two ways to identify elements as a *drop zone,* or in other words, accept draggable elements. Note that the first method is recommended, as it is supported by the most web browsers.

### The dragenter, dragover, and dragleave Event Methods

The first and primary method involves simply assigning drop-point elements a specific class name, such as dropzone, and then using that class name in JavaScript to register listener functions for your drag-and-drop events. Overall, this method gives you more control over the entire drag-and-drop process, but it involves a bit more JavaScript work.

```
<element class='dropzone'>...</element>
```

When using this method, all of your drop zone elements should listen for the dragenter, dragover, dragleave, and drop events in JavaScript, described later in this section in the subsection "Browser Event Workflow."

### The dropzone Attribute Method

The alternative method involves using the new dropzone attribute. As of July 2011, none of the major web browsers support this attribute, but once implemented, it will allow you to simplify the dragenter, dragover, and dragleave events. Its value is a series of parameters that define the drop-point element's behavior:

```
<element dropzone='feedback kind:type'>...</element>
```

The *feedback* parameter can be copy, move, or link and sets the mouse icon effect. Only one feedback value can be specified, but if unspecified, it defaults to copy. The *kind* parameter is a single character that states the acceptable data type. Use f for accepting files dragged from the desktop and s for accepting data strings. *type* is the MIME type of the data accepted. Multiple *kind:type* parameters can be specified, if required.

continued ➤

For example, if you were copying image files dragged from the desktop, the `dropzone` attribute would be `dropzone='copy f:image/png f:image/jpeg f:image/gif'`. If you were moving a data string, use `dropzone='move s:text/plain'`.

When using this method, all of your drop zone elements only need to listen for the `drop` event in JavaScript, described later.

## Browser Event Workflow

The following lists the events triggered during the in-browser drag-and-drop process, in order.

### dragstart

The `dragstart` event occurs on the element that has the `draggable='true'` attribute set. When you register this event listener on a draggable element, you will be notified when the user has clicked down and initiated the drag-and-drop process.

Your registered `dragstart` event function can be used to fade out the `draggable` element object, to use `event.dataTransfer.setData()` to store supplementary information in the dragged item, and to assign a drag image under the mouse cursor.

### drag

The `drag` event occurs on the element that has the `draggable='true'` attribute set. When you register this event listener on a draggable element, you will be persistently notified while the user is actively dragging something.

This event is not commonly used but can be if you need to know exactly where the draggable element is on the web page, as it is being dragged.

### dragenter

The `dragenter` event fires for every element the mouse drag *enters* across the web page. Most web page elements you will not be interested in, so you can isolate your `dragenter` activity by registering an event listener only on drop zone elements.

Your registered `dragenter` event function can be used to highlight a drop zone element area, which provides a visual cue to the user that the element being dragged can be dropped here.

### dragover

The `dragover` event is very similar to `drag` and `dragenter`, except that this event fires continuously only while the user drags and hovers over a drop zone element on the web page. Naturally, this can produce a lot of event noise, so you can focus on appropriate `dragover` activity by registering an event listener only on drop zone elements.

The purpose of this event is to set the drop effect for the user feedback as the user actually moves the mouse. In most cases, your registered `dragover` event function should call `event.preventDefault()` — which allows you to define this `dragover` process — and then set `event.dataTranfer.dropEffect` to either `move`, `copy`, or `link`.

### dragleave

The `dragleave` event is also very similar to `dragenter`, except it fires for every element that the mouse drag *leaves* across the web page. Again, most elements will be uninteresting, except for those that you have already registered as `dragenter` and `dragover` event listeners.

Your registered `dragleave` event function can be used to remove the `dragenter` highlight on a drop zone element area.

### drop

The `drop` event occurs on the drop zone element where the user releases the mouse button. This allows you to identify where exactly the user successfully completed the drag-and-drop process and to launch the appropriate JavaScript code to process the user's action.

Your registered `drop` event function can be used to verify that a drop action was appropriate, such as if the dragged element is compatible with the dropped element. This can be done by comparing the elements directly and running the `event.dataTransfer.getData()` method, which accesses the content that was originally stored using `event.dataTransfer.setData()` in your `dragstart` event function. Your registered `drop` event function should call `event.preventDefault()`, which notifies the DOM that you are providing the drop validation process.

### dragend

The `dragend` event occurs after the user releases the mouse button. This differs from the `drop` event as `dragend` fires from the draggable element, not the drop zone element. In other words, `dragend` occurs regardless of whether the drag-and-drop process completed successfully or not.

Your registered `dragend` event function can be used to undo what the `dragstart` function did, cosmetically speaking. For example, if `dragstart` faded out the `draggable` element object, `dragend` should restore it.

## External Event Workflow

The HTML5 drag-and-drop process can work outside of the web browser. This means that objects can be dragged from the desktop into your web page, and vice versa. When this happens, the previously described event workflow changes slightly.

### Dragging Objects out of a Web Page

Only the `dragstart` and `dragend` events fire when the drag-and-drop process begins and finishes. All other events are omitted because the drop point is outside of the web browser. The information you store in `event.dataTransfer.setData()` will then be transferred to your operating system. It is then up to the desktop or application to interpret that data correctly.

### Dragging Objects into a Web Page

Only the `dragenter`, `dragover`, `dragleave`, and `drop` events fire when dragging something from your desktop into your web page. All other events are omitted because the drag start point is outside of the web browser. The information being brought into your web page can be read using `event.dataTransfer.getData()`, which is usually a path to the local file.

To begin supporting HTML5 drag and drop in your website, you must first instruct the web browser which HTML objects are actually draggable. Fortunately, this is very easy with the advent of a new global attribute appropriately named `draggable`. To activate this, set its attribute value to `true`:

```
<element draggable='true'>...</element>
```

All elements identified as draggable will start firing off `dragstart` and `dragend` events. Listening for these will allow your code to launch when the user begins and completes the drag-and-drop process, relative to the element being dragged.

Using jQuery's selectors and its `each()` method, registration for this event is very easy to do:

```
<script type='text/javascript'>
  $('[draggable=true]').each(function(){
    this.addEventListener('dragstart',
  onDragStart, false);
    this.addEventListener('dragend',
  onDragEnd, false);
  });
</script>
```

If you are using jQuery, your code can replace `addEventListener(event, function, false)` with jQuery's `bind(event, function)` method. However, if you do this, the `event` that is provided to your function will change from the browser's native `MouseEvent` object into jQuery's modified `Event` object. Be aware of this as a drag-and-drop specific object will not be where you expect it to be, as described in the section "Handle the Drag-and-Drop Events" later in this chapter.

## Specify Objects to Drag

**1** In an HTML file, type **draggable='true'** on all HTML elements that you want to drag.

**Ⓐ** Optionally, type **<output id='log'></output>** to define a location to log drag-and-drop activity.

**2** Go to your `<script type='text/javascript'>` block or a JavaScript file loaded after jQuery.

**3** Scroll to a JavaScript `$(function(){...});` group or create one if it does not yet exist.

**4** Type **$('[draggable=true]'). each(function(){.**

**5** Type **this.addEventListener ('dragstart',** *onDragStart***, false);.**

**6** Type **this.addEventListener ('dragend',** *onDragEnd***, false);.**

**7** Type **});.**

**8** Type **function *onDragStart*
(event) { }.

**9** Type **function *onDragEnd*(event)
{ }.

**B** Optionally, type **$('output#log').
append( event.type + "<br>" );**
into each function to log the
drag-and-drop event as it occurs.

**10** Save your HTML and JavaScript
files.

**11** Load your HTML file in an HTML5
web browser.

The draggable objects appear as
normal objects.

**12** Click and hold a draggable object
and move the mouse.

**C** The `dragstart` event fires.

**13** Release the mouse button.

**D** The `dragend` event fires.

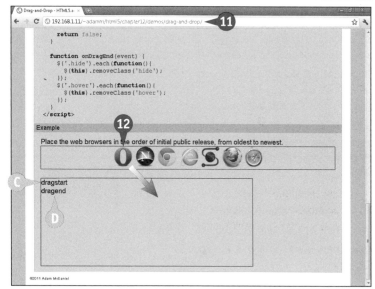

---

## APPLY IT

A third event can be used to monitor the dragging activity as the mouse moves, aptly called `drag`. If you register for this event in the same way you register for `dragstart` and `dragend`, you will see the `drag` event fire repeatedly while actively dragging the object.

You can also alter the mouse cursor displayed over all draggable elements very easily. This allows the user to identify that an HTML object can be moved.

**TYPE THIS**

```
[draggable=true] {
  cursor: move;
}
```

**RESULT**

When the mouse hovers over the draggable object, the mouse cursor changes. The following shows the cursor on Windows, Mac OS X, and Linux using Internet Explorer 9, Safari, and Chrome.

# SPECIFY A DROP ZONE

In order to support drag and drop in HTML5, you will require at least one element to accept draggable elements. Although there is a `dropzone` attribute that you could use, as described in the section "Introducing Drag and Drop in HTML5," it is not currently supported by any HTML5 web browsers. Instead, you can assign a `dropzone` CSS class to one or more elements and then use jQuery to add the event listeners, as shown in the preceding section, "Specify Objects to Drag":

```
<element class='dropzone'>...</element>
```

Note that you do not actually need a CSS rule with the name `dropzone` in order to use it as a CSS class. Because jQuery's selector will match all elements that identify themselves with the `dropzone` class, this is more than sufficient to apply the two primary drag-and-drop events, `dragover` and `drop`.

These events will allow your code to launch when the user hovers over a drop zone and completes the drag-and-drop process relative to the drop zone:

```
<script type='text/javascript'>
  $('.dropzone').each(function(){
    this.addEventListener('dragover',
onDragOver, false);
    this.addEventListener('drop', onDragDrop,
false);
  });
</script>
```

Define these immediately after you register for the `dragstart` and `dragend` events.

## Specify a Drop Zone

① Specify one or more draggable objects, plus the optional `<output id='log'>` tag, if preferred.

**Note:** See the preceding section, "Specify Objects to Drag," for more information.

② Type **class='dropzone'** on all HTML elements that you want to identify as drop points and accept draggable objects.

**Note:** In this example, the drop zone is an invisible bar in between each icon. Because the drag-and-drop process allows you to move icons across a page, an icon can only be moved to a location that is not occupied by another icon.

③ Go to your `<script type='text/javascript'>` block or a JavaScript file loaded after jQuery.

④ Type **$('[.dropzone]').each (function(){.**

⑤ Type **this.addEventListener('dragover', onDragOver, false);.**

⑥ Type **this.addEventListener('drop', onDrop, false);.**

⑦ Type **});.**

**8** Type **function *onDragOver*(event) { }**.

**9** Type **function *onDrop*(event) { }**.

Ⓐ Optionally, type **$('output#log').append( event.type + "<br>" );** into each function to log the drag-and-drop event as it occurs.

**10** Save your HTML and JavaScript files.

**11** Reload your web page.

In this example, the drop zone appears as space in between each icon.

**12** Click and hold a draggable object and move the cursor over a drop zone element.

Ⓑ Following dragstart, the dragover event fires repeatedly as the cursor travels over a drop zone element.

**13** Release the mouse button.

In this example, the drop event does not fire. This is because the dragover event is not yet managed properly.

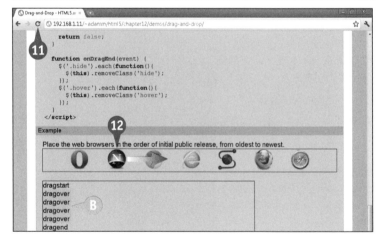

The dragover event works just like the drag event, firing repeatedly while over a drop zone element. In fact, the two will fire in tandem until you either leave a drop zone element or let go of the mouse button.

The purpose of dragover firing repeatedly is to allow you to access the event object's mouse pointer location during the drag-and-drop process. In your onDragOver() function, you can use event.pageX and event.pageY to access the pointer coordinates relative to the web page. If you need to know the coordinates relative to the drag-and-drop elements, use jQuery's offset() method described in Chapter 10, "Drawing

with the HTML5 Canvas," as the same technique applies to any HTML element.

If you simply need to know when the user enters and leaves the drop zone, there are two additional events that you can use, dragenter and dragleave. Both are described later in this chapter in the section "Visually Enhance the Drag-and-Drop Experience" because they are best suited for applying visual enhancements using CSS to the drag-and-drop process, but if you simply want to add logging capabilities to the drag-and-drop process, they are perfect for this stage.

After you have the draggable and drop zone elements established and functions registered for the drag-and-drop events, you are ready to provide the JavaScript code to handle the events' transactions. There are three stages in the drag-and-drop workflow described in this section, and all three are required to fully support drag and drop in your website.

Stage one of three, *handling the drag-start event,* consists of three parts: First, store the source drag element into a global variable; second, specify which type of drop effects are allowed; third, store any data that will be passed from this draggable object into the drop zone element:

```
var srcDragElement;
function onDragStart(event) {
  srcDragElement = this;
```

```
event.dataTransfer.effectAllowed = effects;
event.dataTransfer.setData(format, data);
}
```

The `srcDragElement` global variable is used because the original draggable object that initiated the drag-and-drop process will be difficult to relate back to when you are ready to drop. `event.dataTransfer.effectAllowed` specifies which drag effects are allowed to be shown back to the user. Allowed values are `none`, `copy`, `copyLink`, `copyMove`, `link`, `linkMove`, `move`, and `all`. The `event. dataTransfer.setData()` method accepts `format` and `data` arguments. The current HTML5 specification states that `format` should be a MIME type, but Internet Explorer 9 will not allow this. Therefore, `text` is used as a legacy fallback to `text/plain`, which is simplest to use when sending stringed content as `data`.

## Handle the Drag-and-Drop Events

### Handle the Drag-Start Event

1 Specify one or more objects as draggable and as a drop zone, plus the optional `<output id='log'>` tag, if needed.

2 Type **attribute='value'** for each draggable element.

**Note:** *If you prefer, you can also use the custom* `data` *attributes, such as* `data-dragme='content'` *and pass this information during the drag-and-drop process. In this example, the* `title` *attribute works well for images.*

3 Go to your `<script type= 'text/javascript'>` block or a JavaScript file loaded after jQuery.

4 Type **var srcDragElement;** to use a global variable to store the current element being dragged.

5 Type **srcDragElement = this;** to assign the element that triggered `onDragStart()`.

242

**6** Type **var data = $(this).attr(*attribute*);** to retrieve the draggable elements' attribute value.

**7** Type **event.dataTransfer.effectAllowed = '*move*';** to indicate that this is a drag-to-move transaction.

**8** Type **event.dataTransfer.setData('text', data);** to assign the data to the `DataTransfer` object.

**Note:** *Other complex MIME types could be used in lieu of* `text`, *but they will break drag and drop in Internet Explorer 9.*

Ⓐ Optionally, log the variable assigned in step **6** to the `$('output#log').append()` method to log the data being sent.

**9** Save your HTML and JavaScript files.

**10** Reload your web page.

**11** Click and hold a draggable object and move the mouse.

Ⓑ Optionally, the content assigned to the `DataTransfer` object is displayed in the output log during the `dragstart` event.

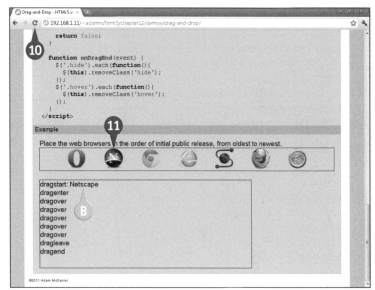

EXTRA

The allowed values for `event.dataTransfer.effectAllowed` may seem a little convoluted, but its purpose is to state to the UI which type of drop effects are allowed by this particular draggable object. The `effectAllowed` property accepts the values `none`, `copy`, `copyLink`, `copyMove`, `link`, `linkMove`, `move`, and `all`, which in turn limit which values are acceptable by the `event.dataTransfer.dropEffect` property, described on the next page.

As described earlier in this chapter in the sections "Specify Objects to Drag" and "Specify a Drop Zone," if you used jQuery's `bind()` method to register your drag-and-drop event handler functions, there is a bug as of jQuery 1.6.1: The original `DataTransfer` object is not imported into jQuery `bind()`'s modified `Event` object. Therefore, you will require the following code fix on every function that uses `event.dataTransfer`:

```
if (!event.dataTransfer && event.originalEvent.
  dataTransfer)
  event.dataTransfer = event.originalEvent.
  dataTransfer;
```

When this bug in jQuery is fixed, this hack will automatically disable itself thanks to the preceding `if` statement.

continued ➤

After processing the `dragstart` event, you need to instruct the browser how to handle the data as it is being dragged across the screen.

Stage two of three, *handling the drag-over event,* consists of two parts: First, cancel the default event using `event.preventDefault()` and by returning `false`; second, specify the appropriate drop effect that will actually be displayed to the user:

```
function onDragOver(event) {
  if (event.preventDefault)
    event.preventDefault();
  event.dataTransfer.dropEffect = effect;
  return false;
}
```

The `event.preventDefault()` and `return false` commands both serve the same purpose but apply to different browsers, yet this code is safe to define on all browsers. Preventing the default action may seem contradictory and pointless, but its purpose is to instruct the browser that this individual function is providing all the functionality for this particular event and that it should therefore avoid the default event actions built into the browser itself. In the case of the `dragover` event, the default actions all relate to the built-in drag-and-drop functionality in the browser's own user interface, such as dragging links into either the URL or tab bars.

The `dragover` event fires repeatedly as the user moves the mouse cursor across the screen while dragging, so you will see this event fire dozens if not hundreds of times during a single drag-and-drop action.

## Handle the Drag-and-Drop Events (continued)

### Handle the Drag-Over Event

**1** Type **if (event.preventDefault) event.preventDefault();** to notify the browser that your `onDragOver()` function is managing the `dragover` event.

**2** Type **event.dataTransfer. dropEffect = 'move';** to inform the user that this action will "move" the draggable element into the drop zone element.

**Note:** *Other possible values are* copy, link, *and* none, *but these must be allowed by* event.dataTransfer. effectAllowed *in* onDragStart().

244

**3** Type **return false;**.

**Note:** *Browsers are inconsistent with how they are to be notified that you are managing the event. Some require* event.preventDefault() *and others require* return false.

**4** Save your JavaScript file.

**5** Reload your web page.

**6** Click and hold a draggable object.

**7** Move the cursor over a drop zone element.

**Ⓐ** The mouse cursor changes to the move effect.

**8** Move your cursor away from the drop zone element.

**Ⓑ** The mouse cursor changes to a neutral, or nontransactional, effect.

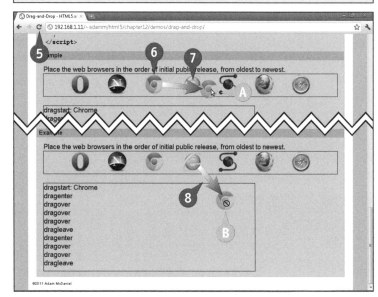

## EXTRA

The HTML5 specification allows for the drop effect to change during the drag-and-drop process. This allows HTML5 developers to produce an interface that mimics an operating system dragging and dropping files into folders.

For example, had you set event.dataTransfer. effectAllowed = 'all' in onDragStart() in the example, you could use this code in onDragOver():

```
if (event.ctrlKey && event.shiftKey)
   event.dataTransfer.dropEffect = 'link';
else if (event.ctrlKey)
   event.dataTransfer.dropEffect = 'copy';
```

```
else
   event.dataTransfer.dropEffect = 'move';
```

Unfortunately, only Firefox 5 supports this code example correctly; there are major problems when tested in Safari 5.0.5, Chrome 14, and Internet Explorer 9.0.1. These browsers allow you to set dropEffect only once; any other changes will be treated as none. Furthermore, Chrome will never convey event.shiftKey while dragging. Finally, to be useful, you must access dropEffect within onDrop(), but all three browsers will always report that dropEffect is none.

continued ➤

**Y**our drag-and-drop events now have a start and middle, thanks to the code from the first two stages, but now you need to instruct the browser on what to do when the user drops the item onto a drop zone element.

Stage three of three, *handling the drop event,* consists of three parts: First, cancel the default event using `event.preventDefault()` and by returning `false`, just as was shown in `onDragOver()`; second, retrieve the data stored in the `DataTransfer` object by the drag-start function, called `onDragStart()` in the example; and third, process the transaction using the stored data and `srcDragElement` by updating the web page:

```
function onDrop(event) {
  if (event.preventDefault)
    event.preventDefault();
```

```
  var data = event.dataTransfer.
  getData('text');
  // Process the completed transaction
  return false;
}
```

Use the `event.dataTransfer.getData()` method to access the data that was originally started in `onDragStart()`. It only allows for a *format* argument. The current HTML5 specification states that *format* should be a MIME type, but Internet Explorer 9 will not allow for this. Therefore, `'text'` is used to simulate text/plain, which is simplest to use when sending stringed content.

While processing the transaction, use the `srcDragElement` variable to identify the original draggable element and `this` to identify the drop zone element.

## Handle the Drag-and-Drop Events (continued)

### Handle the Drop Event

**1** Type **if (event.preventDefault) event. preventDefault(); and return false;** to notify the browser that your *onDrop()* function is managing the `drop` event.

**Note:** *Browsers are inconsistent with how they are to be notified that you are managing the event. Some require* `event.prevent Default()`, *and others require* `return false`.

**2** Use `event.dataTransfer. dropEffect` to identify the drop effect applied in *onDragMove()*.

**A** Optionally, log the data retrieved in step **2** with the `$('output#log'). append()` method to monitor the `dropEffect` used.

**3** Use `srcDragElement` to identify what draggable element was picked up.

**4** Use `this` to identify the drop zone the user dropped the element into.

**5** Apply any testing logic between the elements to identify if the user performed an acceptable drag-and-drop action.

**6** Use `event.dataTransfer.getData('text')` to access the original data packet stored in `onDragStart()` related to the draggable element.

**ⓑ** Optionally, log the data retrieved in step **6** to monitor the draggable element's data.

**7** Apply any changes to the web page to show the user the final result of the action.

**8** Save your JavaScript file.

**9** Reload your web page.

**10** Click and hold a draggable element over a drop zone element.

**11** Drag the draggable element over a drop zone element and release the mouse button.

**ⓒ** The drag-and-drop action is processed by `onDrop()`. A message is displayed, and the icons shift.

**ⓓ** Optionally, the drop effect value is displayed in the output log.

**ⓔ** The source draggable element's assigned data is displayed in the output log.

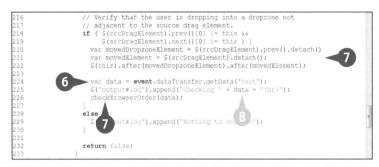

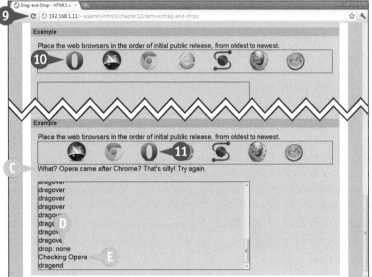

Unfortunately, when tested for this book, only Firefox 5 returned the correct `dropEffect` value; Chrome 14, Safari 5.0.5, and Internet Explorer 9.0.1 returned `none`, making this property useless in an `drop` event function. Hopefully, this will be fixed in future browser releases as drag-and-drop modifiers become better understood by HTML5 web developers.

Also, you can amend multiple `DataTransfer` blocks using `setData()` and then retrieve them using `getData()`. This is done by specifying a different MIME type for each data block.

In addition, the `DataTransfer` object also supports a `clearData()` method. You can use this to wipe the active data memory at the end of the drag-and-drop process. Rather than use it within a function like `onDrop()`, use a function like `onDragEnd()`. Its use is not required, as it will be automatically cleared when the user browses away from your web page, but it is a good practice as a general cleanup if the user will be remaining for an extended period.

Along with doing this, you may also want to set `srcDragElement = undefined`.

With a working drag-and-drop interface, you can visually spice up the click, drag, and drop actions performed by the user. This, like all other cosmetic changes to HTML, happens in the realm of CSS:

| Event | Effect |
|-------|--------|
| dragstart | Applies the hide class; use setDragImage() to set an image under the mouse cursor. |
| dragenter | Applies the hover class. |
| dragleave | Removes the hover class. |
| dragend | Removes the hide and hover classes. |

The hide CSS class will apply to the draggable element as it is being dragged. You can do so by creating a CSS declaration that modifies the source element's dimensions or opacity. Removing this class will automatically restore its default display properties.

The hover CSS class will be used to indicate that the user's cursor is currently dragging an element over a drop zone. This could apply a border around the drop zone, make it flash, or apply a simple animation that expands the area, making it appear to "make room" for the object to be dropped. Again, removing this class will automatically restore the original display properties of the drop zone.

event.dataTransfer.setDragImage() can be used to set the floating cursor image while the drag is active. Unfortunately, this does not always produce the desired effect. You need to verify if the setDragImage() method exists before running it.

## Visually Enhance the Drag-and-Drop Experience

① Type **.hide { opacity: *0.5*; }** to create a hide CSS class.

② Add and remove the hide class in the *onDragStart()*, *onDragLeave()* (not shown), and *onDragEnd()* functions.

③ Test for the setDragImage() method.

④ Type **event.dataTransfer. setDragImage( *image, x, y* );** to set the drag image under the mouse cursor.

**Note:** *If you are dragging an image element, you can use the* this *variable.*

⑤ Type **.hover { width: *64px* }** to create a hover CSS class.

⑥ Add and remove the hover class in the *onDragEnter()*, *onDragLeave()* (not shown), and *onDragEnd()* functions.

**Note:** *jQuery's* each() *method is used to locate all elements that still have the* hover *class. This is required within* onDragEnd() *if the drop attempt was successful.*

⑦ Save your JavaScript file.

```
146  .hide {
147      opacity: 0.5;
148  }
149  .icon {
150      cursor: move;
151  }
```
index.html      146,13    53%

```
182      function onDragStart(event) {
183          var data = $(this).attr('title');
184
185          srcDragElement = this;
186          event.dataTransfer.effectAllowed = 'move';
187          event.dataTransfer.setData('text', data);
188          $('output#log').append(event.type + ": " + data + "<br>");
189
190          $(srcDragElement).addClass('hide');
191          if (event.dataTransfer.setDragImage)
192              event.dataTransfer.setDragImage(this, this.width/2, this.height/2);
193
194      }
```
index.html      187,1    69%

```
239      function onDragEnd(event) {
240          $('output#log').append(event.type + "<br>");
241
242          $(srcDragElement).removeClass('hide');
243      }
```

```
149  .hover {
150      width: 64px;
151  }
152  .icon {
153      cursor: move;
```
index.html      146,11    52%

```
192              event.dataTransfer.setDragImage(this, this.width/2, this.height/2);
193      }
194
195      function onDragEnter(event) {
196          $('output#log').append(event.type + "<br>");
197
198          $(this).addClass('hover');
199      }
200
```
index.html      196,33    69%

```
242
243      function onDragEnd(event) {
244          $('output#log').append(event.type + "<br>");
245
246          $(srcDragElement).removeClass('hide');
247          $('.hover').each(function() {
248              $(this).removeClass('hover');
249          });
250      }
```
index.html      250,1    88%

**8** Load your HTML file into an HTML5 web browser.

**9** Click and drag an element away from its current location.

**A** The hide class is applied.

**10** Hover over a drop zone element; do not let go.

**B** The hover class is applied.

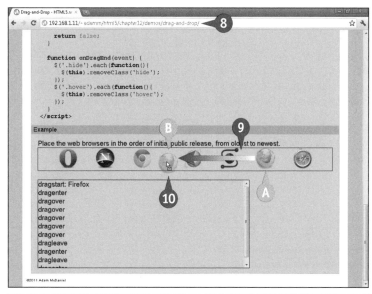

**11** Move the mouse and hover over a different drop zone element.

**C** The hover class is removed from the first drop zone element.

**D** The hover class is applied to the second drop zone element.

Release the mouse button.

In this example, the onDrop() event processes the drag-and-drop transaction and updates the web page.

**E** The hover and hide classes are removed.

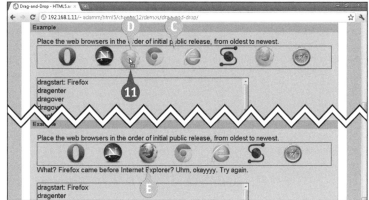

## EXTRA

There are dozens of drag-and-drop plug-ins other developers have made for the jQuery platform. You can browse a complete list at the jQuery Plug-ins page at http://plugins.jquery.com/projects/plugins/drag-and-drop/. The majority of them are not HTML5's version but instead use the mousedown, mousemove, and mouseup events.

But there is nothing wrong with that. These plug-ins will support the major web browsers, including older versions; however, these implementations did require a lot more work upfront than what is described in this chapter. The whole point behind HTML5 drag and drop is that it is being provided by the browser as an additional layer of infrastructure. Although support right now is buggy, the amount of work required to create a visually appealing drag-and-drop experience as described in this chapter is a fraction of managing the mouse events.

So, pick your poison. Do you select the lesser-work but lesser-supported HTML5 drag and drop or spend the time and code it manually with lower-level functions, increasing complexity for such a simple, intuitive interface? Support for HTML5 drag and drop will get better over time, especially because all the major web browser platforms are onboard the WHATWG bandwagon.

# Introducing Client-Side Storage in HTML5

Client-side storage allows websites to store and retrieve information on your computer, using a controlled API secured by the web browser.

For many years now, websites' only option for client-side storage was the HTTP cookie. The poor cookie, despite its flaws, has been used and abused since its introduction in 1994. When used properly, a cookie is a very useful tool to facilitate online authentication, shopping, and advertising. When used improperly, such as not including a server-side IP comparison, an expiry date, and any domain or path restrictions, a cookie can be a useful tool for a watchful Big Brother.

Essentially, a cookie is nothing more than a virtual license plate that allows a site to efficiently identify you among a sea of millions of users at a glance. Detractors argue that cookies carry viruses, cause identity theft, and can slow down your computer. This is no more true than a license plate can cause your vehicle to get dirty, stolen, or crash.

However, this chapter is not about cookies but about the latest HTML5 proposals that endeavor to move browsers beyond them. The Web Applications Working Group, working under the W3C banner, has proposed four new APIs to provide client-side storage: a "better cookie" model, two relational-database models, and a browser–file system hybrid model.

## The Web Storage API

The Web Storage API is available in two flavors, *session storage*, in which the database is active only as long as the browser tab is open, and *local storage*, in which the database is written right to disk.

### A Better Tasting Cookie

The idea behind the Web Storage API is basically the same as the HTTP cookie, except that the HTML5 designers wanted to solve some of the problems inherent in the original cookie model. Specifically, the JavaScript API is much simpler to use than the `document.cookie` interface, and it is less susceptible to the same cookie attacks.

However, it is unfortunate that the Web Storage standard did not cover an extension to HTTP, as server-side CGI programs cannot set Web Storage content directly; it must be done through a JavaScript program.

Also, the Web Storage API can only handle strings natively. However, as shown in this chapter, it is possible to store numbers, arrays, and basic objects by serializing them with the helper utilities `JSON.stringify()` and `JSON.parse()`.

The Web Storage API is extremely weak at handling large amounts of data, so if you need to store nested objects, or very long strings, use the Indexed Database (IndexedDB) API instead.

The full Web Storage specification can be found at the W3C page at www.w3.org/TR/webstorage/.

### Browser Support

The Web Storage API is available in all the latest HTML5 web browsers. For pre-HTML5 browsers, the only release that has support is Internet Explorer 8.

If support is lacking, you can always fall back to cookies or implement both as a redundant backup of the information that you are storing on the user's web browser.

## The IndexedDB API

IndexedDB is a JavaScript API that allows you to store generic objects in different databases and object stores, granting the capability for a Web application to have a local database that is always available, regardless of being online or offline.

### An Indexable Object Store

The IndexedDB API offers a very flexible, transaction-based place for you to store your objects, called an *object store*. Multiple object stores can exist in a single database, but the database itself is specific to the browser and your domain.

The IndexedDB API's strength is its capability to handle large, copious amounts of structured data. It can even be indexed by assigning a primary key, called a *key path*, or additional index properties that will result in fast speed lookups.

The IndexedDB specification can be found at the W3C page at www.w3.org/TR/IndexedDB/.

### Browser Support

The IndexedDB API is supported as of Firefox 4 and Chrome 11. Other browsers have expressed interest, particularly Microsoft Internet Explorer, which is working on an integration effort, but despite the poor adoption rate today, the IndexedDB API looks to become the standard HTML5 will eventually settle on.

Developer Arun Ranganathan wrote a very good article for Mozilla promoting the IndexedDB API, which compares it to the other client-side storage models and is available at the Mozilla Hacks page at http://hacks.mozilla.org/2010/06/beyond-html5-database-apis-and-the-road-to-indexeddb/.

## The Web SQL Database API

The Web SQL Database API turns a web browser into a *relational database* within JavaScript.

### SQL Commands in JavaScript

The deprecated Web SQL specification can be found at the W3C page at www.w3.org/TR/webdatabase/.

### Browser Support

The Web SQL Database API is currently supported on many WebKit browsers, such as Chrome, Safari, and Android, plus the Presto browsers, Opera and Opera Mobile. However, officially, the W3C deprecated the specification in November 2010, meaning that its adoption by other web browsers effectively has halted. Although support is likely to continue in WebKit and Presto, sites that have implemented the Web SQL Database API are encouraged to migrate to the IndexedDB API.

The decision to deprecate the Web SQL Database API was made partly due to the higher learning curve of the SQL language, its rigid schema design, and the overall API complexity — all problems that the IndexedDB API attempts to avoid.

## The FileSystem API

HTML5's FileSystem API enables you to access a *sandboxed* area of your user's local file system. This means that your website can store and retrieve files without accessing the core workstation's file system. This is great for larger binary files that are not appropriate for the Web Storage or IndexedDB APIs.

Typical features associated with file systems, such as directories and subdirectories, plus reading, writing, listing, copying, moving, and renaming files are all standard in this new API. Files are created using a new `BlobBuilder` interface and then downloaded as a traditional file using a new `filesystem:` URL scheme. Because the API is still restricted to the browser and web application, the goal by the specification developers is to make it so that third parties can access the sandboxed file system without going through excessive measures.

Currently, only Chrome 9 and later supports the FileSystem API, and even this is only experimental. As a result, this topic is not covered in this book.

You can find additional information about the FileSystem API at its W3C working draft page at www.w3.org/TR/file-system-api/.

The Web Storage API is designed to store simple stringed values in two ways — long term to disk using `localStorage` and short term to the current browsing session using `sessionStorage`. You can use the Web Storage API to mirror or replace cookies as it has an inherently higher level of security and privacy features and is much easier to set and retrieve in JavaScript than cookies are.

There are several different ways to store data in the Web Storage API. The recommended way is by using the `setItem()` method on the intended storage interface:

```
localStorage.setItem(key, string);
sessionStorage.setItem(key, string);
```

Because the storage interface emulates an associative array, the following code can be used instead, if you prefer:

```
localStorage[key] = string;
sessionStorage[key] = string;
```

Or, if your `key` does not begin with a number, you can simplify this even further by assigning `string` to `localStorage.key` or `sessionStorage.key`.

All variables passed into the Web Storage API will be converted into a string; therefore, if you need to store a number, array, or basic object, use `JSON.stringify()` to flatten the variable into a string:

```
string = JSON.stringify(object);
```

Unfortunately, JSON will destroy the object's constructor and prototype; therefore, you cannot use the Web Storage API to store complex objects.

## Store Data Using the Web Storage API

**1** Open a JavaScript file in a text editor or an HTML file within a `<script type='text/javascript'>` block.

**2** Type **sessionStorage.setItem(key, value);** to store a `value` as a string into session storage under the identifier `key`.

**Note:** `setItem()` does not return anything.

**3** Type **localStorage.setItem(key, value);** to store a `value` as a string into local storage under the identifier `key`.

**Note:** To use the Web Storage API, only one of `sessionStorage` or `localStorage` is required; use whichever is most appropriate for your application.

**Note:** The same `key` can be used in `sessionStorage` and `localStorage` to store independently controlled values.

**Note:** If `key` is reused under the same storage cache, its `value` will be updated.

```
51  <mark>sessionObject</mark> = JSON.parse(sessionStorage.getItem(<mark>key</mark>));
52  </code></pre>
53      <h5>Example</h5>
54      <style>
55      article.example {
56          margin: 10px;
57      }
58      </style>
59      <script type="text/javascript">
60          $(function(){
61              var count = 0;
62              sessionStorage.setItem('sessionCount', ++count);
63          });
64      </script>
65      <article class='example'>
66          <p>
67              You have visited this web page <output id='sessionCount' class='bold'>at
68              least one</output> time<output id='sessionCountPlural'></output>
69              this browser session, and <output id='localCount' class='bold'>at least one
70              time<output id='localCountPlural'></output> with this browser.
71          </p>
72      </article>
73      </section>
74      <footer>
75      &copy;2011 Adam McDaniel
76      </footer>
77  </div>
78  </body>
79  </html>
```

```
51  <mark>sessionObject</mark> = JSON.parse(sessionStorage.getItem(<mark>key</mark>));
52  </code></pre>
53      <h5>Example</h5>
54      <style>
55      article.example {
56          margin: 10px;
57      }
58      </style>
59      <script type="text/javascript">
60          $(function(){
61              var count = 0;
62              sessionStorage.setItem('sessionCount', ++count);
63
64              count = 0;
65              localStorage.setItem('localCount', ++count);
66          });
67      </script>
```

Optionally, type **JSON.stringify( )** to convert a number, array, or object into a string and store it into the Web Storage API.

**Note:** *In this example, the* count *variable is a number to be encoded as a string using* JSON.stringify()*.*

**Note:** *It is safe to use* JSON.stringify() *on a string.*

**Note:** *All Web Storage values that use* JSON.stringify() *must use* JSON.parse() *to access the original value, as described in the following section, "Retrieve Data from the Web Storage API."*

④ Save your JavaScript or HTML file.

⑤ Load your HTML file in an HTML5 web browser.

The local storage now holds *value* under the *key* identifier.

The session storage now holds *value* under the *key* identifier.

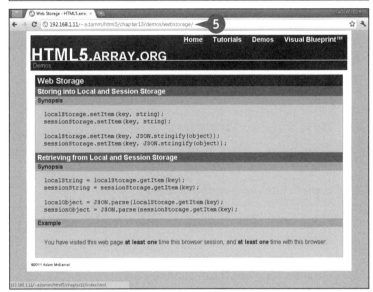

---

You can delete keys one of two ways: either by removing individual keys with removeItem() or by clearing the entire storage cache with clear().

| **TYPE THIS** | | **RESULT** |
|---|---|---|
| localStorage.removeItem(*key*); | → | The only *key* identifier in the localStorage cache is deleted for the web page's domain. This can also be used for sessionStorage. |

| **TYPE THIS** | | **RESULT** |
|---|---|---|
| localStorage.clear(); | → | The entire localStorage cache is deleted on the web page's domain. This can also be used for sessionStorage. |

Of course, all sessionStorage content will be automatically deleted when the browser session ends, which happens by closing the current tab or the entire browser window.

The W3C Web Storage specification states that localStorage expiry can be managed by the web browser, either by treating localStorage as sessionStorage or by providing a way for the user to access the cache and manually delete it per web domain.

Retrieving data from the Web Storage API is just as easy as storing it. The only thing you need to be careful of is that the context of what you access will be retrieved as a string, so if you are expecting a number or object type, some post-retrieval conversion is required.

All Web Storage events occur relative to the user's current domain. This means that if a user visits your website at www.mycompany.com/path/to/storage.html, anything stored there can be accessible only from other JavaScript code running within www.mycompany.com.

There are different ways to retrieve data stored in the Web Storage API:

```
string = localStorage.getItem(key);
string = sessionStorage.getItem(key);
```

This will return `null` if `key` is not yet used in either the `localStorage` or `sessionStorage` caches. Because

the storage interface emulates an associative array, you may retrieve the string with `localStorage[key]` or `sessionStorage[key]`. Or, if your `key` does not begin with a number, you can simplify this even further with `localStorage.key` or `sessionStorage.key`.

These methods will return `undefined` if the `key` does not store a value.

It is also important to note that the data returned will always be a string, regardless of how you saved it. Therefore, if you need to retrieve a number, array, or object, use `JSON.parse()` to convert it from a string back into its original format:

```
object = JSON.parse(string);
```

Because JSON will not provide an object constructor and prototype, use the IndexedDB API to store complex object types.

## Retrieve Data from the Web Storage API

Ⓐ Optionally, type **sessionStorage. getItem(key)** in a conditional test to check if a session storage *key* exists.

① Type *value* = **sessionStorage. getItem(key);** to retrieve a *key*'s *value* as a string from the session storage cache.

Ⓑ Optionally, type **localStorage. getItem(key)** in a conditional test to check if a local storage *key* exists.

② Type *value* = **localStorage.getItem(key);** to retrieve a *key*'s *value* as a string from the local storage cache.

Ⓒ Optionally, type **JSON.parse( )** to convert a JSON string retrieved from the Web Storage API back into an original number, array, or object.

**Note:** *You can safely call* `JSON.stringify()` *and* `JSON.parse()` *for all basic value types.*

Ⓓ Optionally, display the values on the web page.

③ Save your HTML or JavaScript files.

```
59      <script type="text/javascript">
60          $(function(){
61              var count = 0;
62
63              if (sessionStorage.getItem('sessionCount'))
64                  count = sessionStorage.getItem('sessionCount');
65              sessionStorage.setItem('sessionCount', JSON.stringify(++count));
66
67              count = 0;
68              if (localStorage.getItem('localCount'))
69                  count = localStorage.getItem('localCount');
70              localStorage.setItem('localCount', JSON.stringify(++count));
71          });
72      </script>
```

```
51      <mark>sessionObject</mark> = JSON.parse(sessionStorage.getItem(<mark>key</mark>));
52      </code></pre>
53          <h5>Example</h5>
54          <style>
55              article.example {
56                  margin: 10px;
57              }
58          </style>
59          <script type="text/javascript">
60              $(function(){
61                  var count = 0;
62
63                  if (sessionStorage.getItem('sessionCount'))
64                      count = JSON.parse(sessionStorage.getItem('sessionCount'));
65                  sessionStorage.setItem('sessionCount', JSON.stringify(++count));
66
67                  $('output#sessionCount').text(count);
68                  if ( count != 1 )
69                      $('output#sessionCountPlural').text('s');
70
71                  count = 0;
72                  if (localStorage.getItem('localCount'))
73                      count = JSON.parse(localStorage.getItem('localCount'));
74                  localStorage.setItem('localCount', JSON.stringify(++count));
75
76                  $('output#localCount').text(count);
77                  if ( count != 1 )
78                      $('output#localCountPlural').text('s');
79              });
80          </script>
                                                        51,1            75%
```

④ Load your HTML file in an HTML5 web browser.

⑤ If following the sample code, click Reload on the web page three more times, loading the page four times.

**Note:** *In this example, the local and session storage houses counters that increase each time the page is loaded.*

Ⓔ In this example, the local and session values increment by four, counting the number of page loads.

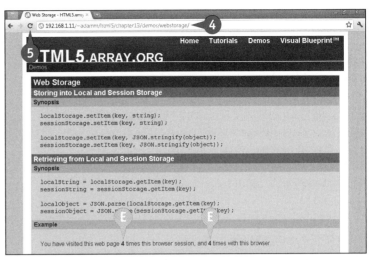

⑥ Open a new browser tab or browser window and load your HTML file again.

Ⓕ The session counter was reset, and the local counter continues from where it left off.

⑦ Close the web browser entirely and restart it. Load up the HTML file once again.

Ⓖ The session counter was reset again; the local counter continues from where it left off.

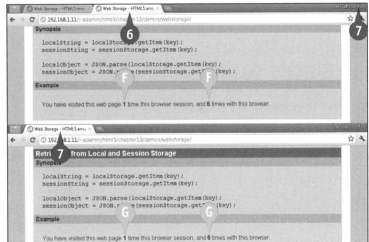

## EXTRA

In Chrome, you can purge any site using local web storage by going into Preferences → Under the Hood → Privacy Content Settings → All Cookies and Site Data and removing entries by domain name.

If you want to see all the keys that are stored in a Web Storage cache, you can retrieve a full list with the following code:

```
for ( i = 0; i < localStorage.length; i++ ) {
  var key = localStorage.key(i);
  var value = localStorage.getItem(key);
  console.log(key + ': ' + value);
}
```

This will enumerate through the size of the local storage cache, identify the key and its value, and display it to the console logger. As before, the `localStorage` interface in this example can be replaced with `sessionStorage` to access its array of session-specific keys and values.

**B**ecause the IndexedDB API is still under heavy active development, Mozilla and WebKit have implemented experimental versions of it by modifying the interface names. The thinking is that when the specification becomes a standard, the final API names will be implemented in the browsers.

As of August 2011, the latest versions of browsers that support the IndexedDB API are Chrome 14 and Firefox 5. So if you were to read the latest IndexedDB specification at the W3C page at www.w3.org/TR/IndexedDB/, you would find that it refers to the object interfaces IDBFactory,

IDBKeyRange, and IDBTransaction, but these objects are nowhere to be found in these browsers.

Therefore, in order to experiment with the IndexedDB API today, you can create an IndexedDB shim that amalgamates the various browser-specific names and create code that uses the standard W3C names.

Obviously, you are assuming an element of risk implementing this API today, in that future versions of Firefox and Chrome will support it differently according to the final W3C specifications. The whole point behind this shim is for experimental testing and to better prepare yourself to adopt the IndexedDB API as a tool when it is finalized, along with the rest of HTML5.

## Using the Correct IndexedDB API

**1** Open an IndexedDB JavaScript file or scroll to the `<script>` tag block.

**2** Type **var indexedDB = window. indexedDB** to use the W3C's IndexedDB API name.

**3** Type **|| window.webkitIndexedDB** to otherwise fall back to WebKit's IndexedDB API name.

**4** Type **|| window.mozIndexedDB;** to otherwise fall back to Mozilla's IndexedDB API name.

**Note:** Now when you use indexedDB in your code, an automatic fallback to the different browser names occurs.

**5** Repeat steps **2** and **3** for the IDBDatabaseException API.

**6** Repeat steps **2** and **3** for the IDBKeyRange API.

**7** Repeat steps **2** and **3** for the IDBTransaction API.

**Note:** Firefox 5 already uses the W3C names for these interfaces.

**Note:** In this chapter, only these four interface names are actually referenced in the code.

**B**efore you can access an IndexedDB object store, you must first open its database context. An IndexedDB database serves two purposes: It houses a series of object stores under a common identification banner, and it serves to offer version control snapshots of the collection of object store schemas at different states.

For the sake of simplicity, and because the IndexedDB API version control is not yet fully supported by browsers, this chapter assumes that the database remains at version 1.0, and no version control is used. "1.0" *is* used when creating an IndexedDB database in the following section, "Create a New IndexedDB Object Store."

```
var db, database = 'myDatabase';
var openDB = indexedDB.open(database);
openDB.onsuccess = function(event) {
  db = event.target.result; };
openDB.onerror = function(event) {...};
```

db is a global variable that stores an IDBDatabase interface to the *myDatabase*. You will be using db throughout the IndexedDB API interaction process, but the identifier is used only when opening the database interface. The db variable is assigned when the database is successfully opened; otherwise, a generic error message is displayed.

Note, you may run db.close() to close the IDBDatabase interface; however, this is unnecessary because the browser closes the database connection automatically when the page unloads.

Using the IndexedDB API is pointless if the user is running Firefox in Private Browsing mode, which will trigger error 6 in event.target.errorCode, and Chrome in Incognito mode, which will allow the API to continue but save nothing to disk.

## Open an IndexedDB Database

1 Type **var db, database = 'myDatabase';** to declare a global database variable and name.

2 Type **var openDB = indexedDB.open (database);** to open the IndexedDB database.

3 Type **openDB.onsuccess = function (event) {** to define code to run when open() is successful.

4 Type **db = event.target.result;** to assign the opened IDBDatabase interface to the db variable.

5 Type **}** to close the anonymous function assignment.

6 Type **openDB.onerror = popupErrorEvent;**.

7 Type **function popupErrorEvent(event) { }** to define generic code to run if an error occurs.

8 Type **alert()** and **console.log()** to display an error message.

*Note: WebKit provides error message descriptions on some failures. You can access one from* event.target. webkitErrorMessage *if it exists.*

```
192        // IndexedDB becomes more stable and supported in more
193        // browsers.
194
195        var db, database = 'myDatabase';
196        var openDB = indexedDB.open(database);
197        openDB.onsuccess = function(event) {
198          db = event.target.result;
199        }
200      })
201      </script>
202      <article class='example'>
203      </article>
204    </article>
205  </section>
206  <footer>
```

```
184        // Merge the various IndexedDB interface names into properly
185        // named variables. Falling back to the Webkit and Mozilla names
186        // makes it possible for Chrome and Firefox to use the same code.
187        var indexedDB = window.indexedDB || window.webkitIndexedDB || window.mozInd
188        var IDBDatabaseException = window.IDBDatabaseException || window.webkitIDBD
189        var IDBKeyRange = window.IDBKeyRange || window.webkitIDBKeyRange;
190        var IDBTransaction = window.IDETransaction || window.webkitIDBTransaction;
191        // This shim is very flimsy. It is very likely to change as
192        // IndexedDB becomes more stable and supported in more
193        // browsers.
194
195        var db, database = 'myDatabase';
196        var openDB = indexedDB.open(database);
197        openDB.onsuccess = function(event) {
198          db = event.target.result;
199        }
200        openDB.onerror = popupErrorEvent;
201
202        function popupErrorEvent(event) {
203          console.log('Error ', event.target);
204          alert('Error:' + event.target.errorCode + ": " +
205            event.target.webkitErrorMessage + "\n(see console log)");
206        }
207      });
208      </script>
209      <article class='example'>
210      </article>
211    </article>
212  </section>
213  <footer>
                                              213,1          97%
```

257

**B**efore creating a new IndexedDB object store, first attempt to read something from it. This will throw an exception error with the code NOT_FOUND_ERR. This is your cue to create the object store by calling db.setVersion() and db.createObjectStore().

Before you begin, you must set an object store name. This can literally be anything, but remember that the information you save to the IndexedDB API will be under this store name, housed within the database name you picked earlier. Because you will be referring to this store name several times, store it as a global variable alongside var db:

```
var objectStore = 'myStore';
```

The store exception test must be placed within the openDB. onsuccess function, after db = event.target.result:

```
try {
  db.transaction(objectStore, IDBTransaction.
  READ_ONLY);
} catch(e) {
  if (e.code == IDBDatabaseException.NOT_
  FOUND_ERR) {
    var request = db.setVersion('1.0');
    request.onsuccess = function(event) {
      db.createObjectStore(objectStore,
        {keyPath: 'id', autoIncrement:
  true});
    };
  };
}
```

In this code, db.transaction() is just a temporary trigger for the exception. It will be replaced later, but it is enough for now to identify when to create a database as e.code is set to NOT_FOUND_ERR.

db.createObjectStore() creates an arbitrary id *key path*, similar to a primary key in SQL, which automatically increments on each object row added to the store.

## Create a New IndexedDB Object Store

**1** Type **var objectStore = 'myStore';** to declare a global name to this object store.

**2** Type **try { } catch(e) { }** to create a try-catch block.

**3** Type **var store = db.transaction (objectStore, IDBTransaction.READ_ ONLY).objectStore(objectStore);** as temporary code to throw an exception error if the object store does not exist.

**4** Type **if (e.code == IDBDatabase Exception.NOT_FOUND_ERR) { }** to test whether the error was the object store not being found and create a new conditional block.

**5** Type **var request = db.setVersion('1.0');**.

**6** Type **request.onsuccess = function(event) { }** to create an anonymous function expression.

**7** Assign an error function for the error event.

8 Type **var store = db.createObjectStore(*objectStore*, {keyPath: 'id', autoIncrement: true});** to create a new object store with an automatically incrementing primary key property named id.

9 Type **console.log(*var*);** at various stages in the creation process to follow along in the console logger.

10 Save your JavaScript file.

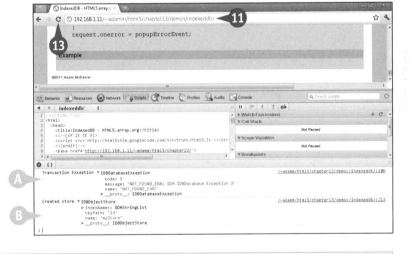

11 Open your HTML file in an HTML5 browser that supports the IndexedDB API.

12 Press Ctrl+Shift+J in Chrome in Windows (Option+⌘+J on Mac OS X) to open the JavaScript console.

Ⓐ The exception error occurred.

Ⓑ The object store is created.

13 Reload the web page.

No exception is thrown; the object store loads normally.

**EXTRA**

You can actually create multiple object stores under a single database and have multiple databases on a single web browser. Although you can communicate to only one database at a time, you can, however, work with multiple object stores in tandem.

In step 5, the setVersion() method is used to handle version control in the IndexedDB database. This method waits for any open file handles to close and can error out if it takes too long. Because the object store is only just being created, this should never fail. Note that the createObjectStore() method can only run within a successful setVersion() response.

In step 8, auto-incrementing the primary key is a design choice and a throwback to relational databases. If you do not want to auto-increment the key path, you must ensure that every object you store in this object store has a unique key path property.

The key path property itself will be useful later with the get(id), put(id), and delete(id) methods. You can use these to retrieve, update, and remove an object from the object store, as described over the next three sections.

# Store an Object Using the IndexedDB API

You can store an object into an IndexedDB object store using the `add()` request method generated by a read-write transaction. Because all transactions run asynchronously, the request/event model allows your code to know when a transaction has completed.

Only an array or generic object can be stored, and not simple strings or numbers. Custom objects that are built with constructors will be destroyed, but their properties and values will survive.

```
function addObject(object) {
  var transaction =
  db.transaction(objectStore, IDBTransaction.
  READ_WRITE);
  var store = transaction.
  objectStore(objectStore);
  var request = store.add(object);
  request.onsuccess = function(event) {...};
```

```
  request.onerror = function(event) {...};
}
```

Typically, when `request.onsuccess` is called by the IDRRequest API, you will know that the object was successfully stored in the database. You can update the web page to notify the user.

If your object store enabled `autoIncrement` when it was created, you must not provide the key path property when using `add()`. Because the purpose of `autoIncrement` is to automatically increment the key path property number, `add()` is managing this itself. However, if `autoIncrement` is disabled, you must provide a key path value into `add()` that is completely unique from all other objects' key path properties stored. This is akin to a relational database in which a primary key must uniquely identify only one record in a table.

## Store an Object Using the IndexedDB API

① Create a new function that accepts an object as a parameter.

② Type **var transaction = db.transaction(*objectStore*, IDBTransaction.READ_WRITE);**.

③ Type **var store = transaction. objectStore(*objectStore*);** to assign the transaction to your object store.

④ Type **var request = store. add(*object*);** to request to add the object to the object store.

⑤ Type **console.log(*object*, *request*);** to monitor the add() object and request.

⑥ Create an anonymous function for the add() request's success event.

⑦ Assign an error function for the add() request's error event.

⑧ Type **object.id = event.target. result;** to ensure that the autogenerated id property is displayed with the object.

⑨ Call a function to display the new object in the web page.

```
221        function popupErrorEvent(event) {
222          console.log('Error ', event.target);
223          alert('Error:' + event.target.errorCode + ": " +
224            event.target.webkitErrorMessage + "\n(see console log)");
225        }
226
227      function addObject(object) {
228        var transaction = db.transaction(objectStore, IDBTransaction.READ_WRITE);
229        var store = transaction.objectStore(objectStore);
230        var request = store.add(object);
231        console.log('addObject', object, request);
232      }
233    });
234  </script>
235  <article class='example'>
236  </article>
```

```
225        }
226
227      function addObject(object) {
228        var transaction = db.transaction(objectStore, IDBTransaction.READ_WRITE);
229        var store = transaction.objectStore(objectStore);
230        var request = store.add(object);
231        console.log('addObject', object, request);
232
233      request.onsuccess = function(event) {
234        // Assign the ID that was autogenerated to the object for rendering
235        object.id = event.target.result;
236        renderObject(object);
237      };
238      request.onerror = popupErrorEvent;
239    }
240
241      function renderObject(data) {
242        var container = $('ol#objects');
243        var li = $('<li></li>');
244        var text = JSON.stringify(data);
245
246        li.attr('id',data.id);
247        li.text(text);
248        container.append(row);
249      }
250    });
251  </script>
252  <article class='example'>
253  </article>
254  </article>
```

`225,13`          `96%`

⑩ Create a way in the web browser to call your "add object" function and provide it with data.

⑪ Construct the object itself.

**Note:** *In this example, the object has three properties with default names of* key1, key2, *and* key3. *The property names and values are customizable by the user.*

⑫ Save your JavaScript file.

⑬ Open your HTML file in an HTML5 browser that supports the IndexedDB API and open its JavaScript console logger.

⑭ Trigger your "add object" function call.

The object is stored in the object store.

Ⓐ The object is displayed on the web page.

Ⓑ The console logger shows the results of the object and request variables.

The first entry added into an object store is assigned id number 1.

## APPLY IT

If you want to update an object that already exists in an IndexedDB object store, replace the add() method described in this section with put(). You will need to specify the key path property so that the IndexedDB API knows which object to update.

**Example**
```
function updateObject(object) {
  var transaction = db.transaction(objectStore,
IDBTransaction.READ_WRITE);

  var store = transaction.
objectStore(objectStore);
```

```
  var request = store.put(object);
  request.onsuccess = function(event) {...};
}
```

So, in this example, the object whose key path is *object*.id will be updated to store *object*. Any properties previously stored in the object store and not specified in put()'s *object* will be deleted. If put() cannot find an object that matches *object*.id, *object* will be added.

You can retrieve objects out of an IndexedDB object store using a *cursor*. This is an enumeration tool that progresses through the list of all objects and returns them to your JavaScript program one by one:

```
function displayObjects() {
  var transaction =
db.transaction(objectStore, IDBTransaction.
READ_ONLY);
  var store = transaction.
objectStore(objectStore);
  var request = store.openCursor();
  request.onsuccess = function(event) {
    if (cursor = event.target.result) {
      renderObject(cursor.value);
```

```
        cursor.continue();
    }
  };
}
```

The `store.openCursor()` method starts the object store retrieval process. For each object, a `success` event fires. You must retrieve the cursor from `event.target.result`, process the cursor's `value` — which is the original object — and then call the cursor's `continue()` method, signaling the next object in the store. When `event.target.result` becomes undefined, the cursor has returned everything.

## Retrieve Objects Using the IndexedDB API

**①** Create a new function for retrieving all objects from a store.

**②** Start a new read-only transaction and retrieve the `IDMObjectStore` interface.

**③** Type **var request = store. openCursor();** to start the record iteration process.

**④** Create an anonymous function for the `openCursor()` request's `success` event.

**⑤** Assign an error function for the `openCursor()` request's `error` event.

**⑥** Type **if (cursor = event.target. result) {** to proceed only if the cursor contains results.

**⑦** Type **console.log('displayObject', cursor.value);** to monitor the `object` returned.

**⑧** Process the cursor object.

**⑨** Type **cursor.continue();** to move onto the next object in the object store list.

**⑩** Type **}**.

**Note:** *In this example, this function can be used to initially display the object store table when the page first loads. This means that the function can replace the temporary code used in step 3 of the section "Create a New IndexedDB Object Store," earlier in this chapter.*

11 Add to the initial `try-catch` block that opens the database for your "display objects" function.

12 Save your JavaScript file.

13 Open your HTML file in an HTML5 browser that supports the IndexedDB API and open its JavaScript console logger.

14 Add entries into the object store and reload the web page.

 The contents of the object store are displayed in the browser.

 The console logger shows the objects being rendered.

---

## APPLY IT

You can use the `IDBKeyRange` interface to create a *range*. This is used to limit the cursor to an upper or lower bound. Use `lowerBound(min)`, `upperBound(max)`, or `bound(min, max)` with `openCursor()`.

**TYPE THIS**

```
var range = IDBKeyRange.lowerBound(id);
var request = store.openCursor(range);
```

**RESULT**

Only objects with a key path value greater than *id* are returned to the cursor.

You can access a single object identified by its key path by calling `store.get()`. This is useful if you do not need to iterate through an entire list of objects just to find one that you can already identify using its key path.

**TYPE THIS**

```
var request = store.get(id);
request.onsuccess = function(event) {
  if (cursor = event.target.result)
    renderObject(cursor);
};
```

**RESULT**

Only the object with a key path value of *id* is returned. If the object cannot be found, `request.onsuccess` will still run, but `event.target.result` will be undefined.

You can delete an object from an IndexedDB object store using the same basic code used to get() it by its key path; however, the get() example earlier in this chapter was a read-only task, and this is a read-write task:

```
function deleteObjectById(id) {
  var transaction =
db.transaction(objectStore, IDBTransaction.
READ_WRITE);
  var store = transaction.
objectStore(objectStore);
  var request = store.delete(id);
  request.onsuccess = function(event) {
    // Update the web page
  };
```

```
  request.onerror = function(event) {...};
}
```

Only the object with a key path value of id is deleted. The process to delete an object may not be instantaneous. Remember that the IndexedDB API runs asynchronously. Therefore, only after you receive the request's success event should you update the web page to state that the object is deleted.

If the object cannot be found, the error event will return event.errorCode 3: "Key does not exist in the object store."

## Delete an Object Using the IndexedDB API

1 Create a new function for deleting an object from an object store.

2 Start a new read-write transaction and retrieve the IDMObjectStore interface.

3 Type **var request = store. delete(id);** to delete the object identified by its key path.

4 Create an anonymous function for the delete() request's success event.

5 Assign an error function for the delete() request's error event.

6 Create a way in the web browser to call your "delete object" function.

7 Save your JavaScript file.

8 Open your HTML file in an HTML5 browser that supports the IndexedDB API, and the console logger.

9 Trigger your "delete object" function.

10 Reload the web page.

The object is permanently removed from the object store.

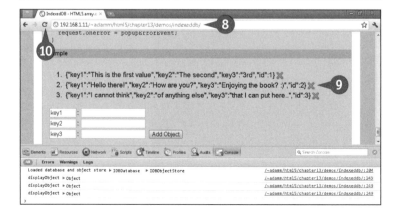

You can delete an entire object store using the same basic code to create one, within a `setVersion()` request, using `deleteObjectStore()`:

```
function deleteObjectStore() {
  var request = db.setVersion('1.0');
  request.onsuccess = function(event) {
    db.deleteObjectStore(objectStore);
  };
  request.onerror = function(event) {...};
}
```

The database version number remains at 1.0 because many HTML5 browsers that do support the IndexedDB API do not properly manage the database version control functionality. The purpose of this is to be able to store multiple versions of data within the same object store within the same database. Ultimately, for most applications, this is overkill; just reassign your IndexedDB database version "1.0" whenever you need to create or delete an object store.

## Delete an IndexedDB Object Store

1 Create a new function for deleting an object store.

2 Type **var request = db.setVersion('1.0');**.

3 Create an anonymous function for the `setVersion()` request's `success` event.

4 Type **db.deleteObjectStore(objectSt ore);** and a **console.log();** message.

5 Create a way in the web browser to call your "delete object store" function.

6 Save your JavaScript file.

7 Open your HTML file in an HTML5 browser that supports the IndexedDB API, and the console logger.

8 Trigger the "delete object store" function.

Ⓐ The database is deleted. A log entry is produced.

9 Reload the web page.

A blank object store is automatically created, if you used the code in the section "Create a New IndexedDB Object Store."

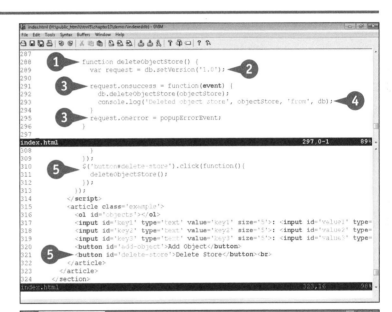

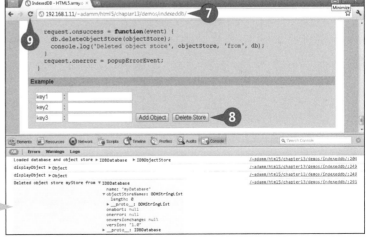

There are two ways to detect whether a browser is online or offline in JavaScript. The first is to query the `navigator.onLine` property, if supported, to give the current state of the network connection media. So if the Ethernet cable is unplugged or the Wi-Fi connection is lost, this property is updated. The second way is to listen to the `online` and `offline` browser events, if supported, to notify you when the `navigator.onLine` property changes.

This is true in most browsers and operating systems, but there are some notable exceptions:

- Internet Explorer 9 does provide the `navigator.onLine` property, but it will not post `online` and `offline` events when it changes.
- Firefox 5 and Opera 11.50 do provide `navigator.onLine` and fire the events, but they are not tied to

the physical media status. Instead, these browsers tie the property and events to a Work Offline option, available on the File menu in Firefox and the Settings menu in Opera.

- Regardless of browser, some Linux distributions tend to completely ignore the external connection media status. So if Ethernet and Wi-Fi are unavailable, the browser still thinks it is online!

Despite these shortcomings, the `navigator.onLine` property and `online` and `offline` events are still useful tools. The events are very standard. To read `navigator.onLine`, use this code:

```
if ('onLine' in navigator) {
  if (navigator.onLine)
    // Browser is currently online
  else
    // Browser is currently offline
}
```

## Identify Whether the Browser Is Online

**1** Open an HTML file in a text editor with jQuery.

**2** Type **The browser is: <output id='browserStatus'>(state unknown)</output>** to provide a location to display the browser status to the user.

**3** Open a JavaScript file loaded after jQuery or scroll to a `<script type='text/javascript'>` block.

**4** Type **if ('onLine' in navigator) { }**.

**5** Type **if ( navigator.onLine ) { } else { }**.

**6** Type ***browserOnline()***; for when `navigator.onLine` is true.

**7** Type ***browserOffline()***; for when `navigator.onLine` is false.

**8** Type **function *browserOnline*() { $('output#browserStatus'). text('online'); }.**

**9** Type **function *browserOffline*() { $('output#browserStatus'). text('offline'); }.**

**10** Type **window. addEventListener('online', *browserOnline*, false);.**

**11** Type **window. addEventListener('offline', *browserOffline*, false);.**

**12** Save your JavaScript file.

**13** Open your HTML file in a web browser.

**A** If the `navigator.onLine` property is defined, the browser's status is displayed.

**14** Disconnect from the network.

**B** If the `offline` event is supported, the browser's status should change.

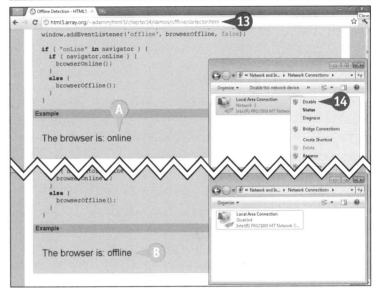

The code in step 2 of this section provides a location in the web page to display the browser status to the user. You may decide not to do this and keep the information internally only. If so, you will be still be notified of browser status changes in the functions created in steps 8 and 9.

Experiment for yourself by changing the computer's physical connectivity, and follow along in the browser's response. Sometimes disabling the physical connectivity using a software setting, such as disabling an Ethernet port in the Control Panel or forgetting about an

associated Wi-Fi access point, is enough to notify the browser that you are online or offline.

Whereas this status detector is suitable for checking the physical connection on most platforms, what do you do if there is no network or Internet connectivity? Network access is also determined by online and offline connectivity, and other factors such as router and ISP settings. Testing for network access is something you need to code yourself. Fortunately, you can use the walkthrough described in the following section, "Identify Whether the Network Is Online."

# IDENTIFY WHETHER THE NETWORK IS ONLINE

Just because the browser is online or offline does not mean that the network connection is. There can be all sorts of connectivity problems between your browser and a website that the `navigator.onLine` property and the `online` and `offline` events will not respond to. The only way to counter this is to use the Ajax core library, `XMLHttpRequest()`, to actually query the website and test for network connectivity in your JavaScript code.

For this to happen, you need to listen for the existing `online` and `offline` events. When the browser is online, test the network. When it is offline, the network is lost:

```
addEventListener('online', testNetwork,
 false);
addEventListener('offline', lostNetwork,
 false);
function testNetwork() {
 // Call XMLHttpRequest()
}
```

```
function lostNetwork() {
 // Network was forced offline
}
```

The `testNetwork()` function will be responsible for calling the `XMLHttpRequest()` code, which in turn will trigger a function to fire off new `netonline` or `netoffline` events. The `lostNetwork()` function only needs to worry about launching the `netoffline` event because if the browser is offline, the network must be offline, too.

Both new events, `netonline` and `netoffline`, will provide for your JavaScript code the current status of the network connection. It will be the `fireNetworkEvent()` function's responsibility to dispatch this event so that JavaScript will know when the network connection is actually good or bad.

## Identify Whether the Network Is Online

① Type **function testNetwork() { }**.

② Type **function lostNetwork() { }**.

③ Type **function testXHR(callback) { }**.

④ Type **function fireNetworkEvent (state) { }**.

⑤ Assign `testNetwork` to `online`.

⑥ Assign `lostNetwork` to `offline`.

⑦ Type **testXHR(fireNetworkEvent)** in `testNetwork()` to use `fireNetworkEvent` as the callback.

⑧ Type **var xhr = new XMLHttpRequest();**.

⑨ Create a `noResponseTimer` to abort `xhr` after 5 seconds.

⑩ Create an `xhr.onreadystate change` function expression to return early if `xhr.readyState != 4`.

⑪ Cancel the `noResponseTimer` when `readyState = 4`.

**Note:** *Status code 4 means that the request is finished.*

**12** Type **if xhr.status == 200) callback(true);** to run `fireNetworkEvent(true)` when the 200 success code is received.

**Note:** *This is the only point where* `fireNetworkEvent()` *will ever run with* `true`: *The user is actually online!*

**13** Type **else callback(false);** to run `fireNetworkEvent(false)` if any other code is received.

**14** Type **callback(false)** if the `noResponseTimer` activates.

**15** Type **xhr.open('GET', '/');** to get your site's base URL to test network access with.

**16** Type **xhr.send();** to launch the `XMLHttpRequest GET` request.

**17** Type **+ '?' + new Date().getTime());** to ensure that a unique URL is required to avoid `XMLHttpRequest` caching issues in Firefox.

**18** Place a `try-catch` block around `xhr.send()`, as required by Firefox.

**19** Type **callback(false);** for when `xhr.send()` throws an exception error in Firefox.

```
 1 function testXHR(callback) {
 2   var xhr = new XMLHttpRequest();
 3   var noResponseTimer = setTimeout(function() {
 4     xhr.abort();
 5     callback(false);       ◄ 14
 6   }, 5000);
 7
 8   xhr.onreadystatechange = function(event) {
12 ► if (xhr.readyState != 4)
10     return;
11
12     clearTimeout(noResponseTimer);
13     if (xhr.status == 200)
14       callback(true);
15     else
16       callback(false);     ◄ 13
17   }
15 ► xhr.open('GET', '/');
19   xhr.send();
20 }
21
22 funct 16 fireNetworkEvent(state) {
23 }
24
25 function testNetwork() {
26   testXHR(fireNetworkEvent);
27 }
28
29 function lostNetwork() {
30 }
```
`1,1            Top`

```
 1 function testXHR(callback) {
 2   var xhr = new XMLHttpRequest();
 3   var noResponseTimer = setTimeout(function() {
 4     xhr.abort();
 5     callback(false);
 6   }, 5000);
 7
 8   xhr.onreadystatechange = function(event) {
 9     if (xhr.readyState != 4)
10       return;
11
12     clearTimeout(noResponseTimer);
13     if (xhr.status == 200)
14       callback(true);
15     else
16       callback(false);     17
17   }
18 ► xhr.open('GET', '/' + '?' + new Date().getTime());
19   try {
20     xhr.send();
21   }
18 ► catch(e) {
23     callback(false);     ◄ 19
24   }
25 }
26
27 function fireNetworkEvent(state) {
28 }
29
30 function testNetwork() {
```
`"network-detector.js" 38L, 765C            1,1            Top`

## EXTRA

The URL that you are testing against must be the same domain you are running your website from, even if you are just building testing code here. The browser applies this restriction to avoid cross-site scripting attacks. So if you were to pick an unrelated URL with `open()` in step 15 in this section, such as www.google.com, it will always fail.

If you must specify a different URL in step 15 than what your JavaScript code runs under, then that website must specifically allow your script to run through a procedure called Cross-Origin Resource Sharing (CORS). This process requires the target web server to grant you permissions so that the `XMLHttpRequest()` function knows that it is allowed to proceed. Although manipulating the web server to accomplish this is outside the scope of this book, you can read about CORS at its W3C specifications page, www.w3.org/TR/cors/.

continued

With the Ajax component finished, if you were to load the JavaScript in a browser right now, the `online` event would launch the HTTP `GET` request and, if successful, would call `fireNetworkEvent(true)`. Otherwise, if the Ajax fails due to a bad URL or no network connectivity or if the browser sends an `offline` event, `fireNetworkEvent(false)` executes.

At this point, you are still missing some key components. First, `fireNetworkEvent()` does not actually do anything yet; it needs to actually dispatch the `netonline` and `netoffline` events. Second, making one Ajax call is fine, but what if the network access changes while the page is currently loaded? You need to be able to dispatch the event by routinely retesting for network access while the browser is online.

Remember, "the browser is online" and "the browser is offline" refer to the browser's state of network access. As described earlier, the browser could be offline because the network cable has been removed, Wi-Fi access is lost, or the user is running in offline mode in Firefox. Naturally, in all three cases, network access is impossible, so you need to cancel the continual testing of the network.

The key problem you are trying to solve is how to identify when the browser has an IP, yet still no Internet access is available. This is the case if the user's router is up but his or her ISP is down, if the user is traveling to a mobile hotspot and needs to provide credentials to get online, or if your own website is down. Specifically, your web application needs to know when the user is connected to your web servers; therefore, you need code to identify any potential network disconnections.

## Identify Whether the Network Is Online (continued)

**20** Type **var networkTimer;** to set up a global timer handle.

**21** Type **networkTimer = setInterval(function(){** to begin an asynchronous repeating code block and assign the handle.

**22** Type **testXHR(fireNetworkEvent);** to launch the same network test again.

**23** Type **}, 30000);** to repeat every 30 seconds.

**24** Type **clearInterval(networkTimer);** under `lostNetwork()` to cancel the repeating test.

**25** Type **var event = document. createEvent('Event');.**

**26** Type **event.initEvent(state, ? 'netonline' : 'netoffline', true, true);** to declare an event that uses `state`, does not bubble, and is not cancelable.

**27** Type **window.dispatchEvent(event);.**

**Ⓐ** Optionally, type **console.log('Firing event', event.type);** to see the event activity in the JavaScript console logger.

```
27 function fireNetworkEvent(state) {
28 }
29
20 ▶ var networkTimer;
31 function testNetwork() {
32   testXHR(fireNetworkEvent);
     networkTimer = setInterval(function(){    21
22 ▶ testXHR(fireNetworkEvent);
     }, 30000);    23
36 }
37
38 function lostNetwork() {
39   clearInterval(networkTimer);    24
40 }
41
42 window.addEventListener('online', testNetwork, false);
43 window.addEventListener('offline', lostNetwork, false);
                                              43,1         Bot
```

```
network-detector.js (H:\public_html\html5\chapter14\demos\offline) - GVIM
File Edit Tools Syntax Buffers Window Help
14       callback(true);
15     else
16       callback(false);
17   }
18   xhr.open('GET', '/' + '?' + new Date().getTime());
19   try {
20     xhr.send();
21   }
22   catch(e) {
23     callback(false);
24   }
25 }
26
27 function fireNetworkEvent(state) {
25 ▶ var event = document.createEvent('Event');
     event.initEvent(state ? 'netonline' : 'netoffline', true, true);    26
27 ▶ window.dispatchEvent(event);
     console.log('Firing event', event.type);
32 }
33
34 var networkTimer;
35 function testNetwork() {
36   testXHR(fireNetworkEvent);
37   networkTimer = setInterval(function(){
38     testXHR(fireNetworkEvent);
39   }, 30000);
40 }
41
42 function lostNetwork() {
43   clearInterval(networkTimer);
                                              42,24        76%
```

**28** Type **var networkStatus;**.

**29** Type **if (networkStatus == state) return; networkStatus = state;**.

**30** Type **testNetwork();** to activate the network tester when `navigator.onLine` is true and if there is no `navigator.onLine`.

**31** Type **fireNetworkEvent(false);** to force the network offline when the browser is offline.

**32** Save your JavaScript file.

**33** Load an HTML page that uses this JavaScript code in a web browser, and open the JavaScript console.

**Ⓑ** A log entry shows the `netonline` event firing.

**34** Sever your network access at your router or web server.

**Ⓒ** After 30 seconds, the `netoffline` event fires.

**35** Reload your web page.

The page should reload from cache and should detect right away that there is no network access.

You can see the actual `XMLHTTPRequest()`s made by right-clicking in the Chrome log panel and selecting the option Log XMLHttpRequests.

If your website is already using `XMLHttpRequest()`, steps 7 to 19 in this section can effectively be merged into your existing code. There is one thing to note, though: Back in step 17, this example adds an arbitrary timestamp onto the URL being requested.

It was alluded in step 17 that this is for cache control reasons. When Firefox cannot establish a network connection, regardless of its Working Offline setting, it will try its best to cache everything. This includes `XMLHttpRequest()` activity, which actually defeats the purpose of what you are trying to accomplish. Testing network connectivity is predetermined on not falling back on the cache.

The timestamp hack fools Firefox into requesting a page that is guaranteed to not be in the cache, thus allowing the network connectivity test to proceed.

When you have two levels of connectivity detection, browser online and offline — which is typically physical media connectivity or in-browser online/offline mode — and network online and offline — which is the actual access online to your web server — you can begin modifying your web application to react properly to both groups of online and offline events:

```
addEventListener('online', function(){
  // The browser has come online.
}, false);
addEventListener('offline', function(){
  // The browser has gone offline.
}, false);
addEventListener('netonline', function(){
  // The network has come online.
```

```
}, false);
addEventListener('netoffline', function(){
  // The network has gone offline.
}, false);
```

Considering that the `netonline` and `netoffline` events are the key events to listen to and they are the most amount of work to tie into according to the section "Identify Whether the Network Is Online," you really need to only listen for their events.

In this code example, all four events are used so that you can watch how they all react to the changing connectivity conditions in real time and in between different web browsers.

## Listen for Online and Offline Events

**①** Open an HTML file that uses your JavaScript code to detect network status.

**②** Type **The browser is: <output id='browserStatus'>(state unknown)></output>** to display the browser's current state on the web page.

**③** Type **The network is: <output id='networkStatus'>(state unknown)></output>** to display the network's current state on the web page.

**④** Type **window.addEventListener ('online', *browserOnline*, false);**.

**⑤** Type **window.addEventListener ('offline', *browserOffline*, false);**.

**⑥** Type **window.addEventListener ('netonline', *networkOnline*, false);**.

**⑦** Type **window.addEventListener ('netoffline', *networkOffline*, false);**.

**8** Type **function** *browserOnline()* **{ $('output#browserStatus'). text('online'); }.**

**9** Type **function** *browserOffline()* **{ $('output#browserStatus'). text('offline'); }.**

**10** Type **function** *networkOnline()* **{ $('output#networkStatus'). text('online'); }.**

**11** Type **function** *networkOffline()* **{ $('output#networkStatus'). text('offline'); }.**

**12** Save your JavaScript and HTML files.

**13** Load your HTML file in a web browser.

The browser and network statuses both report "online."

**14** Disconnect your router or disable your web server.

**A** After a set timeout, network access reports "offline."

**15** Disconnect your Ethernet or Wi-Fi cable.

The browser and network statuses both report "offline."

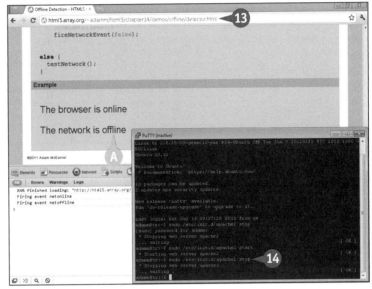

Note that the example in this section merges the `navigator.onLine` tests from the first two sections of this chapter ("Identify Whether the Browser Is Online" and "Identify Whether the Network Is Online") into one basic call. This way, both `browserOnline()` and `testNetwork()` run when the `navigator.onLine` property is true, and `browserOffline()` and `fireNetworkEvent(false)` run when it is false.

Earlier in this chapter, the section "Identify Whether the Browser Is Online" experiments with changing the

computer's physical connectivity to observe the browser's response. If you perform that same process with the code in this section, you should find that the network status mirrors the browser's status.

Of course, that functionality is not everything; you also need to verify that the network connectivity responds. While you are testing, you may want to decrease the `setInterval()` value used in the `testXHR()` loop. This will help you get faster responses from changing your network connectivity status.

# Introducing the Application Cache

The application cache, or *AppCache,* is a new HTML5 feature that can be very useful, yet very frustrating. It is the final piece of the puzzle that transforms a simple web page into a full-blown web application, but until you fully understand how it works, you may be led to believe that your site has permanently lost all connectivity, even though the browser is technically online!

Implementing the AppCache means that your site can be made to run regardless of network connectivity. The AppCache needs to be downloaded only once while online and is then available any time after that, regardless of connectivity state, and always at the same URL. This process is actually so transparent and convincing that you could be traveling on a airplane and open www.*mysuperwebapp*.com, and an onlooker would be fooled into thinking that you have gained high-speed Internet access!

You will still need to implement the online and offline detector, as described earlier in this chapter. This is useful to identify when the users do actually come back online, and whatever activities they performed and stored into their local IndexedDB database (see Chapter 13, "Storing Data Using a Client-Side Database") while offline need to be synchronized with your web server. This process, while outside the scope of this book, is what turns your user's browser into an active participant in the cloud, which is available anywhere you need it and still available when you cannot connect to it.

## Browser Support

The Application Cache API is supported by nearly all the HTML5 web browsers, both mobile and desktop. The only exception is currently Internet Explorer 9; however, support is likely to be added by Internet Explorer 10.

If you were to implement the Application Cache API today, browsers that do not support it should properly ignore it — that is, as long as your AppCache JavaScript code properly identifies when the AppCache API is available.

## Implementing the Application Cache

The Application Cache API can simply be implemented using a manifest file; however, you will also need supporting JavaScript events and methods in order to update the locally AppCached copy. You can view the WHATWG Application Cache specification at www.whatwg.org/specs/web-apps/current-work/multipage/offline.html.

### The Manifest File

The AppCache is activated when you create a manifest file and apply it to your html element on all pages in your web application:

```
<!doctype html>
<html manifest='webapp.appcache'>
```

Your *webapp*.appcache file summarizes all the online resources that you want to cache on the user's browser.

```
CACHE MANIFEST
file1.html
file2.js
file3.css
file4.jpg
```

Normally, the browser caches online resources as the user navigates to them. When the AppCache manifest is implemented, all resources in it are cached at once. This means that the user needs to visit only the first page of your site once in order to cache the entire web application for offline use.

The application cache will always be active after it is implemented, serving manifest content all from the locally cached copy, regardless of network connectivity state and regardless of the online copy of your website. This means that even if you change any of the manifest's files on the web server or disable the manifest file in the html element, its previous version is still active in the web browser — that is, until the cache is swapped in JavaScript. Until you fully understand this "always local" feature, you may find it to be one of the more frustrating "bugs" of the application cache.

## The AppCache API

You can easily detect for Application Cache API support by running the following test:

```
if ('applicationCache' in window) {
    applicationCache.update()
}
```

This is required before you decide to implement either AppCache method.

### applicationCache.update()

The update() method checks the network for an updated manifest file and downloads it if it is changed, along with any updated resources available on the web server.

When working, this method launches the AppCache events, which you can use to create a progress bar or other effect for large-scale application cache downloads.

### applicationCache.swapCache()

When the updateready event fires, you can run swapCache() to actually apply the new cache on the website. This application process applies only to new resource requests — for example, when the page reloads or when the user follows a link to another AppCached web page.

## AppCache Events

You can use events to follow along in the AppCaching process. Note that if you listen for an event on a browser that does not fully support AppCache, it will simply never fire. Likewise, you can listen for events without using any AppCache API JavaScript at all, as AppCaching will automatically kick in when the manifest file is loaded via the html element.

### checking

The browser is actively checking the web server for a new manifest file.

### noupdate

The browser has identified that there is no new manifest file available.

### downloading

The browser has started downloading the manifest file and its referenced resources.

### progress

The browser has started downloading an individual resource file. Note that the supplied ProgressEvent object provides event.loaded and event.total. This represents the current file count downloading and the total to download each time the progress event fires. You could use this to create a moving progress bar element, described in Chapter 3, "Using New HTML5 User Interface Tags and Attributes," for large AppCache downloads.

### updateready

The browser has finished downloading the AppCache resources, which can now be swapped into the live browser session with applicationCache.swapCache().

### cached

The browser has applied the AppCache automatically for the first time.

### obsolete

The manifest file is no longer available; the AppCache is deleted, and the website returns to live-download mode.

### error

There was a failure downloading a resource identified by the manifest.

The AppCache uses a manifest file to represent how all the resources — the HTML, JavaScript, CSS, and other files — your website provides are to be made available when the user is disconnected from the Internet. In its most basic form, the manifest file is structured like this:

```
CACHE MANIFEST
file1.html
file2.js
file3.css
file4.jpg
...
```

Save this file with a `.manifest` extension and reference it in the root `html` element's `manifest` attribute on all static web pages — specifically, all of your *.html files:

```
<!doctype html>
<html manifest='mysite.manifest'>
```

When the user visits any page with an AppCache manifest while online, it will download the resource files referenced and store them locally for offline access.

In the Chrome Inspector, you can use the Resources panel to examine the AppCache and verify that your manifest file is working.

It is very important to note that if the AppCache resources change after the manifest has been initially established, a special JavaScript procedure is required in order to instruct the browser to update the AppCache. See the following section, "Update the Application Cache," for more information.

## Create an Application Cache Manifest

**1** Open a blank file in a text editor.

**2** Type **CACHE MANIFEST**.

**3** Type **# Version 1**.

**Note:** Actually, this version number is not for version control. If you ever change any resource files after the AppCache is established, you must change the manifest file, too. Incrementing a version number is just a cheap way to modify the manifest without actually modifying it and allowing the web browser to re-download it!

**4** Enter the static HTML, JavaScript, CSS, and image files that you want to cache.

**Note:** In this example, the only page being AppCached is a subdirectory demos/offline, but its dependencies are actually located up two directories.

**Note:** If you are using a jQuery CDN, as described in Chapter 10, "Drawing with the HTML5 Canvas," or any other third-party-hosted script, specify its full URL here.

**5** Save your AppCache manifest as *mysite*.manifest.

⑥ Open an HTML file that you want to cache.

⑦ Type **manifest='*mysite*. manifest'**.

⑧ Save your HTML file.

⑨ Repeat steps **6** to **8** for all other static HTML files that you want to use with AppCache.

⑩ Open a caching HTML file in an HTML5 browser and open the JavaScript console.

🅐 The manifest is downloaded.

🅑 The manifest files are downloaded and cached.

⑪ Click Resources.

⑫ Click the Application Cache ▶.

🅒 The files currently in the AppCache are displayed with their cache type.

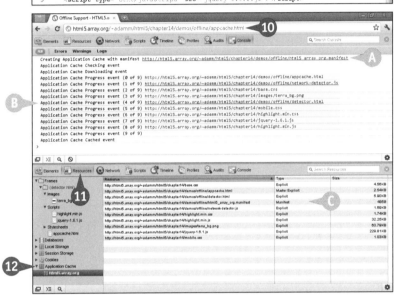

It is possible to create a more complex manifest file that defines manifest sections for which pages should be cached explicitly, which dynamic pages should use a static fallback, and which pages should be ignored by the AppCache entirely. These three cache types are identified by the headers CACHE, FALLBACK, and NETWORK in the manifest file and can be placed in any order. If you do not use any manifest sections after the first line, CACHE is assumed.

**TYPE THIS**

```
CACHE MANIFEST
# Version number
CACHE:
index.html
jquery.js
offline.html
FALLBACK:
login.cgi offline.html
account.cgi offline.html
NETWORK:
/media/
```

→

**RESULT**

In this example, the index.html and jquery.js files are cached normally; however, the files login.cgi and account.cgi, if accessed while offline, will display offline.html. Furthermore, unless anything else is specified, the /media/ directory will be omitted from the cache entirely.

As the user browses your website, files will be cached regardless using standard HTTP procedures — that is, except for content under the NETWORK section. In addition, only when the manifest file itself is updated will files referenced in it be updated without the user specifically visiting.

# UPDATE THE APPLICATION CACHE

You may notice a very strange bug in the pages you store under the application cache. None of them are updating, despite the web server providing an updated file and manifest. At the risk of sounding clichéd, this is not a bug; it is a feature!

The AppCache is designed to supersede all network activity for resources. Effectively, after a file is AppCached, it will always be served from the browser's local copy. So how do you force the application cache to update?

When your page loads, listen for the AppCache `updateready` event, and when it fires, swap the new cache in:

```
if ('applicationCache' in window) {
  applicationCache.
 addEventListener('updateready', function() {
    applicationCache.swapCache();
  },false);
}
```

The `swapCache()` method will install the downloaded copy into the AppCache database, but for the user to actually see the new content, the page must also be reloaded.

Every time your AppCached page loads while the browser is online, the manifest file is downloaded. If the manifest changed, the `updateready` event will fire, which notifies your code to swap the current cache with the new cache. After this, you can run `location.reload()`.

Unfortunately, this can cause your page to double-load, which can be ugly. To counter this, you can launch the manifest download at any time by running `applicationCache.update()`, which in turn will also trigger `updateready` if a new manifest is available.

You could implement this `update()` method in a button the user clicks or in a `setInterval()` repeater that runs every 10 or 20 minutes. If you choose the latter, use `confirm()` to verify that the user *wants* to reload.

## Update the Application Cache

### Update on Web Page Load

**1** Type **if ( 'applicationCache' in window) { }**.

**2** Type **var appCache = applicationCache;**.

**3** Type **appCache.addEventListener ('updateready', function() { }, false);**.

**4** Type **appCache.swapCache();**.

**5** Type **location.reload();**.

### Update Automatically at a Set Interval

**6** Type **setInterval( function() { }, milliseconds );**.

Ⓐ Optionally, type **appCache.autoUpdate = 1;**

Ⓑ Optionally, type **if ( ! appCache. autoUpdate || confirm('Update found. Reload?').**

**7** Type **appCache.update();** to trigger an AppCache manifest download and update check.

**8** Save your JavaScript file.

9. Load your AppCache manifest file.

10. Increment your version number to force a manifest update to re-download AppCache resources.

11. Save your manifest file.

12. Load your AppCached HTML file in your web browser and open a JavaScript console.

13. Type **applicationCache.update();** and press Enter.

14. Type **applicationCache. swapCache();** and press Enter.

The latest manifest is updated and swapped into the cache.

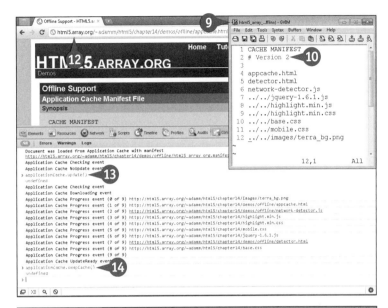

15. Reload your web page.

16. Repeat steps **9** to **11** and wait for the `setInterval` timeout from step **6**.

The automated call to the AppCache `update()` method runs.

● A confirmation prompt appears, showing a new version is ready.

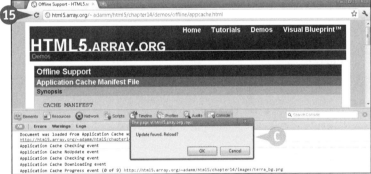

You may be wondering about the purpose of steps 9 to 14 in this section. How can you implement a page that listens for `updateready` and then calls `swapCache()` to refresh the AppCache, when the page itself is currently frozen and AppCached?

The simplest answer is to verify that your manifest has changed, open up a JavaScript console, and run the `applicationCache.update()` and `application Cache.swapCache()` commands by hand. After reloading one more time, your newest AppCached files should now be visible in the browser, which includes this new JavaScript to monitor the `updateready` event!

Steps 9 to 14 are very important if in the future you happen to break your own JavaScript within the AppCache and cannot trigger an automated reload. Effectively, incrementing the version number, reloading, and manually running these two functions should always force the browser to refresh its AppCache.

Given the worst-case scenario, if even this does not work, you can delete the manifest file itself and reload your page to unfreeze it, or in Chrome you can go to the internal URL, chrome://appcache-internals/, and remove your site's AppCache manually.

As described earlier in the section "Create an Application Cache Manifest," your AppCache manifest file can be configured with a FALLBACK section. This can be used to describe a cached file that will be displayed to the user in place of caching the primary file while the user is offline.

This is an excellent way to provide a fallback to dynamic CGI code that requires the server to deliver content while the user is offline; instead of displaying a cached web page that says "Sorry, this web page is available only while connected to the Internet."

In supporting web browsers, the DOM fires off specific events when the browser notices that the network connection has gone offline and comes back online.

Specifically, in your online-only web page, you can use the offline event to reload the browser and switch to the offline fallback page. Likewise, in your offline web page, you can use the online event to reload the browser and switch back to the online-only page. These events are the same ones described earlier in the section "Listen for Online and Offline Events."

Earlier, when you created the manifest, you also created a version comment. The reason for this is to notify web browsers that the AppCache resources have changed, simply by making an arbitrary change to the manifest itself — like changing a comment. Granted, in this particular section, you do not *need* to modify the version comment because the manifest file list is being updated, but it is a good habit to get into. See the section "Update the Application Cache" for more information.

## Create a "Website Offline" Fallback Page

**1** Open your AppCache manifest file in a text editor.

**2** Type **network-detector.js** to add code from earlier in the chapter to the AppCache.

**3** Type **offline.html** to cache the "Website Offline" page itself.

**4** Type **FALLBACK:** if you do not yet have a fallback section.

**5** Type *online-only.cgi* **offline.html**.

**6** Increment your manifest's version number and save the file.

**7** Create a new HTML web page in a text editor.

**8** Display a message that the web page is not accessible offline.

**9** Import the network-detector.js script created earlier in this chapter.

**10** Type **addEventListener('netonline', function(){ location.reload(); }, false);** to have the offline page listen for the online event and reload itself.

**11** Save your file as offline.html.

**12** Open your CGI script to edit its HTML and JavaScript code output.

*Note:* Do not apply the AppCache `manifest` *attribute to your CGI script output! Otherwise, it will invariably be cached and display while offline!*

**13** Import network-detector.js.

**14** Type **window.addEventListener ('netoffline', function() { location.reload(); }, false);**.

**15** Save your CGI script.

**16** Load a web page that uses your changed AppCache manifest file while online.

The application cache is updated.

**17** Load your CGI script.

The CGI script is displayed normally.

**18** Take the network or browser offline.

The CGI script reloads the URL.

Ⓐ The offline.html page appears under the CGI script's URL.

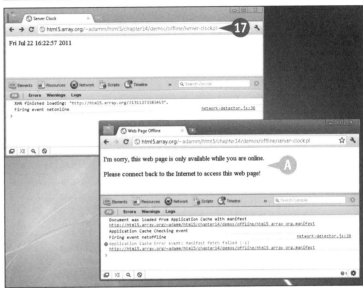

---

APPLY IT

The "Website Offline" fallback page is not limited to dynamic web pages; it can be used to redirect images, music, movies, or any other content that can be loaded directly in the browser. The trick is to create the offline version of the file in the same format as the original source, yet still hint to the user that a connection is required to get the full file.

**TYPE THIS**

```
CACHE MANIFEST
# Version 4
index.html
offline-image.jpg
offline-sound.mp3
offline-movie.mp4
FALLBACK
sunset.jpg offline-image.jpg
piano.mp3 offline-sound.mp3
mywedding.mp4 offline-movie.mp4
NETWORK
*
```

➔

**RESULT**

The web page index.html is cached normally for offline use. If you assume that it also contains the HTML tags `<img src='sunset.jpg'>`, `<audio src='piano.mp3'>`, and `<video src='mywedding.mp4'>`, these multimedia files will not be cached. Instead, when index.html is viewed offline, the offline versions of the picture, music, and movie will be displayed. These could represent a lower-resolution image, a very brief music clip, or a movie with a single frame that displays, "This movie can be viewed only while online."

# DISPLAY A SPECIFIC LOCATION WITH GOOGLE MAPS

You can use the Google Maps API to display a custom map on your own web page, zoomed and centered on latitude and longitude coordinates that you specify. By typing in your own coordinates, you do not need to use any GPS or Geolocation API methods on the user's web browser, but you will still need to identify the coordinates yourself.

You can easily determine a pair of coordinates by opening Google Maps, at http://maps.google.com; clicking ⚙; clicking Maps Labs; and enabling the LatLng Marker feature. After this is active, you can simply right-click any location in Google Maps and click Drop LatLng Marker. The further you zoom in on a map, the more accurate the returned coordinates.

After you have created a working map with hard-coded latitude and longitude coordinates, you can add the Geolocation API, described later in this chapter in the section "Understanding Geolocation and GPS Services," or the Google Geocoding API service, to convert a normal street address into latitude and longitude coordinates. However, if you have never used the Google Maps API before, get the map itself working with static data first before you add in either feature.

For more information on the features provided by the Google Maps JavaScript API, go to http://code.google.com/apis/maps/documentation/javascript/. The Google Geocoding API is described at http://code.google.com/apis/maps/documentation/geocoding/.

## Display a Specific Location with Google Maps

**1** In an HTML5 file, type **<script type='text/javascript' src='http://maps.google.com/maps/api/js?sensor=false'></script>** to import the Google Maps JavaScript API.

**Note:** *Because you are providing specific latitude and longitude data, no sensor is used; therefore, the* sensor *parameter is false.*

**2** Create a local JavaScript function called initmap.

**3** Type **onload='initmap()'** in the <body> tag.

**4** Type **var latlng = new google.maps. LatLng( latitude, longitude );** to set your map's latitude and longitude values.

**5** Type **var options = { zoom: 4, center: latlng, mapTypeId: google. maps.MapTypeId.ROADMAP };** to zoom in on your LatLng coordinates with a roadmap overlay.

**Note:** *The zoom level can be a number from 0 to 21, in which 5 is state level, 11 is city level, and 15 is street level.*

**6** Type **var map = new google.maps.Map ( document.getElementById ( 'map_canvas' ), options );**.

**Note:** *If you have jQuery loaded, you can use* Map( $('div#map_canvas'), options ).

**7** Type **<div id='map_canvas' style='width: *width*; height: *height*'></div>** to create the display map object.

**Note:** *The* width *and* height *variables can be hard-coded pixel values for now.*

**8** Save your HTML file.

**9** Load your HTML file in a web browser.

The Google Maps API initializes.

**A** A map is rendered, centering on your latitude and longitude coordinates.

**10** Use your mouse cursor to navigate around the map.

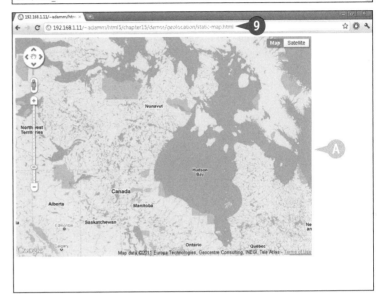

```
13          mapTypeId: google.maps.MapTypeId.ROADMAP
14      };
15
16      var map = new google.maps.Map( document.getElementById(
17          'map_canvas' ), options );
18      }
19      </script>
20  </head>
21  <body onload='initMap()'>
22      <div id='map_canvas' style='width:700px; height:500px'></div>
23  </body>
24  </html>
```

## APPLY IT

The Google Maps API is very flexible; you can even place landmark icons at specific coordinates on your custom map. This is very useful if you run a business and want to announce where your office is located, relative to the city roads.

In step 7 of the example in this section, the map object that was returned by the google.maps.Map() constructor allows you to manipulate your map in just this way.

### TYPE THIS

```
var marker = new google.maps.Marker({
  position: latlng, map: map, title: "Head Office"
});
var infowindow = new google.maps.InfoWindow({
  content: "<p>Our head office is located
  at:<br><address>123 Fake Street<br>Whale Cove,
  Nunavut, Canada</address></p>"
});
google.maps.event.addListener(marker, 'click',
  function() {
  infowindow.open(map, marker);
});
```

### RESULT

A marker is displayed, and when it is clicked, it displays the HTML code from the content property.

The Geolocation API, a new feature for HTML5, is managed by an official W3C specification. It allows for a standard way for websites to access location-specific data about the user, provided that the user consents to the request and the hardware support is available. This process uses multiple methods to retrieve the user's coordinates, via GPS or other geolocation services, and makes the information available over JavaScript.

The website can then choose to process that information in the user's web browser or send it using an Ajax or form submission callback to the web server for server-side processing.

This is an invaluable tool used by many location-specific websites, such as Google Maps, foursquare, Flickr, and Twitter, again, provided that the user allows the site to do so and the web browser hardware supports it. Remember, this is to be used as a convenience to the user: If the Geolocation API is not available, all of these example web apps still work perfectly fine. But if the user wants any location-specific content, that information will need to be provided manually.

## Web Browser Interface

Web browsers that support the Geolocation API provide a new object over JavaScript, `navigator.geolocation`, that you can interface with.

### Hardware Interface

Mobile web browsers supply data to `navigator.geolocation` through built-in GPS radios, cell-tower location detection, or a combination of both. Many of these devices offer a way for the user to disable support and to save battery life, and as such the API will not be available.

Desktop web browsers supply `navigator.geolocation` with information gleaned primarily from public IP addresses, Internet service provider hints, and Wi-Fi connection information, if available. These sources may not provide as detailed or accurate results like true GPS, but if available, they should provide a neighborhood-sized location area for the user to reference.

### Prompting the User for Access

When the Geolocation API is initialized, a notification prompt is displayed to the user. Only when the user agrees to the request for location information will the browser grant it to the JavaScript program provided by the website.

The user's preference is then usually remembered for that website, so if you decline once, you should not be re-asked on that domain until you reset your privacy settings.

### Disabling Geolocation

Geolocation can easily be disabled by the user at various levels, depending on the device. For example, iOS devices allow the user to disable geolocation on the entire device or only for specific applications. Many web browsers allow users to disable geolocation for all websites or only for specific websites.

Some systems default to geolocation being off, without presenting any prompts at all.

If you are having any problems using the Geolocation API on any device or you want to change your preference setting, verify in your operating system control panel and your web browser settings the state of geolocation support.

## Geolocation API

The Geolocation API runs in three basic states: requesting, displaying a successful request, and displaying a failed request.

### Requesting Coordinates

When you are ready to request coordinates from the browser, launch the Geolocation API method getCurrentPosition():

```
navigator.geolocation.getCurrentPosition(successHand
    ler, failureHandler, optionMap);
```

When the request attempt is completed, either the *successHandler* function or *failureHandler* function is executed.

An optional *optionMap* can be used to specify additional configuration properties to fine-tune the specific request.

| Option Property | Description |
|---|---|
| enableHigh Accuracy | A Boolean that means the application wants the highest accuracy available for the coordinate results. This may consume additional power and is off by default. |
| timeout | An integer to adjust the timeout for a pending request to fail. |
| maximumAge | An integer indicating the age of the last-known cached position. If the last-returned position's timestamp exceeds this value, a new position query is forced. |

A similar method is also available, watchPosition(), which uses the same parameter structure. This method persistently watches the user's current location and executes a callback handler every time the position changes. This method returns an identifier that must be passed to a clearWatch() method in order to halt the process.

### Successful Request Callback

If a position becomes available before the timeout, the browser executes the *successHandler* callback function and provides one argument, a position object. You can then access the information retrieved from the Geolocation service using this object.

The object returned will contain the following properties:

- coords.latitude — The degrees latitude.
- coords.longitude — The degrees longitude.
- coords.accuracy — The number of meters accuracy to the coordinates returned.
- coords.altitude — The number of meters above the earth's average surface level.
- coords.altitudeAccuracy — The number of meters accuracy to the surface level altitude.
- coords.heading — The degrees from true north.
- coords.speed — The speed in meters per second.
- timestamp — A Date object timestamp.

Naturally, depending on the method used to retrieve the user's position, some data may not be available. For example, IP addresses cannot reference altitude, speed, or heading, but mobile phones with GPS radios can. The property stores null in the fields that are not available.

### Failed Request Callback

If a position cannot be discovered, the browser executes the *failureHandler* function with an error object as its argument.

The object returned will contain the following properties:

- message — A plain-text message describing the error.
- code — The error code.

The object may report that the Geolocation service is unavailable or that the request has timed out.

## Fallback Support

The Geolocation JavaScript API wrapper is a third-party library that coordinates access to the various geolocation and GPS services on different devices. For browsers that support the W3C's Geolocation API, that is used; for some older browsers, the Google Gears API is used. For mobile operating systems such as those using Android, BlackBerry, iOS, Palm, Windows Mobile, and Nokia hardware, the GPS API is interfaced with and is emulated using the Geolocation API's methods and objects.

For a full list of supported platforms, see http://code.google.com/p/geo-location-javascript/wiki/SupportedPlatforms.

To access the user's current location, the browser needs to support the Geolocation API or an equivalent fallback, and the user needs to allow access to your website.

One of the fallbacks, Google Gears, was designed by Google to provide a multitude of features prior to when the HTML5 specification took hold. In today's HTML5 web browsers, Google Gears is obsolete, but it does provide a useful fallback for pre-HTML5 web browsers, especially those that do not understand the Geolocation API.

The Geolocation JavaScript Library is a useful tool that bridges the interface discrepancies between the W3C's Geolocation API, Google Gears, and some mobile web browsers' JavaScript GPS interfaces. Once implemented, you can use this single library to access all major Geolocation-like interfaces.

Download the libraries http://code.google.com/apis/gears/gears_init.js and http://geo-location-javascript.googlecode.

com/svn/trunk/js/geo.js and save them into your website directory.

After you have both libraries loaded, you can access the Geolocation API, or fallback APIs, using the following code:

```
if (geolocation_position_js.init()) {
  geo_position_js.getCurrentPosition(
    successHandler, errorHandler);
}
```

If the `init()` method fails, no API was accessible, so an appropriate error message can be displayed to the user. If it succeeds, the *successHandler* and *errorHandler* parameters are functions that are to be called after an API has successfully retrieved the user's coordinates or if there is a failure.

*successHandler* provides a position object that holds the actual coordinate data.

## Request the User's Current Location

**1** Download the `gears_init.js` and `geo.js` libraries.

**2** Load the libraries in an HTML file.

**3** Type **if ( geo_position_js.init() ) { }**.

**4** Type **geo_position_js.getCurrentPosition ( geo_success );** if `init()` returns true.

**5** Type **else { ... }** to inform the user that no geolocation support or fallback is available.

**6** Type **function geo_success( position ) { ... }**.

**7** Access the user's degrees latitude and longitude.

**8** Display the information to the user.

**Ⓐ** Optionally, type **, geo_failure** to specify a failure callback handler.

**Ⓑ** Optionally, type **function geo_failure ( error ) { ... }** to access an `error.message` and `error.code`.

**9** Save your HTML file.

286

**10** Load your HTML file in a web browser.

**C** A notification bar requests that the user allow the site to know his or her location.

**11** Click **Allow**.

**Note:** *Opera may request that you agree to Google's Terms of Service, which is strange as there is no Google location service involved here.*

**Note:** *If you do not allow the request to proceed or you want to revoke access, you must go into your browser's preferences to reset the geolocation permissions setting.*

The user's current position is retrieved.

**D** The latitude and longitude coordinates are displayed.

**E** In Chrome, the ⊙ icon appears when the Geolocation API is active.

Although web applications written for mobile HTML5 web browsers can gain a new perspective on their users' surroundings, by providing relevant data to nearby shops, services, and attractions, for example, a significant population of mobile users will be left out in the cold with the current code in this section.

Users who own Android 2.2 to 3.1 devices — and possibly later versions, too, but this was the latest Android release as of August 2011 — require a specific option when calling the `getCurrentPosition()` method:

```
geo_position_js.getCurrentPosition(geo_success, geo_failure, { enableHighAccuracy: true });
```

According to the Geolocation API specification, the `enableHighAccuracy` option instructs the API to provide the best-possible GPS results. Normally, if a device does not support this much detail, the option is ignored, but if it does, it can result in higher power usage and a delay in getting results.

Earlier in this chapter, the section "Display a Specific Location with Google Maps" discusses how to use Google Maps to display a location. After you can locate the user, as explained in the preceding section, "Request the User's Current Location," it is possible to inject that information directly into a Google Maps JavaScript API object.

This is useful if you want to provide an interactive map that compares the user's current location to another location, such as a corporate office or an attraction. Although the code in this example shows how to get the user's location and set a marker, you can modify it by repeating step **6** below — with absolute latitude and longitude coordinates — and steps **9** and **10** — with unique variable names.

In order to do so, you will need to make some changes to the earlier Google Maps example code. First, you must tell the Google Maps API that you are now using a sensor to access its information.

Second, it may take some time for GPS coordinates to be retrieved, but this should not inhibit displaying a general high-level map when the page loads. So display the map first and then update it by panning and zooming in when the coordinates are available.

Finally, set a `marker` and `infowindow` object at the user's location, indicating that his or her location has been successfully detected. Also, add a `click` event to the marker so that it opens the information window.

## Display the User's Current Location with Google Maps

**1** Open an HTML file that uses the Google Maps JavaScript API to create a map object.

**2** Type **sensor=true** in the `src` attribute URL parameter that loads the Google Maps JavaScript API.

**3** Type **zoom: 3** to move the default zoom level to the country level.

**4** Remove any `marker` or `infowindow` objects for now.

**5** Initialize `geo.js`; create a local function that has the `position` object.

**6** Create a new `LatLng` object using `position.coords.latitude` and `position.coords.longitude`.

**Note:** *Because the map is already initialized, you can call* `map` *object methods to alter the current map display.*

**7** Type **map.panTo( latlng );** to move the map and center on the new coordinates.

**8** Type **map.setZoom(8);** to zoom in on the new location.

```
1  <!doctype html>
2  <html>
3    <head>
4      <meta name='viewport' content='initial-scale=1.0, user-scalable=no'>
5      <script type='text/javascript' src='jquery-1.?.min.js'></script>
6      <script type='text/javascript' src='gears_in?.?'></script>
7      <script type='text/javascript' src='geo.js'></script>
8      <script type='text/javascript'
9        src='http://maps.google.com/maps/api/js?sensor=true'></script>
10     <script>
11       function initMap () {
12         var latlng = new google.maps.LatLng( 63, -100 );
13         var options = {
14           zoom: 3,
15           center: latlng,
16           mapTypeId: google.maps.MapTypeId.ROADMAP
17         };
18
19         var map = new google.maps.Map( document.getElementById(
20             'map_canvas' ), options );
21       }
22     </script>
23   </head>
24   <body onload='initMap()'>
25     <div id='map_canvas' style='width:700px; height:500px'></div>
26   </body>
27 </html>
```

```
19         var map = new google.maps.Map( document.getElementById(
20             'map_canvas' ), options );
21
22         if ( geo_position_js.init() ) {
23           geo_position_js.getCurrentPosition( function(position){
24             latlng = new google.maps.LatLng( position.coords.latitude,
25               position.coords.longitude );
26             map.panTo(latlng);
27             map.setZoom(8);
28
29           });
30         }
31       }
32     </script>
```

**9** Create new `marker` and `infowindow` objects indicating that this is the user's detected position.

**10** Add the `click` event listener on the `marker` to open `infowindow`.

**11** Save your HTML file.

**12** Open your HTML file in a web browser.

The map is rendered with a generic, country-level location.

The Geolocation API requests and then identifies your location coordinates.

The map pans and zooms in on your location.

A marker appears at your location on the map.

**13** Click the marker.

Ⓐ A pop-up message appears.

---

## APPLY IT

Because the Geolocation API example in this section is pure JavaScript, everything happens on the web browser: There is no real way for you as the website owner to retrieve this information without leveraging some additional technology, such as Ajax, to send it to your web server.

jQuery provides some useful Ajax helper methods that make implementing this functionality easier.

### TYPE THIS

```
jQuery.post("/cgi-bin/location-listener.pl",
            position, function(data){
  return $('div#map_canvas').after(data);
});
```

### RESULT

A listener CGI script located at `/cgi-bin/location-listener.pl` is launched in the background, after `getCurrentPosition()` has populated the `position` object. The object is serialized and sent as a parameter to the CGI script.

Note that this example simply sends the data to the server and, when successful, injects the response output immediately after the `<div id='canvas'>` tag block.

Creating an appropriate CGI script to listen to Ajax requests is beyond the scope of this book. For a good example, see the book *Perl and Apache: Your visual blueprint for developing dynamic web content,* published by John Wiley & Sons, 2010.

# INTRODUCING WEB WORKERS

**W**ith Web Workers, you can split computationally expensive tasks into separate JavaScript threads and communicate to them independently from the main JavaScript program actually running in a web page.

The workers themselves are clones of the JavaScript runtime environment, so nearly all built-in methods and functions are available, but there are some restrictions on what they can do. For example, a worker cannot access the normal browser window directly, including the window and document objects, nor the DOM itself, so its perspective on the browser's HTML rendering process is nil. Web Workers do have access to the `navigator` and `location` objects, though, so they can discover what the browser is running and its current URL; however, this information is read-only.

The strength of the workers is to facilitate processing commands so that they can be outsourced from the browser's rendering process. This avoids locking the user interface while a resource-intensive task is working, allowing your web application to use the user's CPU more efficiently.

There are two types of Web Workers available — dedicated workers, which imply a single parent and worker process, and shared workers, which imply multiple parents accessing a single worker process. The dedicated model is much more common and described in this chapter; however, the differences between implementing the two are documented here.

The Web Workers specification is described in the Web Applications 1.0 document managed by WHATWG. You can access the latest version of this specification at www.whatwg.org/specs/web-apps/current-work/complete/workers.html.

## Dedicated Worker Setup and Communication

The following describes how to build a Web Worker and how it communicates with the parent thread.

### Dedicated Worker Code

The Web Worker code exists as a standalone file, separate from your main JavaScript code. Because the worker is response-based, there is just one "main" function that listens for input from the main thread and sends a response back.

### Listening for Input Messages

In order for your worker to do anything useful, you need to define a function that runs when a Web Worker message event occurs. A message event signifies a command from the parent to the worker and allows the worker to send additional data as instructions:

```
function onMessage( event ) {
  var input = event.data;
  ...
}
```

The `onMessage()` function will receive one argument, the `event` object, which can be used to access the data packet produced by the parent. In fact, literally, the input data is accessible from `event.data`.

Before you can use this function to process the input message, you must tie it in with an event listener. This will instruct the web browser what to do when a message event type is received by the worker thread — execute the `onMessage()` function:

```
self.addEventListener( 'message', onMessage, false
  );
```

The third parameter, `false`, indicates that this non-normative DOM event must not bubble up the DOM tree. The `addEventListener()` was originally created to enable you to override or amend existing event types, such as `click` and `submit`, in which case it was desirable to add new functionality to an event when the user triggered a click or submit process, for example.

Because Web Worker code is very specific about who listens to what, you will avoid conflicts with multiple workers in your DOM by always specifying `false` in this function in the worker and later in the parent.

### Sending Output Messages

When your worker is ready to send a response message back to the parent, it does so by using `self.postMessage()`. The content being sent can be anything, such as a variable or an object. Be aware that posted event data objects are copied and not shared like a C pointer:

```
function onMessage( event ){
  var input = event.data;
  var output = {};
  ...
  self.postMessage( output );
}
```

Note that multiple output messages can be posted from a single `input` message event. This can be useful if you want to send a progress report back to the parent detailing what stage of a calculation the worker is currently at — and then the final result when completed.

### Parent Code

The following describes how to launch a Web Worker and how to communicate with it.

### Load the Worker

Now that your Web Worker code is defined and stored in a file, you can import that file into your main JavaScript code using the `new Worker()` constructor. This will return a worker object that is used for communicating to the new thread:

```
var worker = new Worker( 'dedicated-worker.js' );
```

At this stage, the worker code is executed; nothing should happen yet as the worker itself is event based. However, if you wanted to, you could specify non-event code, such as an initialization routine, in the worker that would be executed right away.

Because each worker produces a worker object, multiple Web Workers can be spawned at once from a single parent. The workers themselves will not be able to see each other, so the parent will have to coordinate all communication. Note that if you use the shared worker model, this idea is reversed: Multiple parents share a single Web Worker thread, and its responsibility is to coordinate communication.

continued ➤

**Listen for Worker Output Messages**

The parent listens for worker output messages in the same way the worker listens for input messages. The only difference is semantics:

```
function onWorkerMessage( event ) {
  var workerOutput = event.data;
  ...
}
worker.addEventListener( 'message', onWorkerMessage,
  false );
```

This `worker.addEventListener()` callback must be established before you actually send the worker any instructions. This is because you must establish the callback procedure before you expect it to be used by posting a message to the worker.

**Send the Worker Input Messages**

After all the pieces are together, you can launch the worker itself by sending it an instruction. The actual data input can be anything, but if you are sending a complex structure, use an anonymous object as the worker input:

```
var workerInput = {};
...
worker.postMessage( workerInput );
```

The worker thread launches, and its `self.addEventListener( 'message', ... )` receives this `workerInput` variable from your main thread. The main thread is now allowed to proceed as `postMessage()` is nonblocking.

**Terminate the Worker**

A Web Worker thread can be terminated at any time by calling the `worker.close()` method in the parent or by calling `self.close()` in the worker itself.

After this is done, the worker cannot be relaunched until the web page is reloaded.

## Shared Worker Setup and Communication

The shared worker model is almost exactly the same as the dedicated worker model, the difference being that there is more than one parent accessing a worker at a time. To facilitate this, a `port` object is introduced.

### Shared Worker Code

The `port` object is used to coordinate communication between different parents. The port that receives the message event must be the same one used to respond:

```
function onMessage( event ) {
  var port = event.ports[0];
  var input = event.data;
  var output = {};
  ...
  self.port.postMessage( output );
}
self.addEventListener( 'message', onMessage, false );
```

An element of delegation needs to be applied within the `onMessage` function in order to make the shared nature of this worker useful. This implies an initialization routine and coordination between what data is shared publicly and privately with each connected parent.

An example of this is beyond the scope of this book; however, a good demonstration is available on the WHATWG specification for shared workers at www.whatwg.org/specs/web-apps/current-work/complete/workers.html#shared-state-using-a-shared-worker.

## Parent Code

Each parent interested in communicating with a shared worker thread must use the `new SharedWorker()` constructor. This will return a worker object that is used for communicating to the new thread:

```
var worker = new SharedWorker( 'shared-worker.js' );
```

As before, the worker's code is executed, but only if it is the first time that this shared worker has been launched. The primary difference between a dedicated and shared worker is a new `worker.port` object. This must be used to access the shared worker.

The `onWorkerMessage()` example callback function described earlier remains the same; only this time, the `worker.port` version of `addEventListener()` must be used to establish the callback:

```
worker.port.addEventListener( 'message', onWorkerMessage, false );
```

Sending messages using `postMessage()` has the same `worker.port` requirement.

```
var workerInput = {};
...
worker.port.postMessage( workerInput );
```

# CREATE A WEB WORKER JAVASCRIPT FILE

Using Web Workers in HTML5 is a very easy way to add in a level of optimization that was not possible a few short years ago. Previously, JavaScript could run in only one thread in the browser, and any CPU-intensive tasks bogged down user interface features. When you split up your CPU-intensive code into a Web Worker JavaScript file, your users can continue using your website while the Web Worker asynchronously works.

To convert existing JavaScript code into Web Worker code, you need to create a conduit that allows for subroutines to be executed by way of event messages. The parent JavaScript thread running in the browser window will send event messages to a listener running on your Web Workers,

and they in turn will send event messages to a listener running in your parent program.

When your Web Worker is first launched, all code that is accessible directly, that is outside of the event messages, will be launched right away. You can use this to initialize your Web Worker and prepare for the CPU-intensive task that will be executed by the user.

In the example code shown in this chapter, to generate actual CPU activity, a stress-tester utility is used as the Web Worker code. This program was originally produced by Yuen Kit Mun for his website Fossil Toys, www.fossiltoys.com/cpuload.html. His version was modified with permission to add in Web Worker functionality.

## Create a Web Worker JavaScript File

Ⓐ In a new JavaScript file, optionally, type **importScripts( 'script.js' );** to import a legacy JavaScript file that you want to convert into a Web Worker.

Ⓑ Optionally, define any initialization routines needed to run when the Web Worker first starts up.

*Note: In this example, the legacy program executes a portion of the DOM that is not Web Worker safe. That function must be overridden and made compatible with the Web Worker runtime environment.*

① Type **function onMessage( event ) {**.

② Type **var input = event.data;** to receive the input object from the parent's message event.

③ Perform a computational task using the input object.

④ Type **}**.

⑤ Type **self.addEventListener( 'message', onMessage, false );** to register an event message callback.

**6** Type **var output = {};** to construct a generic `output` object.

**7** Store the results of the message event calculation in the `output` object.

```
cpuload-worker.js (H:\public_html\html5\chapter16\demos\web-workers) - GVIM
File  Edit  Tools  Syntax  Buffers  Window  Help
 1 /* Import a local copy of CPU Stress Tester program produced by Yuen Kit Mun
 2  * from Fossil Toys - http://www.fossiltoys.com (used here with permission) */
 3 importScripts( 'cpuload.js' );
 4
 5 /* The cpuload report_back() function makes direct calls to the DOM to
 6  * report calculation activity to the web browser. Since this is not
 7  * compatible with Web Workers, we must override it and use our own version
 8  * of this method to post a message back to the parent. The parent thread
 9  * will recieve the event message and display the calculation. */
10 report_back = function( inelement, intext ) {
11   var output = {};
12
13   output.field = inelement;
14   output.value = intext;
15
16 };
17
18 /* CPU Load uses the function setdutycycle() to configure its intensity
19  * level and begin calculations. Since the user triggers the configuration
20  * and startup, and the user event launches on the parent, the parent must
21  * instruct the worker to run the function. */
22 function onMessage( event ) {
23   var input = event.data;
24
25   setdutycycle( input.setLoad );
26 }
27
28 /* Activate the message event listener on the worker thread */
29 self.addEventListener( 'message', onMessage, false );
                                                           17,0-1        All
```

**8** Type **self.postMessage( output );** to send the output object back to the parent as a message event.

**9** Save your JavaScript file as *program*-worker.js.

Your Web Worker JavaScript file is now ready to be linked into your web application.

```
cpuload-worker.js (H:\public_html\html5\chapter16\demos\web-workers) - GVIM
File  Edit  Tools  Syntax  Buffers  Window  Help
 1    port a local copy of CPU Stress Tester program produced by Yuen Kit Mun
 2     rom Fossil Toys - http://www.fossiltoys.com (used here with permission) */
 3 importScripts( 'cpuload.js' );
 4
 5 /* The cpuload report_back() function makes direct calls to the DOM to
 6  * report calculation activity to the web browser. Since this is not
 7  * compatible with Web Workers, we must override it and use our own version
 8  * of this method to post a message back to the parent. The parent thread
 9  * will recieve the event message and display the calculation. */
10 report_back = function( inelement, intext ) {
11   var output = {};
12
13   output.field = inelement;
14   output.value = intext;
15
16   self.postMessage( output );
17 };
18
```

The example in this chapter demonstrates an event-driven Web Worker that initializes itself and then listens for incoming message events from its parent, eventually sending messages back as the need arises. Although this is the most common way that you can use Web Workers, it is not the only way.

Specifically, if you were to forgo the `self.addEvent Listener()` code and message event function, the Web Worker shown in this section could be instructed to launch its CPU-intensive code as soon as it is loaded in the parent process.

Although the event message and listener model is the most convenient medium for interprocess communication in JavaScript, if you communicate with the Web server, too, you will need to add in another protocol method. For asynchronous connectivity, the `XMLHttpRequest` object will always work, or you can try the new WebSockets protocol, described in Chapter 17, "Communicating with WebSockets."

# LINK A WEB WORKER TO YOUR WEB APPLICATION

To use a Web Worker in your website, your mainline JavaScript program, known as the *parent thread,* must construct the `worker` object from a constructor and its source code. This object can then be used to communicate to the worker by way of event messages.

The event message syntax used in the parent program is almost identical to the Web Worker code, barring a couple differences. First, the initial call to the constructor forms a `worker` object that facilitates communication, whereas the Web Worker within aptly uses `self` for communication. Second, your parent program has the capability to listen to runtime errors caused by the worker thread. Although this may not help you with debugging *per se,* if an issue occurs in loading the worker, your parent can be notified.

The actual messages that you send between the parent and worker threads can be anything from simple numbers to complex objects. Here is a warning, though: `postMessage()` copies the message to the `addEventListener()` callback as it traverses threads, which means that data structures are duplicated in memory. So if you are really concerned about JavaScript efficiency, your code is probably already sending simple variables or data objects, and nothing overly complex.

Note that this chapter describes using a dedicated Web Worker, as this is the most common use case. You could use the alternative shared Web Worker model, which supports multiple parent threads — or to be more specific, browser windows — communicating to a single Web Worker memory stack. This shared worker model does not support communicating to different browser programs or hardware; to do this, you would require WebSockets and a web server program to coordinate traffic.

## Link a Web Worker to Your Web Application

**1** Open an HTML file or JavaScript file run by an HTML file.

**2** Type **var worker = new Worker ( 'program-worker.js' );** to initialize a new Web Worker process using *program*-worker.js.

**3** Type **function onWorkerError ( event ) { ... }** to receive any error messages.

**4** Type **worker.addEventListener ( 'error', onWorkerError, false );** to register an event error callback.

**⑤** Type **function *onWorkerMessage*
( event ) { }** to receive any
worker messages.

**⑥** Type **var workerOutput = event.
data;** to read the worker's event
message.

**Ⓐ** Optionally, perform a display task
using the worker output message.

**⑦** Type **worker.addEventListener(
'message', *onWorkerMessage*,
false );** to register the event
message callback.

**⑧** Type **var *workerInput* = {};** to
construct a generic worker input
object.

**Ⓑ** Optionally, store commands for the
worker in the input object.

**⑨** Type **worker.postMessage
( *workerInput* );** to send a message
event with the object to the worker.

**⑩** Save your HTML or JavaScript file.

Your main JavaScript program is now
linked to the Web Worker thread.

```
122        <script type='text/javascript'>
123          $(function(){
124            /* Load the cpuload.js wrapper, cpuload-worker.js, which
125             * provides the code to make the legacy program Web Worker
126             * compatible. */
127            var worker = new Worker( 'demos/web-worker/cpuload-worker.js' );
128
129            function onWorkerError( event ) {
130              $('output#error').html( 'ERROR: Line ' + event.lineno + ' in ' +
131                event.filename + ": " + event.message );
132            }
133
134            function onWorkerMessage( event ) {
135              var workerOutput = event.data;
136
137              $('output#' + workerOutput.field).html( workerOutput.value );
138            }
139
140            worker.addEventListener( 'error', onWorkerError, false );
141            worker.addEventListener( 'message', onWorkerMessage, false );
142
143            /* Set the 0% button to light-green right away, as the cpuload code
```

```
140            worker.addEventListener( 'error', onWorkerError, false );
141            worker.addEventListener( 'message', onWorkerMessage, false );
142
143            /* Set the 0% button to light-green right away, as the cpuload code
144             * is not active when the script first loads */
145            $('button.cpuload[data-percent=0]').addClass( 'bold' );
146
147            /* Respond to click events for the five buttons, forward the
148             * data-percent attribute value to cpuload.js */
149            $('button.cpuload').click(function(){
150              var percent = $(this).attr( 'data-percent' );
151              var workerInput = {};
152
153              /* Set the clicked button to light-green */
154              $(this).addClass( 'bold' );
155              $(this).siblings().removeClass( 'bold' );
156
157              workerInput.setLoad = percent;
158
159              /* Ready! Send the command to the Web Worker to activate */
160              worker.postMessage( workerInput );
161            });
162
163            // Define the "jquery-waves" animation routine.
```

---

As soon as your main JavaScript code executes `new
Worker()` in step 2 of this section, the new JavaScript
thread is spawned and its global code, if any, is
executed. This happens automatically and
asynchronously from your main JavaScript program.
After that point, the thread will sit idly by, waiting for
you to post a message, as in step 9, or for the main
JavaScript program to close.

An interesting feature of the parent/worker relationship
is that Web Workers themselves can spawn their own
subworker threads. Simply duplicate the process

described in this section in your worker file and create a
new subworker script to communicate with. This can be
useful if a task your worker is charged with becomes
blocking and you want to spawn a third JavaScript thread.

Do not abuse this privilege. Even though workers are
threaded to run concurrently, the user still has a finite
amount of processor resources. For example, if you have
the urge to use JavaScript to calculate pi to 10,000
digits, you should at least leave some processor cycles
for the user to play a game such as HTML5 Angry Birds,
http://chrome.angrybirds.com, in another browser tab.

After you have a worker and parent JavaScript code set up, you can launch the Web Worker process in your web application.

It is important to note at this stage what to expect from Web Workers. They will not automatically access new system resources, better utilize extended or expanded memory, or make your web browser 100% crash safe. In fact, they will make debugging using tools such as the Chrome Inspector impossible to use as no direct interaction with the rendered web browser itself is allowed. You are kind of working in a black-painted room with the lights out.

Web Workers' sole purpose is to move your CPU-intensive code into a different JavaScript thread, outside the main-line user interface, so that the user does not need to stare at a frozen browser window and can still use the UI JavaScript code on your site.

In case there is a problem with the Web Worker code, an error message handler was created that will relay any runtime errors back to the parent. This is convenient because, as mentioned, it is impossible to tie a debugger, such as the Chrome Inspector or Firebug, into a Web Worker process.

For this example site, a relatively complex jQuery animation is used as a demonstration of a UI task that needs to run alongside the Web Workers task. In other words, with the processor-intensive task in its own thread, this jQuery animation should move very smoothly.

But what if Web Workers are not available? Your program should still be able to run, at least. See the next section, "Falling Back for Non–Web Worker Browsers," to learn how to reenable legacy programs in a non–Web Worker environment.

## Launch a Web Worker Event from Your Web Application

① Open an HTML file with the worker and parent JavaScript code set up in an HTML5 web browser.

**Note:** *See earlier sections in this chapter for more information.*

The parent JavaScript process initializes.

The worker JavaScript process initializes.

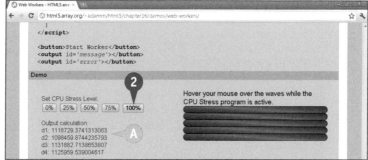

② Trigger a Web Worker event message from the browser interface.

Ⓐ The Web Worker listener event launches, triggering a CPU-intensive task.

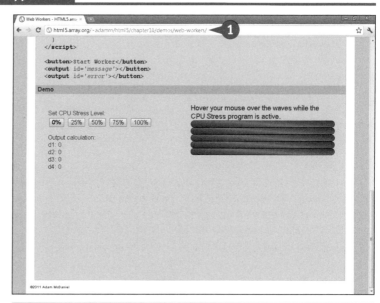

③ Launch the Task Manager in Windows (or the Activity Monitor in Mac OS X) to see the web browser CPU usage.

Ⓑ This is the browser CPU load of the Web Worker.

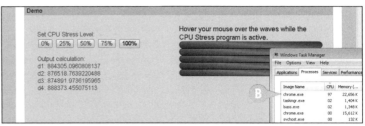

④ Trigger the parent JavaScript that manipulates the browser UI.

**Note:** *In this example, jQuery's* `hide()` *and* `show()` *methods animate content as it fades in and out of view. This generates CPU load on the browser's UI thread.*

The website remains quick and responsive while the Web Worker is active.

Ⓒ The overall CPU usage is shared between the Web Worker and the UI animation threads.

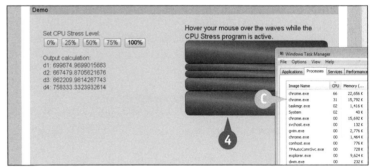

## APPLY IT

When you move to a new web page, close the browser's tab or close the browser entirely. All running JavaScript threads related to your web page will end. Although you do not have much control over the parent thread, you can send a signal to a new Web Worker thread to terminate. This will help you free up system resources used by the worker as it executed its program.

Such is the case when the worker has finished its task but the main web page or application is still active.

**TYPE THIS**

Type this in the parent JavaScript:
`worker.terminate();`

**RESULT**

If the parent process at any time calls `worker.terminate()`, that worker will terminate and free its resources.

**TYPE THIS**

Type this in the worker JavaScript:
`self.close();`

**RESULT**

If the worker process at any time calls `self.close()`, it will terminate and free its resources.

If either action happens, the original `worker` object in the parent is voided and now unusable. If the parent wants to use the worker again, it will have to be created again using the `new Worker()` constructor.

W hen your Web Worker code is functioning properly, what do you do about the users who have not yet upgraded their web browsers? You still want these users to use your website, despite the known issues running processor-intensive code. By activating Web Workers, you have cut off these legacy users entirely!

First, you will need to split up your CPU-intensive code into two separate files, one that provides Web Worker functionality and one that does not. This is actually already demonstrated in this chapter, as the previous sections show a legacy program running the original code and another running the Web Worker setup code.

Next, in your parent script, you will need to detect whether Web Worker support is available. This can be done easily using the Modernizr library, available at www.modernizr.com. When you detect that Web Workers are unavailable, your program must not call any Web Worker–dependent code, such as `addEventListener` or `postMessage()`, and instead import the original legacy program and run it locally.

In the examples in the earlier sections, the cpuload-worker. js file ran a function called `importScripts()` to import the cpuload.js code. Unfortunately, this function is available only in the context of a Web Worker and is not available in your main code. Instead, you can use jQuery's `get()` and `globalEval()` methods to perform the same functionality!

## Falling Back for Non–Web Worker Browsers

**1** Open your parent JavaScript file.

**2** Download and import the Modernizr library.

**3** Type **var worker = undefined;** to create a variable outside of the Modernizr test to hold the `worker` object.

**Note:** Be sure to remove the `var` before the `new Worker()` constructor.

**Note:** Because this variable stores the `worker` object handle, it will remain undefined if it cannot use Web Workers.

**4** Type **if ( Modernizr.webworkers ) { ... }** around your Web Worker setup process.

**5** Type **else {** to provide initialization code when Web Workers are not available.

**6** Type **jQuery.get( srcURL, function ( data ) { jQuery.globalEval( data ); });** to import the legacy source code into the main thread.

**A** Optionally, display a message to the user that Web Workers are not available and execution may be slow.

**7** Type **}**.

**8** Type **if ( worker ) { … }** around all
`worker.postMessage()` calls.

**9** Type **else { … }** to execute the
legacy functions directly.

**10** Call the function required to launch
your imported code.

**11** Save your JavaScript file.

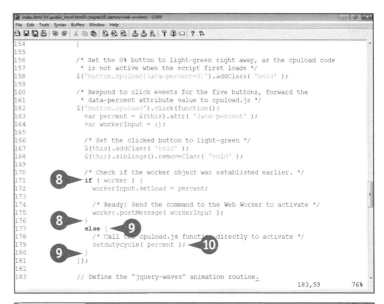

**12** Load your code in a non–Web
Workers browser.

***Note:*** *You can simulate single-thread
execution in any browser: Change step **4**
to* if ( false ) { … } *and reload.*

**B** Optionally, an error message
appears, warning there is no Web
Worker support.

**13** Trigger the CPU-intensive task.

**14** Trigger the browser UI animation.

The website slows down significantly
while CPU load is high.

**C** The Task Manager reports only one
process active, using CPU resources.

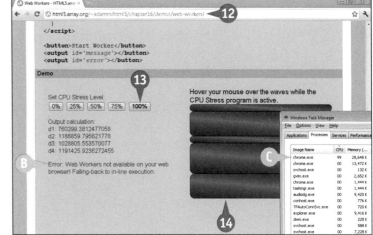

## EXTRA

Web Workers, like all new HTML5 features, should be
as transparent to the end user as possible, regardless of
the web browser version. Of course, there is an
unwritten statute of limitations; no self-respecting
website today will tout Netscape 2.0 compatibility, but
at the very least, you should respect that HTML5 is a
newer technology, and users are still using Internet
Explorer 6, Firefox 3.0, and so on.

On the other hand, you do need to ask yourself if this
legacy functionality is worth it. A CPU-intensive task
running inline will only produce a bad impression of

your website. It may be best to simply deny this support
and include a message saying, "Upgrade your web
browser, please."

It all depends on who your target audience is and what
other HTML5 features you have already implemented
to date that do not provide seamless backward
compatibility. Such is the case with the Canvas API, the
new form input fields, the Geolocation API, and so on. It
is not the end of the world to simply deny these users
access to your site, at the cost of the potential audience
size, at least until these users upgrade.

# Introducing WebSockets

When the Internet and the HTTP protocol were first conceived, information transfer was envisioned to be one way, web server to web browser, and the information on the server rarely changed. As the Internet matured, dynamic web page technology was developed, delivering updated content as soon as the user requested it. This was nice, but what if the website wanted to deliver new data after the page loaded, and have it trickle onto the web page itself without reloading?

Ingenious web developers figured they could keep the HTTP connection alive after the initial connection attempt. New information could flow to the user over an HTTP session that launched seconds or even minutes earlier and never closed. However, many firewalls and proxies took exception to this practice, either by buffering the overall response or, figuring the web server simply crashed or forgot about the user, by killing the connection. This left the user stranded in a state of midpage download.

Later, even more ingenious web developers discovered a little-known JavaScript API called *XMLHttp* in Internet Explorer, soon adopted as *XMLHttpRequest* in other browsers, and christened *Ajax,* an acronym for asynchronous JavaScript and XML. With this, JavaScript could make asynchronous HTTP requests to the server after the initial page load. This was great! It gave birth to many of the first web applications, notably Gmail and Google Maps. However, even Ajax was not without its flaws. As the browser was still responsible to make pull requests to the web server, if there was no new data available, the browser would not know until it asked. An efficient network-push model was still not available.

Even under Ajax, bidirectional communication between the server and browser, also known as *full duplex,* was still being emulated under HTTP, itself a *half-duplex* protocol. This resulted in even more overhead and latency: additional JavaScript on the browser and inefficient network traffic.

HTML5's WebSockets are designed to finally solve this problem. They combine the low-level and efficient communications inherent with Unix-like network sockets with Ajax-like asynchronous transactions. This full-duplex protocol significantly reduces JavaScript complexity, minimizes the per-transaction payload, and lowers the overall network latency to provide a true network-push interface.

---

## Browser Support

The original idea for WebSockets was promoted by Google engineers to WHATWG in 2007, in time for inclusion in an early draft of the HTML5 specification. As a direct result, Chrome has always had the best level of support. Today, the WebSockets API is available as of Safari 5, iOS Safari 4.2, Firefox 4, and Opera 11. Unfortunately, although Firefox 4 and Opera 11 initially touted support, in December 2010 their support was disabled by default due to concerns over protocol handshake security. The procedure on how to reenable these browsers for testing purposes is described later in this chapter in the Extra section of "Interact with a WebSocket Service."

In the long term, it is very likely that this problem will be fixed and the WebSocket API will be adopted by all major web browsers — even Microsoft has plans to include it for Internet Explorer 11. Therefore, you can still investigate and develop for it today, but limit your rollout to Chrome and Safari users.

## WebSockets API on a JavaScript Client

The WebSockets API is very straightforward: It initializes the object to connect, registers handler functions to receive incoming events, sends messages, and terminates when finished.

### Initialize the Connection

If the web browser supports WebSockets, you can initialize it by creating a new object, specifying the WebSocket service URL as a parameter:

```
var ws = new WebSocket(wsURL);
```

This returns a `WebSocket` object that you can use to register functions for incoming transactions, to send outgoing messages, and to terminate the connection.

### Register Event Listeners

There are four response event types that can be triggered by a WebSocket service — `open`, `close`, `message`, and `error`. You should register a handler function that will run as soon as such an event arrives on the web browser client:

```
ws.addEventListener('open', onOpen, false);
ws.addEventListener('close', onClose, false);
ws.addEventListener('message', onMessage, false);
ws.addEventListener('error', onError, false);
```

The `open` and `close` events trigger only once, immediately after the client/server connection is established and after it is terminated. You must define the handler functions `onOpen` and `onClose` as they will allow you to know when it safe to send a message to the server and to communicate to the end user the current status of the WebSocket connection.

The `message` event will trigger whenever a message is received from the server. You must define the handler function

`onMessage` to respond appropriately to the event. This function could be as simple as echoing the server message back to the end user.

If a problem occurs on the server or in the communication protocol, the `error` event triggers. Use this to attempt to reopen the connection, or at the very least to let the user know that there was a problem.

All four events supply an `event` object as the only parameter to the function handlers. You can use this to access details about the event as it was received.

### Send Messages

Whenever you want to send to the WebSocket service a message, use the `send()` method on the connected WebSocket object:

```
ws.send(message);
```

The message will be interpreted by the server, so be sure to follow any formatting that is required by the server to which you are connecting.

### Close the Connection

You can choose to disconnect the WebSocket connection at any time by calling the `close()` method on the connected WebSocket object:

```
ws.close();
```

It is a good practice to terminate the connection when the web page unloads. This way, the server is not left assuming that the connection is still active and can free its resources.

## WebSockets API on a Web Server

There are already a few server-side technologies that can be used to create WebSocket services:

- Perl — Uses the Mojolicious framework, http://mojolicio.us/.
- PHP — Uses the `phpwebsocket` module, http://code.google.com/p/phpwebsocket/.
- Apache/Python — Uses the `mod_pywebsocket` extension, http://code.google.com/p/pywebsocket/.
- Node.js — Uses the Socket.IO frameworks, http://socket.io.

# CREATE A WEBSOCKET CLIENT

To connect to a WebSocket service running on a web server, you will need to create a WebSocket client that runs on the user's web browser that supports the WebSockets API.

Before initializing a connection, you will need to verify if the browser supports the WebSocket API by testing for the `window.WebSocket` object. If it exists, you can establish the connection to a WebSocket service using a ws://*hostname*/*path* URL:

```
if ( 'WebSocket' in window ) {
  var websocket = new WebSocket(wsURL);
```

The returned object is then used to register an event listener for each of the four event types, `open`, `close`, `message`, and `error`:

```
websocket.addEventListener(eventtype,
  function, false);
```

Each event handler function will receive an `event` object parameter when the event fires. For the `open` and `close` event types, this object goes unused, but for the `message` and `error` event types, the object contains a `data` prototype with a message from the WebSocket server.

Upon the receipt of the initial `open` event, your program is allowed to communicate to the service by sending it messages using `websocket.send(message)`.

The WebSocket connection can be terminated at any time by sending a terminate signal with `websocket.close()`. The `close` event will be received when the server acknowledges the termination signal or closes the connection itself.

## Create a WebSocket Client

① In a JavaScript block, type **if ( 'WebSocket' in window ) { }** to check if the browser does support the WebSocket API.

② Type **var *websocket* = new WebSocket ( *wsURL* );** to initialize the object and connect to the WebSocket service.

Ⓐ Optionally, type **else { ... }** to notify the user that the WebSocket API is not supported.

③ Type **websocket.addEventListener ('open', *onOpen*, false );** to register an `open` event handler function.

④ Type **websocket.addEventListener ('close', *onClose*, false );** to register a `close` event handler function.

⑤ Type **websocket.addEventListener ('message', *onMessage*, false );** to register a `message` event handler function.

⑥ Type **websocket.addEventListener ('error', *onError*, false );** to register an `error` event handler function.

**7** Type **function *onOpen*() { }** to define the open event function.

**8** Type **function *onClose*() { }** to define the close event function.

**9** Type **function *onMessage*() { }** to define the message event function.

**10** Type **function *onError*() { }** to define the error event function.

**8** Optionally, type **$(window).unload ( function() { websocket.close(); });** in the onOpen() function.

**Note:** *This will register a handler function to the* unload *event. It will disconnect the WebSocket connection if the user navigates away from the page. This is not required, but it is a courtesy to the server so that it can free resources.*

**11** Save your HTML or JavaScript file.

This web page now supports a basic WebSocket client.

## APPLY IT

The initialization process can occur as soon as the web page loads or when the user clicks a connect button. If you chose a manual connect method, any premature calls to WebSocket methods such as websocket. addEventListener() will be ignored and trigger a JavaScript error.

### TYPE THIS

```
<script type='text/javascript'>
  $(function(){
    $('button#connect').click(function(){
      var wsURL = $('input#wsURL').val();
      // Test for window.WebSocket, connect to wsURL,
      // and register event functions.
    });
  });
</script>
<input type='text' id='wsURL'>
<button id='connect'>Connect</button>
```

### RESULT

The Connect button can now be used to establish a WebSocket connection. Within the $(*selector*).click() function, register all other WebSocket event listeners and define the supporting function handlers and optionally a Disconnect button function handler.

After you have created a WebSocket client framework, you can begin to tie outgoing messages as soon as the *onOpen()* function has started. This function will be run by the *open* event, after the connection handshake process is complete, indicating that a connection is active.

Because WebSockets are a full-duplex protocol, you can technically send a WebSocket message at any time to the server, after, that is, you have established a successful connection, of course. There is not much point in limiting your outgoing messages to *only* the *onOpen()* function, unless the WebSocket service does not require any additional messages.

Therefore, you need a way to be able to send commands, but only while online. This is accomplished by creating a new Message field and Send button. Using jQuery, it

is simple to trigger the *websocket.send(message)* command when the button is pressed.

But how do you stop the user from clicking the Send button until the connection has come online?

This is where two new CSS classes called *useWhileOnline* and *useWhileOffline* come into play. When you assign any input or button element either class name, jQuery can be made to automatically disable elements labeled *useWhileOnline* while offline and disable elements labeled *useWhileOffline* while online. When the connection status changes, the logic is reversed! Because you can only go online via *onOpen()* and go offline via *onClose()*, it makes sense to put your jQuery calls here.

Naturally, when the JavaScript client web page first loads, you default to an offline state. jQuery must ensure that all *useWhileOnline* classed elements are disabled right away.

## Send WebSocket Messages

**①** Open an HTML file that is already configured as a WebSocket client.

**②** Type **<input class='useWhileOnline' type='text' id='message'>**.

**③** Type **<button class='useWhileOnline' id='send'>Send</button>**.

**Note:** *Add* class='useWhileOffline' *to the input and Connect button elements and* class='useWhileOnline' *to the Disconnect button element.*

**④** Go to the <script> tag or a JavaScript file sourced by this HTML file.

**⑤** Wrap the connection block around the jQuery-ready function, if you have not done so already.

**⑥** Type **$('button#send').click(function(){**.

**⑦** Type **var message = $('input#message'). val();**.

**⑧** Type **websocket.send( message );**.

**⑨** Type **});**.

Your WebSocket client can now send messages to the server.

```
150          function onError() {
151          }
152      </script>
153      <article class='example'>
154          <div>
155              <input class='useWhileOffline' type='text' id='wsURL'
156                  value='ws://html5.array.org:3000/time'>
157              <button class='useWhileOffline' id='connect'>Connect</button>
158              <button class='useWhileOnline' id='disconnect'>Disconnect</button>
159          <div>
160          </div>
161              <input class='useWhileOnline' type='text' id='message'>
162              <button class='useWhileOnline' id='send'>Send</button>
163          </div>
164      </article>
```

```
113  <script type='text/javascript'>
114      var websocket;
115  $(function() {
116      $('button#connect').click(function() {
117          if ( 'WebSocket' in window ) {
118              var wsURL = $('input#wsURL').val();
119
120              websocket = new WebSocket(wsURL);
121
122              websocket.addEventListener('open', onOpen, false );
123              websocket.addEventListener('close', onClose, false );
124              websocket.addEventListener('message', onMessage, false );
125              websocket.addEventListener('error', onError, false );
126          }
127          else {
128              alert("Oh noes~! WebSockets are not supported on " +
129                  "your browser!\n(I know!!!!)");
130          }
131      });
132
133      $('button#disconnect').click(function() {
134          websocket.close();
135      });
136
137      $('button#send').click(function() {
138          var message = $('input#message').val();
139          websocket.send(message);
140      });
141  });
142
                                                              113,1        76%
```

**10** Type **$('.useWhileOnline').attr ('disabled','true');** to disable all `useWhileOnline` elements.

**11** Type **$('.useWhileOffline').remove Attr('disabled');** to enable all `useWhileOffline` elements.

*Note: These functions set the default for when the page first loads. The latter function is unnecessary as nothing should be disabled yet, but this makes the code look cleaner.*

**12** Type **$('.useWhileOnline').removeAttr ('disabled')** in the `onOpen()` function.

**13** Type **$('.useWhileOffline').attr ('disabled','true')** in the `onOpen()` function.

**14** Type **$('.useWhileOnline').attr ('disabled','true')** in the `onClose()` function.

**15** Type **$('.useWhileOffline').removeAttr ('disabled')** in the `onClose()` function.

**16** Save your HTML or JavaScript file.

The buttons that require a WebSocket connect are only clickable when online, and vice versa.

```
113        <script type='text/javascript'>
114 _      var websocket;
115        $(function() {
116          $('.useWhileOnline').attr('disabled','true');
117          $('.useWhileOffline').removeAttr('disabled');
118
119          $('button#connect').click(function() {
120            if ( 'WebSocket' in window ) {
```

```
140        $('button#send').click(function() {
141          var message = $('input#message').val();
142          websocket.send(message);
143        });
144      });
145
146      function onOpen() {
147        $(window).unload(function() {
148          websocket.close();
149        });
150
151        $('.useWhileOnline').removeAttr('disabled');
152        $('.useWhileOffline').attr('disabled','true');
153      }
154
155      function onClose() {
156        $('.useWhileOnline').attr('disabled','true');
157        $('.useWhileOffline').removeAttr('disabled');
158      }
159
160      function onMessage() {
161      }
162
163      function onError() {
164      }
165    </script>
166    <article class='example'>
167      <div>
168        <input class='useWhileOffline' type='text' id='wsURL'
169            value='ws://html5.array.org:3000/time'>
                                                    169,1        89%
```

---

The online and offline classes are used as a convenience to the user and are technically not required to use WebSockets. Because they control the state of the `disabled` attribute in the button and input elements, they can be used to show the user which UI components are available when the WebSocket connection is offline and which components are enabled when a connection is online.

As a result, the only element that is clickable while offline is the Connect button. When it is clicked and you go online, it is impossible to connect to anything else, so the Connect button is disabled. Granted, multiple WebSocket connections can be opened in tandem, but for the sake of this example, only one is allowed at a time.

Remember that the `websocket.send()` method, and subsequently the Send button, can be called only when the WebSocket API has sent the `open` event. This is why in the example you remove the `disabled` attribute on the input and button elements only in the `onOpen` function and then re-add the attribute in the `onClose` function.

After you have a WebSocket client that can send messages to a WebSocket service, it makes sense to display the service response messages back to the web browser. Additional information, such as the connection status, error messages, and outgoing messages, is useful to display, too. The best way to do this is to create an `output` element and use jQuery's `append` method to inject information into it. You also can use jQuery's `scrollTop` method to ensure that the window is always showing the last entry, which appears at the bottom of the scrollable window.

Because the `<output>` tag can potentially scroll down the screen, it is a good idea to use the CSS `overflow` property.

This enables you to limit the height and width and have the message automatically scroll down within a nested window.

Remember that this is a convenience process for you when developing your HTML5 web application. Displaying the message activity enables you to easily monitor and debug the WebSocket communication between the browser and the server. For a production web application, a WebSocket implementation should be entirely transparent to the end user.

The purpose of WebSockets is to be a faster and more efficient version of Ajax. Therefore, any website that uses Ajax today should be able to transition to WebSockets, theoretically. This section helps you understand that transition process.

## Display WebSocket Messages

**1** Open an HTML file that is already configured as a WebSocket client.

**2** Type **<output id='*log*'></output>** to provide an output window that displays WebSocket activity.

**3** Go to the `<style>` tag or a CSS file sourced by this HTML file.

**4** Type **output#*log* {**.

**5** Type **height: *200px*;** to set the output log window height.

**6** Type **width: *500px*;** to set an arbitrary output log window width.

**7** Type **overflow: auto;** to enable automatic scrolling.

**8** Type **display: block;**.

**9** Type **}**.

⑩ Go to the `<script>` tag, or a JavaScript file sourced with this HTML file.

⑪ Type **function** *logMessage*(message) **{ }**.

⑫ Type **$('output#*log*').append ('<li>'+*message*).scrollTop(9e9);**.

⑬ Type *logMessage*('Sent: ' + **message);** in `$('button#send). click()`.

⑭ Type *logMessage*('Connected'); into the *onOpen*() function.

⑮ Type *logMessage*('Disconnected'); in *onClose*().

⑯ Type **event** as the parameter for *onMessage*() and *onError*().

⑰ Type *logMessage*('Received: ' + **event.data);** in *onMessage*().

⑱ Type *logMessage*('Error: ' + **event. data);** in the *onError*() function.

⑲ Save your HTML or JavaScript file.

Your WebSocket client can display its activity log directly within the web page.

After your WebSocket client has all its components in place, you will be ready to connect to a WebSocket server, as described in the next section, "Interact with a WebSocket Service," and monitor the communication activity log.

Going back to this example briefly, in the *logMessage*() function in step 12, log messages are appended to the scrollable `$('output#*log*')` element, but an odd technique is used that should be explained. Because the log file is always being appended to, it

makes sense to always see the end of the scrollable log area. jQuery ensures that the visible scrolling area is always positioned at the bottom of the element, but the way this works is a bit of a jQuery hack. By calling `$(*selector*).scrollTop(9e9)`, you are instructing the browser to scroll to the 9,000,000,000th pixel from the top of the *selector* element, but because that element position will never be found, effectively this means, "scroll to the bottom."

Although it is outside the scope of this book to describe how to create a WebSocket service online, there are several examples available online that have open ports to which you can connect. The companion website for this book has a few demonstration WebSocket services active to which you can connect:

- ws://html5.array.org:3000/relay — Relay WebSocket Service — This service relays any incoming messages back to all other clients currently connected.
- ws://html5.array.org:3000/time — Time WebSocket Service — This service broadcasts the current server time every second while connected. Any messages sent are echoed back in uppercase.
- ws://html5.array.org:3000/news — News Ticker WebSocket Service — This service accepts an incoming category message and then streams the news.google.com category's RSS feedback.

All three of these services post a message to the client as soon as it connects. This message introduces the service and then either starts sending data, as is the case in the Time WebSocket Service, or provides some simple plain-text instructions as to how to proceed. At a minimum, your WebSocket client program needs to be listening to the message event so that it can receive the initial server message.

These WebSocket services were written using Mojolicious, a Perl WebSocket framework, specifically for this chapter of the book. The source code is available at http://html5.array.org/demos/websocket/services.html.

After you have all the pieces of the puzzle in place, you can begin using your JavaScript WebSocket client.

## Interact with a WebSocket Service

**1** Open a WebSocket client HTML file in a supported WebSocket browser, such as Google Chrome.

The input and button elements all appear.

**Note:** If you configured a manual Connect button, it should be the only button that is not disabled when the page first loads.

**2** Type a WebSocket service URL into the input field, if you created one.

**3** Click the Connect button, if you created one.

**Note:** If you do not have a wsURL input and a Connect button, you will need to modify the new WebSocket(wsURL) JavaScript code, save, and reload the page.

The WebSocket client connects to the WebSocket service.

**A** A log message indicating that the WebSocket is connected appears.

**B** Other log messages start streaming in.

**4** Type a message into the input field.

**5** Click Send.

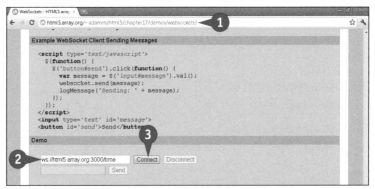

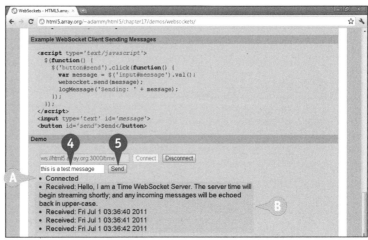

The WebSocket client sends the message to the server.

● The outgoing message is displayed in the output log element.

● The incoming response message is displayed.

Additional incoming messages continue after the initial outgoing message.

**6** Click the Disconnect button, if you created one.

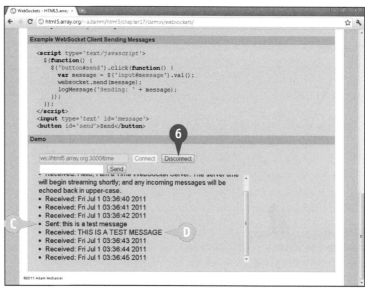

The connection between the WebSocket client and server is broken.

● A log message indicating that the WebSocket is disconnected appears.

The input field and the Send and Disconnect buttons become disabled.

*Note: Navigating away from the web page will also disconnect the WebSocket connection; the `onClose()` function will fire, and a log message will be written to a page that will imminently disappear.*

If the initialization fails, the user may be running a web browser that has support, but that support may be disabled by default. Such is the case with Firefox 5 and Opera 11.50. Later versions of these browsers may also be affected.

In Firefox, you can activate WebSockets by going to the internal URL about:config, filter for websocket preferences, and enable the `network.websocket.enabled` and `network.websocket.override-security-block` preferences:

In Opera, go to the internal URL opera:config, search for **websocket**, and enable the Enable WebSockets check box.

Naturally, these hidden configuration options are designed for developers to investigate WebSockets; they are not intended for end users to actually use them quite yet. You could display instructions to users of these browsers; just be sure that you detect the browsers and respective versions correctly! Do not promote these instructions for users running an older Firefox or Opera release or Internet Explorer.

# Introducing Desktop Notifications for Chrome

U sing the Google Chrome web browser, it is possible to display a subtle notification pop-up window on the user's desktop from your web application. This will enable you to get the user's attention if your web application is running in the background and the user is focused on another program.

Currently, this Chrome-specific feature is not a part of any HTML5 specification. Its documentation is available at The Chromium Projects page at www.chromium.org/developers/design-documents/desktop-notifications/api-specification/, but it is subject to change the closer it gets to being accepted by the W3C.

There is a version of this API available at the W3C as an *editor's draft,* meaning that it has not yet been officially submitted to the W3C and is a work-in-progress. Written by the Google engineer who originally designed the Desktop Notifications API, the specification is titled *Web Notifications,* and it is available at the W3C Public CVS Repository page at http://dev. w3.org/2006/webapi/WebNotifications/publish/.

This chapter describes the Desktop Notifications API as it is currently available in Chrome but not the Web Notifications API.

## Web Browser Support

To detect if the user's web browser supports the Desktop Notifications API, simply check if the object `window. webkitNotifications` exists in the DOM:

```
if ( 'webkitNotifications' in window ) {
   // Desktop Notification API is available
}
else {
   // Desktop Notification API is not available,
   // attempt an alternative method.
}
```

For alternative notification implementations, see the subsection "Alternative Implementations," later in this section.

## Notification Workflow

Displaying desktop notifications is a three-step process. First, you must use the NotificationCenter interface to check if the user has made a decision to grant display permissions to your website. If no decision has been made, the site must request permission.

If permission has been denied, the API will not continue. Only if the user removes the deny decision in the browser preferences will this check-and-request process restart.

If permissions have been granted, the second step is to create an instance of the Notification interface and establish the contents of the pop-up notification message.

The third and final step is to actually launch the Notification instance on the user's desktop and to handle any callback function events. These events launch when the notification is displayed, clicked, and closed and if there is an error.

312

## Desktop Notifications API

The draft Desktop Notifications API is not yet standard, which is why its parent object is `window.webkitNotifications`. After it is accepted as an HTML5 specification, it will likely migrate to `window.notifications`, but its current name and interface will likely be kept active for legacy reasons.

### NotificationCenter Interface

The NotificationCenter interface contains four methods used to prepare for displaying a notification message to the user:

```
window.webkitNotifications.checkPermission()
```

The `checkPermission()` method verifies if the user has already granted permission to the website to launch desktop notification pop-ups. If it returns 0 (zero), permission is granted, so the next step is to call either `createNotification()` or `createHTMLNotification()`. If it returns 1, call `requestPermission()` to request permissions from the user. Any other API request will be ignored. If it returns 2, permission has been denied. All other API requests will be ignored.

```
window.webkitNotifications.requestPermission()
```

The `requestPermission()` method can be executed only in the context of a user event, such as the user clicking a link. For this reason, the user must consciously be interacting with the website before the request notification even appears. This method is the only one with this restriction; all others in the API can be called automatically by the website as each requirement for a desktop notification occurs in your web

application. The `request` method triggers an information bar (infobar) that slides down just below the bookmarks bar.

The user must click Allow in the infobar before the remainder of the API may be used. From this point on, `checkPermission()` will return only 0 or 2 until the user removes the permission setting.

Continue creating the actual notification instance only if `checkPermission()` returns 0.

```
message = window.webkitNotifications.
    createNotification(icon, title, content)
```

The `createNotification()` method enables you to build a simple notification pop-up that has an *icon* image URL, a *title* text string, and a *content* text string. No HTML code is allowed any parameter.

```
message = window.webkitNotifications.
    createHTMLNotification(URL)
```

The `createHTMLNotification()` method is more flexible; with it, you can reference an internal or external URL and have it appear in the desktop notification pop-up window.

Both functions return an instance of the Notification interface that is used to launch the pop-up itself.

continued ➤

### Notification Interface

An instance of the Notification interface is what you use to launch the actual notification message window when it is required and to define callback functions that will execute as specific notification window events occur.

```
message.show()
```

The `show()` method launches the actual notification instance on the user's desktop. If there are too many notifications currently open, this will queue it to launch when space is available.

The actual width and height of the pop-up window is not customizable. The default is 300 pixels wide and between 45 and 160 pixels tall. The height expands depending on how much text needs to be displayed. Usually, only three notification windows can appear at once on Windows and Mac OS X desktops and four on Linux desktops; the actual number depends on desktop screen size.

```
message.cancel()
```

The `cancel()` method closes the pop-up message if it is visible, removes it from the `show()` queue if it is not yet displayed, calls the `onclose` event, and destroys its Notification instance.

```
message.ondisplay = function() { ... }
```

The `ondisplay` property stores the event listener function executed when the display is actually launched on the user's desktop. This may or may not happen immediately after `show()` is called, depending on how many notifications are currently active and cannot be immediately displayed.

```
message.onclick = function() { ... }
```

The `onclick` property stores the event listener function executed when the user clicks the display notification pop-up.

```
message.onclose = function() { ... }
```

The `onclose` property stores the event listener function executed when the user closes the display notification pop-up or when `cancel()` is called.

```
message.onerror = function() { ... }
```

The `onerror` property stores the event listener function executed if the display notification pop-up fails to launch after `show()` is called.

## The Future of the Desktop Notifications API

Because the Notifications API is in a state of heavy development, the interfaces and methods described in this chapter may not be the same as what you will find in a future web browser version. As of August 2011, if you were to browse the W3C's specifications regarding the Notifications API, you will find that it discusses an interface that is very different.

### Requesting Permission

The permission request component of the current NotificationCenter interface has been moved into a completely new specification, simply called the *Feature Permissions API*. It is anticipated that other HTML5 features may join desktop notifications here, such as the Geolocation and FileSystem APIs.

As the API is still in flux, I cannot give a code example here. However, if you are interested in the plan for this new API, an editor's draft is available at the W3C page http://dev.w3.org/2009/dap/perms/FeaturePermissions.html.

### The Notification Constructor

The previous NotificationCenter and Notification interfaces will be merged into the new Web Notifications API. As a result, the methods used to generate and display a notification window will be simplified:

```
var notification = new Notification(icon, title,
    content);
notification.show();
```

In this new API, the display event was renamed to show, and the click, close, and error events and the cancel() method are all maintained. If you want to review the latest Notifications API specification, see the W3C working draft page at www.w3.org/TR/notifications/.

Essentially, the latest development version of Chrome as of when this book was written, Chrome 14, contains an experimental version of the Desktop Notifications API, as it is described in this chapter, and not the version described by the Notification constructor. Therefore, feel free to try it out to see if it works for your web application. If it does, pay special attention to future versions of your browser to ensure that the code you write today works tomorrow. Just remember that with any HTML5 experimental API, there is no guarantee.

## Alternative Implementations

There are some alternative implementations of the desktop notifications feature for non-Chrome browsers; however, the APIs they follow do not conform to what is described in this chapter.

### Google Gears

The Google Gears plug-in has proposed similar functionality in its JavaScript API but appears to have stagnated. This is unfortunate as it could have filled a good niche of pre-HTML5 web browsers including Internet Explorer 6 to 8, Firefox 1.5 to 3.6, and other mobile browsers. There is a design document available at the Google Code page at http://code.google.com/p/gears/wiki/NotificationAPI; however, it looks like Google has abandoned this route in favor of its native Desktop Notifications API.

### Yip

Yip is a Firefox extension that allows you to receive notifications that are triggered by third-party desktop APIs, such as Growl on Mac OS X, Snarl on Windows, and libnotify on Linux. Therefore, coding your web app for Yip allows anyone with its Firefox extension to launch desktop notifications. You can learn more at http://abcdefu.wordpress.com/2009/06/09/introducing-yip-an-unified-notification-system-for-the-web/.

### Firefox Mobile

Firefox has recently implemented its own simpler Desktop Notifications API based on Google's specification, only available on the Android version of Firefox Mobile. This feature is documented at the Mozilla Developer Network page at https://developer.mozilla.org/en/DOM/Displaying_notifications.

**B**efore you can display a Desktop Notifications API pop-up window in Chrome, you must request permission from the user using an infobar. An *infobar* is a subtle slide-down prompt that appears underneath the URL bar and asks the user a question. The user must grant permission for your web app to use the API; otherwise, all other desktop notification calls will be ignored.

This ensures that the user actually wants the desktop notification feature active, avoiding the problems associated with rampant abuse of unwanted pop-up windows in the late 1990s and early 2000s.

Although you can call the `checkPermission()` method at any time, you can call `requestPermission()` only on a `click` event performed by the user. You can use jQuery to easily leverage such an event:

```
var notifyAPI = window.webkitNotifications;
if ( typeof notifyAPI == 'object' &&
       notifyAPI.checkPermission() == 1 ) {
  $('div#configure-notify span').
  click(function(){
     notifyAPI.requestPermission();
  });
} else {
  $('div#configure-notify').remove();
}
```

The `checkPermission()` call returns 1 if the user has not made a decision about access, 0 if permission is granted, and 2 if permission is denied. To provide a good user interface, remove the `configure-notify` object if the Desktop Notifications API is not supported or if `checkPermission()` returns anything but 1.

## Request User Permission to Display Desktop Notifications

**1** Open an HTML5 or JavaScript file that uses the jQuery library.

**2** Type **var *notifyAPI* = window. webkitNotifications;** to access the API with a shorter variable name.

**3** Type **if ( typeof *notifyAPI* == 'object' && *notifyAPI*.checkPermission() == 1 ) { } else { }.**

**4** Type **<div id='*configure-notify*'><span class='*fake-link*'>Click here</span> to configure desktop notification messages.</div>.**

**Note:** *Create a* `fake-link` *class to make this* <span> *tag look like a normal hyperlink.*

**5** Type **$('div#*configure-notify* span'). click(function() { *notifyAPI*. requestPermission(); });** to request permissions when the span is clicked.

**6** Type **$('div#*configure-notify*'). remove();** to remove the request permission message when access is granted or denied.

**7** Save your file.

(8) Open your HTML file in Google Chrome.

(9) Click the link that will pull up your desktop notification permission request.

(A) An infobar appears and asks if you want to allow or deny desktop notifications.

**Note:** *If the user simply closes the infobar,* checkPermission() *will continue to return 1 because no decision has been made.*

(10) Click Allow.

**Note:** *Users can revoke permissions in Chrome's preferences: Click* 🔧 ➔ *Preferences* ➔ *Under the Hood* ➔ *Privacy* ➔ *Content Settings* ➔ *Notification* ➔ *Manage Exceptions.*

(11) Reload the page.

(B) In this example, the configure request is gone.

**Note:** *Reloading is required because of how the sample code flows. Unfortunately, in this version of the Desktop Notifications API, there is no event that fires after the user clicks Allow.*

## APPLY IT

You can easily show the user what the current setting is by changing your logic slightly. In the sample code, you would split the typeof *notifyAPI* and *notifyAPI.* checkPermission() tests, so if the former is true and the latter is not equal to 1, you can override the <div id='configure-notify'> block to display the status; otherwise, you can remove the link as the API is unavailable.

**Example**
```
if ( typeof notifyAPI == 'object' ) {
  var perm = notifyAPI.checkPermission();
  if ( perm == 1 ) {
```

```
    // jQuery request permission click event
  } else {
    $('div#configure-notify').html(
      "Desktop notifications are currently " +
      (perm == 2 ? "disabled" : "enabled") +
  ".");
  }
} else {
  $('div#configure-notify').remove();
}
```

# LAUNCH A DESKTOP NOTIFICATION MESSAGE

After permission has been granted, you can trigger a desktop notification pop-up message at any time in your web application. Naturally, the whole point in displaying a desktop notification is to get the user's attention when your web application is running in the background. This implies some sort of Ajax-like activity that triggers the launch. The Gmail service is a good example of this implementation. Simply leave Gmail running in the background and as new mail arrives, a desktop notification message makes the announcement.

```
var notifyAPI = window.webkitNotifications;
if ( typeof notifyAPI == 'object' &&
     notifyAPI.checkPermission() == 0 ) {
  var notifyMessage = notifyAPI.
 createNotification(iconURL, title, content);
  notifyMessage.show();
}
```

Because `createNotification()` can be called at any time, such as during an Ajax callback, it is a good idea to repeat the object type discovery test and verify that `checkPermission()` is 0, indicating the user has granted you permission to display notifications. It is not possible to repeat the `requestPermission()` method if it returns 1.

The object returned by the `createNotification()` method is a member of the Notification interface. With it, you can call the `show()` method to actually pop up the notification message.

Notification windows can be closed when you run the `cancel()` method or when the user clicks the Close button on the notification itself.

## Launch a Desktop Notification Message

① Open an HTML5 or JavaScript file that uses the jQuery library.

② Identify an Ajax or other asynchronous event that you want to trigger a notification.

**Note:** In this example, a jQuery `click()` method is used as a stand-in for an incoming Ajax event callback. Because clicking this span element will pop up notifications, use this for testing purposes only.

③ Type var **notifyAPI** = window. **webkitNotifications;**.

④ Type if ( typeof **notifyAPI** == 'object' && **notifyAPI.checkPermission()** == 0 ) { ... } to check if permission is granted.

⑤ Type var **notifyMessage** = **notifyAPI. createNotification(** to create an instance of the Notification interface.

⑥ Insert the URL for an icon image.

⑦ Insert the desktop notification title.

⑧ Insert the desktop notification content.

⑨ Type );.

**318**

**⑩** Type ***notifyMessage*.show();** to launch the desktop notification message.

**⑪** Save your file.

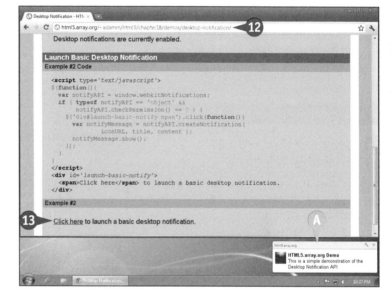

**⑫** Open your HTML file in Google Chrome.

**⑬** Trigger your desktop notification event.

**Ⓐ** A desktop notification window appears, separate from the calling browser window.

## EXTRA

As mentioned earlier, usually only three notification windows can appear at a time on Windows and Mac OS X desktops and four on Linux desktops, depending on the user's desktop screen size. If there are additional Notification instances created and launched, they will be queued to open when you run `show()`. When the user closes an existing notification message while over this limit, the oldest message in the queue will be retrieved and displayed.

The size of the display area for a single line of `title` and `content` is 300 pixels wide, 45 pixels tall. If additional lines are required, the maximum height grows to 160 pixels tall. After that, a scroll bar appears in the desktop notification window itself.

Depending on the operating system, there are some subtle differences in the notification window itself. The following shows the same notification window code running on Linux and Mac OS X desktops.

# Customize the Desktop Notification UI

If the basic notification window structure is too plain for you, you can customize it by launching an HTML notification window with a custom URL. Simply save your notification message into a separate web page, and it will be displayed as the notification window content.

You use the same check permissions and display procedures to create your custom desktop notification UI as described earlier in this chapter, except that you replace createNotification() with createHTMLNotification() and specify the URL as the only argument:

```
var notifyAPI = window.webkitNotifications;
if ( typeof notifyAPI == 'object' &&
     notifyAPI.checkPermission() == 0 ) {
  var notifyMessage = notifyAPI.
 createHTMLNotification(URL);
```

```
  notifyMessage.show();
}
```

Do not use any hyperlinks in your custom notification web page! If you use any, Chrome will render the new page within the notification window itself. Although you may think that the target='_parent' global attribute would correct this problem, Chrome does not identify the original web app browser window as the _parent window, which is a bug as of Chrome 14. At best, you could use an arbitrary target name to open a new browser tab, but the original web app browser page cannot be redirected to the link reference.

Instead, use the onclick event callback described in the following section, "Listen for Desktop Notification Events," and refrain from using any hyperlinks in your custom desktop notification UI.

## Customize the Desktop Notification UI

① Perform steps **1** to **4** from the preceding section, "Launch a Desktop Notification Message."

② Type **var *notifyMessage* = *notifyAPI*.createHTML Notification(.**

③ Insert the URL to the notification web page.

**Note:** *In this example, the URL is a relative link to the same subdirectory as this page because of an earlier* <link href='../../'> *in the* <head> *block.*

④ Type **);.**

⑤ Type ***notifyMessage*.show();** to launch the custom desktop notification message.

⑥ Save your file.

**7** Create a new HTML5 file.

**8** Define your notification message.

**9** Save the HTML file so that it is accessible from the URL used in step **3**.

**Note:** *You can create a CGI script and call it in step **3** to create a dynamically generated custom error message. Make sure that the URL you specify includes any query-string parameters required.*

```html
custom-notification.html - (H:\publi...r18\demos\desktop-notification) - GVIM
File Edit Tools Syntax Buffers Window Help

 1 <!doctype html>
 2 <html>
 3   <head>
 4     <title>Custom HTML5 Notification</title>
 5     <style>
 6       @font-face {
 7         font-family: ubuntu;
 8         src: url(ubuntu-r-webfont.ttf), url(ubuntu-r-webfont.eot);
 9       }
10       body {
11         background-image: -webkit-linear-gradient( left, white, blue );
12         text-align: center;
13       }
14       div {
15         display: inline-block;
16         background: white;
17         box-shadow: 0px 0px 10px 0 black;
18         border: 1px solid black;
19         border-radius: 10px;
20         padding: 5px;
21         font-family: ubuntu, arial;
22       }
23     </style>
24   </head>
25   <body>
26     <div>This is a custom HTML5<br>
27       notification message!!</div>
28   </body>
29 </html>

                                                    29,7        All
```

**10** Open your HTML file in Google Chrome.

**11** Trigger your desktop notification event.

**A** A custom desktop notification window appears, separate from the calling browser window.

```
Desktop Notification - HTM ×
← → C  ⎈ html5.array.org/~adamm/html5/chapter18/demos/desktop-notification/           ☆ ⚲

    if ( typeof notifyAPI == 'object' &&
       notifyAPI.checkPermission() == 0 ) {
    $('div#launch-basic-notify span').click(function(){
      var notifyMessage = notifyAPI.createNotification(
          iconURL, title, content );
      notifyMessage.show();
    });
    $('div#launch-custom-notify span').click(function(){
      var notifyMessage = notifyAPI.createHTMLNotification( URL );
      notifyMessage.show();
    });
    }

  </script>
  <div id='launch-basic-notify'>
    <span>Click here</span> to launch a basic desktop notification.
  </div>
  <div id='launch-custom-notify'>
    <span>Click here</span> to launch a custom desktop notification.
  </div>

Example #2

Click here to launch a basic desktop notification.
Click here to launch a custom desktop notification.
```

This is a custom HTML5 notification message!!

Regardless of whether a basic or custom desktop notification window is on-screen, the user has the opportunity to configure where the window appears on the desktop and revoke access just in case the web application is abusing its desktop-notification privileges.

The display area can be configured by clicking the tiny 🔧 icon in the top right of the corner of the notification pop-up itself and selecting Choose Position.

This setting will be remembered for future desktop notification messages.

# Listen for Desktop Notification Events

You can define custom JavaScript callback functions at specific events to be executed as the Desktop Notifications API interacts with the user. There are four events in the Notification interface for which you can listen:

```
notifyMessage.ondisplay = function() { ... };
notifyMessage.onclick = function() { ... };
notifyMessage.onclose = function() { ... };
notifyMessage.onerror = function() { ... };
```

The `ondisplay` event is called whenever the notification message is actually displayed on the desktop after calling `show()`. This will allow you to know if a delay occurred caused by too many messages on-screen.

The `onclick` event is called whenever the user clicks the message itself. It is a good idea to call *notifyMessage*.

`cancel()` to close the notification window after receiving an `onclick` event; this allows the user to indicate to your web application that he or she has read the message.

The `onclose` event is called whenever the message is closed, either by the user clicking the Close button or by calling *notifyMessage*.`cancel()`.

The `onerror` event is called if there is a problem in launching the event to the user's desktop. You may want to display an error message in the main web page so that when the user returns to your web application, he or she will be notified that a notification attempt was made and has failed.

## Listen for Desktop Notification Events

**1** Open an HTML5 or JavaScript file that triggers desktop notifications.

**2** Type *notifyMessage*.**onclick = function() { ... };** to define code that runs when the message is clicked.

**3** Type *notifyMessage*.**onclose = function() { ... };** to define code that runs when the message is closed.

**Note:** *In this example, jQuery's* `append()` *method is used to log in the browser when an event occurs.*

**Note:** *If you receive an* `onclose` *event without an* `onclick` *event, assume that the user has ignored the message.*

**Ⓐ** Optionally, type *notifyMessage*.**ondisplay = function() { ... };** to define code that runs when the message is displayed.

**Note:** *The order here is irrelevant, but it looks nicer in chronological order: display, click, close.*

**Ⓑ** Optionally, type *notifyMessage*.**onerror = function() { ... };** to define code that runs if the message has a problem.

**4** Save your file.

**5** Open your HTML file in Google Chrome.

**6** Trigger your desktop notification event.

A desktop notification window appears, separate from the calling browser window.

**C** The `ondisplay` event fires.

**7** Click the notification message.

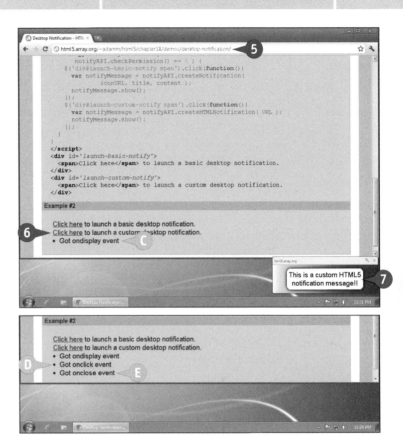

**D** The `onclick` event fires.

**Note:** *In this example,* `notifyMessage.onclick` *calls* `notifyMessage.cancel()`.

**E** The `onclose` event fires.

**Note:** *If the user clicks* ⊠, *only the* `onclose` *event will fire.*

## APPLY IT

Technically, all of the event functions in this example are optional; however, `onclick` and `onclose` are strongly recommended if you want the desktop notification to respond to the user.

It is possible to automatically close a lower-priority notification message by executing `notifyMessage.cancel()` after a delay that begins when the `notifyMessage.ondisplay` event fires. This will automatically hide the pop-up, without acknowledging that the user has seen or responded to it.

### TYPE THIS

```
notifyMessage.ondisplay = function() {
  setTimeout(function() {
    notifyMessage.cancel()
  }, 5000);
};
```

### RESULT

The desktop notification pop-up automatically exits after five seconds. If a `notifyMessage.onclose` callback function is defined, it will also be triggered at this time.

If the user closes your web application while a notification window is active, it is impossible for you to respond to any events, even queued events like this `setTimeout()` example. The notification window will remain open until the user closes it, or Chrome itself.

# HTML5 Reference

This appendix contains much of the information from *HTML: The Living Standard,* as of August 2011. You can find the latest version of the HTML specification at the WHATWG page www.whatwg.org/specs/web-apps/current-work/multipage/.

The following are the different HTML tag categories:

- Metadata tags — These describe the configuration elements in how content appears in the browser.
- Sectioning tags — These provide the HTML5 semantic page layout and define the context for content to appear.
- Grouping tags — These group similar content blocks together, such as paragraphs and lists.
- Phrasing tags — These control inline text blocks within a parent sectioning or grouping tag.
- Embedding tags — These import external content, such as an image, plug-in, movie, sound, or canvas.
- Table tags — These define a tabular structure for content to appear.
- Form tags — These provide a way to define input and output fields to communicate with a web server or JavaScript process.
- Interactive tags — These provide interactive features that the user manipulates on the web page.

The following is a list of all HTML tags identified by category:

| HTML Tags | Category | Description |
|---|---|---|
| `<!-- comment -->` | (none) | Text comment ignored by the browser |
| `<!doctype>` | (none) | The HTML document type (DTD) |
| `<a>` | Interactive, Phrase | A hyperlink |
| `<abbr>` | Group, Phrase | An abbreviation |
| `<address>` | Group, Phrase | A physical address |
| `<area>` | Group, Phrase | An image map area |
| `<article>` | Group, Section | An article of content |
| `<aside>` | Group, Section | Text related to the main content |
| `<audio>` | Embed, Group, Interactive (`controls` attribute), Phrase | A playable sound file |
| `<b>` | Phrase | Keywords requiring attention |
| `<base>` | Metadata | The default URL context for relative links |
| `<bdi>`, `<bdo>` | Phrase | Text with bidirectional isolation and override |
| `<blockquote>` | Group, Section | Quoted text |
| `<body>` | Section | All web page content |
| `<br>` | Phrase | A forced new line in the same group |
| `<button>` | Form, Interactive, Phrase | A clickable button |
| `<canvas>` | Embed, Group, Phrase | A custom drawing object |
| `<caption>` | Table | A caption for a table |
| `<cite>` | Phrase | A referenced title of a work |
| `<code>` | Phrase | An example computer code or command |
| `<col>`, `<colgroup>` | Table | Group of one or more columns |
| `<command>` | Metadata, Phrase | A `<menu>` command |
| `<datalist>` | Group, Phrase | A list of suggestions for a form input |
| `<dd>`, `<dl>`, `<dt>` | Group | A series of terms with descriptions |

| HTML Tags | Category | Description |
|---|---|---|
| `<del>`, `<ins>` | Group, Interactive, Phrase | Content deleted or inserted |
| `<details>`, `<summary>` | Group, Interactive, Section | A shortened summary of a larger body |
| `<dfn>` | Group, Phrase | A new term definition |
| `<div>` | Group | A generic division of content |
| `<em>` | Group, Phrase | Additional emphasis |
| `<embed>` | Embed, Group, Interactive, Phrase | Embeddable content |
| `<fieldset>` | Form, Group, Section | A collection of similar fields |
| `<figure>`, `<figcaption>` | Group, Section | A supporting image, table, chart, or code block |
| `<footer>` | Group, Section | The bottom portion of a section |
| `<form>` | Form, Group | A collection of input fields to submit |
| `<h1>`, `<h2>` ... `<h6>` | Group, Heading | A multilevel text heading |
| `<head>` | (none) | A container for all other metadata for the web page, such as the title |
| `<header>` | Group, Section | The leading portion of a section |
| `<hgroup>` | Group, Heading | A series of headings |
| `<hr>` | Group | A line break between paragraphs |
| `<html>` | (none) | The root of the web page |
| `<i>` | Group, Phrase | Text with an alternative voice or mood |
| `<iframe>` | Embed, Group, Interactive, Phrase | A window that nests external web pages |
| `<img>` | Embed, Group, Interactive (`usemap` attribute), Phrase | An image |
| `<input>` | Form, Group, Interactive (`type` attribute, not `hidden`), Phrase | An input element |
| `<kbd>` | Phrase | A keyboard command |
| `<keygen>` | Form, Interactive, Phrase | A private/public key generator |
| `<label>` | Form, Group, Interactive, Phrase | A common name for a form input |
| `<legend>` | Phrase | Preamble for a `<fieldset>` tag |
| `<li>` | Group | A list item |
| `<link>` | Group (`itemprop` attribute), Metadata, Phrase (`itemprop` attribute) | Imports externally linked content |
| `<map>` | Group, Phrase | An image map |
| `<mark>` | Group, Phrase | Highlight text |
| `<math>` | Embed, Group, Phrase | A group of MathML elements |
| `<menu>` | Group, Interactive (`type` attribute is `toolbar`) | A horizontal or vertical menu list |
| `<meta>` | Metadata | Supplementary website configuration |
| `<meter>` | Group, Form, Phrase | A static progress bar |

continued

| HTML Tags | Category | Description |
|---|---|---|
| `<nav>` | Group, Section | A group of navigational links |
| `<noscript>` | Group, Metadata, Phrase | Text for when JavaScript is unavailable |
| `<object>` | Embed, Group, Form, Interactive (`usemap`), Phrase | An embeddable object |
| `<ol>`, `<ul>` | Group | An ordered and unordered list |
| `<optgroup>` | Form, Interactive | A group of similar `<option>` types |
| `<option>` | Form, Interactive | An option in a `<select>` list |
| `<output>` | Group, Form, Phrase | Display program output |
| `<p>` | Group | A paragraph of text |
| `<param>` | (none) | A parameter for `<object>` |
| `<pre>` | Group | Preformatted text |
| `<progress>` | Form, Group, Phrase | A dynamic progress bar |
| `<q>` | Phrase | A quote from another source |
| `<ruby>`, `<rp>`, `<rt>` | Group, Phrase | Display literal and phrasing content for other languages |
| `<s>` | Phrase | Content that is no longer accurate or relevant |
| `<samp>` | Phrase | The sample output from a `<code>` example |
| `<script>` | Metadata | JavaScript code |
| `<section>` | Section | A section of content |
| `<select>` | Form, Group, Interactive, Phrase | A selectable list of `<option>`s for form input |
| `<small>` | Phrase | Secondary text, like fine print |
| `<source>` | Embed | Alternative sound or movie source files |
| `<span>` | Phrase | A generic span of text |
| `<strong>` | Phrase | Text with additional importance |
| `<style>` | Metadata | CSS code |
| `<sub>`, `<sup>` | Phrase | Subscript and superscript text |
| `<svg>` | Embed, Group, Phrase | SVG code |
| `<table>` | Group, Table | A table |
| `<tbody>` | Table | The table's body of content |
| `<td>`, `<th>`, `<tr>` | Table, Section | A table cell, header cell, and row |
| `<textarea>` | Form, Group, Interactive, Phrase | A multilined text form input |
| `<thead>`, `<tfoot>` | Table | The table's header and footer |
| `<time>` | Phrase | A time or date |
| `<title>` | Metadata | The web page title |
| `<track>` | Embed | A track of audio |
| `<var>` | Phrase | A variable for equations |
| `<video>` | Embed, Flow, Interactive (`controls` attribute), Phrase | A playable movie file |
| `<wbr>` | Phrase | A word break opportunity |

**E**very element in HTML supports a group of *global attributes*. These enable you to configure elements' styling, user interaction, writing system, language, and pragmatic data.

The HTML5 specification says browsers should allow global attributes to apply to nonstandard HTML elements. This provides a vital level of forward compatibility: If an HTML5 web browser encounters a post-HTML5 web page, at the very least the newly defined tags can still be stylized and controlled in the JavaScript DOM.

Note that these global attributes do not apply to metadata tags, described in the next section, "HTML Metadata Tags," but they do implicitly apply to all other HTML tags described in this appendix.

The following are all HTML global attributes grouped by their class, current as of the WHATWG HTML specification as of August 2011. For an updated list, see the WHATWG page at www.whatwg.org/specs/web-apps/current-work/multipage/elements.html#global-attributes.

## CSS Attributes

The CSS global attributes allow you to locate specific HTML objects in CSS selectors and stylize your website according to your design and layout preferences.

| Attribute | Description |
| --- | --- |
| class | Assigns a CSS class name directly to an element. |
| id | Assigns a single identifier to an element. |
| style | Assigns arbitrary CSS declarations to an element. |

Actually, id is not strictly a CSS attribute, but it is most often used as one. Its main purpose is to easily identify HTML objects in the JavaScript DOM; however, if you use jQuery, you can easily use any CSS-style selector.

To stylize class and id elements, a CSS selector must be constructed and one or more CSS rules used to declare a CSS property and specific value. See Chapter 4, "Styling with CSS3," for more information.

continued ▶

# HTML GLOBAL ATTRIBUTES (continued)

## User Interaction Attributes

The user interaction global attributes allow you to configure an element to interact with the user in new and interesting ways without any — or in the case of drag and drop, with very little — supporting JavaScript.

| Attribute | Description |
| --- | --- |
| accesskey | Creates a keyboard shortcut to a specific element. |
| contenteditable | A Boolean to identify text in an element block that can be edited by the user. |
| contextmenu | Allows for configuration of a drop-down `<menu id='name'>` tag to appear when an element with `contextmenu='name'` is clicked. |
| draggable | Specifies whether an element can be clicked and dragged by the user. Possible values are `true`, `false`, and `auto`. |
| dropzone | Specifies an element that accepts a draggable element to be dropped and what happens. Possible values are `copy`, `move`, `link`. |
| hidden | A Boolean to hide an entire element or an element block and all its children. Equivalent to the CSS declaration `display: hidden`. |
| spellcheck | A Boolean to identify text in an element block to be checked for spelling errors. |
| tabindex | Allows for a specific navigation focus order when pressing Tab. |

You can read more information about HTML5 user interaction at the WHATWG page at www.whatwg.org/specs/web-apps/current-work/multipage/editing.html.

For more information on drag and drop, see Chapter 12, "Using Drag and Drop in HTML5."

## Text and Language Attributes

The text and language global attributes provide subtle hints to the web browser about the language the web page text uses and allows for brief descriptions assigned to elements as required.

| Attribute | Description |
| --- | --- |
| dir | Configures the direction of text given the language — `rtl` is right to left of an element block; `ltr` is left to right and the default. |
| lang | Identifies an element block as written in a specific language. |
| title | Assigns a simple text description to an element. |

The `lang` attribute is useful if you need to specify multiple languages in a single web page, using the language's two-character name. If an entire web page is written in one specific language, declare the language in the metadata tag `<meta http-equiv='content-language' content='lang'>` or use the `lang` attribute directly very early on the main HTML tag: `<html lang='lang'>`. The implied default is `lang='en'`.

The `dir` attribute is useful only for languages that flow right to left, such as Hebrew or Arabic. If the entire web page is written in either language, use it alongside `lang`, as in `<html lang='he' dir='rtl'>`. Otherwise, if the writing direction changes midpage, you can assign it to individual `<article>` or `<p>` tags as needed. Note that `dir='ltr'` is the implied default.

The `title` attribute appears as a subtle pop-up on any standalone element, or element block and its children, that appears when the user hovers the mouse cursor over it.

## Microdata

The HTML5 microdata specification allows you to label content to describe the specific type of information, using a standard format. The idea is similar to a lightweight directory access protocol (LDAP) database. The microdata provides the database schema, and the HTML code provides the database values. The purpose is to make human-readable HTML easier to parse by automated programs and to identify facts and data.

HTML5 web browsers themselves may not have microdata capabilities, but they are not the target platform. Microdata is useful for companies such as Google to parse websites for vital information, providing better search optimization.

| Attribute | Description |
|---|---|
| itemid | Creates a unique identifier of the item in the DOM. |
| itemprop | A child element's item property name that is defined in the itemtype URL. |
| itemref | An element not a descendent of itemscope can be assigned an itemtype via itemid. |
| itemscope | A Boolean that creates a microdata item and indicates that a child element's itemprop attribute can be referenced back to this parent. |
| itemtype | A URL to a vocabulary that describes the item and its properties, assigned to the parent with the itemscope attribute. Prebuilt common microdata specs, such as person, product, and organization, are available at http://data-vocabulary.org. |

Microdata is defined by the WHATWG specification document located at the WHATWG page at www.whatwg.org/specs/web-apps/current-work/multipage/links.html#microdata.

For more information on how to use microdata, also known as *rich snippets,* see Google's Webmaster Tools Help page at www.google.com/support/webmasters/bin/topic.py?topic=21997.

# HTML Metadata Tags

The HTML metadata tags describe the configuration specific to your website and not specific content that appears in the browser. In other words, they describe how content should appear and how your website should be portrayed to automated programs in the outside world, but not the actual content.

Most HTML metadata tags should come before the `<body>` tag group; however, there are a few exceptions: The comment tag, `<script>` tag, `<link>` tag, and `<style>` tag can appear anywhere in your website.

Note that these HTML metadata tags do not accept any of the global attributes defined earlier.

## `<!doctype>`

The `<!doctype>` tag is a special preamble tag to your HTML web page. Called a *document-type definition* (DTD), it instructs the web browser which standards-mode rendering method it should use to display your web page. Prior to HTML5, the DTD could get very long because it was also required to specify the public identifier and system identifier for the version of HTML the website was written in. For example, if you wanted the Transitional DTD from HTML 4.01, you were expected to introduce a web page with the following:

```
<!doctype html public "-//W3C//DTD HTML 4.01 Transitional//EN" "http://www.w3.org/TR/html4/loose.dtd">
<html>
   ...
</html>
```

In HTML5, this was simplified greatly. You need to specify only a very short DTD prior to all other HTML tags:

```
<!doctype html>
<html>
   ...
</html>
```

The DTD must appear exactly once, as the first line of your web page, immediately followed by the `<html>` tag group.

## `<!-- ... -->`

The `<!-- ... -->` tag is a special pseudo-tag that allows you to create comments in your web page. It can technically appear nearly anywhere in the body of your HTML source, as long as it is after the DTD. The comment tag can wrap around nearly anything, such as text or even other HTML tags, and will be ignored by all web browser rendering engines:

```
<!doctype html>
<!--
   This web page is Copyright (c)1999
   Most rights reserved
-->
<html>
   ...
</html>
```

## `<html> ... </html>`

The `<html>` tag group represents your entire HTML web page:

```
<!doctype html>
<html manifest='filename'>
  ...
</html>
```

It accepts one optional attribute, `manifest`, that allows you to define which resources should be cached locally by the user's web browser. For more information on how the manifest and ApplicationCache works, see Chapter 14, "Providing Offline Access to Web Applications."

## `<head> ... </head>`

The `<head>` tag group holds all other metadata for the web page, such as the `<title>`, `<meta>`, `<script>`, and `<style>` tags. No actual formatting or content should appear in the `<head>` block:

```
<!doctype html>
<html>
  <head>
    ...
  </head>
```

This block is followed by the `<body>` block, which defines your web page content.

## `<title> ... </title>`

The `<title>` tag group defines the title of your web page. It must appear within the `<head>` block:

```
<head>
  <title>Title of your web page</title>
  ...
</head>
```

This value is typically used when users bookmark your website and is displayed in the operating system user interface next to the browser's icon.

continued ➤

## \<base>

The optional `<base>` tag defines the default base URL and browsing context for the entire web page. It may appear only once within the `<head>` block:

```
<head>
  ...
  <base href='url' target='target'>
  ...
</head>
```

The `href` attribute specifies the web page base URL. This is useful for resolving relative URLs specified by the web page within hyperlinks, images, or any other embeddable content.

The `target` attribute identifies the default browsing context for the entire page. This context specifies where hyperlinks and forms open when they are clicked. Possible values are _blank, _self, _parent, _top, or your own custom name. This is most often used when every link on a web page opens up a new pop-up window or when every link on a popped-up web page opens on its parent. Remember that individual links and forms can also be assigned the `target` attribute, but when `target` is set in `<base>`, it is the web page default for all links.

## \<link>

The `<link>` tag defines any externally linked content, such as CSS files, that should be imported into your web page. Multiple link tags may be used, one for each imported file, but all should appear within the `<head>` block. It is possible to use `<link>` later in your web page outside of `<head>`, but this is not a good practice.

```
<head>
  ...
  <link rel='linktype' media='mediatype'
  type='mimetype' sizes='hhxww' href='url'
  hreflang='lang' title='title'>
  ...
</head>
```

The `rel` attribute, if defined, identifies the relationship between this web page and the external resource by way of specific link-type keywords, described later in the subsection "Relationship Link Types." In other words, this controls the type of functionality the link definition provides. Multiple relationships to your page can be defined with multiple `<link>` tags, each with a specific `rel` attribute.

The `media` attribute specifies which presentation media type the resource applies to, such as screen, print, or television; a complete list is described later in the subsection "Media Types." If omitted, its value defaults to `all`, meaning that the link applies to all media types.

The `type` attribute indicates the MIME type of the file that will be loaded by the `href` URL. For example, if you are loading a `rel='alternate'` RSS feed, you would set `type='application/rss+xml'`.

The `sizes` attribute may be used only with `rel='icon'`. It specifies the sizes of the icons available in the `href` file for visual media.

The `href` attribute refers to the external file that will be loaded into the web page. If you are using `rel='stylesheet'`, then `href` should link to a CSS file; if you are using `rel='icon'`, then `href` should link to an ICO file; and so on.

`hreflang` identifies the language the `href` URL uses, if any. Most often this is formatted as a two-character language code, such as `en`, or optionally is followed by a dash and a two-character capitalized region, such as `en-US`. If you provide an externally linked web page in multiple languages, each one will need its own `<link>` tag, and the user's browser will select which one is most appropriate.

The `title` attribute refers to the title of the external resource.

## Relationship Link Types

The most commonly used link types are as follows:

- `stylesheet` — All primary style sheets that you want to load should use this `rel` type.
- `icon` — You can define a website icon through this `rel` type. It will appear alongside the site `<title>` content in the operating system, web browser, and bookmarks.
- `alternate` — You can specify alternative ways of viewing your website, such as an RSS feed, or even combine it with an alternative style sheet to define auxiliary style sheets. You should use the `title` attribute as well to provide a basic description of what the alternative is that you are loading.

These less-commonly used link types are not as well supported by most browsers but are still valid:

- `author` — Links to the web page author's home page.
- `help` — Links to a general help page for the web page.
- `license` — Links to the page's license or copyright file.
- `first, last, next, prev, up` — Link to pages in a booklike web page, such as the first page, last page, next page, previous page, and table of contents, respectively.
- `pingback` — Specifies the address of a pingback server, often used by blogging systems such as WordPress.
- `prefetch` — Allows you to preload a URL in the browser's cache. When the user clicks the URL linked in the web page, the linked page loads directly from cache.
- `search` — Indicates that the referenced page provides a search form specifically designed for the website.
- `sidebar` — Defines a URL that is intended to be shown in a sidebar interface, if available in the web browser.

## Media Types

The `media` attribute must be set to one of the following types:

- `all` — Indicates any media type.
- `braille` — A Braille feedback device.
- `embossed` — A Braille printer.
- `handheld` — A handheld device, such as a mobile phone or tablet.
- `print` — A printout copy on paper.
- `projection` — A PowerPoint-style presentation slide.
- `screen` — A regular computer screen.
- `speech` — A text-to-speech translation; replaces the `aural` media type.
- `tty` — A monospace character device, such as a teletype or terminal.
- `tv` — A television screen.

You can also create a media query by combining one or more media types with a basic logic statement. As described in Chapter 1, "Introducing HTML5," you can use this to create a style sheet specifically targeted to smaller handheld devices:

```
<link rel='stylesheet' media='screen' href='base.
  css'>
<link rel='stylesheet' media='screen and (max-width:
  320px)' href='mobile.css'>
```

This will load base.css for all screen media and mobile.css for all screen media smaller than 320 pixels wide. If you viewed this web page on alternative media, such as print, neither CSS file would be loaded.

You can also use media queries within a CSS file directly.

## `<style>` ... `</style>`

The `<style>` tag group defines the CSS rules that apply only to the web page. It normally appears only within the `<head>` block, but it can be used anywhere in your web page:

```
<head>
  ...
  <style type='text/css'>
    /* Define your CSS rules here */
  </style>
  ...
</head>
```

For additional information on how the CSS rules are structured, see Chapter 4.

## <script> . . . </script>

The <script> tag group defines any additional scripting code and external files, usually JavaScript, in your web page. It normally appears within the <head> block but may be used anywhere in the <body> block if you need to coordinate the execution of code with specific HTML elements:

```
<head>
  ...
  <script type='text/javascript'>
    /* Include your JavaScript code here */
  </script>
  <script type='mimetype' src='URL'></script>
</head>
```

The type attribute indicates the MIME type of the code itself; in the case of JavaScript, this is text/javascript. The src attribute, if used, refers to an external script or library that you want to import into your web page. If you do specify the src attribute, do not define any code within the <script> tag block.

If JavaScript is disabled on the user's web browser, you can use the text-level tag <noscript> to define content that should appear in place of JavaScript execution. Note that <noscript> is not valid as a metadata tag within the <head> block.

## <meta>

The <meta> tag defines any other configuration that your website requires to render properly but cannot be represented by any of the aforementioned tags. When used, all meta tags must appear within the <head> block, and they may contain a combination of the attributes name, http-equiv, content, and charset; at a minimum, at least one attribute must be specified per <meta> tag:

```
<head>
  ...
  <meta name='name' content='content' http-equiv='equiv' charset='charset'>
  ...
</head>
```

The name attribute can be one of the following keywords and then described with content:

- application-name — A short string describing the web application name.
- author — The name of one of the web page authors. You can use multiple instances of <meta name='author' content='full name'>, one for each author.
- description — Descriptive text that describes the web page. Only one <meta> tag can define a description.
- generator — A string that describes which software program was used to generate the website's HTML code, if one was used.
- keywords — A string of comma-separated words that describes search keywords relevant to the website content. Note this is a legacy metadata configuration; modern search engines no longer use its value due to rampant abuse, so this can be omitted without penalty.

Additional keywords are maintained by the WHATWG at http://wiki.whatwg.org/wiki/MetaExtensions.

The `http-equiv` attribute converts the `meta` element into a *pragma* directive, which allows you to provide additional HTTP header information via the `content` attribute. The possible values for `http-equiv` are the following and then described with `content`:

- `content-language` — Specifies the default language of the current web page.
- `content-type` — Allows you to set the character encoding declaration; however, this value is maintained for backward compatibility; use the `charset` attribute described below instead.
- `default-style` — Sets the name of the default alternative style sheet set. This is useful when you have multiple CSS files that are alternative ways to display the web page and you want to assign a name to the default CSS file that is loaded first.
- `refresh` — This acts as a timed refresh rate, allowing you to reload this web page, or another web page, automatically after a short time has elapsed.
- `set-cookie` — This allows you to set arbitrary HTTP cookies in the web page itself. Use this if the pragma should be limited; instead, set cookies in JavaScript or in the HTTP headers by way of a CGI program directly.

Additional keywords are maintained by the WHATWG at http://wiki.whatwg.org/wiki/PragmaExtensions.

The final `charset` attribute represents the character encoding the website itself. It cannot be combined with any of the other `<meta>` attributes and must be specified only once:

```
<!doctype html>
<html>
  <head>
    <meta charset='UTF-8'>
    ...
  </head>
  <!-- The rest of the document may now use UTF-8 characters. -->
```

This attribute is designed to be a simpler way to represent the following pre-HTML5 pragma directive:

```
<meta http-equiv="content-type" content="text/html; charset=UTF-8">
```

Both are equivalent, but most pre-HTML5 browsers such as Firefox 3.5 and Internet Explorer 8 understand the simpler attribute.

# HTML Sectioning Tags

Sectioning tags are the pinnacle of the semantic layout, which was introduced in HTML5. They do not tend to support any local attributes but do fully support global attributes. As such, they can and should be manipulated via CSS. The semantic layout is demonstrated in Chapter 2, "Getting Started with HTML5 Page Layout."

All HTML sectioning tags support the standard global attributes, described earlier in this appendix in the section "HTML Global Attributes."

## &lt;body&gt; ... &lt;/body&gt;

The `<body>` tag group represents the main content of the web page. It is used exactly once, directly after the `<head>` block:

```
<!doctype html>
<html>
  <head>
    ...
  </head>
  <body>
    ...
  </body>
</html>
```

Note the closing `</body></html>` tags should be the final two tags referenced at the end of your HTML file. All other HTML tags described from here on in this appendix can be used only within this `<body>` tag group.

## &lt;header&gt; ... &lt;/header&gt;

The `<header>` tag group represents a group of introductory or navigational components. It typically appears directly after the `<body>` block begins but can be used anywhere within `<body>`:

```
<body>
  <header>
    Website header content
  </header>
  ...
</body>
```

## &lt;footer&gt; ... &lt;/footer&gt;

The `<footer>` tag group represents a footer for sectioning content; it typically contains information about its section such as the author and even secondary-level navigational components. It typically appears directly before the `<body>` block ends but can be used anywhere within `<body>` or just prior to the end of any section-related tag:

```
<body>
  ...
  <footer>
    Website footer content
  </footer>
</body>
```

## `<section>` . . . `</section>`

The `<section>` tag group represents a generic section of a web page, where a section is a grouping of content, typically with a heading. It can be used multiple times anywhere within the `<body>` block:

```
<body>
  ...
  <section>
    A section of content...
  </section>
  ...
</body>
```

## `<nav>` . . . `</nav>`

The `<nav>` tag group represents a section of a page that links to other pages or to parts within the page: a section with navigation links. It can be used multiple times anywhere within the `<body>` block:

```
<body>
  ...
  <nav>
    Links or a navigational menu...
  </nav>
  ...
</body>
```

## `<article>` . . . `</article>`

The `<article>` tag group represents a single web page, application, or object that is independent from other articles. This could be a blog post, a newspaper article, a program, or any other piece of content. It can be used multiple times anywhere within the `<body>` block. Often multiple `<article>` tags are used within a `<section>` block that is dedicated to house all articles:

```
<section class='articles'>
  <article>
    The first article...
  </article>
  <article>
    The second article...
  </article>
  ...
</section>
```

continued ➤

## `<h1> ... </h1>, <h2> ... </h2> ... <h6> ... </h6>`

The `<h1>` to `<h6>` tag groups represent headings for sections, in order of hierarchy. They can be used multiple times anywhere within the `<body>` block but are often used to introduce new topics or subtopics in articles. The first heading in your web page typically receives the `<h1>` tag, optionally followed later by the subheading `<h2>` tag and so forth, or by a new `<h1>` tag indicating a new higher-level topic:

```
<article>
   <h1>The main heading</h1>
   Introduce a new topic...
```

```
   <h2>The second-level heading</h2>
   Expand on the first topic with a sub-topic...
   <h2>A new second-level heading</h2>
   Expand on the first topic with another
sub-topic...
   <h1>A new top-level heading</h1>
   Introduce a completely new topic...
   ...
</article>
```

## `<hgroup> ... </hgroup>`

The `<hgroup>` tag group represents the heading of a section. It can be used anywhere within the `<body>` block but should be used only as the immediate parent object of multiple, successive heading tags:

```
<article>
   <hgroup>
      <h1>The main heading</h1>
      <h2>The second-level heading</h2>
   </hgroup>
   Introduce a new topic and sub-topic...
   ...
</article>
```

## `<aside> ... </aside>`

The `<aside>` tag group represents a section of a page that is related to the main content but is still considered separate from that content. For example, if newspapers were like websites, `<aside>` would be used for featured quotes, advertisements, or references. It can be used multiple times anywhere within the `<body>` block. Often, `<aside>` is used within an `<article>` block:

```
<article>
   Article text...
   <aside>Some additional quote about the
article...</aside>
   More article text...
</article>
```

## `<address> ... </address>`

The `<address>` tag group represents any contact information relevant to the current section. It is typically used once near the end of a `<body>` or `<article>` block:

```
<article>
   ...
   <address>
      To contact the author of this article, email <a
href='mailto:jsmith@mycompany.com'>John Smith</a>.
   </address>
</article>
```

Note that it is typically used for an email address, telephone number, or other contact information. It is not intended for postal addresses unless that is the only way to contact the web page author.

Grouping tags are designed to group similar blocks of text or content together under a tag group, such as a paragraph or a figure, or to split up a series of similar groups with a subtle effect, such as a line.

All HTML grouping tags support the standard global attributes, described earlier in this appendix in the section "HTML Global Attributes."

## `<p> . . . </p>`

The `<p>` tag group represents a paragraph of text. Although normal paragraphs segregate sentences into like-minded topics and flow, the physical separation can be manipulated via CSS to the point that the paragraph itself is no longer distinguishable.

Even if you have a single sentence of only a few words, if it is to display as a standalone block of text, wrap it in the `<p>` tag group.

One or more `<p>` blocks can appear anywhere within the `<body>` block. If you are following the semantic layout paradigm, you may find that the largest collection of paragraphs appear within `<article>` blocks:

```
<body>
  <p>See below for articles:</p>
  <article>
    <h1>Welcome to my site</h1>
    <p>This is the first paragraph of text. It
  introduces new ideas and topics in the form of
  multiple sentences.</p>
    <p>This is the second paragraph of text. It
  should expand on one of the ideas introduced in
  the first paragraph. Subsequent ideas may be
  elaborated on in additional paragraphs.</p>
    ...
  </article>
</body>
```

## `<hr>`

The `<hr>` tag represents a break in between multiple paragraphs. Often rendered as a single vertical line, it can be used to transition to another topic within the same section by displaying a type of a pause that spans an entire line of text:

```
<p>paragraph text</p>
<hr>
<p>paragraph text</p>
```

## `<pre> . . . </pre>`

The `<pre>` tag group represents preformatted blocks of text. Normally, all whitespace around elements and text is trimmed; however, when wrapped in `<pre>` spacing in the HTML, source code is displayed literally in the web browser:

```
<pre>
This text
   displays
      exactly as it appears
         in HTML source.
</pre>
```

## `<blockquote> . . . </blockquote>`

The `blockquote` tag group represents quoted text, possibly from an external source. It typically is rendered with a small indent:

```
<p>"The Raven" - by Edgar Allen Poe - describes a
   lonely evening when the narrator laments for his
   life and love, only to be visited by a raven that
   questions, confuses, and finally mocks him by
   uttering only a single word.</p>
<blockquote>
   Quoth the raven, "Nevermore".
</blockquote>
```

continued ➤

**339**

## `<ol><li> . . . </ol>`

The `<ol>` tag group represents an ordered list. This appears as incrementing numbers for each item in the list. The `<li>` tag within represents a single list item and can be used multiple times, once for each item in the list.

To create a subnumbered list, simply nest another `<ol>` tag group as a new list item:

```
<ol>
  <li>Ordered item #1
  <li>Ordered item #2
  <ol>
    <li>Ordered item #2.1
    . . .
  </ol>
  <li>Ordered item #3
  . . .
</ol>
```

## `<ul><li> . . . </ul>`

The `<ul>` tag group represents an unordered list. Bullets appear for each item in the list. The `<li>` tag within represents a single list item and can be used multiple times, once for each item in the list.

To create a subbulleted list, simply nest another `<ul>` tag group as a new list item:

```
<ul>
  <li>Bulleted item #1
  <li>Bulleted item #2
  <ul>
    <li>Bulleted item #2.1
    . . .
  </ul>
  <li>Bulleted item #3
  . . .
</ul>
```

## `<dl><dt> . . . </dt><dd> . . . </dd></dl>`

The `<dl>` tag group is a series of title-description groups represented by one or more sets of `<dt>` and `<dd>` tag groups; the `<dt>` tag group represents the title portion of a specific definition in a description list, and the `<dd>` tag group represents the text portion of a specific description:

```
<dl>
  <dt>Term #1</dt>
  <dd>First Description for Term #1</dd>
  <dd>Second Description for Term #1</dd>
  <dt>Term #2</dt>
  <dd>First Description for Term #2</dd>
  <dd>Second Description for Term #2</dd>
  . . .
</dl>
```

Note that the closing `</dt>` and `</dd>` tags are optional but recommended.

## `<figure> ... </figure>`

The `<figure>` tag group represents additional content that describes an image, table, chart, code, or other object that typically coincides with paragraphs of text:

```
<figure>
   <img src='photo.jpg'>
</figure>
```

The figure is not rendered as anything specific in the browser but instead acts like a semantic layout tag, making it easy for you to customize its layout in CSS.

## `<figcaption> ... </figcaption>`

The `<figcaption>` tag group can be included in a `<figure>` block to define caption text that describes the nearby figure object. Only one caption should be used per figure. This tag also acts like a semantic layout tag; however, it does have some default formatting that can easily be overridden in CSS:

```
<figure>
   <img src='photo.jpg'>
   <figcaption>A description of the photo image.</figcaption>
</figure>
```

Note that the `<figcaption>` tag may be referenced below or above the referenced image, table, chart, or object.

## `<div> ... </div>`

The `<div>` tag group is like a wildcard. It represents anything you want it to that does not fit within any of the previously described HTML block tags. It has no inherent formatting; therefore, it is most commonly used in stylizing HTML content using CSS. For this to happen, either one of the `class` or `id` global attributes should also be used; very rarely will you ever see `<div>` without one of these attributes on a website:

```
<div class='center red'>This is centered red text.</div>
```

The `<div>` tag was most popular in sites designed for HTML 4.01 and earlier. With the advent of the semantic layout in HTML5, tags such as `<header>`, `<footer>`, `<section>`, `<article>`, and `<figure>` should be used in place of `<div class='header'>`, `<div class='footer'>`, and so on. In fact, if you think about it, these HTML5 semantic layout tags are rendered the same way as `<div>` tags: as nothing but simple blocks; therefore, they also require CSS. The only difference is that in HTML5, new semantic tags have specific names to identify their use and context.

# HTML Phrasing Tags

bjects created using *phrasing tags,* also known as *text-level tags,* appear inline with each other within a parent sectioning or grouping tag. This means that if you string a series of these tags one after another, they will be rendered from left to right and top to bottom in the web browser. In other words, a phrasing tag will never force a new line unless it runs out of room on its current line.

All HTML phrasing tags support the standard global attributes, described earlier in this appendix in the section "HTML Global Attributes."

## `<a> . . . </a>`

The `<a>` tag group represents a clickable hyperlink to another web page, website, or URL. Text within the tag appears to the user as clickable, by way of underlined, blue text. Note that the default rendering of hyperlinks can easily be overridden in CSS.

```
<p>To learn more about this topic, you can <a
href='URL'>click here</a> to read follow-up
documentation.</p>
```

At a minimum, the `href` attribute should be used to specify where the hyperlink directs the user. If `href` is not used, the simpler `<a>text</a>` block can be used as a placeholder for a link to come later.

When you use `href`, you can use these additional attributes:

- `hreflang` — Describes the language of the target `href` URL.
- `media` — Describes what media type the target web page is designed for. This uses the same configuration as the `<link media='type'>` tag described earlier, except that this

applies only to this particular hyperlink.

- `ping` — Assigns a supplementary URL that will be notified when the user follows the link.
- `rel` — Assigns a link-type keyword to the hyperlink itself. This uses the same configuration as the `<link rel='type'>` tag described earlier, except that this applies only to this particular hyperlink.
- `target` — Assigns a name to the browsing context the link will be used for. This uses the same configuration as the `<base target='context'>` default described earlier, except that it overrides on a per-link basis.
- `type` — Describes the MIME type encoding of the target `href` URL.

The `href`, `target`, and `ping` attributes reflect what happens when the user follows the hyperlink. The `rel`, `media`, `hreflang` and `type` attributes describe what can be found at the other end of the hyperlink.

## `<em> . . . </em>`

The `<em>` tag group represents additional emphasis on the text included within it:

```
<p>Sometimes a form of <em>emphasis</em> is required to get a specific point across.
```

When rendered, this tag may make text display in italics by some web browsers, but this is not guaranteed and should not be used as such. Instead, if you simply want to italicize text without specifying emphasis, use the CSS definition `font-style: italic`.

## `<strong> . . . </strong>`

The `<strong>` tag group represents additional importance on the text included within it:

```
<p><strong>ERROR:</strong> Invalid user name or password. Please try again.</p>
```

When rendered, this tag may make text display in bold by some web browsers, but this is not guaranteed and should not be used as such. Instead, if you simply want to bold text without specifying importance, use the CSS definition `font-weight: bold`.

## \<small> . . . \</small>

The \<small> tag group represents secondary text, such as fine print, which is often useful in licenses, disclaimers, or caveats. However, if the page you are producing contains nothing but one big license or disclaimer, use normal text.

```
<p>This toy uses 4 AA batteries <small>(batteries not included)</small></p>
```

## \<s> . . . \</s>

The \<s> tag group represents content that is no longer accurate or relevant but that you still want to display *because* it is no longer accurate. It may be immediately followed by contradictory text that corrects the irrelevant content:

```
<p>You can buy this product for <s>$129.95</s>
$59.95, but only for a limited time!</p>
```

When rendered, this tag will display text with a line through it, called *strikethrough,* but this is not guaranteed and should not be used as such. Instead, if you simply want to display a strikethrough line through text without specifying relevancy, use the CSS definition `text-decoration: line-through`.

## \<cite> . . . \</cite>

The \<cite> tag group represents an external title of work that is referenced by your web page:

```
<p>My first book, <cite>Perl and Apache: Your visual
blueprint for developing dynamic Web content</
cite>, was published in 2010 and is available at
Amazon.com.</p>
```

When rendered, this tag may display text in italics by some web browsers, but this is not guaranteed and should not be used as such. Again, if you simply want to italicize text without citing a source, use the CSS definition `font-style: italic`.

## \<q> . . . \</q>

The \<q> tag group represents content quoted from another source. The idea is similar to \<blockquote> except that it appears inline with other text, typically rendered only with double quotes. If the source can be referenced from another website, the `cite` attribute may be used to link back to that website:

```
<p>In February 2011, the W3C CEO Jeff Jaffe said,
<q cite=' http://www.w3.org/2011/02/htmlwg-pr.
html'>Today we take the next step, announcing 2014
as the target for [HTML5].</q></p>
```

Note that this should not be used as a replacement for double quotes but only if quoting an external source — and optionally using the `cite` attribute along with the \<cite> tag.

## \<dfn> . . . \</dfn>

The \<dfn> tag group represents the first time a new term is introduced on a web page or site. Typically, the remainder of the paragraph or section will go on to provide a definition of the term. Additional uses of the term do not require the \<dfn> tag to be re-referenced, as the term has already been established.

You can also set the `title` attribute, which will be interpreted as a direct expansion of the acronym:

```
<p>The new <dfn title='element names that provide
self-explanatory context'>semantic layout</dfn> in
HTML5 refers to a new class of elements that are
purely designed to help you understand where and
how text is defined in your web page and its
context. All semantic tags must appear within the
<body>...</body> container tag group.</p>
```

continued ➤

## `<abbr>` . . . `</abbr>`

The `<abbr>` tag group represents an abbreviation or acronym. It may be found within a `<dfn>` tag group by providing a new definition and attribute at the same time. Additional uses of the acronym do not require the `<abbr>` tag to be re-referenced, as the acronym has already been established.

You can also set the `title` attribute, which will be interpreted as a direct expansion of the acronym:

```
<p>The <dfn><abbr title='World Wide Web
  Consortium'>W3C</abbr></dfn> produced the first
  <dfn><abbr title='hypertext markup language'>HTML</
  abbr></dfn> standard document. Follow-up versions
  of HTML were produced by the W3C and other
  parties.</p>
```

## `<time>` . . . `</time>`

The `<time>` tag group represents an absolute time on a 24-hour clock or a precise date with an optional time and time zone as a `datetime` attribute. The text within the time tag can be arbitrarily structured, or, in other words, human readable:

```
<time datetime='2011-06-16'>June 16, 2011</time>
<time datetime='2011-06-16T04:11:00-0600'>June 16,
  2011, 4:11am</time>
```

Note that the format for `datetime` can be either $yyyy-mm-dd$ to reflect a simple date or $yyyy-mm-ddThh:mm:ssTZ$ to reflect a full date timestamp with a time-zone offset.

## `<sub>` . . . `</sub>`, `<sup>` . . . `</sup>`

`<sub>` represents subscript text, and `<sup>` superscript text. This will be rendered with smaller text below and above normal text, respectively. This can be useful in scientific and mathematical formulas and to provide footnotes in text:

```
<p>The molecular formula for Butane is C<sub>4</sub>H<sub>10</sub>, it has a density of 2.48 kg/m<sup>3</sup>
  in a gaseous state.</p>
```

## `<code>` . . . `</code>`

The `<code>` tag group represents a small portion of computer code, such as a function name, keyword, or computational statement. The text within can be used as the subject in a sentence of normal text or can be wrapped in `<pre>` and a monospaced font to show larger portions of preformatted, sample code:

```
<p>You can call the <code>init()</code> function from the <code>System</code> object to initialize the API at
  program startup.</p>
<pre><code style='font-family: courier'>
int main( void ) {
  char* handle;
  handle = System.init();
}
</code></pre>
```

When rendered, this tag may display the text in a sans-serif font in some web browsers, that is, unless you override it.

## `<var>` . . . `</var>`

The `<var>` tag group represents a variable, either in a mathematical or computational context or as a placeholder term:

```
<p>The Pythagorean Theorem is written as <var>a</var><sup>2</sup> + <var>b</var><sup>2</sup> = <var>c</var><sup>2</sup>.</p>
```

Variables typically appear italicized.

## `<kbd>` . . . `</kbd>`

The `<kbd>` tag group represents user input, such as from a keyboard or keypad:

```
<p>To exit out of the Vi editor without saving the file, type <kbd>ESC</kbd> to return to command mode, then <kbd>:q!</kbd> and press Enter.</p>
```

This tag causes the text to change to a monospaced font in some browsers. You may want to consider adding additional CSS formatting to make it more obvious to the user; for example, command-line text inputs could be described with white text over a black background, akin to input on a terminal prompt.

## `<samp>` . . . `</samp>`

The `<samp>` tag group represents sample output from a described `<code>` program or from an external process:

```
<p>If you run the command <kbd>sudo whoami</kbd> and press Enter, the whoami program will print <samp>root</samp> and exit.</p>
```

Like `<kbd>`, this tag also causes the text to change to a monospaced font in some browsers. You should consider differentiating it so that the user can easily identify that it is sample output. Even simply adding border: 1px solid black will help.

## `<i>` . . . `</i>`

The `<i>` tag group represents text with an alternative voice or mood. This could be used to represent an alternative speaker, language, or idiom. If used as another language, include the global attribute lang:

```
<p>Despite many shortcomings, the manager's <i lang='fr'>savoir-faire</i> was his ability to respond appropriately to any situation.</p>
```

The legacy formatting of this tag, italicizing text, is still used by nearly all web browsers. However, do not use this tag if you simply want to italicize text for different reasons. Instead, consider `<em>` or use the CSS declaration font-style: italic.

continued ➤

## `<b>` . . . `</b>`

The `<b>` tag group represents text in which attention is being drawn to keywords, without marking them with any extra importance:

```
<ol>
   <li>Head north on <b>1st Street</b> toward <b>Hwy 401</b> for 500m.
   <li>Turn right onto <b>Hwy 401</b>. Continue to follow for 15km.
   <li>Take <b>exit 125</b> for <b>35th Street</b> eastbound.
</ol>
```

The legacy formatting of this tag, bolding text, is still used by nearly all web browsers. However, do not use this tag if you simply want to bold text for different reasons. Instead, consider `<strong>` or use the CSS declaration `font-weight: bold`.

## `<u>` . . . `</u>`

The `<u>` tag group represents text with an unarticulated nontextual annotation. Sometimes this can be useful for labeling proper names or misspelled text:

```
<p>Spelling <u>erorrs</u> are among the most common surface errors as well as the most easily <u>correked</u>.</p>
```

The legacy formatting of this tag, underlining text, is still used by web browsers; therefore, do not use this tag where the text could be confused with an underlined hyperlink.

## `<mark>` . . . `</mark>`

The `<mark>` tag group represents text that should be highlighted for reference purposes:

```
<blockquote>
   Spelling <mark>erorrs</mark> are among the most common surface errors as well as the most easily
   <mark>correked</mark>.
</blockquote>
<p>The original author forgot to the fix the spelling of the words <q>errors</q> and <q>corrected</q>.</p>
```

The `<mark>` tag is displayed with a yellow background, just like an actual highlighter pen.

## `<noscript>` . . . `</noscript>`

The `<noscript>` tag group can be used to specify content that will appear when JavaScript is disabled. On browsers that have JavaScript enabled, this tag and its contents will be ignored:

```
<script type='text/javascript'>
   // Render the cool graphic animation
</script>
<noscript>You need to have JavaScript enabled to view the animation</noscript>
```

## &lt;ruby&gt;&lt;rt&gt; . . . &lt;/rt&gt;&lt;/ruby&gt;

The &lt;ruby&gt; tag group allows for phrasing content to be marked with ruby annotations, which means supplementary text that is displayed alongside of base text. This is commonly used in East Asian languages as a guide for pronunciation. The &lt;rt&gt; tag group follows the foreign spelling and describes the correct pronunciation using a format that is understood by the reader:

```
The capital city of Japan is:
<ruby>
   東 <rt>tō</rt>
   京 <rt>kyō</rt>
</ruby>.
```

When rendered by supporting web browsers, the ruby block will appear as: "The capital city of Japan is 東京."

## &lt;rp&gt; . . . &lt;/rp&gt;

The &lt;rp&gt; tag group provides parentheses around ruby text around a ruby annotation. This is useful for browsers that do not understand the &lt;ruby&gt; and &lt;rt&gt; tag annotations as a way to provide brackets around the &lt;rt&gt; phrasing content. Browsers that do understand ruby will ignore the &lt;rp&gt; tag. To extend the previous example, &lt;rp&gt;(&lt;/rp&gt; and &lt;rp&gt;)&lt;/rp&gt; can be added as follows:

```
The capital city of Japan is:
<ruby>
   東 <rp>(</rp><rt>tō</rt><rp>)</rp>
   京 <rp>(</rp><rt>kyō</rt><rp>)</rp>
</ruby>
```

When rendered by nonruby supporting browsers, the ruby block will appear as: "The capital city of Japan is 東(tō) 京(kyō)."

Supporting web browsers will still render the pronunciation above the base text.

## &lt;bdi&gt; . . . &lt;/bdi&gt;

The &lt;bdi&gt; tag group represents text that is isolated for the purposes of bidirectional text formatting. This is useful if you need to embed a short word or sentence that moves in the opposite direction to the body of your web page, such as Hebrew or Arabic, or if you are accepting user-generated content that could appear in either format:

```
<p>Enter your name in English or Hebrew: <bdi><input type=text name='name'></bdi></p>
<p>The value you submitted was: <bdi>My Name</bdi>.
```

continued ➤

## `<bdo> . . . </bdo>`

The `<bdo>` tag group represents an override for the default bidirectional text formatting. For this to work, the `dir` attribute must set `ltr` for left-to-right or `rtl` for right-to-left text direction:

```
<p>This is an example of <bdo dir='rtl'>text that
  appears backwards</bdo> when displayed to the
  user.</p>
```

The end result is that every character is written backward; however, the line formatting itself is still the default, so it could start from the left of the line and move to the right. The appropriate context for this would be if you wanted to embed right-to-left text, such as Hebrew or Arabic, within normal left-to-right text.

Note that the result of this tag differs from any element using the global attribute `dir`. For example, if you write the same example as `<p dir='rtl'>`, the line appears right to left, and the words are reversed, but the ordering of the characters stays the same.

## `<span> . . . </span>`

The `<span>` tag group is like a wildcard element. It represents anything you want it to that does not fit within any of the previously described HTML inline tags. Essentially, it is `<div>`'s inline cousin. It has no inherent formatting; therefore, it is most commonly used in stylizing HTML content using CSS. For this to happen, either one of the `class` or `id` global attributes should also be used; very rarely will you ever see `<span>` without one of these attributes on any other website.

```
<p>Welcome to the <span class='bold blue'>City
  Police</span> website.</p>
```

## `<br>`

The `<br>` tag represents a simple line break without transitioning into a new display block. This is useful for line breaks that are a part of the single content group, such as addresses and poetry:

```
<p>Visit the Currency Museum of Canada at:<br>
<address>245 Sparks Street<br>
Ottawa, Ontario<br>
Canada</address></p>
```

Older websites often used multiple `<br>` tags in succession to force several new lines and begin a new paragraph. Never do this; use the `<p>` tag group as directed.

## `<wbr>`

The `<wbr>` tag represents a line break opportunity. Natural line breaks occur only when a word reaches the end of the line; however, you will not be aware of how wide the user's browser is, especially if you are displaying a very long word. This tag can be used to provide hints to the browser as to acceptable line break points, if required for spacing reasons:

```
<p>In the Dutch language, compound words can be formed to limitless length. For example, the word <i lang='nl
  '>vervoerder<wbr>saansprakelijk<wbr>heidsver<wbr>zekering</i> means <q>liability insurance carrier</q>.</p>
```

**H**TML embedding tags allow you to import content from separate files into your web page document by specifying a form of a URL on an embed tag. This could be an image, a movie, a Flash animation, and so on.

Some embedding tags do not accept separate files but instead allow you to embed separate code; this is the case with the `<math>` tag group to create MathML code and the `<svg>` tag group to create scalable vector graphics.

All HTML embedding tags support the standard global attributes, described earlier in this appendix in the section "HTML Global Attributes."

## `<img>`

The `<img>` tag represents an image that you can load into your web page. It takes a multitude of attributes, but at a minimum, you need to specify `src` to identify the source file. When you load an image, it is formatted to appear inline with other content. To make it appear standalone, like its own paragraph, wrap `<figure>` around it. The file format of your image depends on what the web browser supports:

```
<figure>
  <img src='photo.jpg'>
</figure>
```

Additional attributes can be included in the `<img>` tag:

- `alt` — This acts as the image fallback content, a text field that describes the image for those who cannot see or load it.

- `crossorigin` — A Cross-Origin Resource Sharing, or CORS, settings attribute. This allows you to load an image from another domain that may require credential authentication.

- `usemap` — Allows you to specify a `<map><area>...</map>` tag group that specifies coordinates linked to URLs. This will create one image that supports multiple URLs based on click location. See `<map>` for more details.

- `ismap` — Specifies that the image is a server-side map. Coordinates are passed to the parent `<a>` hyperlink target that identify where the user clicked on the map.

- `width` — Specifies the display width of the image.

- `height` — Specifies the display height of the image.

Note that if only one of `height` or `width` is specified, the image is scaled to match the value. If both are specified, the image's original aspect ratio may be lost.

## `<map><area> . . . </map>`

The `<map>` tag group allows you to specify multiple geometric areas of an image that are clickable. The `<area>` tag, which appears within the `<map>` group, identifies the general shape of the area, coordinates of the area, and URL. To tie the image map to an image, use the `<img>` tag's `usemap` attribute:

```
<figure>
  <img src='canada.jpg' usemap='#provinces'>
</figure>
<map name='provinces'>
  <area shape="poly" coords="22,365,252,365,249,494,318,581,216,581,201,590,130,545" href="british-columbia.html">
  <area shape="poly" coords="253,365,365,365,365,582,319,582,250,492" href="alberta.html">
  <area shape="rect" coords="366,366,459,581" href="saskatchewan.html">
  ...
</map>
```

The `<map>` tag group accepts only a `name` attribute. This matches the image's `usemap` attribute but without the # character.

continued ▶

The <area> tags within accept multiple attributes:

- shape — The basic shape of the coordinates specified. The value can be circ for a circle, poly for a polygon, or rect for a rectangle. If omitted, it defaults to a rectangle shape.

- coords — A series of (x, y) values joined by commas that construct the shape on the image map. Note that (0, 0) is the top left of the image.

- href — The hyperlinked URL the user will transition to when the specified coordinate area is clicked.

- hreflang — Describes the language of the target href URL.

- alt — Acts as description of this clickable area of the image.

- target — Identifies the default browsing context for the entire page. This context specifies where hyperlinks and forms open when they are clicked. Assigns a name to the browsing context the link will be used for. This uses the same configuration as the <base target='context'>

default described earlier, except that overrides on a per-link basis.

- ping — Assigns a supplementary URL that will be notified when the user follows the link.

- rel — Assigns a link-type keyword to the hyperlink itself. This uses the same configuration as the <link rel='type'> tag described earlier, except that it applies only to this particular hyperlink.

- media — Describes what media type the target web page is designed for. This uses the same configuration as the <link media='type'> tag described earlier, except that it applies only to this particular hyperlink.

- type — Describes the MIME type encoding of the target href URL.

The href, target, and ping attributes reflect what happens when the user follows the hyperlink. The rel, media, hreflang, and type attributes describe what can be found at the other end of the hyperlink.

## <iframe> . . . </iframe>

The <iframe> tag group represents a nestable browsing window. Essentially, you can use this to import and restrict a completely separate HTML into a virtual box in the current web page. Content within the starting and ending tags appears in browsers that do not support the <iframe> tag:

```
<iframe seamless src='otherpage.html' >
   The iframe element is not supported by your
   browser!
</iframe>
<iframe sandbox srcdoc='<p>This is
   &quot;sandboxed&quot; HTML content</p>'></iframe>
```

The following attributes are available:

- src — A URL to the external web page or file.

- srcdoc — Simple HTML code that will appear in the iframe. Note that only one of src or srcdoc may be specified. If any quotes appear within srcdoc, they must be specified with &quot;. Otherwise, they could conflict with parsing the tag itself.

- name — If specified, this attribute allows you to identify the iframe object in the JavaScript DOM.

- sandbox — Enables additional restrictions over the imported content, if supported by the web browser. Essentially, if you are loading a web page from a source you do not trust, specify this attribute with at least one of the following values:

  - allow-same-origin — Allows for the main site to access the sandboxed DOM, but not vice versa.

  - allow-top-navigation — Allows the sandboxed iframe to change the URI of the parent.

  - allow-forms — Allows the use of forms within the sandboxed iframe.

  - allow-scripts — Allows JavaScript to run inside the iframe.

- seamless — Specifies that the iframe should be seamlessly integrated into the web page.

- width — Specifies the display width of the iframe.

- height — Specifies the display height of the iframe.

## \<embed\> . . . \</embed\>

The \<embed\> tag group represents an external resource that can be included in your web page. The content between the starting and ending tags will appear only in browsers that do not support the embed element or could not load the embedded item itself:

```
<embed src='demo.swf' type='x-shockwave-flash'
  allowfullscreen='true'>
    The embed element is not supported by your browser!
</element>
```

The following attributes are available:

- src — The URL of the external file that will be embedded.
- type — Describes the MIME type encoding of the target src URL.
- width — Specifies the display width of the iframe.
- height — Specifies the display height of the iframe.

Any additional attributes specified ad hoc will be sent to the embedded resource as parameters.

## \<object\> . . . \</object\>

The \<object\> tag group represents an external resource that can be included in your web page. Depending on the attributes specified, this can be an image, a nested browsing context, or a resource processed by a plug-in.

It may sound like \<embed\> and \<object\> are very similar, and this is actually true. Whereas \<object\> is useful for maintaining legacy support for pre-HTML5 web browsers, \<embed\> provides a simpler syntax to create embedded objects, but only for supported web browsers.

The content between the starting and ending tags will appear only in browsers that do not support the object element or could not load the object itself:

```
<object data='http://www.externalsite.com/widget.
  html'
        type='text/html-sandboxed'>
  The external object is not supported by your
  browser!
</object>
```

The following attributes are available:

- data — The external resource URL that will be processed.
- type — Describes the MIME type encoding of the target data URL.
- typemustmatch — A Boolean that specifies that the type attribute must match the server-side MIME type supplied by the external resource.
- name — If specified, this attribute allows you to identify the external object in the JavaScript DOM.
- usemap — Allows you to specify a \<map\>\<area\>... \</map\> tag group that specifies coordinates linked to URLs. This will create one image that supports multiple URLs based on click location. See \<map\> for more details.
- form — Allows you to associate a form on the main web page with input elements found in the external object.
- width — Specifies the display width of the iframe.
- height — Specifies the display height of the iframe.

Optional parameters can be specified with the \<param\> tag.

## \<param\>

The \<param\> tag can be used to apply optional parameters to the \<object\> tag group. This is useful if you need to provide additional context to the plug-in or external URL that is being embedded or objectified:

```
<object type='application/x-shockwave-flash'>
  <param name='movie' value='http://www.video.com/
  movies/12345.swf'>
  <param name='allowfullscreen' value='true'>
  Flash is not supported by your browser!
</object>
```

Two attributes are supported, name and value, which are provided to the external source in the form of key/value pairs.

continued ➤

## &lt;video&gt; . . . &lt;/video&gt;

The &lt;video&gt; tag group enables you to play videos or audio files with captions. The content between the starting and ending tags will appear only in browsers that do not support the video element:

```
<video src='movie.avi' controls>
   Your browser does not support HTML5 video, please
   download the <a href='movie.avi'>AVI</a> of the
   free movie.
</video>
```

The following attributes are available:

- src — The URL of the external video file.
- crossorigin — A CORS settings attribute. This allows you to load an image from another domain that may require credential authentication.
- poster — Specifies an image URL that appears in the video frame before the video starts to play.
- preload — Specifies how the media may be preloaded in the browser, if supported by the browser, before the user starts playback:
  - none — Do not preload any data. Download content only after the user starts playback.

- metadata — Download only metadata content, such as the video dimensions, duration, tracks, channels, and the first video frame.
- auto — Begin downloading the entire file and cache it locally in the browser.
- autoplay — A Boolean attribute that determines that the media can start playing immediately after the page loads; however, this can be overridden by a user preference on the browser, if available. Implies preload='auto'.
- mediagroup — Allows you to synchronize multiple videos by sharing an arbitrary value.
- loop — A Boolean that loops the media playback.
- muted — A Boolean that sets the default volume level on playback to muted.
- controls — A Boolean that enables built-in video controls, provided by the browser itself.
- width — Specifies the display width of the video.
- height — Specifies the display height of the video.

## &lt;audio&gt; . . . &lt;/audio&gt;

The &lt;audio&gt; tag group allows you to play audio files. The content between the starting and ending tags will appear only in browsers that do not support the audio element:

```
<audio src='music.mp3' controls>
   Your browser does not support HTML5 audio, please
   download the <a href='music.mp3'>MP3</a> of the
   free song.
</audio>
```

The following attributes are available:

- src — The URL of the external audio file.
- crossorigin — A CORS settings attribute. This allows you to load an audio file from another domain that may require credential authentication.
- preload — Specifies how the media may be preloaded in the browser, if supported by the browser, before the user starts playback:

- none — Do not preload any data. Download content only after the user starts playback.
- metadata — Download only metadata content, such as the duration, tracks, and channels.
- auto — Begin downloading the entire file and cache it locally in the browser.
- mediagroup — Allows you to synchronize multiple audio files by sharing an arbitrary value.
- loop — A Boolean that loops the media playback.
- muted — A Boolean that sets the default volume level on playback to muted.
- controls — A Boolean that enables built-in audio controls, provided by the browser itself.

## `<source>`

The `<source>` tag enables you to specify alternative sources for the `video` and `audio` elements. Because HTML5 web browsers do not all support the same source formats, this method is recommended because browsers will attempt to load the first source file and, if it is not understood, attempt the second, and so on. This tag is designed to replace the singular use of `<video src='file'>` or `<audio src='file'>` attributes. In other words, the `<source>` tag and `<video src>` or `<audio src>` attributes are mutually exclusive:

```
<video controls>
  <source src='movie.avi' type='video/msvideo;
codecs="xvid, mp3"'>
  <source src='movie.mp4' type='video/mp4;
codecs="mp4v, mp4a"'>
  <source src='movie.ogg' type='video/ogg;
codecs="theora, vorbis"'>
```

```
  Your browser does not support HTML5 video, please
download the <a href='movie.avi'>AVI</a>, <a
href='movie.mp4'>MP4</a>, or <a href='movie.
ogg'>OGG</a> versions of the free movie.
</video>
```

The following attributes are available:

- `src` — The URL of the external video or audio file.
- `type` — Describes the MIME type encoding of the target `src` URL. Additionally, a `codecs` parameter can be amended to specify how the external file is encoded.
- `media` — Describes what physical media resources the video applies to using a valid media query. See the earlier subsection "Media Types" in the section "HTML Metadata Tags" for more information on formatting.

## `<track>`

The `<track>` tag allows media elements to use timed text tracks. This is loaded from a separate external file and runs parallel to the main media resource playback. This tag must be specified within a `<video>` block:

```
<video src='movie.avi' controls>
  <source type='video/msvideo; codecs="xvid, mp3"'>
  <track kind='subtitles' src='movie.en.vtt'
srclang='en' label='English Subtitles' default>
  <track kind='subtitles' src='movie.fr.vtt'
srclang='fr' label='French Subtitles'>
</video>
```

The following attributes are available:

- `kind` — Specifies the type of information that this track provides:
  - `subtitles` — A transcription or translation of the dialogue. Useful when the sound cannot be understood, such as foreign languages.
  - `captions` — A transcription or translation of the dialogue, plus sound effects, music cues, and other audio information. This is useful for deaf and hard-of-hearing users.
  - `descriptions` — Textual descriptions of video content. This is useful for blind users, when it is synthesized into an audio track.
  - `chapters` — Chapter titles, useful for navigation.
  - `metadata` — Content that should be interpreted by supporting JavaScript, if required. Not presented by the web browser directly.
- `src` — The URL of the external text track data.
- `srclang` — The language of the text track data.
- `label` — Provides a user-readable title for the track.
- `default` — A Boolean that sets one particular track to be the default, if the user's preferences do not specify a default.

continued

## <canvas> ... </canvas>

The <canvas> tag provides browsers with a bitmap canvas that can be used for rendering graphics, animations, and other custom visual elements in real time. It is designed to be a flexible replacement for the proprietary Flash plug-in. The element itself is highly dependent on JavaScript to do anything useful, so there is very little you actually need to specify in HTML. The content between the <canvas> starting and ending tags will appear only in browsers that do not support the canvas element:

```
<canvas id='myCanvas' height='500' width='200'>
  <figure>
    <img src='image.jpg'>
    <figcaption>
      Your web browser does not support the HTML5
canvas.
      A static image is displayed instead.
    </figcaption>
  </figure>
</canvas>
```

The following attributes are available:

- width — Specifies the display width of the canvas.
- height — Specifies the display height of the canvas.

It is strongly recommended that you assign the global attribute id, too, as this is the most appropriate way to identify a canvas object in JavaScript.

It is also recommended that the canvas should not be used for static images or for elaborate content that can be marked up in HTML and CSS. It is, of course, most useful for dynamically generated visual content, interactive content, and embedded content in place of Flash.

See Chapter 10, "Drawing with the HTML5 Canvas," for more information about using the canvas in JavaScript.

## <math> ... </math>

The <math> tag group can be used to access Mathematical Markup Language (MathML) elements and embed complex mathematical formulas into your HTML web page. For a complete summary of all MathML elements and how to use them, see the W3C page at www.w3.org/TR/MathML/.

## <svg> ... </svg>

The <svg> tag group can be used to access Scalable Vector Graphics (SVG) elements and embed dynamic vector graphics into your HTML web page. For a complete summary of all MathML elements and how to use them, see the W3C page at www.w3.org/TR/SVG/.

# HTML Table Tags

The HTML table tags allow you to define a simple or complex grid-based structure in your web page. When compared to HTML 4.01 and earlier, the `<table>` tag has gone through a major purge. Nearly all of the display attributes previously allowable under HTML table tags, such as `border`, `cellpadding`, `cellspacing`, and `width`, are no longer valid. You must use CSS to define these properties in HTML5.

Some alternatives to the HTML table structure include the CSS Flexible Box Model and CSS multi-column layout, both described in Chapter 6, "Creating Boxes and Columns with CSS3."

All HTML table tags support the standard global attributes, described earlier in this appendix in the section "HTML Global Attributes."

## High-Level Table Structure

The following describes the table tags that can appear only once and establishes the basic table structure before any table data can be specified.

### `<table>` ... `</table>`

The `<table>` tag group represents a simple or complex table, filled with one or more rows and columns. The table itself is most often a child of a section tag, described earlier in this appendix in the section "HTML Sectioning Tags," such as `<article>`, `<figure>`, or simply `<body>`. It could be a child of a group tag, but with the exception of `<div>`, this is relatively rare:

```
<table>
</table>
```

In HTML 4.01 and earlier, tables could be stylized using HTML attributes such as `cellpadding`, `cellspacing`, `frame`, `rules`, and `width`. These attributes have been deprecated in HTML5 and should not be used. Instead, you must style a table using CSS.

There is one attribute that is still valid on `<table>`, but its meaning has changed since HTML 4.01: `border`. In HTML5, if its value is 0, this table is likely a *layout table,* meaning that it is used across the entire web page in place of the semantic layout and CSS. If its value is 1 or not specified, it is most likely a *nonlayout table,* meaning that it shows only data.

### `<caption>` ... `</caption>`

The `<caption>` tag group represents an optional display block that summarizes the table. It can be as small as a few words or as large as a few paragraphs using multiple `<p>` blocks:

```
<table>
  <caption>A description of this table</caption>
</table>
```

The caption will always appear at the top of the table, unless you override it using the CSS declaration `caption-side: bottom`.

### `<colgroup><col>` ... `</colgroup>`

The `<colgroup>` tag group helps you to declare a table's column groups. This optional tag should appear early in the table structure; its only allowed predecessor is `<caption>`.

Not all columns need to be in a group, but it can be useful if you want to stylize a column group specifically with only one CSS rule. This is done by using the global attribute `id` or `class` on either `<colgroup>` or `<col>`:

```
<table>
  <caption>A description of this table</caption>
  <colgroup><col><col span='number'>...</colgroup>
</table>
```

The `span` attribute may be used on `<col>` to expand a specific style to multiple columns. Or `span` can be applied to `<colgroup>`, but only if there are no child `<col>`s within.

If you do not require any special column CSS styling, you can omit the `<colgroup>` and `<col>` tags entirely.

continued

## Table Rows and Cells

Individual rows and cells constitute the core table data. This is the information that will appear within the grid layout provided by HTML tables.

### `<tr> ... </tr>`

The `<tr>` tag group represents a single vertical table row. It is required for every row in the table but should come after the `<colgroup>` tag group, if it is used. You can repeat the `<tr>` tag group for as many rows as required by your table:

```
<table>
   <caption>A description of this table</caption>
   <colgroup><col><col span='number'>...</colgroup>
   <tr>
     ...
   </tr>
   ...
</table>
```

### `<th> ... </th>`

The `<th>` tag group represents a single table header cell and can be found only within a `<tr>` tag group. Each time it is repeated in a `<tr>` parent block, a new horizontal header cell is created, right to left. The total number of cells per row should match the `<colgroup><col>...</colgroup>` schema if used; otherwise, it should match the total of all other `<tr>` and `<td>` members per row in this table. If not, the table will appear incomplete with missing cells.

```
<table>
   <caption>A description of this table</caption>
   <colgroup><col><col span='number'>...</colgroup>
   <tr>
     <th>...</th>
     <th colspan='number'>...</th>
     ...
   </tr>
   ...
</table>
```

The `colspan` attribute instructs a cell to span multiple columns in that row. In addition, a `rowspan` attribute may be specified to allow a single cell to grow downward and span multiple table rows. For each subsequent `<tr>` row that is interfered with, there will be one less `<th>` or `<td>` cell that can be specified.

Cells that use the `<th>` tag center text in bold as a way of differentiating themselves from the regular `<td>` cells. This can easily be overridden using CSS.

### `<td> ... </td>`

The `<td>` tag group represents a single header cell and can be found only within a `<tr>` tag group. Each time it is repeated in a `<tr>` parent block, a new horizontal cell is created, right to left. The total number of cells per row should match the `<colgroup><col>...</colgroup>` schema if used; otherwise, it should match the total of all other `<tr>` and `<td>` members per row in this table. If not, the table will appear incomplete with missing cells.

Its usage and implementation is exactly like the `<th>` tag group, except that `<th>` is typically used only as the cells in the first table row or the first column:

```
<table>
   <caption>A description of this table</caption>
   <colgroup><col><col span='number'>...</colgroup>
   <tr>
     <th id='col1'>...</th>
     <th id='col2' colspan='number'>...</th>
     ...
   </tr>
   <tr>
     <td headers='col1'>...</td>
     <td headers='col2' colspan='number'>...</td>
     ...
   </tr>
   ...
</table>
```

The `colspan` attribute instructs a cell to span multiple columns in that row. In addition, a `rowspan` attribute may be specified to allow a single cell to grow downward and span multiple table rows. For each subsequent `<tr>` row that is interfered with, there will be one less `<th>` or `<td>` cell that can be specified.

New in HTML5 is the `headers` attribute. This optional feature allows you to establish a clear link using a common name between a data cell's `header` attribute and a header cell's `id` attribute: the `<td headers='name'>` tag and `<th id='name'>` tag. There is no visual change to establishing this link when the table is rendered, but it does make parsing the table easier for automated programs.

## Grouping Rows by Header, Body, and Footer

It is possible to define which rows make up the table header, body, and footer. If you implement this, it helps you to clarify how each `<tr>...</tr>` group is used in the table, as some rows may be column descriptions, some column data, and others column summaries.

The benefit of using these tag groups is that they allow you to create row groups, just as `<colgroup>` is used to create column groups, for the purpose of CSS styling.

If you do not require any special row group CSS styling, you can omit these tags entirely.

### `<thead>`

The `<thead>` tag group represents one or more rows of cells that define the column labels.

Only one `<thead>` tag group should be defined — and only after the `<caption>` and `<colgroup>` tags, if used, and before `<tbody>`, `<tfoot>`, and additional `<tr>`s. Only one `<thead>` tag group may be used within `<table>`:

```
<table>
  <caption>A description of this table</caption>
  <colgroup><col><col span='number'>...</colgroup>
  <thead>
    <tr>
      <th>...</th>
      <th colspan='number'>...</th>
      ...
    </tr>
  </thead>
  <tr>
    <td>...</td>
    <td colspan='number'>...</td>
    ...
  </tr>
  ...
</table>
```

### `<tbody>`

The `<tbody>` tag group represents the body of actual data for the table. As many `<tr>` rows as required can be defined within this group:

```
<table>
  <caption>A description of this table</caption>
  <colgroup><col><col span='number'>...</colgroup>
  <thead>
    <tr>
      <th>...</th>
      <th colspan='number'>...</th>
      ...
```

```
    </tr>
  </thead>
  <tbody>
    <tr>
      <td>...</td>
      <td colspan='number'>...</td>
      ...
    </tr>
    ...
  </tbody>
  ...
</table>
```

The `<tbody>` tag group may be repeated throughout `<table>`, essentially creating multiple batches of subtable rows.

### `<tfoot>`

The `<tfoot>` tag group represents one or more rows of cells that either repeats the column labels or defines the column summaries, if required.

This tag group can be used only after the `<caption>`, `<colgroup>`, `<thead>`, and `<tbody>` blocks, if used, as the bottom row or rows of the table. It should be the last tag group before `<table>` ends:

```
<table>
  <caption>A description of this table</caption>
  <colgroup><col><col span='number'>...</colgroup>
  <thead>
    <tr>
      <th>...</th>
      <th colspan='number'>...</th>
      ...
    </tr>
  </thead>
  <tbody>
    <tr>
      <td>...</td>
      <td colspan='number'>...</td>
      ...
    </tr>
    ...
  </tbody>
  <tfoot>
    <tr>
      <td>...</td>
      <td colspan='number'>...</td>
      ...
    </tr>
  </tfoot>
</table>
```

# HTML FORM TAGS

**A**ll HTML form tags support the standard global attributes, described earlier in this appendix in the section "HTML Global Attributes."

## Basic Form Structure

From a high level, an HTML form requires only an appropriately created `<form>` tag group. All other tags can be used only within this group.

### `<form>` ... `</form>`

When defining an HTML form, you must configure where the submitted data is to be sent to, which is the URL defined in the `action` attribute, and how it is to get there, which is the method attribute. After that, you still need to be concerned with the CGI program that will be accepting the form input so that you can process the user's form submission request.

```
<form action='URL' method='method'>
</form>
```

Several attributes are available to forms. If you are creating a JavaScript-only form, you do not need any additional attributes; but if you do communicate with a server-side CGI, you need to specify `action` at minimum.

- `accept-charset` — Identifies the preferred character encoding method of the server-side CGI program.
- `action` — A URL of the server-side CGI program that will accept the submitted form data.
- `autocomplete` — A Boolean that controls whether any submitted data may be cached in the browser and repopulated if this form is reused.
- `enctype` — The encoding type of the content attributes. Possible values are as follows:
  - `application/x-www-form-urlencoded` — The default form encoding method, if `enctype` is unspecified.
  - `multipart/form-data` — Useful if uploading files within the form, but not much else.
  - `text/plain` — Backward compatible to older CGI programs, but not recommended as submitted data could be misinterpreted.
- `method` — The method that the data will be submitted over HTTP. Possible values are as follows:
  - `get` — Use the HTTP `GET` method.
  - `post` — Use the HTTP `POST` method.

- `name` — A simple identifier to help locate the form in the DOM.
- `novalidate` — A Boolean that disables all built-in validation routines specified in HTML5.
- `target` — Identifies the browsing context when the form is submitted.

### `<fieldset>` ... `</fieldset>`

The `<fieldset>` tag group represents a collection of similar fields and other inputs. For example, if your web page asks for registration information from the user, you may use one field set for personal details, such as the first and last name, another for contact details such as email address and phone number, and another for mailing details, such as street, city, zip code, and country.

Simply put, the `<fieldset>` tag enables you to subdivide complex forms into categories and style each accordingly:

```
<form method='method' action='URL'>
    <fieldset>
    </fieldset>
    ...
</form>
```

When rendered by the browser, a `<fieldset>` group appears like a gray box around all child fields and text. This can of course be customized in CSS.

### `<legend>` ... `</legend>`

The `<legend>` tag group provides preamble text for the field set. It appears in the top-left corner, overlapping the box graphic:

```
<form method='method' action='URL'>
    <fieldset>
        <legend>Title of this field set</legend>

    </fieldset>
    ...
</form>
```

## Form Fields

The form fields allow the user to insert data into the form itself, directly within the browser window. This data will be included when the form is submitted.

### <label> ... </label>

The <label> tag group represents an input field's common name for a form input. Although optional, this helps the browser understand that the text is associated with a specific field input:

```
<form method='method' action='URL'>
  <fieldset>
    <legend>Title of this field set</legend>
    <label>
      Field Label:
    </label>
    ...
  </fieldset>
  ...
</form>
```

<label> accepts two optional attributes:

- form — Links a label to a specific form from outside of a <form> block.
- for — Links a label to an input, if that input is not defined within the <label> block.

### <input>

The <input> tag provides a way for the user to insert data into the form. It may appear standalone anywhere inside of the <form> block or within a <label> block, thus turning it into a *labeled control*. This means that the user can click the labeled text, and it is the input that is actually selected. This can provide some usability improvements to complex forms:

```
<form method='method' action='URL'>
  <fieldset>
    <legend>Title of this field set</legend>
    <label>Field Label:
      <input type='type' name='fieldname'>
    </label>
    ...
  </fieldset>
  ...
</form>
```

### Input Attributes

- accept — Acceptable MIME types for file input fields.
- alt — An alternative text description for image input fields.
- autocomplete — Allows the browser to store the form results for future reference.
- autofocus — A Boolean that sets an element to be focused when a page first loads.
- checked — A Boolean that sets a radio or check box input field to be on by default.
- dirname — Applies a new name field that specifies the input text's direction, left to right (ltr) or right to left (rtl).
- disabled — Disables the input element so that the user cannot change or use it in the form itself.
- form — Specifies a parent form element identifier, if this input element is not defined under a specific <form> tag group.
- formaction — Sets an alternative form action URL to submit the form to with a submit input button.
- formenctype — Sets an alternative form enctype setting when submitting the form with a submit input button.
- formmethod — Sets an alternative form method setting when submitting the form with a submit input button.
- formnovalidate — Sets an alternative form novalidate setting when submitting the form with a submit input button.
- formtarget — Sets an alternative form target setting when submitting the form with a submit input button.
- height — The height of the input field, measured in pixels.
- list — Links into a <datalist> identifier.
- max, min — The acceptable minimum and maximum values a number input field can accept.
- maxlength — The maximum number of characters the input field can accept.
- multiple — A Boolean that allows for multiple values to be entered and submitted into a single text field.
- name — The name of the input field used for CGI submission.

continued ➤

- pattern — A regular expression pattern that sets the acceptable input text formatting.
- placeholder — Temporary text that appears in the input field until the user starts typing.
- readonly — A Boolean that specifies the input field cannot be changed.
- required — A Boolean that specifies the input requires a text value.

- size — The width of the input field, measured by the number of characters to display at once.
- src — Specifies the source URL for an image input button.
- step — The stepping amount that a number input field increments or decrements by.
- type — The input element's type.
- value — The default value for the input element.
- width — The width of the input field, measured in pixels.

The following input types are accessible with the type attribute. Those that are new in HTML5 are described throughout Chapter 7, "Creating HTML5 Form Inputs."

### Text-Based Input Types
- email — An email address.
- number — A number or number range.
- password — A password.
- search — A search query.
- tel — A telephone number.
- text — A generic text string.
- url — A URL.

### Time-Based Input Types
- date — A date string.
- datetime — A date and time string.
- datetime-local — A date and time with a local timezone string.
- month — A month number.
- time — A time string.
- week — A week number.

### Complex UI Input Types
- color — Provides a pop-up color selector, new for HTML5.
- range — Provides a slider bar, new for HTML5.

### Other Input Types
- button — Provides a clickable button. The value attribute defines the button's text.
- checkbox — Provides a check box input.
- file — Provides a way to specify a local file to be uploaded. It is displayed as a text-like field that opens a dialog box to browse the user's local file system. It is recommended that you use enctype='multipart/form-data' in the parent form to ensure that large files can be accepted.

- hidden — Hidden from the user entirely; useful to pass arbitrary data into the form that is not visible to the user.
- image — Provides a clickable button that is displayed as an image identified by the src attribute.
- radio — Provides a radio button. Multiple radio buttons can share the same name attribute, but only one can be selectable.
- reset — Provides a button to reset the form to its default state. The value attribute defines the button's text.
- submit — Provides a button to submit the form. The value attribute defines the button's text.

## Selection Pull-Downs

The <select>, <optgroup>, and <option> tag groups define an input field that can be pulled down by the user as a form input. This helps to save space in the form by displaying only the current selection, rather than the whole list.

### <select> . . . </select>

```
<form method='method' action='URL'>
  <fieldset>
    <legend>Title of this field set</legend>
    <label>Field Label:
      <select name='fieldname'>
      </select>
    </label>
    ...
  </fieldset>
  ...
</form>
```

## &lt;optgroup&gt; ... &lt;/optgroup&gt;

```
<select name='fieldname'>
  <optgroup label='group text'>
  </optgroup>
  ...
</select>
```

## &lt;option&gt; ... &lt;/option&gt;

```
<select name='fieldname'>
  <optgroup label='group text'>
    <option value='value'>option text</option>
    ...
  </optgroup>
  ...
</select>
```

## &lt;datalist&gt; ... &lt;/datalist&gt;

The &lt;datalist&gt; tag group is similar to &lt;select&gt;, except that it applies its pull-down list into a text input element directly, linked by the list attribute value. Only after the user begins to type in the text field will a filtered version of the &lt;datalist&gt; options appear.

```
<form method='method' action='URL'>
  <fieldset>
    <legend>Title of this field set</legend>
    <label>Field Label:
      <input type='type' name='fieldname'
  list='listname'>
      <datalist id='listname'>
        <option value='value'>text</option>
        ...
      </datalist>
    </label>
    ...
  </fieldset>
  ...
</form>
```

## &lt;textarea&gt; ... &lt;/textarea&gt;

The &lt;textarea&gt; tag group represents a multilined text input field:

```
<form method='method' action='URL'>
  <fieldset>
    <legend>Title of this field set</legend>
    <label>Field Label:
      <textarea name='fieldname' rows='number'
  cols='number'>
      </textarea>
    </label>
    ...
  </fieldset>
  ...
</form>
```

## &lt;keygen&gt;

The &lt;keygen&gt; tag represents a dynamic public-private key generator. This can be used to validate the server's response. The public version of the key is submitted with the form, and its private counterpart is stored locally in the browser:

```
<form method='method' action='URL'>
  <fieldset>
    <legend>Title of this field set</legend>
    <label>Field Label:
      <keygen name='fieldname'>
    </label>
    ...
  </fieldset>
  ...
</form>
```

continued ➤

## Data Submission and Display Feedback

The HTML tags that are used to submit a form usually appear as the last components of the `<form>` block. At minimum there should be a button that submits the form. It is not uncommon to see all of the following elements appear outside of a `<form>` block, as is the case when the data being submitted and displayed is being handled only by JavaScript.

### `<button>`

The `<button>` tag represents any type of clickable button.

```
<form method='method' action='URL'>

    ...

    <button type='buttontype' name='buttonname'
    value='buttontext'>
</form>
```

### Button Types

- button — A generic button, useful for JavaScript-only data submission. If `type` is undefined, this is the default.
- submit — A form submit button. This is the same as `<input type='submit'>`.
- reset — A form reset button. This is the same as `<input type='reset'>`.

### `<output>` . . . `</output>`

The `<output>` tag represents a placeholder for data that will appear later. Such is the case of an Ajax form or a JavaScript-only submission.

```
<form>
    ...
    <button type='buttontype' name='buttonname'
    value='buttontext'>
    <output name='outputfield'></output>
</form>
```

### `<progress>` . . . `</progress>`

The `<progress>` tag group represents a moving progress bar indicating an action the user is waiting for. This element is a JavaScript-only output mechanism and not used within `<form>` blocks.

```
<progress value='valuenumber' max='maxnumber'>
    Total progress is valuenumber of maxnumber
</progress>
```

The content between the `<progress>` starting and ending tags will appear only in browsers that do not support the `progress` element.

### `<meter>`

The `<meter>` tag group represents a static progress bar indicating a snapshot in time and does not typically change after the page has loaded. This element is a JavaScript-only or static HTML output mechanism and is not used within `<form>` blocks.

```
<meter value='valuenumber' max='maxnumber'>
    Total progress is valuenumber of maxnumber
</meter>
```

The content between the `<meter>` starting and ending tags will appear only in browsers that do not support the `meter` element.

# Symbols

# A

# B

# Index

# Index

# Index